Made by the USA

Made by the USA

The International System

Alex Roberto Hybel

palgrave

MADE BY THE USA
© Alex Roberto Hybel, 2001

First published 2001 by
PALGRAVE
175 Fifth Avenue, New York, N.Y.10010 and
Houndmills, Basingstoke, Hampshire RG21 6XS.
Companies and representatives throughout the world

PALGRAVE is the new global publishing imprint of St. Martin's Press LLC Scholarly and Reference Division and Palgrave Publishers Ltd (formerly Macmillan Press Ltd).

ISBN 0-312-23892-4 hardback

Library of Congress Cataloging-in-Publication Data
Hybel, Alex Roberto.
    Made by the USA : the international system / by Alex Roberto Hybel.
    p. cm
    Includes bibliographical references and index
    ISBN 0-312-23892-4
    1. United States—Foreign relations. 2.United States—Foreign economic relations 3. International relations. I. Title.

E183.7.H94 2001
327.73—dc21
                                                        00-069224

A catalogue record for this book is available from the British Library.

Design by Westchester Book Composition

First edition: April 2001
10 9 8 7 6 5 4 3 2 1

Printed in the United States of America.

To

Susan Eckert Lynch

Contents

Preface

The political analyst is part storyteller, part conjecturer. He or she tries to capture a slice of political life by imposing on the story his or her own theoretical perspective. Since the United States's conception as a state, analysts have sought to explain the development of its foreign policies by highlighting different "causes." Some analysts have identified its strategic and/or economic interests as the dominant causal forces, others have focused on its predominant values, a third group has underscored the political struggles between the domestic organizations responsible for designing foreign policies, and a fourth group has concentrated on the psychological nature or the information-processing attributes of its leaders. Although my objectives in this book are similar to those of my predecessors, the conceptual framework I designed does not fit neatly into any of their theoretical constructs.

My argument is built on the premise that the global system is constantly undergoing change, which is spawned by tensions generated by contradictory forces originating from different international and domestic sources. Despite the fact that every state in the global arena would prefer to create an international system that caters to its own interests, only a handful can partially fulfill this goal. Success in this kind of endeavor is dictated by the extent to which an entity's power and domestic structure make it possible for its leaders both to understand the nature of the contradictory forces that dominate the international system and its own domestic environment at different times, and to deal effectively with the tensions these forces induce. Based on this theoretical device, I delineate the steps taken by the United States during the nineteenth and twentieth centuries to, first, become a world power and, subsequently, forge the type of international system that would help address its needs and interests. I use the same conceptual framework to posit a series of predictions about the foreign policies the United States is likely to pursue during the first 25 years of the new millennium, the tensions that are likely to erupt in the global system, the effects the tensions are likely to have on the stability of the international system and the interests of the United States, and the likelihood that the United States will retain its standing as the international system's chief entity.

In light of the above remarks, the reader might be inclined to assume that I wrote this book with a very small audience in mind. Such was not my hope. As one who has spent much of his professional life in the academic world, I have always placed equal value on my roles as scholar and professor. Likewise, I have always tried to use one role to complement the other. I wrote this book hoping to stimulate interest among both international politics/foreign policy theorists and practitioners, and undergraduate and graduate students. Among those who are well versed in the foreign policies of the United States, there will be some who will contend that I could have used less information to back my theoretical arguments. In a sense, they are right. Most of the information I present in this book was derived from a wide range of published sources and is common knowledge among U.S. foreign policy analysts. From them, I ask their indulgence, and their concentration on the nature and content of my arguments. I hope that those with inquisitive minds, but who are relatively new to the field of study, will use this book to acquire a better understanding of an important aspect of U.S. history, and to learn about a new theoretical perspective.

My last contention calls for a minor proviso. I did not write this book with the intent of covering the entire spectrum of the United States's international activities during the past two centuries. For instance, the reader will notice that I discuss the foreign policies of the United States toward Europe in much greater detail than those toward Africa and Latin America. By placing different emphases on different regions, I do not mean to suggest that some areas are more important than others. My decision to discuss certain regions at great length and to cover others sporadically was dictated by the intensity of the tensions that emanated from them. In the future, some of the areas I touched upon only briefly could become the primary instigators of severe international tensions; in that case, analysts would be forced to gauge their effect on the international system and to depict the way its most powerful entities attempt to defuse them.

The idea for the book was born in 1994. In that year, and in 1995, I helped direct two conferences at Connecticut College. The conferences were designed to identify and evaluate the various effects, both positive and negative, that the globalization of the market economy had generated since the end of the Cold War. I am grateful to many of the conferences' participants, especially William Smith, Richard Falk, Mwesiga Baregu,

Claire Gaudiani, Marion Doro, Maria Cruz-Saco, Julie Fischer, Mary McGinn, James K. Onoh, Julia Kushigian, Ann Elizabeth Harrison, Anthonia C. Kalu, Nirvana A. E. Khadr, Steven Lamy, Hernan Martinez, Azim A. Nanji, and Francis Fox Piven, for their insightful contributions. The conferences could have not been held without the generous support from the Carnegie Corporation of New York, The Andrew W. Mellon Foundation, and the Rockefeller Brothers Fund. I received additional financial support, in the form of travel grants, from Connecticut College's R. F. Johnson Funds.

I am indebted to John Odell, Sidney Drell, Robert Peurifoy, William Rose, David Patton, Ronald Steel, and the anonymous reviewers, for their constructive critiques of the manuscript. Many of my former students also played important roles. Alexander Thompson, who served as my research assistant before leaving for his graduate education at the University of Chicago, contributed extensively to the writing of chapter 7. Hagen Maroney, likewise, helped me develop a better understanding of the new economic and financial challenges faced by Latin American states. In addition, I am thankful to the students in my international relations theories and foreign policy seminars for their willingness to read incomplete versions of the manuscript and for providing helpful comments. As in the past, Barbara Peurifoy, my mother-in-law, helped me edit the manuscript.

I would have never been able to complete this work without the unwavering love and support from my wife Jan, and our two daughters Sabrina and Gabriela. As I sat in front of my computer every morning for nearly two years, always wondering whether I would have a productive day, I knew that ten hours later I would be returning to an environment filled with joy and laughter. This knowledge made my work astonishingly easy.

I extend my final expression of gratitude to Susan Eckert Lynch. Susan has been a major constructive force at Connecticut College for many years. As an alum and a member of the Board of Trustees, she played a leading role during Connecticut College's last fund-raising campaign. She helped set the tone by creating the endowed chair that I now hold. Her function, however, has transcended that of an important trustee and financial contributor. Her warmth, friendship, and commitment to my academic development has made me appreciate the value of being associated with a small, reputable, liberal arts institution. I dedicate this book to her.

Alex Roberto Hybel
Stonington, Connecticut

INTRODUCTION

The United States and the Changing Nature of the International System

The Intellectual Challenge

The end of an era is ordinarily supervened by uncertainty. As the United States and the Soviet Union closed the doors on the Cold War in the late 1980s, some U.S. foreign policy analysts claimed that American hegemony was a thing of the past. Hard data seemed to back their declaration. By the end of the Reagan administration, the United States's gross national debt had jumped from $995 billion to $2.9 trillion, and its annual deficit stood at $152 billion. Conditions did not improve during the next three years. Under George Bush's leadership, the United States economy endured a recession, and by 1992 the federal government's cumulative debt had surpassed $4 trillion and the annual deficit had risen to $290 billion.[1] Based on analyses of the potential capabilities of entities such as China, Japan, the European Union, Russia, India, and Indonesia, some observers also predicted that by the year 2020 the structure of the international system would be multipolar and that the rivalry between the dominant powers would induce instability.[2]

By the start of the second half of the 1990s, a new group of experts wondered whether some of the doubts voiced earlier about the fate of the United States might have been premature. The United States still possessed the most powerful and most advanced military in the world, and its economy had again become the envy of its most ardent international competitors. And yet, it took only two new international crises in the late 1990s, one financial and the other military, to once more persuade some critics that the United States was destined to lose its economic and strategic dominance, and that the international economic and security systems were about to undergo radical transformations. Not surprisingly, by the end of the first half of 1999, as the economies of many Asian countries showed new signs of growth, the United States's economy continued to prove its resilience, and Serbia signaled that it was finally ready to comply with the United States and NATO's Kosovo demands, many pundits yet again began to question the earlier conclusions.

The fate of a hegemon cannot be augured just on the basis of an examination of its most recent experiences, its ability to contend with the latest international crises, and the potential capabilities of its closest rivals. To foretell a hegemon's future, it is also crucial to conduct a historical assessment of its capacity to deal with a series of domestic and international challenges under a wide range of circumstances, and to learn from its accomplishments and failures. My ultimate objective in this book is to explain why the United States will most likely manage to preserve its superpower status for decades to come. To accomplish this goal I will focus on the United States's two-century struggle to become the globe's dominant entity, alter the structure and nature of the international security and economic systems, and protect its hegemonic standing.

The Analytical Framework

Throughout history, the international system has wavered between stability and instability, between peace and war. Changes in the international system have been induced by tensions generated by the collision between contradictory forces. The contradictions were sometimes generated by forces originating in the international system itself, at other times by forces emanating from rival states, and at other times by forces springing from both locations.

The contention that contradictory forces generate changes in the international arena has its roots in ancient Greece, and was elaborated by Hegel and Marx many centuries later. Hegel and Marx viewed history as an impersonal process, moving toward some ideal telos. For Hegel, history reflects the progress of freedom; for Marx, it is defined by the dynamic of economic development that gives rise to clashes between classes struggling for control of the state. Hegel tried to apply his conceptual structure to every aspect of reality, intertwining religion and metaphysics, psychology and value, and being and time; Marx used his analytical framework to design a principle of economic and political revolution.[3] The application of dialectic logic to the study of foreign policy does not depend on the assumption that an ideal telos awaits, or on the assertion that only a very narrow set of dynamic contradictory forces induces change. Instead, it is built on the neutral supposition that history is contradictory and changing, is undergoing processes of opposition and integration, and is defined by the actions from different subjects attempting to find solutions to the tensions that evolve from the contradictions flowing from a wide range of sources.[4] During the years just preceding the start of the First World War, for instance, the forces of nationalism surging from the Ottoman Empire, the Austrian-Hungarian Empire, and the newly created Balkan states collided with the drive by several powers either to preserve or offset Europe's balance-of-power system. The Cold War period, on the other hand, was the result of a tension that had its origins in the bipolar rivalry between two states with opposing ideologies.

International tensions propel the international system's principal states to design policies that attempt, at minimum, to alleviate the costly effects spawned by contradictory forces and, at maximum, to replace the system with one that serves more effectively their own separate needs and interests. Each of the system's chief states is seldom able to react to the tensions emanating from the international arena as a single, rational, national actor whose interests are determined solely by its standing in the international system. Instead, each responds as an entity led by a small number of decision-makers who are rarely free to act without first gauging the way other states would interpret and respond to their actions, and who on most occasions are armed with inconclusive information and hindered by a series of psychological and information-processing limitations.[5] These domestic and personal conditions, rather than generating a clear conception of a state's national interest, provoke diverse opinions about the nature of the international challenge and its domestic and international implications, and about the foreign policy that should be designed and implemented. Moreover, in each instance the leaders' final decision is dictated not only by the potential effects it would have on the state's place in the international system, but also on a wide range of other interests, both domestic and international.

The ability of a state to increase its political and economic power, or to lessen the costs occasioned by the tensions afflicting the international system or its own domestic system, is a function not just of its relative military and economic capabilities, but also of the attributes of its domestic political and economic systems. Domestic political and economic systems can be differentiated along a wide range of factors, many of which are not transferable from one system set to the other. There are two factors, however, that are applicable to both political and economic systems: their levels of competitiveness and openness.

Political systems vary according to the extent to which the actions of the government can be contested. In the Soviet Union, for instance, the Communist Party never authorized any other party to openly contest its power and policies. To note that a political system is competitive is not to assert that it is also fully open. For years, Switzerland had one of the world's most fully developed systems of political competition; and yet, until not long ago, women were not authorized to participate in national elections. An open and competitive political system is one in which its citizens have the same, relatively unimpaired, legal opportunities to support or contest the conduct of the government, and one in which no individual or party can control the government for an indefinite period of time.[6] Democracy, which is the term normally assigned to an open and competitive political system, has its counterpart in the economic arena in the form of the open market.[7] Markets can differ with regard to the freedom that different people (or organizations) have to enter the market, and in the extent to which different individuals (buyers or sellers) can influence the terms of economic exchange. Stated in terms that are analogous to those used to differentiate political systems, markets vary according to their "degree of openness and the intensity of the competition among producers and sellers." Thus, "a perfect or self-regulating market is one that is open to all potential buyers and sellers and one in which no buyer or seller can determine the terms of exchange."[8]

Markets affect every aspect of the societies that encompass them. Markets that are very open and highly competitive place emphasis on the efficient allocation of labor, land, and capital in order to promote technological and other types of innovations and bring about economic growth. The underlying rationale for this process is greater economic wealth. Democracies make it possible for their citizens to decide who will lead them, what issues their leaders will address, and what policies their leaders should implement. Though all democracies must grapple with economic issues, the degree of emphasis they place on them and the way they contend with them differ markedly depending on their markets' levels of openness and competitiveness. In a democracy paired with a very open and highly competitive market system, the leaders and citizens of the state will invariably place an inordinate amount of emphasis on the execution of domestic and foreign policies that nurture the conditions that enhance the likelihood of uninterrupted economic growth.[9]

The alignment of an open market with a democracy has two additional interrelated effects. The cohabitation of open and competitive political and economic systems has a major positive effect on the state's willingness to reflect on past errors and address them expeditiously. A democracy, like any other political system, will commit political errors. In a democracy, however, because of its openness and competitiveness, the drive to find the underlying causes of an error will be greater than in a closed political system. Though the search for the cause of an error does not guarantee its discovery, the chances for discovery are null if an inquiry is not forced or initiated. Because an authoritarian state bases much of its authority on infallibility, it is less prone to conduct an objective analysis of past errors than is a democratic state.[10] Similarly, market competition, which forces producers eager to prosper to find higher levels of productive efficiency and technology, also propels them to address costly errors that, if unresolved, could hamper their ability to remain competitive.

The Proposition

All great powers eventually become lesser powers. It is improbable that the United States will become history's sole exception. Still, it is highly unlikely that the United States will experience such a fate in the near future. The openness and competitiveness of the United States's domestic political and economic systems enabled it to become the international system's dominant state and to retain its status even in the face of ponderous external and internal challenges. So long as the United States does not alter the structure of its domestic systems, it will remain the international system's most puissant actor for the next quarter of a century.

The analysis of the foreign policies of the United States during the past two centuries discloses a fallible international actor. It reveals an entity not always able to comprehend the nature of the contradictory forces besetting the international system, not always willing to use its power to prevent the accumulation of contradictory forces or to abate those already in existence, and not always adept at anticipating the consequences of some of its actions as it responded, or failed to respond, to the tensions emanating from the international arena. It also unveils, however, an international party inclined to examine and redress its past errors, and determined to carry out the steps necessary to become the world's most dominant international entity and protect its leadership.

Always attentive to the domestic repercussions of its foreign policies, Washington consistently confronted the future by gauging the costs the United States had encountered in its immediate past. A costly past experience generally elicited responses designed to avert its recurrence. On such occasions, it was not unusual for Washington to opt for the path of less domestic resistance; but that path, in turn, often generated new, unexpected, costs. When such an outcome resulted, Washington, constantly attuned to the U.S. public's disposition, drew up new policies designed to revert it. On the whole, possession of an open and competitive domestic system did not prevent the United States from committing grave foreign policy errors; it did, however, enhance its ability to reveal them before they became unbearably costly.

Structure of the Book

In the next seven chapters I analyze the unfolding of the foreign policy of the United States during the past two centuries. In chapter 1, I discuss the origins of the nineteenth century European balance-of-power system, the contradictions and tensions it generated as its structure corroded, the manner in which its steady breakdown helped the United States broaden its political and economic power, and the effects the nature of the United States's domestic political and economic systems had on its drive to increase its own power. I close the chapter with an analysis of the international conditions that induced the 1914 war, the opportunities the war and the international system afforded the United States, and the United States's domestic conditions that impelled its leaders to reason that it would be in its interests to enter the war. In chapters 2 and 3, I focus on the 1919–1941 period. I start with descriptions of the goals sought by the major powers at the end of the war, the peace agreement they designed, and the effects the peace agreement had on them. I then move to an analysis of the world economic depression and its effects on the international system and on two of its most troublesome actors, Germany and Japan. I also discuss the way the United States responded to developments in the international arena in the 1930s, and the way its internal political and economic conditions influenced its responses. In chapter 4, I describe the post–Second World War international system envisioned by Roosevelt and explain why the United States fell somewhat short in shaping it in the manner he had hoped. I then discuss the genesis of the Cold War and the tensions it started to generate between the United States and the Soviet Union. In chapter 5, I spell out the evolution of the Cold War, the contradictions it spawned within the United States, and the effects these contradictions had on its foreign policies. In chapter 6, I focus on the United States's attempts to find a new equilibrium after the end of the Vietnam War, and on the turbulent domestic and international effects of these efforts. I also explain, via a comparison of the domestic political and economic systems of the United States and the Soviet Union, why the former emerged victorious from the Cold War, while the latter witnessed its own demise. In chapter 7, I discuss the United States's 1990s doctrine of enlargement, and the contradictions and tensions the doctrine either originated or helped intensify in different regions of the globe. I also speculate about how these contradictions and tensions are likely to affect the stability of the international system, and why the United States should be able to cope with them effectively.

CHAPTER ONE

The Rise of a New International Giant

International Opportunities And Domestic Conditions

The most important outcome of the First World War was the emergence of the United States as the international system's dominant state. This development begs the question: How did a nation, which at the start of the nineteenth century was unsure that it would be able to survive in an anarchical international system, become its most commanding member in a little over a century? In this chapter, I propose that the United States's unique domestic political and economic systems both spawned pressures on, and freed, its leaders to expand its territory and increase its international political and economic influence. These conditions alone, however, could not have been enough to help transform so radically the power of the United States. To reach the zenith of the international system, the United States was aided by its territorial remoteness and an international system that had been created to guarantee that no single European state would become too powerful.

The anarchical nature of the international system forces every newly born state to try to enlarge its power in order to lessen the ability of other states to exploit its initial weakness. Until quite recently, any state that sought to expand its power tried to do so by attempting to augment its territorial control and its international political and economic influence. A state that initiated this task had no reason to cease it until the marginal costs of additional changes become equal to, or greater than, their marginal benefits.[1] A state's commitment to expanding its power was determined by the opportunities rendered by the international system, and by the effects the expansion was likely to have on the interests of its most powerful domestic groups and individuals. During much of the nineteenth century, states tried to augment their powers by increasing the size of their territories. The leaders of states assumed that by enlarging their territories they would also be able to increase their international political and economic influence. At least two external factors typically affected the propensity of states to attempt to enlarge their territories. Generally, they gauged the external benefits that the control of additional territories would bring about, and the level of external opposition they would encounter in their drive to enlarge their territories. The greater the benefits they calculated they would amass and the lower the level of external opposition they expected to encounter, the greater their determination to expand their territories.

Not all states responded in the same manner to the same set of external opportunities and constraints. Different types of domestic political, economic, and social arrangements created different forms and levels of incentives by having different effects on a state's initiative and capacity to adapt to specific environmental opportunities and changes.[2] The domestic structure of the United States during the nineteenth century was very effective at fostering initiative and adapting to specific international opportunities and constraints, largely because it combined the characteristics of the democratic and market systems. Before I describe and explain the effects of the United States's domestic structure on its foreign policy, however, I must delineate the nature of the international system the United States responded to during the first half of the nineteenth century and describe the objectives its creators had hoped it would fulfill.

In Search Of A Less Violent International System

The eighteenth century is often referred to as the Age of Enlightenment or the Age of Reason. Heartened by Isaac Newton's scientific theories, some of Europe's greatest thinkers believed they would also be able to discover rules of rational behavior for human society. But the relationship between human societies of different states did not buttress this sentiment. Though the European states had succeeded in moderating their anarchic tendencies, the principal powers continued to battle one another. Disillusioned by these developments, some of Europe's chief political thinkers proposed the establishment of a balance-of-power system. The system, they suggested, would be created to restrict the power and territorial ambitions of international actors, and would be controlled by no more than five powers.[3]

Some ideas take a long time to germinate into palpable realities. The idea of creating a balance-of-power system did not assume the form of concrete policies until the actions of one of Europe's dominant parties threatened the power of its equals. The French Revolution set a mild spark. But it was not until 1812 that Napoleon, who had become Europe's most dominant leader, forced the other main European leaders to form a grand alliance to stop him. Following Napoleon's defeat, the victors gathered in Vienna to give shape to Europe's balance-of-power system. The architects of the new system made it clear that its driving rationale would be to resist any effort at unilateral domination. The attainment of this end, they agreed, was dependent on their joint ability to offset an attempt by any one state to expand its strength beyond a certain assumed level, and upon their adeptness at keeping the German states disunited. With Britain as the acknowledged dominant power, it was natural for them to assume that Russia, France, and Austria would strive to further augment their own capabilities. However, they did not apply this assumption to the German states. They expected the German states "to serve as a kind of shock absorber and hence had to remain disunited in the interests of peace, preserving the 'balance through an inherent force of gravity.'"[4] Moreover, they presumed that, disunited, no one single German state would ever become powerful enough to fracture the equilibrium forged by the principal states.

The likelihood that an international political system will achieve the ends for which it was designed depends on the correctness of its assumptions and on its capacity to cope with unforeseen developments. By the middle of the nineteenth century, Europe's balance-of-power system was already braving its first set of strains. Russia, which had elicited the respect of its peers during the early part of the century, found itself struggling to regain it. Initially, as European leaders looked toward Russia, they held in awe the vastness of its territory and population. This attitude was reinforced when Saint Petersburg responded to Napoleon's invasion of Russia by marching its own troops to the gates of Paris in 1814. The image of Russia as a state being led by a stable regime was solidified in 1848 when, with Britain, it managed not to acquiesce to the flames of revolution that spread throughout much of Europe. This image, however, did not reflect accurately Russia's domestic condition. First, it did not take into account that Russia had been losing ground at an alarming pace in the economic and technological race with its major European rivals. Between 1830 and 1850, its per capita GNP increased only from $170 to $175, while Britain's went up from $346 to $458, and France's from $264 to $333.[5] Second, the image did not consider that the benefits Russia obtained from its vast territory and large population were in part enfeebled by its lack of access to an open sea. It was enclosed by ice on the north and east and by the land masses of Asia and Europe on the south and the west. Its only warm-water ports were on the Black Sea.[6] The Ottoman Empire, however, controlled access from the Black Sea to the Mediterranean Sea. It was in this part of the world that Russia would ultimately expose its military and economic weaknesses.

In 1853, Saint Petersburg moved its troops to the borders of Moldavia and Wallachia and sent a commission to Constantinople to demand the right to protect Orthodox Christians everywhere in Turkey.[7] When the commission failed to extract an agreement from Constantinople, Saint Petersburg ordered Russian troops to occupy Moldavia and Wallachia. Constantinople responded by declaring war on Russia in October. Russia gained the upper hand in November by destroying the Turkish fleet. This development did not fare well among British and French leaders, and in March 1854 they declared war on Russia. Their rationales for going to war differed. The leaders in London were convinced that the only way they would be able to bring about a modicum of stability in the Near East was by defeating Russia decisively. Louis Napoleon, on the other hand, hoped to use a war alliance with Britain, and the eventual defeat of Russia, as means to alter the 1815 European system. The war came to an end when Russia conceded that it could not win and signed a peace agreement in Paris on March 30, 1856.

For Russia the outcome of the conflict proved to be a blessing in disguise. When Britain and France forced Saint Petersburg to cede territory to Moldavia and accept the neutrality of the Black Sea,[8] Russia's leaders recognized that its power was inferior to that of its rivals and that unless it altered its ways it would have to sacrifice its standing in the European system. As noted by one of Russia's leaders in the aftermath of the war, Russia could not deceive itself any longer, for it was "both weaker and poorer than the first-class powers, and poorer not only in material but also in mental resources, especially in matters of administration."[9] Saint Petersburg initiated a series of radical changes designed to enhance Russia's ability to compete in the military and economic arenas. Its newly born determination was partially reinforced by the knowledge that yesterday's enemies sometimes become tomorrow's allies. In 1858, Russia's Czar Alexander II received a letter from Louis Napoleon stating that if Saint Petersburg helped modify aspects of the 1815 treaty, Paris would respond in form with regard to the Treaty of Paris.

France, Russia's potential partner, had also been experiencing some major challenges. Though during the first half of the century France's power was greater than Prussia's or Austria's, it did not compare favorably with Britain's or Russia's. Several problems impaired France's standing in the European continent. First, it had to cope with the fact that all the other great European powers had united to prevent France's attempt to become Europe's hegemon in 1814-1815 and subsequently had constructed a postwar international system designed to block any future attempts by France, or any other international entity, to resurrect such a foreign policy. Second, its army did not compare favorably with Russia's nor did its navy with Britain's. And third, its economy no longer possessed the vitality that it had at the beginning of the century. During this period, Britain's and France's manufacturing output were almost at the same level, but 30 years later Britain's was 182.5 percent of France's, and by the end of the next 30 years it had risen to 251 percent. France's problems were temporarily compounded by developments in 1848. In the early months, students and workingmen took to the streets to condemn the political and economic policies of the French government. Following a confrontation with French troops that resulted in the deaths of some 50 people, new demonstrations ensued. Unable to withstand the political pressure from below, King Louis Phillipe abdicated and fled to England. His departure was followed by the establishment of a provisional government that, based on its composition, seemed to signal its members' determination to transform France into a republic and address the economic and social needs of the "common man." This perception proved to be mistaken. By May of the same year, with a new National Constituent Assembly in place, it became evident that though the new France would be a republic in political attitude, it would be predominantly conservative in social philosophy.[10] By year's end, France had a new president in the person of Prince Louis Napoleon. Four years later, he was proclaimed emperor of the French people.

Napoleon III came to power committed to transforming Paris into Europe's diplomatic capital. He believed that to achieve this end he would have to revive France's economy. He launched a series of economic policies designed to promote the establishment of new industry and the framing of public works to reduce unemployment. On the international front, he was determined to alter the settlement imposed on France in Vienna in 1815, and to create a new international order. This new order would have as its foundation the principle of national self-determination. According to Napoleon, a Europe based on fulfilled nationalist aspirations and satisfied national interests would bring harmony and prosperity to the continent and inspire universal respect toward the country that animated the transformation.[11] Napoleon's first major foreign policy adventure pitted France against Russia in 1854. The Crimean War enhanced his international prestige and prepared the way for a future understanding between France and Russia.[12]

Before Russia and France could develop a new understanding, other issues had to gain visibility and intensity. As an empire's power ebbs, rival entities witnessing the process scheme to find ways to fill the power vacuum that inevitably results. In the middle of the nineteenth century, Prussia was by far the lesser of the major powers. Its fortunes experienced a major change with Otto von Bismarck's ascendancy to the role of minister-president in September 1862. Bismarck understood that for his country to augment its power it would first have to fight a weakened Austria for leadership over the German people, who still remained divided into a myriad of principalities. The issue was resolved at the battle of Königgrätz, where the Prussian army crushed its Austrian counterpart on July 3, 1866.[13] Bismarck did not use the victory to humble Austria. As he would explain to those who wanted to impose an opprobrious peace treaty on Vienna: "We [Prussians] are not the only inhabitants of Europe, but live in it with three other powers that detest us and envy us."[14]

One of the powers that particularly concerned Bismarck was France. Shortly after the end of the Austrian-Prussian war, Paris initiated a series of policies designed to both challenge Prussia's newly acquired status and build a set of alliances that would better France's defensive capabilities. The final outcome of Prussia's and France's rivalry was a war that resulted in France's defeat in late 1870. The consequences of the war were monumental. To begin with, it led to the dethroning of Louis Napoleon and the creation of a new French republic. More importantly, it destroyed the merit of the primary assumption that had helped sustain the balance-of-power principle—a disunited and weak Germany. In 1871, the German states united under the leadership of a single monarch.[15] The effect of this event was experienced immediately. As a united state, Germany instantly became more powerful than its neighbors on the continent, and by the beginning of the twentieth century's second decade it was challenging Britain's hegemony.[16] Germany's unification and increased strength spawned two interdependent responses. To Germany's own leaders, it signaled that other European countries either would search for ways to protect themselves from future attempts by Germany to increase its own power at their expense, or would attempt to weaken Germany's newly acquired strength. To counter these possibilities, Germany sought refuge in the formation of intricate, and in some instances secret, alliances.

Power begets counter-power. Though in 1815 Europe's leaders failed to envision a Europe in which a united Germany would become the dominant continental power, it would have not been difficult for them to comprehend this development had they been present during the last quarter of the nineteenth century. It is likely, however, that had they been alive they would have been astonished by the effects nationalism had on the structure of the international system. Humans have always defined themselves in relation to a relatively narrow reference point. A point of reference relied on by inhabitants of different regions has been the nation and its outgrowth—nationalism. In its simplest form, nationalism refers to the doctrine that perceives a nation's interests as separate from the interests of other nations or the common interests of all nations. It is a cultural artifact that can be used to command profound emotional legitimacy and to incite action.[17] Though nationalism emerged as a normative concept in Europe in the eighteenth century, it did not become a dominant international force until the middle and second half of the nineteenth century, following the revolutionary upheavals of 1848 and the emergence of a unified kingdom in Italy and a new empire in Germany.[18]

Depending on the internal nature of the state, nationalism could act either as a strengthening or a debilitating force. In instances in which there was a close correspondence between the legal and the cultural entity—that is, between the state and the nation—nationalism could be used by the state to augment its international power. When the state was inhabited by more than one nation, when the legal system did not effectively represent the various nationalities, and when the power of the state was limited, nationalism threatened to undermine the ability of the state to keep its dominance over the different national groups. In Europe, almost nowhere did the state lines follow the lines of nationality, and every state faced, to some degree, opposition from one or more national groups. Britain was burdened by the Irish question, and France and Germany by Alsace and Lorraine. But no European power feared the destructive forces of nationalism more than the leaders of the Austrian Empire and the Ottoman Empire.

Among the European states, the Austrian Empire ranked second in territory, third in population, fourth in foreign trade, and fifth in industrial output. Furthermore, it had an efficient civil service, a strong army, and a stable government. However, behind this picture of grandeur and stability lingered a potential source of discord: a population divided into many nations. The Congress of Vienna of 1815 sought to restore thrones, states, and boundaries. Austria, or more specifically the Habsburg Empire, had different forms of jurisdiction over a vast territory encompassing a wide range of nationalities. It presided over the very loose German confederation of 39 states, had direct control of lands in northern Italy, had annexed both Lombardy and Venice, and had granted the key Italian duchies of Modena and Parma to its own princes. Moreover, its own territory was occupied by German, Magyar, Czech, Ruthen, Polish, Rumanian, and Serbo-Croatian nationals.

One of the first signs that the Habsburg Empire was built on a house of cards came about not within the empire itself but within another empire threatened by a similar condition: the Ottoman Empire. In 1833, after an extended nationalist revolt that lasted through most of the 1820s and drew the support of Russia, France, and Britain, Greek rebels secured the creation of an autonomous Greek monarchy under the suzerainty of the Ottoman Empire. For Austria, the warning could not have been more ominous. The parturition of modern Greece signified not simply the birth of a new state but the genesis of a nation-state from an empire made up of many nations. The forces of nationalism were slow to gain momentum in Austria. But finally, on March 3, 1848, a little over a week after rioting had broken out in the streets of Paris and just a few days after Louis Phillipe had abdicated the French throne, a Hungarian aristocrat by the name of Lajos Kossuth demanded in Budapest an end to the "unnatural political system" that ruled Austria.[19] By the month's end, the Austrian government had granted Hungary a set of "March laws." The laws abolished censorship, ended the nobility's exemption from taxation, and proclaimed equality before the law. Developments in Hungary were followed immediately by demonstrations in Vienna, Prague, Milan, and Venice. In Frankfurt, Germans called for freedom of the press and the creation of a constitutional national government. These actions, however, did not germinate into immediate, tangible changes. Just as France's revolutionary drive was to be tamed by the autocratic actions of its new ruler, Louis Napoleon, Budapest was to learn in a very short time that Vienna was not yet ready to acquiesce to the forces of nationalism. In April 1849, Hungary declared its independence from the Habsburgs, only to find itself back under Austrian dominion by August of that same year.

Though the forces of change instigated by the 1848 French Revolution did not immediately trigger within the Habsburg Empire the domestic changes longed for by their champions, they openly revealed that unless the empire abated the divisive effect of nationalism, it would corrode Austria's standing among the European powers. In fact, 1848 marked the beginning of nationalism's "shaping mass personalities and producing their inevitable conflicts."[20] But nearly 20 years would have to pass before the Habsburg monarchy would finally accede to changes in its domestic political structure. In 1866, after being soundly defeated by the German kingdom of Prussia and thereby losing his role in Germany and Venice, the Habsburg ruler was forced to turn his attention inward. Cognizant that the war had debilitated the Austrian Empire, the Magyars, the most important national group because all of its members resided within the empire—in contrast to the Italians, Germans, Rumanians, Serbs, and Poles, most of whom lived outside it—demanded the creation of a Hungarian state within the monarchy, but ruled by Magyars. In 1867, the Habsburg emperor acquiesced to their demands and authorized the formation of two independent states. Austria and Hungary would be united under his rule as king-emperor by a treaty that regulated their commercial and financial relations; established joint administrative institutions responsible for defense, foreign affairs, and finance; and provided for a common army. The Austrian Empire, thus, managed to avert its own demise by transforming itself into the Dual Monarchy.[21] The cure, however, also exposed the intensity of the empire's malady. It immediately revealed that the future of the monarchy would be to a significant extent captive of the forces of nationalism. But it would take nearly 50 years for the world to learn that there was no cure for an empire that owed much of its power to the control over rival nationalities.

It is impossible to understand the nature of the international system brought into being by the major European powers, and the tensions it generated as the nineteenth century unfolded, without taking into account the role played by Great Britain. By the middle of the eighteenth century, France and Great Britain were the international system's two principal entities. Though France was the dominant actor in continental Europe and the more powerful of the two, Britain, with its mastery of the high seas, was not far behind. As the last half of the century evolved, Britain's economic might began to grow at a faster pace than France's. Historically, technological advance has been continuous and incremental over time. However, occasionally major technological innovations occur, and when they do they tend to converge in both time and space. The innovative technologies of the first phase of the Industrial Revolution, during the second half of the eighteenth century, appeared primarily in Britain. Benefited by rich veins of coal, deposits of iron, and a resourceful and energetic population, Britain took the lead in the development of textiles, iron, and steam power, and in a relatively short period became the world's first industrial nation. By the middle of the nineteenth century, with a manufacturing output that was greater than Russia's and France's combined and more than four times bigger than Austria's or the German states', and with a per capita level of industrialization that was equal to Austria's, France's, the German states', the Italian states', and Russia's combined, Britain had become the world's economic hegemon.[22]

With the defeat of Napoleon in the early part of the nineteenth century, the major European powers created a balance-of-power system meant to prevent any state from attaining universal domination. The creation and protection of the system, at least during its first 40 years, could have not been realized without Great Britain's active involvement. Britain's determination to create and support the balance-of-power system had a simple rationale. With the advent of the Industrial Revolution and during the first half of the nineteenth century, Britain used its industrial and financial power to design an interdependent world economy based on free trade, equal treatment, and nondiscrimination. This international economic system had enabled Britain to become the world's leading economic power. To help protect it, Britain used the balance-of-power system. [23] The balance-of-power system required that the major powers in Europe keep each other in check and that Britain, because it did not have any direct interests at stake on the continent, play an objective balancing role. So long as the main parties on the continent of Europe focused primarily on balancing each other's power, Britain was able to direct its attention, without great difficulty, to its overseas economic interests. Britain, however, was not willing to stake its own economic future on such a fragile condition. Though Britain's military power was markedly inferior to that of the major European powers, its navy was greater than those of France, Russia, and Spain combined. This strength made it possible for Britain to control the "five keys" that "lock up the world"—Gibraltar, Singapore, Dover, the Cape of Good Hope, and Alexandria—and to restrain Europe's access to the outside world.[24]

In short, by the middle of the nineteenth century there were two complementary international subsystems, both of which were dependent on Britain's power and actions. Politics within continental Europe were dictated by a balance-of-power system created and protected by its major members, with Britain serving as the external enforcer. With the passage of time, as the system started to experience contradictions and tensions not envisioned by its designers, their ability and willingness to preserve it abated. Outside Europe, Britain, the proprietor of the world's most powerful navy, created an international economic system intended both to curb the involvement of its major European rivals and to serve its own industrial core via the supply of cheap food, raw materials, and markets. This system also endured appreciable contradictions and tensions, but they did not arise until later. The existence of these two systems and the manner in which they evolved had a major effect on the development of the foreign policy of the United States during the nineteenth century.

The Intersections Between The International System, Democracy, The Open Market, And The Foreign Policy Of The United States

"[T]he United States was conceived as a creature of foreign relations."[25] To this assertion one should add that it was the structure of the international system during the nineteenth century that enabled the United States to incorporate so much new territory so rapidly and at so little personal cost.[26] This enlargement, however, did not come about without a powerful domestic impetus. In the next few sections I will delineate the steps the United States took to expand its territory, and explain the manner in which its political and economic structures impelled its leaders to take advantage of the opportunities afforded by the international system. Before I conduct these tasks, however, I must outline the nature of the United States's political and economic structures.

The Nature of Democracy

It has been stated that the "history of democracy is largely an account of the pursuit of liberty."[27] The statement, if taken out of context, could help create the wrong impression, mainly because the contemporary concept of freedom was unknown in antiquity. In Ancient Greece, the idea of each individual's development of his own private moral code without reference to the state was unthinkable. As Hannah Arendt put it, free will was a "faculty virtually unknown to classical antiquity. . . . In Greek as well as Roman antiquity freedom was an exclusively political concept."[28] Arendt's distinction is critical. The Greeks did not conceive of man as an individual with a private self, with a legitimate private space conceived as the "moral as well as the juridical projection of the single human person."[29] The modern conception of freedom, which gained ground in the wake of the Reformation after the seventeenth century and is often referred to as "freedom from" (the state), assumes that man is more than a citizen of the state; he is a private self with the freedom to be different and to dissent.[30] In order for the individual to be able to practice this type of personal freedom, the state, which exists as a supraordinate entity, must protect the individual against any attempt on its part to abuse its power or use it arbitrarily. This form of protection permits the individual to choose, and it is guaranteed, as John Locke reminded us, by laws.

Democracy, or more specifically, liberal democracy, is bounded also by a second component: equality. To examine this concept and its meaning, I must first focus on a common misconception. The claim that men are entitled to equal rights and opportunities because they are in fact equal, does not hold. Equality is not natural, inequality is. Equality does not result if things are allowed to follow their course; equality can result only from the acts of an external agent. The Greeks and Romans entertained the concept of equality without ever assuming that men were the same, alike, or equal. Instead, they derived it from the belief, suggested initially by Aristotle and then repeated by Brunetto Latini, that "he who wants to establish justice tries to make equal the things that are unequal."[31]

The drive to make unequal things equal has assumed different forms through the years; it started as a juridical-political form of equality ("to everyone the same legal and political rights"), and in its most contemporary incarnation it called for economic sameness ("the same wealth to each and all"). For present purposes it is not important to discuss the evolution and significance of the different forms of equality. It suffices to note three things. First, though "freedom from" and juridical-political equality belong to separate categories, together they function as the foundation of liberal democracy. Second, as one moves from juridical-political equality to economic sameness, one moves from a form of equality that tolerates diversity to an equality that challenges diversity. And third, the movement from the first form of equality to the last one can ensue only by increasing the power of the state, that is, by reducing the capability of individuals to be different.

In what ways do "freedom from" and juridical-political equality serve as the foundation of liberal democracy? Without the presence of both conditions, political competition and political participation would be unrealizable; and without the presence of political competition and political participation, democracy would be impossible. When discussing the role of competition in democracies, most analysts concentrate on the competition that takes place among political leaders for the people's support. Joseph Schumpeter, for instance, postulates a competitive theory of democracy in which he contends that the "democratic method is that institutional arrangement for arriving at political decisions in which individuals acquire the power to decide by means of a competitive struggle for the people's vote."[32] Giovanni Sartori expands on Schumpeter's theory by noting that a contemporary democracy is a mechanism that generates an open polyarchy whose competition in the electoral market ascribes power to the people and specifically enforces the responsiveness of the leaders to the led.[33] Though I agree that one of the critical ingredients of a democracy is the competition that ensues between political leaders for the people's support, this view of competition is constricted and, as a result, misleading. Politics, in a democracy, is a matter of competition between groups at different levels, with different interests. Government is the focal point for pressure from competing interest groups, and its task is to design a policy that reflects the highest common factor of demands.[34] In a democracy there is never one interest group with the power to consistently determine the outcome of every single issue. Instead, a number of interest groups compete to influence those in government as to who should get what, when, and how, and their success varies across time and from one issue to another.

If competitiveness in politics is desirable, can it be assumed that the greater the level of competitiveness in a democracy, the greater the likelihood it will thrive?[35] No, particularly among newly born states. The type of electoral system a newly born state institutes can have a major effect on the level of competitiveness its democratic political system experiences. A newly born state that is not severely divided along racial, religious, or ethnic lines is bound to be well served by the adoption of a plurality electoral system, that is, a winner-takes-all type of electoral system. Such an electoral system tends to encourage the configuration of centripetal forces. One of the most common effects of the establishment of a plurality electoral system is the development of a two-party system. In a two-party system, the two competing entities understand that to win, when the spread of opinion is small and its distribution single peaked, they must vie for the support of the voters at the center of the spectrum of opinions.[36] This simple dictum was understood by the founding fathers of the United States. Convinced that too much political competitiveness, fostered by personal liberty, would spawn factions, they sought to design a system that would curb its scope. Via the establishment of a winner-takes-all type of electoral system, they automatically curbed the number of parties that would emerge throughout the nineteenth century, with each of the parties attempting to amalgamate as many groups, interests, and demands as possible.

A two-party system cannot succeed under all types of societies. Its chances of success are markedly greater the smaller the spread of opinion within a society. Its success in the United States during the nineteenth century can be attributed in no small measure to the narrow dispersion of opinions of its members.[37] As an entity with a short history, inhabited, at least during its early years, by a very small population, most of whom lived east of the Appalachian mountains and were immigrants or descendants of immigrants from the Anglo-Saxon and Germanic countries of northern and western Europe, the United States found itself relatively free of the divisions that often afflict newly created states. With its independence finally acknowledged by the major European powers and the nature of its constitution mostly resolved, by the second decade of the nineteenth century the people of the United States were finally able to focus most of their energies on the betterment of their own personal economic welfare. This commitment, and the basis for its development, was aptly stated by Alexis de Tocqueville when he wrote:

> Perhaps there is no country in the world where fewer idle men are to be met than in America, or where all who work are eager to promote their own welfare. . . . An American tends to his private concerns as if he were alone in the world. . . . The inhabitants of the United States alternately display so strong and so similar a passion for their own welfare and for their freedom that it may be supposed that these passions are united and mingled in some part of their character. [T]hey believe . . . that their chief business is to secure for themselves a government which will allow them to acquire the things they covet and which will not debar them from the peaceful enjoyment of those possessions which they have already acquired.[38]

The Nature of the Market

Why this unrelenting commitment among Americans to the promotion of their own private economic welfare? Each society needs an orderly economic system for the allocation of resources. Without an economic system people would fight among themselves for scarce resources, and social order would break down. An economic system is bounded by the set of arrangements a society creates to allocate resources. In its simplest form, an economic system refers to the set of ownership, resource allocation, incentives, and decision-making arrangements used by a society to address economic issues. In a society, the factors of production may be owned by private individuals, by the government that represents society, or by both. The allocation of resources can be determined either by the forces of supply and demand or by government planners. The economic system may use economic, moral, or threatening incentives to induce individuals to work and produce. And the level of decision making may vary from a system in which the individual participants make their own decisions, to one in which the decisions for the individuals are made by government officials at the local, regional, or national level.

Different types of economic systems have different types of political, economic, and social effects. Presently, the most common economic system is the market economy. A market is to economics what democracy is to politics. A market economy is an established arrangement in which buyers and sellers come together to exchange particular goods and services on the basis of relative prices. Markets differ, and have differed, with regard to the freedom granted to individuals to enter the market and the extent to which buyers and sellers can determine the terms of exchange. A self-regulating, or perfect, market is one in which all interested buyers and sellers are free to participate and in which no buyer or seller can determine the terms of exchange. Notwithstanding the fact that a market can never attain perfection, its ability to approximate perfection is invariably determined by the actions of the political system under which it exists. A market cannot be self-regulating if the political system entitles the government to become a market's sole player, or if the political system does not authorize the government to prevent a single private supplier from becoming the sole determiner of the terms of exchange within a market.[39]

All democracies are open-market economies.[40] This association is not coincidental, since the two are the materialization of constitutional liberalism. In its earliest development, constitutional liberalism was a movement designed to enlarge and protect the liberties first of nobles, and then of a merchant middle class, by imposing constitutional restrictions on the prerogatives of government. The personal liberties sought by these groups reached beyond the right to be different and to dissent, as dictated by each person's conscience. A significant portion of the type of personal liberty they sought was the freedom to engage in trade, to set up their own enterprises in order to pursue the gains of trade, and to keep as much of their own earnings and assets as possible. Democracies, in other words, were created to win and protect various types of liberties, with private property, free enterprise, free contract, and occupational choice being among the most significant. The end result of the drive to secure these freedoms has been competition—competition between individuals free to decide what they want to do with their own energies and skills in both the political and economic arenas.[41]

The Effects of Domestic Political and Economic Competitiveness on U.S. Foreign Policy

It is not uncommon for analysts to assert that the American public pays little attention to foreign policy, and that elections are seldom determined by foreign policy issues. Both statements could be highly misleading, particularly if they persuade the reader to assume that, historically, U.S. decision-makers formulated foreign policies free of domestic pressures. U.S. decision-makers have always been conscious of existing and potential domestic pressures during the formulation of foreign policies. These pressures have emanated from different interest groups, depending on the nature of the issue. During the nineteenth century, however, most of the pressures on the political parties originated from domestic groups with competing economic interests.

From its early days as a nation, the United States understood that if it ever hoped to become a powerful international entity it first had to ensure its own survival, and that it could accomplish this end only by taking advantage of its geographical remoteness and by developing a unique relationship with Europe. In his presidential farewell address, George Washington reminded Americans that their country's "detached and distant situation" invited and enabled them to pursue "a different course," and warned them that were the United States to implicate itself "by artificial ties in the ordinary vicissitudes of [Europe's] politics or the ordinary combinations and collisions of [Europe's] friendships or enmities," it would not be able to prosper and become a powerful nation.[42] As the nation matured, this sentiment was reaffirmed by subsequent presidents. Thomas Jefferson admonished Americans to shun "entangling alliances" with other nations, and in the 1820s James Monroe endorsed the original principle by stating that "[i]n the wars of the European powers in matters relating to themselves [the United States has] never taken any part, nor does it comport with [its] policy to do so."[43]

Eschewing alliances never meant shunning the international arena. Each leader fully sensed that to protect the national sovereignty and independence of the United States he would have to be actively involved in international political, economic, and commercial affairs. Equally as significant, nearly each president believed that the United States, with a population almost doubling every 25 years, had to expand its power in the international arena whenever the opportunity arose. Thomas Jefferson was the first to voice this belief in a letter to James Madison in 1801, in which he stated:

> However our present situation may restrain us within our limits, it is impossible not to look forward to distant times, when our rapid multiplication will expand beyond those limits, and cover the whole northern, if not the southern continent, with a people speaking the same language, governed in similar forms, and by similar laws; nor can we contemplate with satisfaction blot or mixture on that surface.[44]

A similar belief was proclaimed some 20 years later by John Quincy Adams, secretary of state under James Monroe, when he remarked that "[t]here are laws of political as well as physical gravitation; and if an apple severed by the tempest from its native tree cannot but fall to the ground, Cuba, forcibly disjoined from its own unnatural connection with Spain, and incapable of self-support, can only gravitate toward the North American Union, which by the same law cannot cast her off from its bosom."[45] By midcentury, this belief had assumed the form of a principle. In 1845,

John L. O'Sullivan, a newspaper publisher from New York, described the nature of the principle in the form of a "manifest destiny." He wrote that it was "the fulfillment of [the United States's] manifest destiny to overspread the continent allotted by Providence for the free development of our yearly multiplying millions." Three years later, O'Sullivan added that the United States had no choice but to continue growing in order to accommodate a population that was doubling every generation.[46]

These beliefs did not exist in a domestic political vacuum. Until about 1815, the U.S. economy was dominated by two groups whose interests, though not always mutually exclusive, differed considerably. The smaller of the two, the shipping-commercial group, was composed primarily of merchants, traders, fishermen, and shipbuilders, as well as bankers and creditors who helped finance the trading and shipping enterprises. Most members of this group conducted their businesses in New England and in the eastern states of the mid-Atlantic areas, and were normally associated with the Federalist Party. The members of this group sought the design of policies that would protect and advance U.S. foreign trade. Specifically, they advocated a peaceful relationship with Great Britain, as most of their trade was with that country. They also supported the establishment of commercial treaties, the creation of a large and effective navy, and subsidies for the fishing industry. Equally as important, the shipping-commercial group vehemently opposed the westward territorial expansion by the United States. They feared that such a move would reduce the labor supply in the east and increase its cost, and that Westerners would, at least initially, produce less for exports and buy fewer European products. Furthermore, they speculated that the expansion would lead to the creation of more agrarian states and thus reduce the political power of the shipping-commercial interest group.

This last concern was justified. Prior to 1815, the largest economic interest in the United States was the farmer-agrarian group, which was made up of small farmers, planters, fur traders, and land speculators.[47] The group included members from the New England and mid-Atlantic states, but most of them resided in the South and the Piedmont valleys of the Appalachians and the Ohio-Mississippi Valley.[48] Though members of this group favored foreign trade, they depended less on this activity than did the shipping-commercial group. For the farmer-agrarian group, one of the most important political-economic issues was the westward territorial expansion of the United States. In pursuit of this goal, they sought and received the support of the Democratic-Republican Party, which between 1801 and 1809 was led by Thomas Jefferson, and between 1809 and 1817, by James Madison.[49]

The rivalry between the two political parties was temporarily silenced when certain members of the Federalist Party denounced the war with Britain, which had been going on since 1812, and threatened to leave the

Union unless New Englanders were granted veto powers over issues regarding commercial matters and the admission of new western states into the Union. Their warning reached Washington in late 1814, just as the city was receiving news that Britain and the United States had agreed on a peace treaty. Americans did not forgive the Federalist Party for this blunder, and in the 1816 elections they placed the presidency and the Congress in the hands of the Democratic-Republican Party. Shortly afterward, the Federalist Party evanesced, as most of its supporters switched their allegiance to the remaining party.

The one-party system came to an end late in the 1820s with the emergence of two parties, both of which had their roots in the earlier parties.[50] The National Republican Party, which soon became the Whig Party, was the political descendant of the Federal Party. Under its new configuration, the party drew most of its support from merchants, shippers, bankers, and creditors. The Whig Party opposed the westward territorial expansion of the United States, while it favored protective tariffs, a national bank, federal aid for internal improvements, and fair treatment of Native Americans. The second party, the Democratic Party, was the offspring of Jefferson's Democratic-Republican Party. Though under its new structure it began to make significant inroads among urban workers, it continued to rely on the support of the farming West and planting South. It also remained committed to a policy of westward territorial expansion and of forcing Native Americans off of land coveted by whites.[51] The new party structure did not alter measurably the power distribution, at least at the executive level. Between 1829 and the end of 1860, the Whig Party controlled the presidency only during two four-year terms.[52] With the Democratic Party at the helm of the federal government most of the time, the agrarian-farmer group in the South and the West campaigned vigorously for low tariffs and territorial expansion.

The actions of these two economic interest groups had arresting effects on the foreign policies of the United States, particularly on its drive to expand southward and westward after independence. In 1801, after Spain had sold the Louisiana territory to France, Jefferson and his secretary of state, James Madison, concluded that if the United States ever hoped to incorporate the region west of the Mississippi all the way to the Pacific, it first had to secure control over the area just purchased by France. Two years later, aware that France was about to go to war against Great Britain once again and that France could ill afford to face at the same time a major dispute with the United States, Jefferson sent Madison to Paris to purchase the Louisiana territory. Prior to dispatching Madison to Paris, however, Jefferson asked his friend, Pierre Samuel Du Pont de Nemours, to warn the French government that if France chose to take possession of New Orleans, the United States would be forced to join forces with Great Britain, and together they would "maintain exclusive possession of the ocean."[53] The transaction between the United States and France was completed in April 1803. For a paltry $15 million, the United States managed to double, almost overnight, the size of its territory. Though originally Jefferson had assumed that the federal government would not be able to purchase Louisiana without a constitutional amendment granting it such authority, he submitted the treaty between France and the United States to the Senate and requested that it be approved. As expected, Republicans from agricultural states in the South and the West pushed for its approval, while most Federalists from the mid-Atlantic states and New England, afraid that the acquisition of the new lands would strengthen the power of their political adversaries, opposed it. The Senate approved the treaty along party lines.[54]

The United States's move southward took another major step at the start of the 1820s. Unburdened by party politics following the collapse of the Federalist Party after the 1816 presidential elections, and aware that Spain was having difficulty neutralizing the independence drive launched by most of its Spanish American colonies and that Great Britain did not want another war with the United States, President James Monroe demanded that Spain relinquish control of Florida and turn over its rights to the Pacific coast. John Quincy Adams, Monroe's secretary of state, left no doubt about his country's determination to fulfill both objectives. In a meeting in 1818 with Spain's minister to the United States, Adams warned that if Spain did not cede Florida immediately, "Spain would not have the possession of Florida to give us."[55] Shortly afterward, with much of its military power depleted, Spain acquiesced to the United States's demands by signing the Transcontinental Treaty.

The southward expansionist drive took an unusual turn in 1823. During his annual message to Congress, Monroe warned that though the United States was not planning to gain control over any of the newly created Spanish American states, it would not tolerate the attempt by any European entity to supplant Spain as a colonial power in the region. Monroe also reaffirmed the United States's commitment to continue abstaining from European wars. Analysts have been at odds regarding the rationale for what has been commonly referred to as the "Monroe Doctrine." Some analysts have claimed that the Monroe Doctrine represented a defense of American security and commerce, while others have contended that it was a reflection of the United States's expansionist tradition. The two arguments do not refute one another.

The Monroe Doctrine had a dual external origin. In 1821, the Russian czar, Alexander I, promulgated an imperial decree that prohibited all foreign vessels from coming within 100 miles of the American northwest coast north of 51 degrees latitude. The United States and Great Britain, which under the convention of 1818 had joint ownership of the territory north from 42 degrees to a line yet undetermined, immediately rejected the imperial decree. It was also around this time that Russia floated the idea of enlisting the major European powers to assist Spain in regaining control of its former American colonies. Britain, which had been profiting from trade with the newly independent Spanish American states, did not welcome Russia's proposal. In 1821, George Canning, Britain's foreign minister, submitted a letter to the United States proposing that jointly they inform the world that neither country intended to gain control of any of the Spanish American countries, and that together they would prevent, if necessary, the attempt by any European power to reduce "the Colonies to subjugation, on behalf or in the name of Spain; or which mediates the acquisition of them to itself, by cessation or by conquest. . . ."[56]

The United States's response to Russia's actions and to Britain's proposal discloses its strategic concerns and long-term objectives. Upon having rejected Canning's proposal for a joint declaration, Monroe announced that the United States would "consider any attempt on their part [the European powers] to extend their system to any portion of this hemisphere as dangerous to our peace and safety."[57] With regard to Russia, Monroe and Adams sensed that the czar was not taking a hard stand on their claims in the Northwest, and they were willing to discuss the matter. With respect to Britain, the two leaders concluded that a joint declaration would be unwelcome and unnecessary. It would be unwelcome because the United States, as the weaker party, would find itself playing a subservient role. It would be unnecessary because Britain could easily act on its own against any of the other European powers that sought to undermine its interests in Spanish America. But this was not all. According to Adams, the agreement proposed by Canning was also designed to prevent the United States from gaining control "of any part of the Spanish-American possessions," particularly of Cuba and Texas. In a discussion that ensued during a cabinet meeting in November 1823, Adams argued that:

> We have no intention of seizing Texas or Cuba. But the inhabitants of either or both may exercise their primitive rights, and solicit a union with us. They will certainly do no such thing to Great Britain. By joining with her, therefore, in her proposed declaration, we give her a substantial and perhaps inconvenient pledge against ourselves, and really obtain nothing in return. Without entering now into the enquiry of the expediency of our annexing Texas or Cuba to our Union, we should at least keep ourselves free to act as emergencies may arise, and not tie ourselves down to any principle which might immediately afterwards be brought to bear against ourselves.[58]

In short, the originators of the Monroe Doctrine took into account the international challenges faced by the United States, the way these challenges affected the interests of both the urban-shipping commercial group and the farmer-agrarian group, and the means the United States had at its disposal to protect and promote these interests. Convinced that sometime in the future the United States would fix its claim on the northwest coast of America and that the czar was not prepared to take a hard stand, Monroe and Adams warned Russia—without making overt threats however—not to take lightly their country's interests. Aware that Britain, on its own, could block the attempt by any European power to undermine its economic interests in Spanish America, and that the United States lacked the power to prevent Britain from intruding in the affairs of the former Spanish American colonies, the two leaders articulated the United States's interests without ever claiming that it would take drastic measures to protect them. Moreover, though they did not design the doctrine in order to alter extensively the actions of the United States toward Spanish America, they sought to ensure that in the short run it would satisfy the interests of its two principal economic groups by opening the possibility for increasing trade with its southern neighbors and annexing additional territories.

Fearful that any direct involvement would induce unwanted and costly results, Washington refused to act against repeated drives by France and Britain to violate the sovereignty of some of its southern neighbors. Washington, however, remained attuned to new territorial opportunities, particularly if they sprang close to its borders. In the middle of the 1820s, Adams, who had succeeded Monroe as president of the United States, tried to annex Texas. Texas, which was part of Mexico's sovereign domain, had become the host to large numbers of American settlers. Adams, knowing well that the southern and western states would welcome the addition, instructed his ambassador to Mexico to try to buy all or parts of Texas. Mexico refused Adams's offer, along with the offer extended subsequently by his successor, Andrew Jackson. In 1830, alarmed by its inability to govern Texas, Mexico enacted a law designed to stop the immigration of Americans into the area, and prohibited the further introduction of slaves. Americans outside and inside Texas were not inhibited by Mexico's decision and continued to immigrate and to bring more slaves. After years of haggling, the Americans in Texas and the Mexican government decided to resort to war to resolve their differences.

The war, which started in 1835 and lasted a year, did not elicit immediately the results hoped for by the leaders of the executive branch. The Americans in Texas exited from the struggle victorious and expressed great interest in becoming part of the United States. However, the executive branch was unable to convince the Senate to support such an act until the mid 1840s. The Whig Party, as it had on so many occasions in the past, opposed annexation. It feared that incorporation of additional territory would lead to the expansion of slavery and thus increase the power of the agricultural sector. Finally, in early 1845, the House and the Senate approved, along party lines, the annexation of Texas as a "slave state." In June of that same year, the Texas legislature voted unanimously to become a member of the United States.

The White House transformed the annexation of Texas into a broader issue. Convinced that Britain would attempt to annex California, and mindful that U.S. commercial and agrarian groups were interested in California, President James Polk sent a representative to Mexico to negotiate its purchase. Upon learning that the mission had failed, and aware that the Mexican government was furious about the annexation of Texas, Polk ordered American troops to cross into Mexico and asked Congress to declare war. In his request, Polk did not refer to his resolve to annex California. The Senate approved the petition almost unanimously. The war came to an end with the Treaty of Guadalupe Hidalgo on February 2, 1848, five months after U.S. forces had marched into Mexico City. The treaty transferred to the United States all the territory of the present states of California, Nevada, Utah, most of New Mexico and Arizona, and parts of Colorado and Wyoming, for the sum of $15 million. This victory, which supervened the agreement Washington had reached with London two years earlier regarding control over the Oregon territory, marked the zenith of U.S. territorial expansion.

The expansionary drive by United States came to a halt at midcentury. Nearly every state experiences a transforming crisis, most likely during its early developmental stage. By the end of the Mexican-American war in 1848, the contradictory forces within the United States had become abundantly clear. During the century's early decades, the South had pressed Washington to increase the United States's territorial power, and had demanded that it authorize the practice of slavery in the newly acquired territories. Originally, opposition to this demand came principally from the North, but with limited effect, largely because the Southern planters and Western farmers had joined forces. However, by the middle of the century, with some 4.2 million immigrants flooding the eastern cities and western lands in just the past 20 years, with the Industrial Revolution enabling the North to develop its economy faster than the South, and with the Northeast further solidifying its power by developing new financial and commercial links with farmers from the Midwest and West, the power balance began to switch. Specifically, the North was able to rely on the support of the West to oppose the annexation of territories when the question was tied to the issue of slavery. The South, cognizant that its power was fading, struggled to find alternative means to protect and promote its economic interests, but with little success. For a brief while it tried to annex Cuba, and actually gained the support of many northeasterners who wanted to expand their trade linkages with the Caribbean. This effort, however, came to naught when the Republican

Party demanded that the issue of slavery be resolved before the United States considered whether to annex Cuba, or any other territory.[59] By this time, the South could no longer count on the support of a united Democratic Party, one that included representatives from both the South and the North. Divided by the issue of slavery, the Democratic Party split twice, first in 1848 and again in 1857-1858. The second breakup proved to be exceedingly costly. With the 1860 presidential election approaching, the Democratic Party, represented by two competing banners, found itself confronting a reinvigorated Republican Party, led by Abraham Lincoln.[60] As it became evident that Lincoln had won a plurality of the popular vote and a majority of the electoral votes, the South prepared to secede. After several futile attempts to prevent the breakup of the Union, the North and the South moved to the battlefields to redress their differences.

With the start of the war, while the South sought to recruit the help of Britain, the North was content to ensure that no single European power would assist its southern rival in the struggle. All in all, the North succeeded with this task, without investing great energy and resources. Though Russia, France, and Britain would have benefited notably from a weakened United States, all three recognized that the North, notwithstanding the Civil War, would be a formidable adversary if challenged. Moreover, the political troubles brewing in many of Europe's principal capitals did not encourage the taking of risks in distant lands.

In sum, by the end of 1865, the United States was no longer the nation that it had been at the start of the century. During the first 50 years of the century, it nearly tripled the size of its territory. This operation had numerous effects, but for present purposes I need to discuss only two. Externally, the successful expansion warned the major European powers that a major entity was surfacing on a continent far from theirs, but not so far that it would be inconsequential. Three external conditions helped the United States enlarge its territory. First, the major European states were, for the most part, too preoccupied with their own affairs to be unduly concerned with the expansionary actions initiated by the United States. Each major European state was so committed to preventing its counterparts from becoming overly powerful that acting against a non-European entity would have meant overextending its resources. Second, and almost as an offshoot of the first condition, the United States was well served by the remoteness of its location. Though the United States was weaker than the most powerful European states, none of the latter, with the possible exception of Great Britain, possessed the resources necessary to engage in a protracted struggle with an entity thousands of miles away. And third, when the United States sought to absorb new territories, the states that controlled them, such as Mexico, were considerably less powerful, or were so preoccupied with problems closer to home that they were amenable to reaching peaceful solutions.

The internal effects of the United States's expansionist drive were both destructive and constructive. Almost since its creation, the United States was divided on whether to try to annex neighboring territories whenever the opportunities emerged, and on whether to empower the incorporated areas to decide if they wanted to authorize the practice of slavery. The tension generated by the opposing camps eventually resulted in a civil war that would last four years. Though the war spawned very high human costs, it also had a positive effect. By channeling new wealth to the North, the war energized the United States's capacity to launch one of the most dramatic economic transformations ever experienced by a state. If in 50 years the United States had nearly tripled the size of its territory, in the next 40 years it would transform itself into the world's most powerful industrial entity. Before I can depict this transformation, however, I need to sketch out the transformation Europe's political arena underwent during the last years of the nineteenth century and the first ones of the twentieth century.

The European Balance-Of-Power System and The Other Effects Of Nationalism

In 1875, Emily Dickinson wrote that luck is not chance, but is earned. Notwithstanding her dictum, it is fair to say that though the United States toiled to bring about its own luck during the last part of the nineteenth century, part of its good fortune originated outside its boundaries. The United States launched its second power drive just as Europe was being forced to cope with a new increase in tension within its own balance-of-power system.

Nationalism had a broader effect on Europe than the one delineated in an earlier section in this chapter. Adjacent to Europe's large and powerful states, there were new states that owed their recent origin to the forces of nationalism. Some of these states were involved in complex and dangerous political games. They often sought to broaden their territorial power by attempting to incorporate territories controlled either by states with similar experiences or by neighboring states trying to govern nationalities with opposing interests. Typically, the most consequential responses to the actions by these new entities were those originated by the more powerful states. Powerful states burdened by the presence of rival nationalities within their own borders aggressively opposed attempts to promote internal discord by states that owed their recent origin to the forces of nationalism. The counteracting multinational states were responding not just to protect their sovereignty; they also were signaling that they would not tolerate the inception of a power vacuum or an attempt by any major state to exploit the situation in order to enlarge its own power. Needless to say, such conduct by the afflicted states was followed almost without fail by an attempt by another major power to exploit the circumstances. If it seemed that the major power attempting to exploit the situation was about to alter the distribution of power in the affected region, a third major power, and sometimes a fourth one, would intervene diplomatically and militarily for the sole purpose of impeding such a development.

The major European powers endeavored to defuse the tensions initiated by the clash between the forces of nationalism and the structure of the international system by repeatedly altering territorial boundaries. Time and again they relied on a simple formula: the redrawing of borders, both of states that owed their recent birth to the forces of nationalism and of a decaying major state inhabited by various nations. The implementation of this formula, however, seldom elicited auspicious results. Invariably, at least one of the newly born states or the major powers would voice dissatisfaction with the latest territorial arrangements and would immediately begin to devise ways to amend it. This form of interaction became so ordinary that after a while the involved parties automatically assumed that if war resulted from their disputes, it would hardly diverge in intensity and length from the preceding one. This phenomenon started in the 1820s but did not gain full momentum until after Germany's victory over France had challenged the balance-of-power structure in Europe.

In August 1875, rebels in Bosnia and Herzegovina, an area lying northwest of Serbia, launched an insurrection against Turkish rule. The rebels, who were Southern Slavs and predominantly Christian, were being supported by the Serbs, who in turn were very interested in expanding their own territory. By October, the Turkish government had managed to impose crushing defeats on the Serbian forces. Serbia immediately appealed for international protection, and in June of the next year Russia responded by moving its forces swiftly toward Constantinople.[61] Turkey was not cowed by Russia's action. Turkish forces moved to the town of Plevna in Bulgaria, where they entrenched themselves. Still, even after a protracted and costly battle, the Turkish defense was not able to offset Russia's superior military power. Russia's military triumph, however, did not translate into a diplomatic victory. When Saint Petersburg set up the peace terms that would have enabled Russia to become the dominant power from the east coast of the Black Sea to the Adriatic Sea, Britain and Austria immediately voiced their objections. Bismarck, who initially had no desire to be pushed into the limelight on Balkan issues, finally agreed to host a meeting in Berlin to help the embattled parties iron out their differences.

The Congress of Berlin, which came to a close in July 1878, failed to quell tensions. Though Serbia gained its full independence from Turkey, it did not gain control over Bosnia and Herzegovina as it had hoped; instead, it learned that the two areas would be ruled by Austria.[62] Montenegro and Rumania were also able to become fully independent states. But Rumania had to relinquish to Russia the Bessarabian provinces it had won control over in 1856. Greece, which had expected to attain authority over Epirus and Crete following the collapse of the Ottoman Empire, came up empty-handed. Britain, which was determined to obstruct Russia's drive to broaden its territorial power, took over Cyprus. This action served Britain's interests well, for it enhanced markedly the potential mobility of its navy in the area.

At first glance it would seem that the spoils of the war were parceled out primarily among the big European states, at the expense of the small Balkan nations aspiring to become full-fledged nation-states. This description is only partially correct. The ire provoked among nationalist groups by the agreements reached at the Berlin Congress was matched by the anger it galvanized among Russian leaders. For them, their gains did not justify Russia's heavy expenditure of money and men during the war. "[I]n Russia the Berlin settlement (and especially the truncation of Greater Bulgaria) was naturally regarded as a great humiliation which damaged the prestige of the czarist regime."[63]

Bismarck immediately recognized that Germany could not afford to overlook Saint Petersburg's anger. He feared that the Russians would go to the French and propose that the two countries form a common front against Germany, as both had been affronted by Berlin's actions since the start of the 1870s. His first step was to sign a defensive alliance with Austria. The alliance's primary clause stipulated that were either party attacked by Russia, the remaining party would assist in the defense of the ally. The second clause stipulated that were either party attacked by a power other than Russia, the other party would, at minimum, remain neutral. Then, to allay Russia's fears and ensure that Saint Petersburg would not seek to counterbalance the Germany-Austria alliance with its own alliance with France, he persuaded both Vienna and Saint Petersburg to revive the old Three Emperors' League treaty. Without identifying the names of potential aggressors, the 1881 treaty was designed to ensure that Austria and Germany would not assist Britain against Russia, and that Russia would remain neutral in a conflict between France and Germany or Austria and Italy.[64] But Bismarck still remained unconvinced that he had done enough to minimize Germany's chances of being overpowered by its European rivals. Thus, a year after signing the Three Emperors' League treaty, he persuaded Austria and Italy to secretly transform the Dual Alliance of 1878 between Germany and Austria into a triple alliance that would include Italy.

The revived Three Emperors' League treaty had a short life. During the Bulgarian crisis of 1885-1887, Russia's and Austria's interests once again clashed. Hoping not to alienate Russia, Bismarck tried to keep his distance from the crisis by claiming that Germany cared neither who ruled

Bulgaria nor what its future held. The crisis, however, persuaded Saint Petersburg not to renew the treaty. Still determined to make sure that Russia would not seek an alliance with France, Bismarck convinced Saint Petersburg to sign a separate agreement with Berlin. The Reinsurance Treaty of June 1887 committed Germany to extend to Russia diplomatic support in the Balkans, thus challenging, if not the letter, at least the spirit of Germany's alliance with Austria.[65]

In 1890, the new German-Russian treaty experienced the same fate the Three Emperors' League treaty had undergone three years earlier. Two factors contributed to the demise of the Reinsurance Treaty. First, shortly after it was signed, Bismarck denied Saint Petersburg the capital it badly needed to reinvigorate the Russian economy, and raised tariffs against Russian exports to Germany. The second factor played a more important role. In 1890, Bismarck, who had been Germany's dominant political figure since the early 1860s, was forced to resign by the new kaiser, Wilhelm II. One of Wilhelm's first decisions after firing Bismarck was to annul the Russian-German treaty. He and his advisers concluded that the treaty was inconsistent with Germany's obligations to Austria.[66] The cancellation of the treaty and Russia's overlying need to find a new creditor led Saint Petersburg to seek assistance from the one state Bismarck had all along feared—France. In 1891, Paris and Saint Petersburg agreed to consult one another in the event either party was threatened by aggression from a third party, and by 1894 they had formalized the agreement into a treaty that stipulated that if either party were to be at war with Germany, the other would extend military support. The treaty also noted that France would assist Russia financially to develop its new industrial program.

Thirteen years after Russia and France had formed an alliance, a highly unexpected party joined them. In 1904, Britain and France signed an entente, which was followed by the signing of a new entente between Britain and Russia three years later.[67] Why would Britain, a state that during the nineteenth century refused to become a member of any alliance that could undermine its independence, be willing to ally itself with two of Europe's major powers? In an anarchical international system, every single state must continuously estimate the existing and potential interests and capabilities of its most immediate rivals. By the end of the nineteenth century, Britain was aware that the United States was moving rapidly to become the international system's most powerful entity and that their rivalry was likely to intensify, particularly in Asia and Latin America. Britain, however, though determined to keep a close watch on the United States, was more alarmed by the behavior of a European state—Germany. Britain's concern had two foundations. First, from an economic standpoint Britain was no longer as strong as it had been earlier in the century. Though its economic output continued to increase, its relative share of the world production had been decreasing since the middle of the second half of the nineteenth century, particularly in relationship to the United States's and Germany's respective economic outputs. This decline affected directly Britain's naval and military strength, which rested on its industrial and commercial preeminence.[68] Second, though since 1871 Germany had been signaling its determination to become and act as a major power, until the removal of Bismarck in 1890, Berlin had also tried to foster the belief among its immediate international rivals that it would not unleash its power aspirations. This policy was altered by Wilhelm II, not long after he fired Bismarck. Wilhelm II made it clear that "Germany had great tasks to accomplish outside the narrow boundaries of Europe."[69]

The kaiser's strategy was not much different from that chosen by some of the other entities that had become major powers by the end of the century. Britain and France, for instance, owed their standing as world powers, in part, to their control over territories outside the European continent. One way Berlin hoped to reach beyond Europe's immediate confines was by enlarging Germany's navy. Berlin's new naval policy worried London, for the latter recognized that Germany had the economic capacity to build a navy that could challenge Britain's naval superiority. Russia's loss to Japan in 1905 did not ease London's concern. The war reduced Russia to the level of a second class power, at least for several years, and as a result swung the military equilibrium in Europe decisively in Germany's direction.[70] The naval race between Britain and Germany gained momentum in very short time, and by 1912 it had become one of their most divisive issues.

Britain was not the only major power pondering the future of its empire. In Russia, as information about the Russo-Japanese war began to filter home, workers from cities in different regions took to the streets to voice class and national grievances. In an attempt to prevent extremists from carrying the day, the Russian czar, Nicholas II, issued a manifesto in late 1905 pledging to establish an Imperial Duma. The Duma would be elected on a broad franchise and be responsible for ensuring the legality of governmental actions. Nicholas's promise materialized only after a major political battle. Initially, only a minority of the working class was franchised, and the czar retained "supreme autocratic power." The newly established Duma, upon demanding more power, was dissolved in July 1906. The second Duma, which was created some 14 months later, had wider representation from the national minorities and leftist parties. This Duma was soon replaced by a third one, which lasted until 1912.[71]

In the meantime, trade unions and political parties throughout Europe were also demanding changes. These organizations rarely adopted the same strategy, and their effects on the political systems varied markedly. In Austria-Hungary, strikes and protest rallies forced the emperor to sanction major electoral reforms in January 1907. In Germany, following mass demonstrations in Saxony and Hamburg in support of suffrage, the trade unions and the Social Democrats agreed to share power in party decisions and to outlaw mass strikes, thus enhancing their overall standing in the German Reichstag. In Britain, the Trades Union Congress decided to engage in political action through the Labour Party. The Labour Party, in turn, rejected class war and the socialization of the means of production and entered into a pact with the Liberal Party to form a common front against the Conservative Party. And in France and Italy, the trade unions battled to assert their independence from the political parties.[72]

These upheavals, though newsworthy, paled in comparison to the chaos that started to brew once again in the Balkans. In 1897, after years of acrimonious disagreements over the way the Balkans should be partitioned, Austria-Hungary and Russia agreed not to initiate actions that might undermine the other. The agreement experienced its first setback in 1903. In October of that year, Serbian officers shot their king, Alexander, his wife, and several other major Serbian officials. Alexander, who had been a client and protégé of Austria-Hungary, was replaced by Peter Karageodjevic, who as a Pan-Serb pro-Russian wanted to end Serbia's dependence on Austria-Hungary and unite under a common state all Serbs and Croatians. After these events, Slav nationalism rapidly gathered momentum. Clubs and secret societies committed to the redemption of Slavs in the southern part of Austria-Hungary and in the adjacent provinces of Turkey grew in number. A series of meetings and congresses in Fiume, Zara, Saint Petersburg, and Prague, all designed to encourage Slav nationalism, were organized between 1903 and 1908.[73]

Austria-Hungary was troubled by these activities. Hungary was particularly concerned with a resolution arrived at by 40 Croatian deputies in early October 1905. At a meeting in Fiume, a city located in the southwestern section of Hungary, they announced that their support for the Hungarian Union was dependent on the acceptance of the Triune Kingdom of Croatia, Slovania, and Dalmatia as an equal partner of the Austrian-Hungarian Monarchy. Twenty-six Serb deputies backed the resolution in the city of Zara a few weeks later. Austria-Hungary viewed these events as an attempt on the part of Russia or Serbia to promote Slav nationalism in Hungary and to provoke division within the monarchy.

Vienna, convinced that its problem in the Balkans would not recede until it subordinated Serbia, decided to exploit Serbia's heavy diplomatic and commercial dependency on Austria-Hungary. The opportunity arose in 1906 when, in an attempt to free its economy from Austria-Hungary, Serbia signed a customs treaty with Bulgaria.[74] Vienna responded by stopping the import of Serbia's largest export, livestock. Vienna's action did not have the intended effect. Within a year's time, Belgrade had managed to develop new trade agreements with Egypt, Germany, Greece, and

Turkey, and to surpass Serbia's pre-1906 foreign trade level. Angered by its initial failure to debilitate Serbia, Vienna announced its intention to build a railroad that would directly link Austria-Hungary with Salonika on the shore of the Aegean Sea. The railroad would bypass Serbia and cut it off from the Adriatic Sea by going through the Sanjak of Novi Bazar, located between Serbia and Montenegro.

Russia and Britain immediately opposed Austria-Hungary's plan, but just as Berlin was joining Vienna to reject the objection, a group of junior officers of the Ottoman Empire stationed in Salonika launched a revolt against the Ottoman Empire's sultan, Abdul-Hamid. The action was designed to stop the despotism of the sultan, the further crumbling of the empire, and the continued intervention by foreign powers. The revolt did not bring about the results intended by its leaders. Almost immediately, Bulgaria declared its independence of the Ottoman suzerainty, Crete joined Greece, and Austria-Hungary announced the annexation of Bosnia-Herzegovina, a region it had administered since 1878. Austria-Hungary's decision elicited a strong reaction from Saint Petersburg. In turn, Berlin, though upset with Austria for not requesting Germany's advice, informed both Belgrade and Saint Petersburg that if they did not accept the annexation, Germany was prepared to join Austria-Hungary in war against them. Russia, still weak from its defeat by Japan, and conscious that neither France nor Britain could come to its aid if a war against Germany and Austria-Hungary were to erupt, had no choice but to accept Vienna's terms.

Austria's victory proved to be elusive, and Berlin realized that Germany had been ensnared by its own accomplishments. Germany's swift military and economic success had forced other powers, specifically France and Russia, to ensure that if either had to face Germany on the battlefield, neither would have to do it on its own. Germany also recognized that both Serbia and Russia had been humiliated by their last concession to Vienna, and that in time they would strive to alter the distribution of territories in the Balkans. These developments convinced Berlin that Austria-Hungary would have to eventually invade Serbia in order to "bring the whole Serb people under the Habsburg scepter . . ." and that Germany's and Austria's military forces had to be prepared to launch simultaneous campaigns against Serbia, Russia, France, and, if necessary, Italy.[75]

The path Europe would take during the early years of the twentieth century was dependent on what Germany did. What Germany did was determined, in no small measure, by its need to protect Austria-Hungary's status as a major power. Austria-Hungary's power was affected by Serbia's nationalist drive. And Serbia's ability to fulfill its nationalist aspiration was affected by whether the leaders of the Ottoman Empire would be able to arrest its downfall. In 1909, the young Turkish military officers, who the year before had demanded that the Sultan change his regime's ways, marched into Constantinople, deposed him, and created a military regime designed to 'Turkify' the empire. One of their first acts was to close all political institutions that had based their organizations on nationality. This measure immediately gained Italy's attention, and it generated strong opposition in the Balkans. For some time, Italy had been wanting to gain control over Libya, one of the Ottoman Empire's remaining provinces in North Africa. Upon deciding that the Ottoman Empire had been weakened by the actions initiated by the Turkish officers, and that an invasion of Libya could be conducted at relatively little cost, Italy invaded the North African province. Italy's assessment was partially correct. Its troops soon defeated the Turkish forces stationed in Libya, but the Libyans refused to surrender and waged an effective guerrilla war. Back in the Balkans, Montenegro, Serbia, Bulgaria, and Greece, aware that the Turks had been further weakened by the need to fight on several fronts at the same time, declared war on Constantinople.

The joint efforts by the small Balkan countries ultimately brought down the Ottoman Empire. Their victory, however, did not generate the rewards they had awaited. Bulgaria, Greece, and Serbia all managed to enlarge the size of their respective territories, but none by as much as it had expected. Serbia, however, was the most displeased. During the war, Serbian troops had gained control over an area called Scutari, on the Adriatic Sea. At the peace negotiations held in London in 1913, the Serbs demanded that the area be made part of Serbia. Vienna vetoed the proposal and supported, instead, the creation of an independent Albania. Belgrade objected, but upon receiving an ultimatum and learning that Saint Petersburg would not stand by its side, it reluctantly accepted the creation of Albania.

Displeasure with the terms of the London agreement was voiced also by two of Europe's most important powers. Saint Petersburg found itself once again on the losing side after failing to support the needs of its principle client in the Balkans—Serbia. Russia was so upset by the failure that one of its leaders wrote to a Serbian counterpart: "Serbia's promised land lies in the territory on present-day Hungary."[76] The Austrians adopted a similar hostile stance. The latest set of events reaffirmed their determination to respond rapidly and forcefully to any new attempt on the part of Serbia to challenge Austria-Hungary's control over the Croatia-Slavonia region in southern Hungary.

The house of cards created by the 1815 balance-of-power system finally tumbled in 1914. On June 28, 1914, Archduke Franz Ferdinand, heir to the Habsburg throne, and his wife were assassinated in the city of Sarajevo. Shortly after the slaying, Austria-Hungary's leaders, with Germany's unqualified support, issued an ultimatum to Serbia demanding almost full jurisdiction over the investigation of the act. The Serbian government faced a monumental dilemma: if it decided to acquiesce to

Vienna's demands, it would sacrifice Serbia's sovereign status; but if it chose to outright reject the ultimatum, it would find itself at war with a much more powerful adversary. In an attempt to free itself from the predicament, Serbia forwarded a compromise that met almost all of Vienna's conditions. Vienna discarded Serbia's attempt at rapprochement and declared war on July 28.

The ultimatum forced Saint Petersburg to conclude that if Austria-Hungary went to war and defeated Serbia, Russia would not be able to regain its lost stronghold in the Balkans. Saint Petersburg also knew that if Russia joined forces with Serbia against Austria-Hungary, Berlin would actively assist Vienna. Thus, on July 30, Saint Petersburg ordered the full mobilization of its troops against Austria-Hungary and, as a precautionary measure, along the Russian-German border. Saint Petersburg's preventive stratagem impelled Germany to counteract immediately. Knowing that a war against Russia would expose Germany's western flank because of Saint Petersburg's defense alliance with Paris, Berlin issued an ultimatum to Paris demanding that it affirm its neutrality during the forthcoming war between Germany and Russia and that it transfer to Germany the custody of two border fortresses as evidence of good faith.[77] Paris rejected Berlin's demand, thus setting the stage for a war between members of two rival alliances.

England was the last major European power to disclose its hand. Its role was deemed critical by the other major European powers. The common sentiment in Europe was that England was the only country with the capability to stop Germany from skewing Europe's existing balance of power. For England, geography meant everything. It would respond aggressively to any attempt by a hostile power to gain control of the coast opposite the English Channel. London had good reason to be resolute on this matter; on more than one occasion, an adversary had used this region as a springboard for an invasion of the British Isles. Germany's attack plan called for the invasion of France through Belgium, thus evoking the threat London was unwilling to tolerate. London's decision to enter the war reaffirmed the belief that Europe would brave a short war. By the onset of the winter snows, however, the war had bogged down in a stalemate on the Western front that would persist until 1917. With no end in sight, the United States finally joined England, France, and Russia in their struggle against Germany and Austria-Hungary. This decision did not break the impasse immediately, but by the end of 1918, Berlin, mindful that the pendulum had swung against Germany, agreed to sign an armistice.

The Final Ascent

Through the early years of the nineteenth century, the United States doggedly endeavored to ensure its own survival. Subsequently it attempted to augment, first, its territorial power, then its economic strength, and finally its military power. It would be senseless to suggest that the United States's forefathers had this course in mind when they admonished Americans to refrain from being drawn into Europe's political squabbles, while they underscored that it was part of the country's destiny to transform itself into a world power. But with the above two axes as a foreign policy guide, it is not surprising that the United States's path to hegemony followed the course it did, considering its domestic political and economic systems, geographical remoteness, and Europe's political quandary.

The Civil War alerted Europe to the presence of a new giant. By the end of the century, the warning had taken on a new meaning. At the start of the Civil War, the United States had a population of 32 million people; 40 years later it had more than doubled to 73 million.[78] In 1860, the United States's world manufacturing output was still behind Britain's, but it was on the verge of overtaking France's and had already surged past Russia's and Germany's.[79] Forty years later, the United States's share of the world manufacturing output was more than three times greater than France's, close to three times larger than Russia's, nearly two times bigger than Germany's, and considerably stronger than Britain's. Equivalent imbalances existed in iron/steel production and energy consumption.[80] These increases, which were accompanied by a spectacular growth in agricultural production, helped bring about, for an extended period, a shift from an unfavorable to a favorable balance of trade.

The United States did not rival its European counterparts in military power. The disparity, however, was intentional. The United States's potential to become a military giant had become evident during the Civil War. Though the war was bloody and costly, it "catalyzed the latent national power which the United States possessed, transforming it (at least for a short while) into the greatest military nation on earth before its post-1865 demobilization."[81] At the end of the Civil War, the United States once again directed its energies toward the development of its economies. Still, the event served to warn the United States's potential rivals that it possessed both the resources and the population to create a formidable military force in a very short time, if any of them sought to undermine its interests.

During the 40 years that followed the Civil War, developments in the United States's political arena assumed a relatively uncomplicated pattern. With Americans still driven by the yearning for material gain, and with the Democratic Party weakened by sectional tensions and the Civil

War, the Republican Party controlled the political system for most of the balance of the nineteenth century, advocating that only through the success of the business community would the nation progress and prosper. Backed by the agricultural Midwest and West, and the business Northeast, the Republican Party championed the implementation of laissez-faire policies that encouraged governmental aid to businesses and few governmental regulations. Convinced that ability and ambition were the two basic ingredients an individual needed to succeed, the Republican Party paid little attention to the plight of workers or farmers.

Until the beginning of the last decade of the nineteenth century, the United States centered most of its economic growth at home. Even during its economic downturns, financiers, manufacturers, railroad entrepreneurs, and farmers believed that abundant economic opportunities existed within its borders. However, as the century came to a close, it became evident that the United States would not be able to sustain the rate of economic growth it had bolstered in the previous decades without reaching outside its domestic market. Between 1893 and 1898, the economy of the United States experienced a severe and double-cycle depression. Its consequences were monumental. As noted by the *Commercial and Financial Chronicle* in August 1893, never before had there been in the United States "such a sudden and striking cessation of industrial activity. . . . Mills, factories, furnaces, mines, nearly everywhere shut down in large numbers . . . and hundreds of thousands of men [were] thrown out of employment."[82] Washington came under immediate pressure from the leading members of the business and financial community to help find new foreign markets. An editorial in the *United States Investor* remarked "that an outlet for surplus stocks becomes an imperative necessity."[83] In 1897, the president of the National Association of Manufacturers noted that many of the manufacturers in the United States "have outgrown or are outgrowing their home markets and the expansion of our foreign trade is their only promise and relief."[84] It did not take Congress and the executive branch long to accept that the continued prosperity of the United States was heavily dependent on its ability to prevail on new foreign markets to open their doors. In 1897, the Republican senator of Indiana, Albert J. Beveridge, conveyed a sentiment that had become quite popular among his colleagues when he stated: "American factories are making more than the American people can use; American soil is producing more than they can consume. Fate has written our policy for us; the trade of the world must and shall be ours."[85] The Department of State did not ignore the cues. In an 1897 release to its various embassies abroad, it noted:

It seems to be conceded that every year we shall be confronted with an increasing surplus of manufactured goods for sale in foreign markets if American operatives and artisans are to be kept employed the year around.

The enlargement of foreign consumption of the products of our mills and workshops has, therefore, become a serious problem of statesmanship as well as of commerce.[86]

By the closing of the nineteenth century, there was no state in the international arena that doubted the United States's capability to broaden its political and economic domains. Prior to that time, the United States had already revealed its edacity for Asia's economic riches by forcing Japan to open its ports to American ships, by purchasing Alaska from Russia, and by pressuring Korea and China to accept an "open trade policy." In the 1890s, the United States annexed the Hawaiian islands, part of the Somoan islands, and the Philippines. It also erased whatever qualms the European states might have had about its resolve and ability to become the Caribbean Basin's and Latin America's principal military and economic actor. For the most part, however, the United States was not interested in the annexation of territory. Its interests were of a different nature. Secretary of State James G. Blaine left very little doubt about the United States's aim when he stated:

[T]he United States has reached a point where one of its highest duties is to enlarge the area of its foreign trade. Under the beneficent policy of protection we have developed a volume of manufactures which, in man departments it overruns the demands of the home market. In the field of agriculture, with the immense population given in it by agricultural implements, we do far more than produce breadstuffs and provisions for our own people. . . . Our great demand is expansion. I mean expansion of trade with countries where we can find profitable exchanges. We are not seeking annexation of territory.[87]

Possibly few political affairs revealed more unerringly the United States's resolve to become the Western Hemisphere's dominant entity than two events in the 1890s. Since the 1840s, London had claimed as British possession the territory between its colony of British Guiana and Venezuela. The claim ran counter to the Monroe Doctrine, but Washington had refrained from enforcing it, mainly because it lacked the means to do so. In the 1890s, when Britain began to reassert its claim, Washington decided that it was time to respond with a warning. In a message to London, Washington noted that the United States, as the supreme entity in the Western Hemisphere, was prepared to enforce the Monroe Doctrine. London, disquieted by Germany's zealous campaign to match, and possibly surpass, Britain's naval and economic power, was forced to accept the United States's secretary of state's claim that the "infinite resources [of the United States] combined with its isolated position render it master of the situation and practically invulnerable as against any or all other powers."[88]

The United States's boasting was not the outcome of a haphazard resolution. As the nineteenth century came to a close, Washington took another major step to make it very clear that the United States was determined to eradicate as much as possible any form of European influence in the Caribbean Basin and Latin America, and to become the region's unchallenged master. In 1898, with the Cuban revolution against Spain raging, President William McKinley asked Congress for the authority to declare war on Spain. By the year's end, the United States had managed to expel the Spaniards from Cuba. With no one to challenge its authority in the Caribbean Basin, Washington forced Cuba in 1903 to incorporate several provisions in its new constitution. The provisions: i) granted the United States the authority to intervene as it wished to protect Cuba's independence, ii) limited Cuba's debt to prevent European creditors from using it as a justification to use force to collect it, iii) awarded the United States a 99-year lease of the Guantánamo naval base, and iv) required the enforcement of a major sanitation plan to make the island more attractive to U.S. investors.[89] The new Cuban government, though terribly unhappy with the United States's demands, had no choice but to accept them. Other Caribbean Basin countries experienced a comparable fate as the first two decades of the twentieth century took hold.[90]

The new century did not mark a major change in the foreign policy of the United States. To the dictum that the new United States needed overseas markets to absorb products from its factories and farms, Theodore Roosevelt, who served as president from 1901 until 1909, added that it also needed overseas capital markets to absorb its surplus capital. Roosevelt also made it abundantly clear that with so much at stake abroad, the United States was determined to use its power to ensure that its economic interests would be fully protected. In his annual message to the Congress, delivered on December 6, 1904, Roosevelt remarked that:

> If a nation [in the Western Hemisphere] shows that it knows how to act with reasonable efficiency and decency in social and political matters, if it keeps order and pays its obligations, it need fear no interference from the United States. Chronic wrongdoing, or an impotence which results in a general loosening of the ties of civilized society, may in America, as elsewhere, ultimately require intervention by some civilized nation, and in the Western Hemisphere the adherence of the United States to the Monroe Doctrine may force the United States, however, reluctantly, in flagrant cases of such wrongdoing or impotence to the exercise of an international police power.[91]

Woodrow Wilson's ascent to the presidency in 1913 reaffirmed the United States's commitment to "dollar diplomacy" and political order. Initially, he seemed ready to break with the past. In October 1913, Wilson promised Latin American countries that the future was "going to be very different." These states, he added, would soon begin to experience "an emancipation from the subordination, which has been inevitable, to foreign enterprise. . . ." He then pledged that their new relationship with the United States would be built on "equality and honor." Wilson did not honor his promises. During his eight-year tenure as president, he sent U.S. forces to Mexico, the Dominican Republic, Cuba, and Haiti to restore political and economic order. Like his predecessors, Wilson understood that the power of the United States was solidly dependent on fostering new international economic opportunities for its markets, and on ensuring the ongoing presence of political order and stability in the new markets. He sought to capture the relationship between both conditions when he wrote:

> The East is to be opened and transformed. . . . the standards of the West are to be imposed upon it; nations and people who have stood still the centuries through are to be quickened, and to be made part of the universal world of commerce and of ideas which has so steadily been a-making by the advance of European power from age to age. It is our peculiar duty . . . to moderate the process in the interests of liberty; to impart to the peoples thus driven out upon the road of change . . . our own principles of self-help; teach them order and self-control in the midst of change.[92]

The 1914 European war generated a series of problems and opportunities for the United States. Though for the most part Washington sympathized with the Allies, in no small measure because they, together with their colonies, had purchased in 1913 approximately 77 percent of all U.S. exports, its chief hope was for the two sides to strike a compromise that would bring the war to an end. Washington did not favor Germany's winning the war because a German victory would mark the triumph of militarism in Europe, destroy Europe's balance of power, and harm U.S. economic interests in Europe. On the other hand, it feared that if the Allies emerged victorious, Russia would become central Europe's dominant entity. For nearly two years, as Wilson attempted to mediate an end to the war, he also rejected suggestions that the United States enter the war on Britain's side. But as time went by, it became harder for his administration not to play favorites. Wilson's tilt toward the Allies first surfaced when he refused to criticize the Allies' food blockade of Germany but denounced Germany's submarine warfare aimed at Allied and neutral ships and demanded its commitment not to attack neutral ships.[93] Germany, determined to prevent the United States from helping the Allies, extended the promise. At about this time, Wilson was forced to reconsider the granting of loans to the belligerents. The United States's two key exports, cotton and wheat, depended heavily on Germany's and Britain's purchasing power. By 1915, the war had abated considerably the purchasing capability of the two European rivals. As a result, both countries approached U.S. financial institutions and applied for loans. Initially, Wilson opposed the requests. But with the U.S. economy suffering a severe slump since 1913, the president was forced to allow loans to be floated to ensure that both Britain and Germany would be able to continue buying American products. Wilson's decision proved to be crucial. During the next two years, the Allies borrowed $2.5 billion; the Central Powers, however, were awarded less than one-tenth that sum.[94]

By 1917, the United States had nearly run out of options. With Russia no longer able to protect its western front, the German kaiser was persuaded by his military advisers to launch an all-out submarine warfare. A military victory, they contended, would empower Germany to annex new territory, force Belgium into neutrality, and set up new naval bases in the Atlantic and Pacific Oceans. The news coming from the other side was also discouraging. In 1916, Wilson, who had hoped to impose a stable and open world economic system at the end of the war without entering it, learned that the Allies had met in secret and decided to create a program designed to neutralize the economic power of the United States. At a meeting in Paris, the French, Russians, Italians, and British agreed to use government subsidies, higher tariffs, and controlled markets to offset U.S. competition. In January 1917, Wilson tried one more time to convince both parties to agree on a "peace without victory" that would include a series of principles such as self-determination for all nations, freedom of the seas, and the elimination of entangling alliances. But his call came too late. On April 2, some two months after Germany had launched total submarine warfare, Wilson asked the U.S. Congress to declare war on Germany.

The End of an Era

To varying degrees, states are prisoners of the international system they inhabit. In 1815, the major European entities created a balance-of-power system designed to restrain the potentially excessive power aspirations of its strongest entities. For the system to fulfill this objective, its principal members had to maintain constant vigilance over each other's political and economic activities, and had to prevent unexpected developments from invalidating the premises on which they had built the system. Though the system's usefulness was eventually nullified by Germany's rapid emergence as continental Europe's most powerful member and by the swift rise of an inflexible form of nationalism, for nearly a century its principal members remained highly attentive to its needs. No single state in the international arena benefited more from Europe's political entanglement than the United States. With Europe's major entities caught in their own web of political intrigues, and with the advantage of its considerable geographical isolation, the United States found itself relatively free to realize its political and economic aspirations throughout much of the nineteenth century and the early part of the twentieth century.

The United States's success in the international arena cannot be attributed solely to the nature of the global system. From its conception, the United States strove to become a powerful international entity. This drive was not aberrant; throughout history, many other entities had had the same aspiration. The United States, however, was structured by a domestic system that was highly unique. It was circumscribed by an economic system that venerated the spirit of economic competition and cultivated the belief that one of the government's main duties was to facilitate the attainment of greater material goods, and by a political system that empowered the people to make demands from their political leaders and forced them to compete for the backing of the people. With the political system buttressing the economic system, the United States was geared to widen its political and economic might beyond its original horizons.

Strong political and economic aspirations generally provoke intense contradictions. A state's internal strength is measured less by its ability to avert internal contradictions than by its capacity to use to its betterment the crises that contradictions often produce. The competitiveness induced by the United States's political and economic systems created the contradictions that brought about the Civil War. However, the Civil War, though costly, gave rise to a new United States, which almost immediately functioned as a more united, more productive, and more powerful nation.

Any state that yearns to become a hegemon will try to change the international system in ways that would enhance its own state interests. The 1914 cataclysmic war afforded the United States the opportunity to impose on the international political arena the vision that had served its own political and economic interests so well for more than a century. Shortly after it failed in its initial attempt to end the war without its direct participation, the United States accepted that its chances of creating a different international system were dependent on whether it agreed to pay the costs of war. The United States finally acceded, and by the end of the First World War it was the only state with the material capability to design a different kind of international system. But did it possess the foresight and will to do so?

CHAPTER TWO

The New Giant's First Major Blunder

The Failings of War

If the intent of war is to help mend the failings of peace, the First World War was a futile tragedy. The war brought to an end the balance-of-power system that had defined the relationships between the world arena's major members for nearly a century. Its demise did not give rise to a less troublesome international system. Instead, it paved the way for the creation of a system that in a 20–year period failed to avert the collapse of the world economy, the rapid ascent of two rogue states, and a second global war. In this chapter I focus on the failed attempts by the United States to alter the nature of the international political system after the end of the 1914 war, and to prevent the collapse of the international economic system in the late 1920s and early 1930s. In chapter 3, I discuss the rebirth of Germany's power under Nazism, Japan's attempts to attain hegemony in the Far East, and the United States's reactions to these developments.

Democracy, Rationality, Preferences, and Experiences

During the nineteenth century, few political leaders and analysts believed that democracies could function as effective entities in a competitive international system. One of the first analysts to sound the alarm was the famous French observer of American society, Alexis de Tocqueville. Though a great admirer of the American political system, Tocqueville remarked that it was in the conduct of foreign affairs that "democracies appear[ed] . . . decidedly inferior to other governments." Influenced by the value the leaders of the major international entities placed on secrecy, detailed negotiations, patience, and the freedom to act rapidly, Tocqueville wrote that a democracy "can only with great difficulty regulate the details of an important undertaking, persevere in a fixed design, and work out its execution in spite of serious obstacles."[1]

Tocqueville was partially right. Like any other type of political system, a democracy is faced with the troublesome task of arriving at decisions rationally. At its most basic level, rationality entails gathering the information necessary to delineate the nature of a problem, ranking preferences, identifying and evaluating objectives and their interrelationships, isolating alternatives and estimating their probable effects, and choosing the alternative with the highest expected utility. Pure rationality is an ideal, unattainable for at least two reasons. First, each decision-maker is a captive of a particular past. Consequently, the manner in which a decision-maker defines a problem is always affected by the inferences he or she derives from certain experiences. Two decision-makers with very different experiences will most likely define the same problem differently. Second, each decision-maker is the carrier of values and beliefs that affect his or her preferences and interpretations of experiences. Two decision-makers with different values and beliefs could very well derive different lessons from the same experiences.[2]

Like the decision-maker, each state is captive of its own past. Decision-makers within a state cannot escape the state's past and their own past whenever they encounter new problems. The way the decision-makers of a state define and address a problem is also affected by their values and beliefs, and by the state's domestic political structure. In an authoritarian state, the only values, beliefs, and inferences derived from experiences that count, in the addressing of a problem, are those of a very small number of decision-makers. In a democratic state, the picture is markedly more complex. Clearly, the values, beliefs, and inferences derived from experiences of the president and his advisers are central. They will have great difficulty in dealing with the problem as they had intended, however, if their values, beliefs, and inferences do not partially correspond with those of the dominant interest groups.

It is inevitable that at some point a decision-maker will make the wrong decision. The error may be induced either by the absence of relevant information or by a diagnosis failure. If the error is caused by a diagnosis failure, it is often spawned by the decision-maker's values and beliefs, reference to inapplicable experiences, or incorrect inferences from experiences. Whatever its basis, it is clear that if the error is costly, the decision-maker will try to correct it without much delay. The state faces similar pressures. Any state that finds itself coping with the costs engendered by a bad policy will be forced to search for an alternative. Simple logic suggests that a democratic state has a better chance than a non-democratic state to recognize past costly foreign policy mistakes, infer the correct lessons from them, and attempt to remedy them. To acknowledge the presence of these favorable conditions in a democratic state, however, is not to suggest that such a state will in every instance be more success-ful than a non-democratic state in formulating the most effective foreign policy. And herein lies one of democracy's most intriguing foreign-policy-making paradoxes. Though it is in the nature of democracy to give serious attention to past errors, the effective execution of the foreign policy process may be encumbered by the powerful emotions generated among its citizens by the memory of costly events.

The United States and Its First Major Failure

A state's ability to decree the rules that will influence the interaction between states in the international system is a function of its relative power and prestige. The two elements are closely connected. A state gar-ners prestige when it uses its power to impose its will on other states, such as during war.[3] Victory forces other international actors to bear in mind the victor's capabilities and willingness to exercise them, particu-larly if the interests of all parties do not concur. Prestige, however, is an amorphous concept, and its value depends not just on the nature and actions of the entity being assessed, but also on those of the assessors. Moreover, an entity can easily squander its prestige if, after a war, it pur-sues goals that are greatly at odds with those sought by those it hopes to influence, or its policies prove to be ineffective.

The international arena in 1919 was ripe for a new leader with a differ-ent set of goals and ideas. Russia had collapsed in revolution, and under its new Bolshevik leaders it had retreated into isolation. Germany, though not decisively defeated during the war, was forced to accept a peace agree-ment that it had neither anticipated nor wanted. France and Britain, though victorious by war's end, found themselves encumbered by ravaged economies and social discontent. And Japan, though acknowledged by many as an important international actor, remained a regional power. That left the United States, an entity barely touched by the war, endowed with a military and economy potent enough to have global effects, and celebrated by millions of people throughout the globe as the country with the vision and moral fortitude to create a less baleful international system.

The goals proclaimed during and after the war by the United States's leader seemed to justify its world standing and reputation. He aspired to design a peace agreement between the warring parties that would help shape a less strained international system, and he endeavored to create an international organization that would make the attainment of such a goal more likely. By 1921 these two ends had come to naught, and the United States was no longer perceived in the same light. To grasp why a nation with so many resources and so many options failed to extricate the world from its tormented past, I will focus on: i) the peace agreement designed by the victors at the end of the war; ii) the accord to create the League of

Nations; and iii) the decision by the United States to cast off the peace agreement and not become a member of the League of Nations.

The End of the War

The First World War began to change direction a few months before President Woodrow Wilson announced that the United States would join forces with the Allies to fight Germany. After weathering several military defeats and much domestic chaos, the Russian czarist regime of Nicholas II came to a crushing end in February 1917. The Provisional Government that replaced it was immediately beset by new losses on the battlefield and a major economic crisis. By October of the same year, the Bolsheviks, led by Vladimir Uliyanov Lenin, took over the city of Petrograd and declared Russia a soviet republic. Though immediately defeated in the elections for the Constituent Assembly, the Bolsheviks held on to power. In January 1918 they dissolved the assembly, and two months later they signed the Peace of Brest-Litovsk with Germany.

The peace treaty with the new Soviet Russia freed Germany to move its troops to France and launch a major assault on Allied forces. By April, German forces had moved to within 40 miles of Paris. But that was as close as they would get. In May, some 200,000 American troops, who had arrived in Europe in December 1917 to train for battle, entered combat. Six months later, after the Allied forces had broken through German lines, Berlin called for a peace agreement. The Germany of late 1918 was no longer the same one that had marched its armed forces against Russia and France in 1914. The military, political, economic, and social demands imposed by the war had inflicted a heavy cost on Germany. By early October, the German government, still under the leadership of Kaiser Wilhelm II, appealed to Wilson for a peace agreement under the terms of the president's Fourteen Points peace plan. Wilson replied that he would not forward the request to his allies until Germany proved that it would lay down its weapons and establish a truly representative government. The kaiser abdicated and was replaced by a democratic government. On November 11, 1918, German representatives signed the armistice, thus bringing the First World War to an end.[4] The signing of the armistice forced Great Britain, France, and the United States to face the laborious task of resolving differences among themselves and with their enemies without resorting once again to armed conflict. To achieve this end they agreed to meet in Paris.

Ostensibly, the representatives of Britain, France, and the United States were to gather in Paris to draft and sign a peace treaty. This intent, however, was partially overshadowed by the fact that each country's leader was firm in his determination to create a peace treaty that reflected his "world vision" and strengthened his country's international standing. The issue that was to most divide them came in the form of the question: Should a balance-of-power system define the nature of the new international system? A corollary to this question was: Should Germany's power be abated? Two philosophies, one representing the past and the other hoping to symbolize the future, clashed immediately.

Both Britain, which had sent 947,000 young men to war to die for their country, and France, which saw much of the war fought on its own land and witnessed the death of 1,385,000 Frenchmen on the battlefield, hoped to create a balance-of-power system in which Germany would not play a dominant role. Britain's recently elected prime minister, Lloyd George, was determined to make sure that his country's domination of the seas would not be imperiled, that its colonies remained firmly under its control, and that Germany was stripped of all its military and economic means of war. As he had remarked while campaigning in 1918 : "We will squeeze the orange [the Germans] till the pips squeak."[5] George's desire for revenge was exceeded by that of his French counterpart, George ("The Tiger") Clemenceau. Clemenceau had been elected prime minister toward the end of 1917, after the French military had failed to score a major victory at Chemin des Dames and massive industrial unrest had erupted throughout France. Fully aware that the French voters had not forgotten the humiliation France had endured under the hands of the Prussians at the end of the 1870 war, Clemenceau promised that he would make "Germany pay." Clemenceau's words contained more than blustery rhetoric. From the moment he assumed power, he was determined to fulfill two international goals. His first objective was to strip Germany of its ability to attack France. His resolve was justified. First, in its northern sector France shared a long, unprotected frontier with Germany, one that had been occupied by German troops on two occasions in less than half a century. Second, Germany's economy had become the strongest in Europe, enabling Berlin to build a very powerful and efficient military. Third, Germany's population was more than one and a half times larger than, and would continue to increase at twice the rate of, France's population. And fourth, France would no longer be able to rely on Russia to serve as an eastern counterweight to Germany's power as it had in the past.[6] The prime minister's second goal was related to his first one. He was adamant that Germany be held responsible for starting the war and be forced to pay reparations for the damages its army had caused in France's northeastern territory. He also demanded French control over Germany's southwestern coal and iron regions.

The beliefs and goals that would influence George's and Clemenceau's stand during the negotiations in Paris were not particularly unique. Though their visions differed markedly from that promoted by the European leaders at the birth of the 1815 system, the incongruity was justified. The last war far exceeded in ferocity the war that preceded the formation of the 1815 balance-of-power system. The 1914–1918 war was "not a limited but a total war that involved the whole of the resources at the command of the participants, and it broke down the old division between the military and civilian parts of society."[7]

If political decisions are anchored to lessons leaders infer from events that resonate in their minds,[8] it should not come as a surprise that the two European leaders had to negotiate with a leader who openly questioned the balance-of-power doctrine. Woodrow Wilson, who as president of the United States was representing a country that had lost in the last war only about one-twentieth the number of men sacrificed by Britain, berated his war partners for wanting to shape a new balance-of-power system based on alliances. In a speech delivered to the United States Senate on January 22, 1917, he asked that all nations "avoid entangling alliances that draw them into competitions of power, catch them in a net of intrigue and selfish rivalry, and disturb their own affairs with influences intruded from without." He emphasized the same point just a few days before he arrived in Paris, where he declared that the war had been fought "to do away with an older order," one which was called "the balance-of-power—a thing in which the balance was determined by the sword which was thrown in the one side or the other; a balance which was determined by the unstable equilibrium of competitive interests; a balance which was maintained by jealous watchfulness and an antagonism of interests which, though it was generally latent, was always deep-seated."[9]

The Paris Peace Conference

On January 12, 1919, representatives of 27 Allied and Associate states gathered in Paris to begin deliberations.[10] Because of their countries' roles during the war, President Wilson, Prime Minister George, and Prime Minister Clemenceau became the principal decision-makers.[11] After several months of intensive discussions, the main parties were able to reach an agreement. The Germans, who had not been consulted during the negotiations, were given 15 days to study the settlement and submit their objections in writing to the Allies. On June 28, 1919, during the fifth anniversary of the Sarajevo assassinations, the Allies and the Germans met in the Hall of Mirrors of Louis XIV's palace, the same place where King Wilhelm I of Prussia had been proclaimed kaiser of a united Germany in 1871, to sign the Treaty of Versailles. If the Allies chose the location to humiliate the Germans, they succeeded; but this effect would prove to be less troublesome than the effect the treaty itself would have.

"The Big Three" designed a treaty that exacted moral, military, territorial, and economic claims on defeated Germany. Article 231 of the treaty stated that Germany accepted responsibility "for causing all the loss and damage to which the Allied and Associated Governments and their nationals have been subjected as a consequence of the war *imposed upon them by the aggression of Germany and her allies.*"[12] As the "Hang the Kaiser" call resonated on both sides of the English Channel, negotiators demanded that William II, who had left Germany for the Netherlands on November 10, 1918, after being forced to abdicate the throne, be tried by an international court for his acts against international morality. Skeptical about the legality of the proposed procedure, the Dutch government rebuffed the request.[13] Notwithstanding this minor setback, the Big Three succeeded in creating a moral foundation for their material claims.

Until quite recently states upheld their power via territory, economic wealth, and military strength. Though, in 1919, Britain, France, and the United States did not completely raze Germany's power, together they sought to ensure that its three pillars would be severely weakened. One of their first measures was to divide Germany's former colonies among themselves and Japan. Originally, Wilson had opposed this action, but under pressure from his allies and Japan, he acquiesced.[14] Of greater significance was the way the three major powers parceled out Germany's own and contiguous territory. Germany was forced to renounce the gains it had exacted from the Russians at Brest-Litovsk, accept the creation of a free Poland and the establishment in Western Prussia of a corridor to provide Poland access to the port of Danzig on the Baltic Sea, return Alsace-Lorraine to France, cede the towns of Eupen and Malmédy to Belgium, and allow plebiscites to determine the future possession of Schleswig and certain districts of East Prussia and Silesia.[15] The most vexing territorial issue was a region on the western side of Germany, strategically located between France and the Rhine River and commonly referred to as the Rhineland. In recognition that this region provided the German military rapid access to France's industrial sector in the northeast and to Paris, Clemenceau proposed that the Rhineland be transformed into an independent sovereign state under French military protection. Both George and Wilson rejected Clemenceau's proposal. The British prime minister remarked that the friction Alsace-Lorraine had generated between France and Germany proved that Europe could not afford to have another perpetual source of strife. In turn, Wilson asserted that the forcible separation of the Rhineland from Germany would violate the principle of national self-determination. As a compromise, the parties agreed to an inter-Allied military occupation of the Rhineland for a period of 15 years and the permanent prohibition against the deployment of German military forces or the construction of fortifications on the territory west of the Rhine.[16]

Having dealt a major blow to Germany's territorial power, the Big Three sought to ensure that it would not have the means to regain it. Their first set of restraints was designed to leash Germany's military power. They bounded Germany's armed forces to a size no larger than

100,000 officers and men, denied its army the right to manufacture military aircraft, tanks, and other offensive weapons, and stipulated that the navy would be limited to a nominal force with no submarines and no vessels exceeding 10,000 tons. Furthermore, they dissolved what they considered to be the breeding places of Prussian militarism: the General Staff, the War Academy, and the cadet schools.[17] Aware that these measures alone would not satisfy Clemenceau, Wilson and George committed the United States and Britain to defend France were it to sustain an unprovoked attack from Germany.

The second set of controls were markedly more complex. On the one hand, they were steered to help France, and to a lesser extent Britain, reconstruct their economies; on the other hand, they were intended to bridle Germany's economy. France was in dire need of a massive infusion of capital from abroad. Initially, it hoped to rely principally on the support of the United States and Britain. During the war, the United States and Britain had delivered coal, oil, wheat, and many other commodities that France had not been able to produce in sufficient quantities. Clemenceau and his French associates were hopeful that the economic partnership that the three major powers had forged during the war would continue after the war. At the time of the armistice he proposed that the victorious Allies revive the idea of a permanent economic bloc, which had already been suggested in 1916, with the United States serving as the principal financier. He also indicated that after France and Belgium had completed their economic revitalization, Germany might be authorized to gradually become part of an Atlantic economic order. Under this plan, though Germany would be expected to contribute to the rebuilding of the areas its armies had destroyed, its financial contribution would have been significantly smaller than that of the United States.[18] Wilson immediately made it clear that the United States was not in the business of forging loans, that the European states would have to rely on their own financial resources to pay for their economic recovery, and that if they wanted financial support from the United States they would have to seek it through private investment channels. The U.S. president also informed his allies that with the war at an end the United States would expect full repayment for the loans it had extended to them.[19] Mindful of France's pressing economic needs, Clemenceau decided to place most of the burden for his country's economic recovery on Germany in the form of reparation payments.[20]

France's attempt to exact reparations from the Germans was not unusual. France had paid Britain 700 million francs after 1815, in compensation for Napoleon's war activities, and had paid Germany 500 million marks after the war of 1870. Having paid twice, it was now France's turn to demand retribution.[21] More importantly, of the Big Three, France not only suffered the largest number of human casualties but also absorbed the highest material costs during the war. France's ten most productive *départements*, located in its northeastern region, had served as the main battleground on the eastern front and had been totally devastated after four years of intensive combat.

As already noted, Clemenceau's determination to secure reparations had more than one origin. After having witnessed with great consternation how easily Germany's economy had overtaken France's during the second half of the nineteenth century, and how Berlin had used this might to forge a German empire, he was determined to make sure that the Germany of the future would never again resemble that of the past. Wilson advocated a less rancorous treatment of Germany. He agreed that Germany had to be held responsible for reparation payments, but he was afraid that if they were made abnormally high, the world would eventually suffer dire consequences. He was convinced that a weak Germany would become a magnet to communist movements, ultimately benefiting no one but Russia. George acknowledged this much, but remained forceful in his advocacy that Germany pay a heavy indemnity. Aware that the damage to civilian property in Britain had been minimal, but determined to make sure that Britain was properly compensated, he demanded that the cost of veterans' pensions and separation allowances be made part of the reparation payments. Some of George's advisers, however, were not convinced that it would be in Britain's economic interests to force on Germany high reparations. One group proposed that since Germany had always been a major market for British manufactured goods, the imposition of high reparations would reduce Germany's capacity to import, thereby denying British industry a very important customer. A second group contended that Germany could pay the high reparations only by generating a major foreign trade surplus. However, were Germany to capture a major share of the foreign markets, then Britain's economy, so heavily dependent on its export trade, would suffer. These concerns and disagreements convinced the principal leaders to delay the declaration of a final figure until 1921, with the proviso that in the interim period Germany pay $5 billion.[22]

The agreement reached by the three principal leaders reflected the vision and philosophy not of the new but of the old world. To begin with, Wilson accepted a peace agreement that relegated Germany to a secondary role. Moreover, in an attempt to persuade Clemenceau that France would be safe even if Germany's productive capabilities were not fully dismantled, Wilson was forced to commit the United States to provide military assistance to France were it to be attacked by Germany. These concessions beg the question: Why would Wilson, the leader of the most powerful entity in the international system, give in to the demands of two troubled and weaker partners? To understand Wilson's decision, I will shift the focus to the League of Nations.

The League of Nations

Less than a year after Wilson announced that the United States would enter the war, he presented a Fourteen Points peace program. The first 13 points delineated the conditions for peace. They emphasized, among other things, the importance of: i) not reaching private agreements, ii) guaranteeing the absolute freedom of navigation outside territorial waters; iii) advancing free world trade; iv) reducing the size of each country's armed forces, v) respecting Russia's right to self-determination, vi) restoring territories lost by Russia, Belgium, France, Rumania, Serbia, and Montenegro during the war, vii) readjusting Italy's, Austria-Hungary's, and the Ottoman Empire's frontiers and granting national groups under their domain security and the opportunity for autonomous development, and viii) forming an independent Polish state. Wilson's most cherished point, however, was the fourteenth one, which proposed the creation of a general association of nations, to be named the League of Nations. It stated: "A general association of nations must be formed under specific covenants for the purpose of affording mutual guarantees of political independence and territorial integrity to great and small states alike." The function of the League of Nations would be not just to implement the peace agreement but also to correct the errors the negotiators might commit during its drafting.[23] Thus, to the extent that the Treaty of Versailles imposed on Germany an agreement that did not harmonize with Wilson's vision, the U.S. president was convinced that the League of Nations would succeed in addressing its errors during the implementation process.

For the League to become an important and effective instrument of international peace, it had to have the firm endorsement of its major signatories. Two conditions diminished markedly the probability of procuring the support of the one state the League most needed—the United States. First, two of the Covenant's articles stipulated, indirectly, that the United States had to follow a foreign policy path different from the one that it had always traveled, and that it had to relinquish part of its freedom as an independent state. Specifically, Article 10, which Wilson referred to as the "heart of the Covenant," and Article 16 threatened the United States's honored tradition not to become entangled in alliances that could hinder its ability to freely formulate its own foreign policy. Article 10 required that each League member pledge "to respect and preserve as against external aggression the territorial integrity and existing political independence of all members of the League." Article 16, in turn, delineated the steps members of the League would have to take to enforce Article 10. Specifically, Article 16 stipulated that if any member of the League resorted to war and disregarded Article 12, 13, or 15, the remaining members would ipso facto consider the action an act of war and would "subject it to the severance of all trade or financial relations, the prohibition of all intercourse between their nations and the nationals of the covenant-breaking State, and the prevention of all financial, commercial, or personal intercourse between the nationals of the covenant-breaking State and the nationals of any other State." It also noted that the League would recommend the types of military steps its members should take "to protect the covenants of the League." Observance of both articles could have forced Washington to act in ways it did not deem appropriate to the interests of the United States in at least two types of cases. As the hegemon in the Western Hemisphere, Washington could have been pressed to relinquish its assumed right to intervene militarily in the domestic affairs of one of its Caribbean Basin neighbors if such a party experienced extensive domestic turmoil or initiated policies that threatened the security, economic, and commercial interests of the United States.[24] As a member of the League of Nations, moreover, Washington could have been compelled to take retaliatory steps against a state that used military force against another party in disregard of the League's covenants but whose actions did not threaten the interests of the United States.

Articles 10 and 16 did not automatically nullify the chances of the United States's becoming a member of the League of Nations. States have been known to modify the core of their foreign policies, particularly if past international actions had proven to be too costly. Conditions in the United States in 1919, however, were quite unique and thus required mindful actions from the League's principal advocate. The United States had just come out of a war that involved the participation of states that had been battling one another throughout much of their histories about matters that to the American public and Congress seemed only tangentially related to their own problems and interests. Under such circumstances, and considering that the Congress and the Executive were under the leadership of rival parties, it would have been prudent for Wilson to seek the advice of, and to involve, his political rivals in the drafting of the Covenant. But that was not the way he handled it. While in Paris, he completed the writing of a covenant for the League on his own, with almost no consultation, and in just ten days. Then, with little warning, he returned to Washington to lobby for the Covenant. Some Republicans in the U.S. Congress began to voice doubts about its merits immediately. Wilson, rather than listening to their concerns, defied them to stand against him by remarking that he would link the peace agreement to the Covenant so tightly that they would have to accept both if they wanted a peace agreement. On March 4, 1919, while Wilson was still in Washington, Republican Senator Henry Cabot Lodge announced that 39 senators, more than the one-third needed to reject Wilson's League, would not accept it as proposed.[25]

Wilson went back to Paris and demanded from his counterparts that they agree on a covenant for the League. He persuaded Clemenceau and George that the Monroe Doctrine was an integral component of the United States's national interest and thus had to be protected. In return, he acquiesced to George's insistence that Britain's domination of the seas could not be compromised, and to Japan's demand that it be authorized to remain in Shantung, a region in China, inhabited by some 30 million Chinese, that had been under German control. Clemenceau and George, conscious that their chances of fulfilling their own goals depended extensively on whether Wilson realized his own objective, agreed to the creation of the League of Nations. Sir Eric Drummond was immediately named the League's first secretary and was charged with the task of establishing an International Court of Justice and an International Labor Office.

By then, however, the future of the League of Nations had already been jeopardized, if not doomed. Wilson returned to the United States, only to be reminded that his vision of the future was not shared by many members of the Congress, particularly since its leaders had been excluded from its design. Two groups resisted his plan. One group, the "Irreconcilables," opposed membership in any kind of organization that would draw the United States to defend the interests of colonial powers such as France and Britain. This group demanded that the United States center its attention on domestic problems and show sympathy for revolutions in places such as Russia and China. The second group, the "Reservationists," led by Lodge, was more sympathetic to British and French interests but feared that Article 10 would lock the United States into acting on behalf of the weakening European powers. Senator Lodge sought to find a compromise by proposing his own set of 14 points, which were immediately rejected by Wilson. On November 19, 1919, less than two months after Wilson had suffered a massive stroke while campaigning for the League in Pueblo, Colorado, the Senate defeated Lodge's revised treaty. On March 19, 1920, Wilson's covenant received the support of the Senate, but the votes (49 to 35) fell short of the required two-thirds. In sum, the belief that U.S. membership in the League would have meant "an increase in contact with the poison-infected areas of the world"[26] won out over the belief that the League was the only antidote that could protect the American people from the "poison of disorder, the poison of revolt" that was roaming through the international arena. Though the loser might have fostered an unrealistic view of the capabilities of the League of Nations, the winner failed to cultivate a practical alternative to an international system that was in desperate need of an entity ready to lead.

Why the Failing?

A state's experience in, and knowledge about, international affairs are critical. The end of the war brought to the bargaining table two very different sets of experiences. Armed with the power and moral authority that typically enshrines victors, President Wilson advocated the destruction of the old balance-of-power system. That type of system, he argued, could not avoid being unstable, for it was kept in place by jealous watchfulness and the antagonism generated by deep-seated interests. As an alternative, he proposed creating an international system bounded by democratic nation-states. He voiced his faith in the rightness of popular judgment in two different ways. During the war he had remarked that its unfolding revealed that the people, not the leaders, were the ones who discerned its true purpose. "The counsels of plain men," he stated, "have become on all hands more simple and straightforward and more unified than the counsels of sophisticated men of affairs, who still retain the impression that they are playing a game of power and are playing for high stakes. This is why I have said that this is a people's war, not a statesmen's. Statesmen must follow the clarified common thought or be broken." On his way to Paris to negotiate the peace agreement he expanded on this point by stressing that the representatives must be "prepared to follow the opinions of mankind and to express the will of the people rather than that of leaders. . . ." Failure to follow public opinion, he added, would lead to "another break-up of the world." [27] To this notion he attached the argument that the world would be markedly less tense if political maps were redrawn according to the principles of national self-determination.

Wilson's message was not new; his rhetoric preceded him for well over a century. Since President Washington's days, one U.S. president after another, and a countless number of secretaries of state, had reproved Europe's balance-of-power system and warned that the United States had little to gain by being drawn into its malignant web. The warnings, however, never impeded U.S. presidents from capitalizing on the constraints imposed by the European balance-of-power system on its principal members to expand the power of the United States in the Western Hemisphere and the Pacific region. Almost as significant, nearly every single expansionary step was accompanied by the claim that no other nation was better equipped than the United States to propagate the seeds of political, economic, and social freedom.

As I have already explained, it is not uncommon for leaders to rely on old approaches to resolve new problems, nor to miss or ignore the differences between past and present events. For much of its first 100 years, the United States had tried to impose its will only on European states that were entangled in political quagmires in their own continent, or on considerably weaker Latin American adversaries. The United States's critical role during the 1914 war convinced Wilson that he would be able to replicate its earlier victories in a very different world scenario. He traveled to Europe disinclined to acknowledge that though its members had been ravaged by the war, they were unprepared to admit that the international system no longer spun around them, and to anoint the United States as its new center.

During his visits to London, Rome, and Paris, hundreds of thousands of well-wishers welcomed Wilson as Europe's savior. They applauded his call for the design of an international system led by democratic nation-states, and for the active involvement of the public on matters of international affairs. Their leaders, though uneasy about the idea of having to appraise how their foreign policies would be received by their publics before they acted, recognized that it was a constraint they had to accept. At the same time, however, they used the drive to democratize the foreign-policy-making process to advocate their own world-order vision. Prime Minister Clemenceau's determination to humiliate Germany and strip it of its ability to attack France again, for instance, mirrored not only his own anger but also that of his people. What is more, he had little faith in the type of international system that Wilson was advocating. As he noted with mordant glee: "God has given man Ten Commandments. He broke every one. President Wilson has his Fourteen Points. We shall see."[28]

The basic intent of any peace agreement is not to humiliate the defeated party but to minimize the likelihood that it will become the cause of the next war. Clemenceau concurred with the second part of this proposition. His strategy was driven by the belief that if the allied forces amputated parts of Germany's economic and military power, its ability to start a new war would be radically reduced. His reasoning, however, was erroneous on several accounts. Clemenceau did not understand that Germany, with its history, political structure, and strategic location, would eventually strive to regain, at minimum, its earlier strength unless the Allied forces completely destroyed its power and committed themselves fully to stop any attempt on the part of its leaders to restore its lost power. To completely eradicate Germany's power and to ensure that the Allied forces would impede any attempt on its part to violate the conditions stipulated in the agreement, Clemenceau would have needed the unwavering backing of the other major negotiators, principally the United States and Britain. Though he knew he lacked their support to impose on Germany such excessive conditions, he decided that a partial attainment of his objectives was preferable to no accomplishment at all. In making this decision, Clemenceau failed to recognize that he was creating a highly contradictory agreement. It was an accord that, on the one hand, magnified Germany's willingness to violate the conditions stipulated in the Covenant as a means of regaining some of its lost power and pride; on the other hand, it did not firmly guarantee that France's allies would come to its aid if Germany decided to resort to war once again.[29]

It may be reasonable to expect a certain measure of wisdom from a leader whose central task was to create a European system that would protect his country from future aggressive acts. However, one can comprehend Clemenceau's loathing, and that of his people, toward Germany, considering the human and material costs it had imposed on France. A similar measure of reluctant absolution, however, cannot be extended to Woodrow Wilson. The U.S. president understood that Clemenceau's proposal to dismember part of Germany would produce a sick, unbalanced Europe, and more wars. As he explained, the United States did not wish to injure "her [Germany] or block in any way her legitimate influence or power. We do not wish to fight her with arms or with hostile arrangements of trade if she is willing to associate herself with us and the other peace-loving nations of the world in covenants of justice and law and fair dealing."[30] And yet, he gave in, and in doing so, he helped plant the seeds that would result in a war that would once again engulf the entire international system.

One should never underestimate the destructive effect of a person's inflated ego. When Wilson traveled to Europe, he was guided by the conviction that his actions were shepherded by God's will, and that his intellectual and moral faculties were so superior to those in the U.S. Congress that he did not need their counsel. It did not take him long to realize that his resolve, and the power of the United States, would not be sufficient to force his allies to create both the kind of international system he wanted and an international organization to help regulate it. Unable, or unwilling, to return home empty-handed, Wilson agreed to compromise on his first goal. Two factors influenced his decision. First, he believed that ultimately the Allies would have no choice but to accept his postwar vision. As he told a close adviser: "When the war is over, we can force [England and France] to our way of thinking because by that time they . . . [will] be financially in our hands."[31] Moreover, he assumed that though the international system the United States and its allies were creating was imperfect, the League of Nations would be able to rectify it in due time.

Wilson's confidence was unwarranted. The peace treaty, along with the decision to become a member of the League of Nations, would have thrust the United States to the center of Europe's destructive political web and reduced Washington's freedom to design its own foreign policies. Neither Americans nor Congress took these prospects lightly. Americans were concerned that by becoming a member of the League of Nations the United States would be drawn into the venomous affairs of decaying political regimes. It is not unreasonable to infer, however, that had Wilson sought the advice of key U.S. senators during his negotiations with the European leaders, the chances of the treaty's receiving the two-thirds support required for passage would have increased considerably.[32] Former presidents who had been successful at annexing territory had always been aware that without congressional support their endeavors would have been thwarted. Moreover, by the time the final vote took place, a significant portion of the American public had started to pressure Congress to approve the treaty. The decision by the U.S. Congress guaranteed that the League of Nations would be born powerless. No institution created to promote and maintain world order can be effective without the active membership of the international system's most powerful entity.

Wilson's actions had other effects besides those I have just delineated. The war generated a strong antiwar sentiment in both the United States and Europe. Though U.S. leaders were not yet ready to seek the public's guidance on matters of foreign affairs, they understood that it would be politically unwise for them to propose that the United States assist far-off nations at war, regardless of how morally fitting or restricted the intended assistance would be. They were cognizant that their constituents were opposed to risking the lives of young American men in wars that did not have a direct bearing on U.S. interests. They remembered the 1920 presidential election and the ease with which the Republican candidate, Warren G. Harding, had defeated the Democratic nominees, Governor James Cox and his running mate, Franklin Delano Roosevelt, both of whom had tried to make the League of Nations a salient issue. Of great interest to the postwar political leaders was Harding's prenomination speech, in which he called for a return to "not submergence in internationality but sustainment in triumphant nationality."[33] Harding's political slogan during the campaign: "Stabilize America first, prosper America first, think America first and exalt America first,"[34] was a blunt rebuttal to the notion that the United States had an obligation to serve as the international system's constabulary. Sixty percent of the American voters who visited the voting booth during the presidential election concluded that Harding's message reflected their beliefs.

Across the Atlantic, Britain's political system experienced a transformation that would also affect its leaders' freedom to direct their country's foreign affairs. In 1921, just three years after all men over 21 years of age had been enfranchised, women over 30 were also granted the right to vote. This change forced Britain's leaders to become more attentive to the voices of their constituents on foreign policy matters. The British people, like their American counterparts, were vehemently opposed to embroiling their nation in the affairs of other states. Thus, when the United States made it clear that it would not fulfill its promise to assist France were it to be attacked by Germany, the British government saw no reason to honor its own pledge. The intensity of the antiwar sentiment in Britain remained unaltered almost until the end of the 1930s, when the people and their leaders were forced to conclude that they had no alternative to war.

Across the English Channel, fate had not been as indulgent with France as it had been with its two former allies. Though the French had absorbed much greater material and human costs during the war than the British and the Americans, and were equally opposed to war, they recognized that their country's border with Germany did not afford them the luxury of indifference to the affairs of its neighboring states. With Britain and the United States unwilling to commit themselves to assist France were it to find itself at war with Germany once again, the French people decided to elect a government whose top priority was to protect their country from war. France's militaristic mentality was disclosed by the November 1919 elections, which resulted in the great victory of the conservative national bloc. Subsequent elections in France were also dictated by the electorate's perception of the candidates' ability to respond effectively to international challenges. This perception experienced a major jolt following France's occupation of the Ruhr. World condemnation of the act forced France to conclude that its combative approach to foreign affairs was not serving its national interest. The person empowered to search for an alternative approach was Aristide Briand, who became France's foreign minister in 1925 and stayed in office until 1932. Briand decided that in view of the new international antiwar mood, the most effective way of protecting France from a German attack would be through agreements and alliances rooted in the League of Nations' system of collective security. Considering that the United States had outright rejected membership in the League of Nations, and that Britain viewed it not as an institution with the authority to act on behalf of its members but as a forum for leaders to address their international differences, France's decision signaled a resigned admission of the limitations of its choices.[35]

In short, rather than paving the road for the development of a more stable international system, the First World War helped accomplish the precise opposite. At a war's end, the loser, in spite of its objections, is typically forced to acquiesce to the demands of the victor, and to assume a subordinate role. How cooperative the loser is in its new role depends on the nature of the peace treaty it has been coerced to accept, and on the nature of its own political system. Notwithstanding its displeasure with the peace treaty, Germany realized that it had to accept it, at least temporarily. Circumscribed by a political system that enabled domestic political entities to use the public ire to espouse radical causes, Germany would eventually discard its subservient guise. Before then, however, the world had to resolve another pressing affair.

The passing of the leadership banner in international politics is seldom a simple procedure. The matter is particularly complex when the bequeathing calls for an interplay between two powerful parties, both victorious in war. A marred international hegemon is unlikely to cede center stage amiably to a rising power, even when it is in the latter's debt and knows that the power realignment is inevitable. Britain, having dominated the international system for nearly a century, was not yet ready to relinquish the baton to the United States. London recognized that without the United States's involvement, Britain would have had great difficulty defeating Germany. London also knew that the power potential of the United States was vastly superior to Britain's, and that it was only a matter of time before this fact became evident to the world. But neither fact made it easier for London to accept its new fate. London's problem was compounded by the United States's behavior.

The measure of leadership is determined not by the nerve to try to achieve an unrealizable goal, but by the readiness to tackle a challenging, conquerable, problem. As the new global power, Washington sought to change the rules of the game overnight. Emboldened by the United States's power and copious earlier feats, Wilson assumed that the world would bow to his vision and will. He never considered that the changes he promoted were excessive and would have forced the European powers to modify radically their own way of thinking and behavior. Nor did he give much thought to the fact that the United States could not enforce them without their explicit approval. Equally as consequential, to thrive in international affairs, the rulers of a democracy must always keep a watchful eye on those they serve at home. As in the international arena, those in the domestic field are hardly ever prepared to accept fundamental foreign policy changes, particularly when they are not consulted. By not enlisting Congress in the design of the treaty, Wilson doomed its approval, hampered the future effectiveness of the United States in the international arena, and helped catapult the international system into a chaotic future. But these were not the only troubles that would torment the United States. As the 1920s unfolded, the international economic system on which Washington had become so dependent began to tumble.

From One Quandary to the Next One

The decision by the United States not to become a member of the League of Nations, and to sign separate peace treaties with Germany and Austria, was not a resolution to abandon the international arena. Influenced by its century-long tradition not to sign alliances that would entangle the United States in the political predicaments of other states, but cognizant that failure to assume a major international role would undermine its capacity to influence the outcome of critical international events and enhance its reputation, Washington set its sight on building a more open and stable international economic system. By the end of the 1920s, however, the United States saw its hopes shattered by the Great Depression, and by its own inability to prevent being engulfed by the tide of economic nationalism that overtook the globe. Without examining both the causes of the Great Depression and the tensions it generated, it is impossible to understand the causes of the Second World War and the role the United States played prior, during, and immediately after the war. Therefore, I am compelled to analyze the Great Depression in some detail.

A Structural Realist Explanation of the Great Depression

It has been suggested that the United States could have, if not averted, at least tempered the global economic depression had it, among other things, kept the international market for distressed goods relatively open and provided countercyclical long-term lending.[36] Structural realism proposes that the foreign economic policy of a state is affected by both the nature of the international economic structure and the state's position within it.[37] The international economic structure is determined by the number and category of states within it. The category of states is captured along two axes. One axis measures a state's relative size, which is determined by that state's proportion of trade. The second axis outlines the state's relative productivity, which is measured by the state's relative output per unit of labor input. The combination of these measures leads to the identification of four types of states: free riders, spoilers, supporters, and hegemonic leaders. Free riders have no effect on the international economic system, simply because they generate a very small proportion of the world trade and their own relative productivity may vary from low to high. Spoilers are drawn to destabilize the international economic system by behaving like free riders, because the proportion of world trade they yield may vary from middle to high and their relative productivity is typically mediocre. Supporters are interested in supporting the liberal economic system, but they cannot always do so because the proportion of world trade they produce may vary from middle to middle-high and their relative productivity may range from middle to high. Hegemonic leaders are interested in protecting and fostering the international economic system, because they supply a high proportion of the world trade and have a very high relative productivity. For present purposes, the two roles that are important are those played by the hegemonic leaders and the supporters.

A hegemon struggles to keep an international economic system open, not because it is altruistic but because the benefits it accrues typically outweigh the costs it absorbs to keep it open. A supporter, on the other hand, because it has fewer resources, is less able to absorb short-term costs and thus is not as inclined to keep the system open. Of great significance to the future and stability of an open international economic system is whether it is inhabited by one or two supporters, when there is no hegemonic leader. When the system lacks a hegemonic leader and has only one supporter, the latter will have no qualms about erecting trade barriers. The single supporter might value export markets but lacks the resources necessary to preserve a liberal international economic system. On the other hand, when the system has no hegemonic leader but has two supporters, the two entities, because of their moderate-to-high relative productivity, will value export markets more than protectionism. These two supporters, however, will sacrifice the openness of their markets if they conclude that by erecting trade barriers at home they will persuade their counterparts to lower them. In short, on a scale of one to three, with one being the least protectionist, structural realists rank first an international economic system with one hegemon, second a system with no hegemon and two supporters, and third a system with no hegemon and one supporter.

International Economic Problems in the 1920s

The theoretical framework I have just delineated has been used to explain the foreign economic policy of the United States between 1913 and 1934.[38] To evaluate its theoretical utility, however, I must first present some of the events the model strives to explain. After the end of the First World War, there was nothing more political in the international arena than economics. The most common effect of the open-market system is competition, which in turn abets uncertainty. The state tolerates some uncertainty so long as its leaders assume that the benefits generated by competition outweigh its short-term costs. The economic uncertainty generated by the war, and the continuing rise in the United States's economic power, had driven Britain, Russia, Italy, and France to meet in Paris in 1916, to reach an agreement designed to protect their economies by organizing trade on a state capitalist basis around exclusive regional blocs.[39] This action ran counter to the type of international economic system Wilson hoped to create after the war.

Since his early days as president, one of Wilson's objectives had been to construct a world system that encouraged self-determination, free trade, and U.S. economic interests. The president believed that tariff duties, which in the past had enabled the United States to help build its economy, were starting to act as barriers to further economic development. In a speech before the Congress in 1913 in which he advocated passage of the Underwood Tariff Act, Wilson remarked that tariffs had to be changed in order "to meet the radical alterations in the conditions of our economic life which the country has witnessed within the last generation." Passage of the act lowered the average rate of duty on all imports to the United States from 20 percent to 8.8 percent, and on dutiable imports alone from 41 percent to 26.8 percent.[40] Five years later he sought to reduce competition for foreign markets between American firms by signing the Webb-Promerene Act. This act authorized American firms to split foreign markets among themselves. He took another major step a year later when he signed the Edge Act, a law designed to encourage American banks to create joint subsidiaries to lend money abroad.[41]

The Harding administration, which came to power in March 1921, did not agree with Wilson that the "Great War" had been fought to eliminate future wars, and that the League of Nations, led by democracies, would help abolish the long-standing dependency on war as an instrument of politics. The new administration believed that wars would persist and that the Great War differed little from previous wars. Furthermore, it contended that the League of Nations was nothing more than a different sort of alliance, one that other states might try to use to assure their own safety but that would not serve the interests of the United States. The Harding administration, however, shared with its predecessor the belief that the United States should attempt to create a more liberal international economic system. Its first secretary of commerce, Herbert Hoover, noted that in order for economic freedom to become the international economic system's new driving principle, the United States had to cultivate the kind of individualism that lay at the core of its own economic and social system.[42] But just as the previous administration had failed to create a more democratic international political system, its successor failed to devise a more open international economic system.

By the time Harding became president, the international arena was already being afflicted by a series of economic problems. As Secretary of State Charles Evans Hughes remarked in 1922, the international problems of the United States were "mainly economic problems." The Harding administration understood that, though by the end of the war the world owed the United States some $3 billion and the American public and Congress were clamoring that Europeans pay their debts, the economy of the United States would suffer unless a significant portion of this money was recycled back to Europe.[43] This issue was contaminated by the reparation costs imposed by the Allies on Germany at the end of the war. In 1920, Prime Minister George, no longer convinced that it would be in Britain's best interests to encumber Germany with such a high economic burden, called for a meeting to see whether a new reparations arrangement could be formalized. The meeting did not effect a new agreement. Also, during this period the smaller European countries, particularly those that had been carved out of the Austro-Hungarian Empire, started to apply higher tariffs in order to protect their new industries. Not to be outdone, Britain adopted a moderate form of imperial preference through the Safeguarding of Industries Act of 1921, and France passed a two-tiered tariff in which the highest duties were applied against countries that imposed high duties on French exports.[44] As if these setbacks were not bad enough, the worldwide economic boom, which had been propelled in 1919 by the need to replace the inventories exhausted by the five-year war, came to an end by the summer of 1920.

Washington did not succumb fully to the higher-tariffs fever afflicting most of Europe. The Harding administration, after coming under intense pressure from American producers who demanded protection from cheap foreign goods, approved the Fordney-McCumber Act in 1922. The effect of the act on tariffs, however, was not as radical as depicted by some historians.[45] The act was passed as a bargaining tool to extend abroad the Open Door policy. It provided the president the authority to impose penalty duties on countries that discriminated against American products. Moreover, though the act imposed tariffs higher than those required by the Underwood Tariff Act of 1913, they remained markedly lower than the tariffs that had been in place between 1890 and 1913.[46] The Harding administration, however, was not successful at using the new act to persuade other states to lower their trade barriers.

Fear, induced by highly chaotic or threatening conditions, can be an exceptional incentive for change. Since 1918, the new Soviet regime had been systematically nationalizing its industries. The socialization of private property became the most critical challenge ever initiated against foreign capital. After failing to force the new Soviet regime out of power, some of the Allies recognized that it would be in their interests to seek a negotiated agreement with Moscow. Britain was particularly interested in resolving the Allies' differences with the Soviet Union, because London hoped to lead the process of Soviet reconstruction. In order to win the cooperation of the other major states, however, Britain needed to find a way to settle the nationalization issue.[47] It was also during this time that London tried, once again, to address Germany's economic maladies. Representatives of the Soviet Union, Germany, and the major Allied states, with the exception of the United States, met in Genoa in April 1922 to discuss means of promoting the economic recovery of Europe in general, and Germany and Russia in particular. Upon realizing that France had no intention of softening its demands and that the United States, though not present, would oppose any attempt to acknowledge the Soviet Union's right to nationalize foreign property, the German and Soviet representatives retired to the city of Rapallo, where they signed an economic agreement. The specific terms of the treaty were less important than the fact that, by signing it, the two countries put the world on notice that their present internal economic woes would not deter them from seeking to reclaim their former power status.[48]

For Germany, the agreement could have not come at a more opportune time. The German mark had been in trouble since 1921, when it slipped to one-fiftieth of its 1914 value. The inflation had more than one cause. Initially, Germany had financed its war effort by selling bonds instead of taxing its people. This debt was compounded by the reparation costs imposed by the allies and by the costs impelled by Germany's own demobilization policy, which involved extending care for the wounded and widowed, and finding jobs for the able. These developments did not abate France's determination to collect reparation costs from Germany. Concluding that he could not tolerate any further the dwindling of German payments in foreign exchange and deliveries in kind to France, Prime Minister Poincaré ordered the French invasion of the Ruhr—Germany's industrial heartland—in January 1923. Poincaré's decision backfired immediately. While Germany's economy took a deeper plunge, with hyperinflation superseding inflation, the rest of the world, including the United States and Britain, scolded France for its action. Finally, in December, after recognizing that hyperinflation suited almost no one, the British, French, and Germans agreed to appoint a commission to consider ways of balancing Germany's budget, stabilizing its currency, and establishing a new and viable level of annual reparations. The commission was to be headed by Charles G. Dawes, who was then serving as the first director of the United States Bureau of the Budget.[49]

In June 1920, a committee appointed by the Allies concluded that Germany should pay 269 billion gold marks (including interest), or $67.25 billion. Germany rejected the figure, and a year later the Allies reduced it to 132 billion gold marks, or $33 billion, at 6 percent interest, with final payments in 1988.[50] To pay for the reparations, Germany decided to print money instead of raising taxes. This action brought about an unprecedented level of inflation and forced Germany's leaders to eventually stop the reparations payments. The Dawes plan, which became effective in March 1924, had two broad and closely interconnected components. Under its first component, Germany's payments were scaled down to $250 million in the first year and increased to $650 million a year by the fifth year. After the fifth year, Germany's annual payments were to vary moderately for the next 45 years from the $650 million sum, according to changes in the index of German prosperity. To facilitate the payment process and to intervene in the event of a serious payment problem, the commission recommended the setting up of a Reparations Agency in Berlin. Germany's ability to meet the agreed payment schedule depended entirely on whether its economy would recover. The second component of the Dawes plan called for the extension of a $200 million loan to be floated in various financial capitals. U.S. private banks agreed to provide slightly over half of the loan; however, when they floated it on the public U.S. market, in just a few days they subscribed over $1 billion, or ten times the amount they had originally expected.[51]

During its early stage, the Dawes plan had much of the effect its drafters had hoped. The plan freed the Reichsbank from the German government and produced an inflow of capital in the form of foreign loans that, during the early phase, were used to revitalize industry. Equally as significant, Germany's foreign minister, Gustav Stresemann, sought to improve his country's world standing by seeking new diplomatic agreements with some of its former enemies. In 1925, he negotiated with France and Belgium the Locarno Treaty, in which Germany recognized the permanence of its boundaries with the two countries as dictated by the Treaty of Versailles. The foreign ministers of the three countries also agreed to renounce the use of war against each other except in self-defense, or in accordance with the League of Nations' Covenant. Moreover, though Germany was still committed to changing its eastern frontiers, Stresemann underscored that his country would seek their modification only through peaceful means, and that it would become a member of the League of Nations if it was awarded a permanent seat on the Council and was exempted from certain of the military obligations dictated by the Covenant. To a Europe tired of the tension that had been swelling since the end of the war, the agreements reached at Locarno seemed to reflect a desire not to repeat past errors.[52]

The Dawes plan also had a noticeable, though short-lived, effect on the country that assumed the central burden for its implementation—the United States. Since the U.S. Congress had decided to reject the Treaty of Versailles and the League of Nations, the reputation of the United States in the international arena had been slipping. Other states acknowledged that the United States had become the world's supreme military and economic power, but felt that it had yet to develop the maturity necessary to become an effective leader. The Dawes plan changed this perception, at least temporarily. The United States became, as a U.S. official remarked, "the creditor nation and [was] trusted in all Europe even where she [was] despised." He also added that this new trust gave the United States a "potential power to straighten [her] affairs over here."[53]

The hopes generated by the Dawes plan did not last long. On October 24, 1929, the world learned that the New York stock market had collapsed. On that date, nearly 13 million shares changed hands at vastly reduced prices. Five days later, more than 16 million shares were traded. The Dow-Jones industrial average, which had reached a high of 381 on September 3, fell to 198 by November 13. These events did not crop up unannounced.[54] From 1924 to 1928, Americans had been drawn to invest in Europe by the high rates of return it offered. In 1928, however, U.S. investors realized that they could make more money by investing in the U.S. stock market. The effect of this realization was monumental. As U.S. overseas investments in Europe fell by $800 million between 1928 and 1929, the Dow-Jones industrial average doubled from 191 in early 1928 to 381 in September of the following year, and peak daily turnovers increased from four million shares in March 1928 to 8.2 million a year later. These transactions could not have come at a more inopportune time. Belgium, for instance, experienced its business cycle peak in March 1929, Germany in April, Britain in July, and Canada and South Africa sometime in the second quarter. In an attempt to retain badly needed foreign investment, many of the major European countries raised their discount interest rate. Italy increased its own in January 1929, Britain in February, and Italy again in March. The Netherlands, Germany, Austria, and Hungary followed the same path shortly afterward, and so did Belgium in July. These hazards had not gone unnoticed among U.S. financial leaders.

For them, the danger lay in the unstable credit that supported the market and the pressure that these loans exerted on credit throughout both the United States and the rest of the world. In early 1929, the chairman of the Federal Reserve Board, Roy Young, warned that unless banks curbed their brokers' loans, which were feeding the speculation in the stock market, the Federal Reserve would take action. Cognizant of the tension generated by these two seemingly conflicting needs, George Harrison, the president of the Federal Reserve Bank of New York, noted that, while developments in the New York stock market called for an increase in the discount rate from 5 to 6 percent, such an action would not benefit the European economy. He hoped that American investors would redirect their investments back to Europe after the rise in the U.S. stock market had been halted. Harrison's hope never materialized. In early August the Board of Governors accepted a recommendation by the president of the Federal Reserve Bank of New York to increase the discount interest rate from 5 to 6 percent, but the decision did not stop the stock market from moving up another notch. Shortly afterward, on September 26, the Bank of England raised its discount interest rate from 5.5 to 6.5 percent. New York banks, with substantial assistance from the Federal Reserve Bank of New York, attempted to support stock market prices by direct purchase, holding back on margin calls, and taking over loans called by outsiders. But on October 3, they learned that withdrawals by foreigners had occasioned a $120 million decline in brokers' loans. On November 1, just a week after the New York stock market debacle, the Federal Reserve Bank of New York lowered its discount interest rate from 6 to 5 percent, and by another half percent two weeks later. European banks, hoping to relieve the financial impact of the crash, pursued a similar path. Between October 29 and the end of the year, the Bank of England reduced its discount interest rate three times; the Netherlands and Norway twice; and Austria, Belgium, Denmark, Germany, Hungary, and Sweden once. The effort did not plug the dam; between October 29 and December 31, some $450 million were withdrawn from New York by foreign accounts.

Following the crash of the New York stock market, U.S. banks began to call in their short-term loans and to cut off new loans. The number of dollars made available by the United States declined by 68 percent between the end of the 1920s and 1933; by 1934 the loans had ceased altogether. Moreover, as investors began to withdraw money from the New York market, firms that had counted on ready access to the New York stock and bond markets started to cut their spending. These actions had devastating effects, both in the United States and abroad. In the United States, industrial production fell by almost 10 percent in a two-month period, and from 1928 to 1932 the gross national product dropped from $104 billion to $56 billion. A significant portion of the drop was absorbed by the auto industry, which in 1931 produced only half the automobiles it had manufactured two years earlier. Abroad, one of the most severely affected countries was Germany. As I already noted, U.S. private institutions had extended loans to Germany since 1924 to help revitalize its economy. German businesses, convinced that U.S. capital would continue to flow, used much of the money it had borrowed on short-term loans for long-term investments. Initially, Germany's economy grew, but by 1929 its productivity had begun to slow down. With the withdrawal of American money from the German economy, the liquid reserves of German banks and businesses came under pressure. What is more, because the foreign loans had to be repaid in foreign currency, the withdrawal jeopardized the German currency by absorbing the gold reserves of the Reichsbank. By the summer of 1931, Germany's gold reserve amounted to only 10 percent of what it had been prior to the start of the crisis.[55] The Germans, cognizant of their country's adverse financial condition, started to withdraw their funds. Since Britain and the United States had invested heavily in Germany's economy, this development translated into major losses to their own banks; these losses, in turn, brought about the implementation of additional credit restrictions.[56]

Conditions in the agricultural world were also bleak. Until about 1866, most of the world relied on the harvest to measure business conditions. During the last part of the nineteenth century, however, Western Europe began to pay less attention to agriculture. Investors and analysts began to relate the business cycle to financial conditions, the state of industrial inventories, expenditure for plant and equipment, or population migration. But this change did not alter the fact that over 67 percent of the world's active population still engaged in agriculture, and almost two-fifths of the world trade was in agricultural products. This was true even in the United States, where in 1929 farming accounted for a quarter of total employment, and farm exports accounted for 28 percent of farm income. In central and southern Europe, and Latin American countries such as Uruguay, Chile, and Argentina, the percentages on both scores were markedly higher.[57]

Agricultural prices started to fall prior to 1929. At the time of the war, most Western European states were unable to maintain their prewar production levels. This gap was filled by non-European states. With the end of the war came the restoration of agricultural production in Europe, which resulted in an increase in world supplies and a drop in agricultural prices. The United States attempted to subsidize its export of wheat in order to maintain the domestic price, but to no avail. Other countries, with economies heavily dependent on agriculture, lacked the financial capacity to hold up the prices for their farmers. During this period, farm debts increased rapidly. In the United States, farm mortgages in 1925 reached $9.4 billion, a debt nearly three times greater than it had been 15 years earlier. The gross debt service for Argentina, Australia, Brazil,

Canada, India, Netherlands East Indies, New Zealand, South Africa, Poland, Rumania, Hungary, and Yugoslavia in 1928–1929 added up to $1.4 billion. Few of the farmers in these countries were in a position to service their debts, if required to do so by the lenders, without experiencing major personal financial losses and generating concrete domestic and international financial pressures.[58]

As I have just noted, exports in the 1920s accounted for a significant portion of many states' incomes. In the 1920s, as today, certain countries were more affected than others by changes in their trading partners' national incomes. The imports of the United States in the 1920s were relatively small; however, because its national income was the largest in the world, its decline helped ravage the economies of its trading partners, especially its European trading partners. By 1935, European trade was down to $20.8 billion from $58 billion in 1928.[59] Between the 1928 to 1933 period, for instance, Denmark's exports fell by more than 55 percent, Finland's by more than 50 percent, and Norway's by more than 45 percent.[60] Unemployment, which was already quite high in Europe through the 1920s, increased further. In the case of Germany, unemployment rose from around 9 percent in the late 1920s to nearly 22 percent in 1933, while in Britain it increased from around 12 to 15 percent. The United States did not fare any better; its unemployment rose from 3.2 percent in 1928 to 24.9 percent in 1932.

The shrinking of credit, the fall in productivity and agricultural prices, the rise in unemployment, and the general collapse of almost every country's economy did not help cultivate, at least during the early years of the Depression, a move toward greater international cooperation. As each state began to accrue greater economic losses, its leaders came under intense domestic pressure to set up measures that would protect the welfare of their citizens. As a result, instead of attempting to negotiate a positive-sum game, the leaders of each state retreated to their national confines and gave birth to a zero-sum game. One of their first measures was to elevate further the protectionist barriers that had been erected after the end of the First World War. Germany, Rumania, and France, to name a few countries, imposed stiff import duties or quotas on imported goods. Britain, the world's bastion of economic liberalism during much of the nineteenth century, passed the General Tariff Act in April 1932, some eight months after the depreciation of the sterling, and four months later it approved the Imperial Protection Agreement. The most harmful step, however, was taken by the country where the stampede had started—the United States.

With intense prompting from Europe, the League of Nations had organized a World Economic Conference in Geneva two years prior to the collapse of the stock market to stop the tariff increase that had been expanding steadily throughout the world since the early 1920s. Though at that time foreign lending could still counterbalance the costs imposed by tariffs, some leaders feared that unless they came up with some type of agreement that curtailed the growth of protectionism, some states might eventually abandon the most-favored-nation treatment. The attempt to abolish the prohibition of imports was so thwarted by demands from different states to insert reservations that addressed their distinct domestic priorities that the agreement was never ratified. Few states would show greater misgivings about lowering trade barriers than the United States. In 1928, as he was campaigning for the presidency, Herbert Hoover, the same person who in the early 1920s had claimed that intellectual freedom could not exist without economic freedom, promised to raise tariffs to help farmers in the United States struggling with falling prices. In March 1929, shortly after he was inaugurated, he called a special session of Congress to address the issue. His request led to the enactment of the Smoot-Hawley Tariff Act in June 1930. With the United States in the lead, protectionist sentiments swept immediately throughout the globe. In short time, one state after another heightened its own trade barriers to insulate its domestic industries in jeopardy.

The United States and the World Market System According to Structural Realism

During the early 1930s, the productivity of both industrial and primary commodities continued to descend, unemployment kept increasing, and credit remained meager. The Depression, however, reached its deepest trough in 1933, just as Franklin D. Roosevelt was replacing Hoover as president of the United States. The 1933 trough marks a good point at which to begin an evaluation of the theoretical utility of the structural realist model.

It has been contended that with Britain no longer able to act as a hegemonic leader, and the United States operating as a supporter, Washington struggled to help keep the international economic system relatively open. Washington started in 1913 by approving the Underwood Tariff Act, a legislation that lowered the average rate of duty on all imports from 20 percent to 8.8 percent. Then, in 1922, as the Europeans began to erect greater trade barriers, Washington tried to dissuade them by passing the Fordney-McCumber Act. Washington hoped to use this act as a way of convincing its trade partners, particularly Britain, that it would be in their interests to lower their own trade barriers. The effort to stabilize the international economic system and the liberal international economic regime came to an end in 1930, when Britain was no longer able to function as a supporter and Washington concluded that the United States lacked the capability to do it on its own.

The structural realist model, as delineated, is encumbered by several shortcomings. First, the model does not stipulate how to ascertain at which juncture an international entity moves from one category to the next one. For instance, according to David Lake, Britain moved from being a hegemonic leader in 1900 to becoming a supporter in 1913, while during that time the United States remained a supporter. During this period Britain's proportion of world trade plunged from 17.5 to 14.1, and its relative productivity decreased from 1.30 to 1.15; meanwhile the United States's proportion of world trade increased from 10.2 to 11.1, while its relative productivity grew from 1.42 to 1.56.[61] The most that one can infer from a close look at the figures is that while Britain's standing in the international economic arena languished, the United States's advanced. These figures, alone, however, cannot tell us why an analyst would decide that Britain qualified as a hegemonic leader in 1900, but not 13 years later. This flaw leads the reader to wonder whether Lake designed the categories in which to place the different international entities independently of their behavior, or whether their behavior influenced his decision as to where to place them.[62]

Second, the structural realist model is static. The model assumes that an actor's location in the international economic system will influence its international economic policies, but does not leave room for the strong possibility that its actions will also be affected by its previous place in the international economic arena, and by its perception of where it believes it will be standing in the near future. Let us put aside, for a brief moment, my previous criticism and consider the United States's and Britain's respective places in the international economic arena in 1913, where each stood prior to that time, and where each assumed it would be standing in the early 1920s. From 1870 to sometime just before 1913, Britain, as a hegemonic leader, experienced a steady decrease in its proportion of world trade and its level of relative productivity, while the United States, a supporter, watched both components undergo significant increases. It is fair to say, thus, that during this period Britain's dependency on free trade declined, and its leaders had no reason to assume that the descent would end shortly. The United States's reliance on free trade, on the other hand, increased considerably starting in the 1890s, when its political and economic leaders concurred that without new foreign markets it would fail to sustain its earlier rate of economic growth. This variance between the two countries helps explain why in 1916 Britain agreed with France to organize trade around exclusive regional trading blocs, while the United States continued to call for the reduction of trade tariffs. It also helps explain why in the early 1920s Britain adopted a moderate form of imperial preference, while the United States tried to use the Fordney-McCumber Act of 1922 to persuade other states not to erect trade barriers.

Based on my last criticism, some analysts might suggest that my alternative perspective cannot help explain why the United States failed to stabilize the international system as it became evident that only its aggressive and constructive involvement would, if not avert the "Great Depression," at least curb its costs. More specifically, they might ask: Why would the United States approve the Smoot-Hawley Tariff Act in June 1930, a law designed to increase tariffs on imports, when some years earlier it had pressured other states to do precisely the opposite and knew that passage of the act would lead other states to erect new trade barriers?

I have repeatedly stated that the United States's answer to an international event is always a function of both its standing in the international arena and the effects its foreign policy are expected to have on its dominant interest groups. Based on the trade policies the United States had been advocating for a number of years, it would be reasonable to infer that its decision in 1930 ran counter to its previous actions. This claim, however, fails to take into account that despite the fact that the United States had advocated for years the opening of foreign markets, and had enacted laws designed to achieve the same end at home, the doctrine did not have a long history, and the change in trade policy in 1930 was in direct response to a change in domestic pressure. Prior to the 1890s, a wide range of domestic economic interests had pressured the U.S. government to erect or maintain trade barriers in order to protect infant industries, or those that lacked the means to compete effectively in the international arena. As these industries grew stronger and the growth of the U.S. domestic market slowed down, many of these industries asked the government to force other states to open their markets. As the 1914 war came to an end, many U.S. industries assumed that their relative strength vis-à-vis those of other industries in the international economic market would give them a significant competitive advantage. For a time, their assumption proved to be correct, and numerous U.S. industries benefited greatly. But as soon as Europe restored its prewar production, the prices of a range of products, including agricultural products, dropped, and many U.S. industries found themselves heavily mortgaged and unable to pay their debts. As this process gained momentum, domestic pressure became so intense that the United States government was forced to approve the Smoot-Hawley Tariff Act. In short, even when a democratic state such as the United States occupies the upper echelons of the international economic system, it is not evident that it will strive to keep it open when its openness has concrete negative effects on strong interest groups at home.

One development that has perplexed analysts has been the decision by the United States not to serve as a lender of last resort in 1930. Analysts have acknowledged that this action would have not prevented the economic depression. Nonetheless, some have suggested that had the United States agreed to assume this responsibility, the Depression would have not lasted as long as it did, nor would it have been as costly. Between 1873 and 1913, Britain kept its foreign lending and domestic investments in continuous counterpoint. Whenever Britain experienced a recession, it increased its foreign lending; whenever it underwent an economic boom, it lowered its foreign lending. Countries that were dependent on British loans were not hurt by its economic booms. During those times, Britain would increase its imports, which would in turn generate an export stimulus abroad. In short, Britain followed the "demand model" by distributing its savings between domestic and foreign markets, depending on their relative demands. The United States behaved quite differently. During the 1920s, its foreign lending, rather than being counterpoised with domestic investment, was positively correlated. During its economic boom in the 1920s, the United States invested heavily abroad. In 1928–1929, before the crash of the stock market, investors started to divert from the boom in foreign bonds that followed the Dawes loan, to the boom in the United States in stocks.[63] However, rather than follow this redirection of investments with an increase in imports, the United States erected additional trade barriers. What is more, by 1934 its foreign loans had dwindled to zero.

The United States's action is not difficult to comprehend. As I noted earlier, for a decision-maker to be able to select the best alternative, she or he must have knowledge about possible options. Such knowledge is typically gained through experience. The United States's experience as a foreign creditor was limited; it started in the 1890s but did not assume major proportions until the start of the 1914 war. But one should also recognize that even if the United States had been able to provide lending of last resort through discounting, it still lacked the mechanism to sustain international lending. The U.S. president could stop lending by government fiat but did not have the authority to get the private market to start lending again after it had stopped. In the 1930s, the international economic system did not have machinery such as the World Bank to replace the private market with public funds.

A Wearisome Beginning

States are prisoners of their respective histories. A state's international experience affects both its leaders' perceptions of, and ability to operate effectively in, the international system. Between 1900 and the 1920s the international system grew in complexity. In the interim, the world emerged from its first global war, witnessed the downfall of empires and the arrival of a new major power, observed the unfolding of a new global political ideology, and underwent a major increase in its level of economic interdependence. Though the United States emerged from the 1914 war as the globe's most powerful military and economic entity, its leaders and people lacked the wisdom and maturity to become the world's new chieftain. For most of its brief existence, the United States had dealt either with powerful actors that were too absorbed by the politics of a distant region to seriously challenge its authority, or with powerless international actors. It had consistently held to the belief that its ability to dictate its own foreign policy course would be impaired if it were to form alliances with major states.

The United States entered the 1914 war guided by unrealistic expectations. Its successful actions under relatively simple circumstances during much of the nineteenth century had convinced its leader, Woodrow Wilson, that after the war the United States would be able to create two international systems, one that would restrain the disposition of states to resort to war, and one that would foster greater trade between states. In his effort to create both systems, he neglected to consider four potential problems. First, he did not take into account that the systems he envisioned might be so different from the one his allies contemplated that they would not accept his conception unconditionally. Second, he failed to take into consideration that though the United States's allies no longer possessed the power of yesteryears, they were still strong enough to force him to be mindful of their own needs and interests. Third, he ignored the possibility that by acquiescing to his allies' demands, jointly they might create one or two systems encumbered by intense contradictions. And fourth, he overlooked that without the active participation of other U.S. political leaders in the peace process, Congress would be disinclined to support a treaty that would alarmingly increase the United States's involvement in the political affairs of other states.

The weight of history did not recede with Wilson's departure from the White House. It was not long before U.S. leaders accepted that their country's economy would suffer unless it helped rejuvenate the world economy. But there was little it could do. Three factors undermined the United States's ability to redress the ills afflicting the international economic system. First, its need to keep the international system open was substantial, but not intolerable. Second, its leaders lacked the experience, knowledge, and organizational structure to keep it open. And third, the design of any long-term economic policy would have undermined the short-term interests of some of its most important interest groups.

As the world economy continued its abysmal performance, the new leader of the United States, Franklin Roosevelt, along with other world leaders, began to wonder about the future of the international economic system. Little did they know at that time that the most perilous threat to the international system would be spawned by the effects the economic changes were starting to have on two countries located at opposite ends of the globe.

CHAPTER THREE

The Humbling of Democracy

Introduction

One of the most difficult tasks faced by a war's victors is to create an international system that can satisfy the interests and needs of its principal protagonists. Failure to accomplish this end results in an increase in tension, which often sparks another major war. The international system that the principal victors sought to create at the end of the First World War had its first significant, damaging effect on its most important state: the United States. Convinced that by becoming an active member of the new international system it would get entangled in the political affairs of corrupt states and lose the freedom to design its own foreign policies, the United States refused to assume the responsibilities typically expected of the system's most powerful member. This action had two distinct, but interrelated, effects. First, it created a major power vacuum within the international system itself. And second, it prolonged the world economic depression and exacerbated its costs.

With a power vacuum at the core of the international system, it was not long before some states would try to capitalize on the condition. A state unsatisfied with the international system may consider altering its structure, but it will be reluctant to try to do so if it estimates that the expected costs will exceed the expected benefits. A state's calculation is heavily influenced not just by its relative power in the international system, but also by the nature of its own domestic political and economic systems, and by its perceptions of its past and the role it should play in the world arena. By the end of the First World War, Japan and Germany faced distinctly different futures. Japan sat at the winners' table, convinced that its power would continue to grow and that in time it would be able to pressure other powerful entities to accept it as Asia's hegemonic leader. On the other hand, the most Germany could hope was for the victors to accept that, as in the past, Europe's stability and development depended on a strong and content Germany, and that this end could be achieved only by freeing Germany from the political, military, and economic restraints it had been forced to accept at the end of the First World War.

Domestic interest groups with extremist agendas find it easier to rise to power in young and troubled democracies than in established and stable democracies. When these groups take over the reins of troubled regimes, whether or not they bring about a change in the structure of the international system depends not just on their ability to augment their countries' military and economic power, but also on the resolve of the international system's leaders to neutralize their actions. In the early 1930s, Japan and Germany, two countries undergoing substantial political and economic turmoil, witnessed the rise to power of domestic interest groups determined to lift their respective countries to the zenith of the international system. With their economies ravaged by the global depression, Japan and Germany found themselves facing a permissive international security system. As they elevated their countries' international standings, they concluded that only two states had the capabilities to deter them from imposing their wills on weaker international entities, and those two were not prepared to pay the costs necessary to accomplish such an end. Encumbered by the costs of the 1914 war and the realization that their respective peoples would not support any action that could lead them to another war, Washington and London were reluctant to warn Japan and Germany that their acts of aggression against weaker states would elicit vigorous retaliation.

The Second World War became a full-scale global war when Japan attacked the United States at Pearl Harbor on December 7, 1941. This war, however, was preceded by two regional wars. The first war began on July 7, 1937, when fighting broke out between Japanese and Chinese forces near Beijing. The second one started in late August 1939, when German forces marched into Poland. These attacks were followed by a series of war declarations and additional attacks and invasions, culminating in the Japanese surprise assault on Pearl Harbor. My tasks in this chapter are twofold. I start with an explanation of Japan's and Germany's political systems during the 1930s and their respective decisions to go to war. I then focus on the foreign policies of the United States and explain why its leaders never tried to persuade Germany and Japan that their hostile acts would provoke Washington to commit itself to the destruction of their power and political regimes.

The Battle for Hegemony in the Far East

Around the middle of the nineteenth century, none of the major powers considered Japan a potential rival. Their lack of concern was justified. Japan's economic development had been severely impeded by a terrain unsuited for significant cultivation and by the absence of natural resources. Moreover, because Japan had been almost completely sequestered from foreign contact from 1638 to 1853, its decentralized feudal oligarchy had never had a reason to consider altering its political, economic, and social systems.

Japan's complacency came to an end in 1853, when Commodore Matthew C. Perry anchored about a quarter of the United States Navy in Japanese waters. Perry's mission was to demand that Japan grant U.S. ships access to Japanese ports. The Japanese government, aware that it lacked the power to reject Perry's demand, caved in. The incident forced Japan to recognize that if it wanted to free itself from the dictates of a foreign power it would have to learn from the foreign intruders to change its ways. In 1868, the Japanese government launched a modernization program that included the adoption of a Prussian-German style constitution that replaced the old feudal domains with a more centralized rule, the reformation of the legal system, the rapid expansion of the educational system, the modernization of both the army and the navy, and the development of heavy industry. These measures helped improve Japan's condition, but because the economic gap between Japan and the major powers was too large for the margin to be narrowed noticeably in a short period of time, Western leaders were slow to recognize its achievements.

The world was forced to take notice in 1894, when Japan, after defeating China in a war over claims in Korea, sought to gain control over Port Arthur and the Liaotung Peninsula. Russia, France, and Germany made it clear that they would intervene together if Japan carried out its intent. The response by the three European powers reminded Japan that it needed to continue modernizing and strengthening its military if it hoped to compete with the major powers. Japan sent an unequivocal signal of its determination to be accepted as a major international player and to become Asia's hegemon when its navy gained a major victory over Russia's navy in the 1904 to 1905 period. The message was heard loud and clear. After 1905, no major power dared to consider an action in the Far East without first giving serious thought to the way Japan's leaders might respond.

By the start of the twentieth century, Japan had already adopted, with some important adjustments, a few Western political practices. Its new constitution, approved in 1889, established a bicameral national assembly. The House of Peers, which was modeled after the British House of Lords, was filled almost entirely by former court nobles, feudal lords, and the members of the new leadership groups. Members of this house either were appointed or inherited their posts. Members to the House of Representatives, the Diet, were elected by 1 percent of the population—male taxpayers who paid more than 15 yen in taxes. From the moment it was created, the Diet used its control over the budget to wrest a share of political power from the governmental cabinets. The cabinet finally gained full dominance in the first half of the 1910s, when it came under the command of the same political party that dominated the Diet. While these changes ensued at the upper levels of the political structure, a set of more "democratic" measures was introduced below. Japan reduced substantially the tax qualification for voting in 1900 and in 1919, and in 1925 it finally gave the vote to all adult males. These changes impressed the democratic Western states so much that they began to relinquish some of the extraterritorial privileges that they had extorted from Japan in the 1850s.[1]

Japan's zeal to "Westernize" its domestic political system was matched by its fervor to become Asia's hegemon. Its leaders never assumed that the Western powers would give in to Japan's dreams freely. The start of the 1914 war in Europe, however, altered markedly Japan's assessment of its own chances in Asia. The Chinese revolution of 1911–1912 had brought down the Manchu dynasty. Its successor, rather than following in the steps of its predecessor and turning to Japan for financial assistance, approached Europe. Tokyo did not welcome China's attempt to reduce its dependency on Japan, but there was little that it could do, until it declared war on Germany in August 1914. As Germany tried to fight a two-front war in Europe, Japan seized all the German possessions in the Far East. More importantly, it decided to take advantage of the military impasse in Europe by presenting to the Chinese government what became known as the "Twenty-One Demands" document. The terms, which when put together amounted to an ultimatum, stipulated the creation of a de facto protectorate in the form of Japanese advisers attached to the Chinese government, as well as the imposition of Japanese control over China's principal natural resources. The United States and Britain immediately demanded that Tokyo rescind its claim for a protectorate but agreed to accept many of its economic terms. In 1916, Britain, Russia, and France formally recognized Japan's wartime gains in East Asia, but the United States did not. Washington feared that such an act would undermine the United States's long-standing commitment to the preservation of its "Open Door" policy for trade and investment in China. After extensive negotiations, Washington and Tokyo reached a mutually satisfactory compromise. Both parties agreed to accept China's territorial integrity and the "Open Door" principle, and to recognize Japan's special interests in China accorded by their geographical proximity. Japan's power aspirations were not satiated by the accord. Though its interest in the way Europe would be partitioned after the war was minimal, its attendance at the Paris Peace Conference and recognition as one of the dominant powers was of great importance to Tokyo. Also of great significance was its success at persuading the major powers during the bargaining sessions to have the League of Nations grant Japan, in the form of a mandate, control over the former German Pacific islands north of the equator, and the same economic privileges previously enjoyed by Germany on the Shantung peninsula of China.

As I have already explained, the focus during the 1920s was principally on Europe's political and economic needs. In Washington, however, there were many leaders who argued that the United States could not afford to become complacent about developments in the Far East, especially in Japan. Their concern was justified. Between 1917 and 1921, Japan allocated over a third of its budget to expanding its naval power. Though this investment would not be enough to propel Japan's navy from its number three world standing to a higher rank, Tokyo estimated that it would be enough to render it immune to U.S. or British naval threats. Tokyo's estimates were partially correct. Japan's alliance with Britain, signed in 1902 and then renewed in 1905 and 1911, restrained, at least for a while, London's eagerness to curb Tokyo's imperial aspirations. The United States, moreover, had to divide its attention, and navy, between the Pacific and the Atlantic Oceans. The Treaty of Versailles, however, freed Washington to place greater emphasis on the Pacific and to develop contingency plans that delineated ways the United States's navy might respond to a Japanese naval threat. Still, Washington had no desire to engage in a costly naval race with Japan. Hence, in an attempt to avert this outcome, and to break the alliance Japan still had with Britain, Secretary of State Hughes persuaded President Harding to convene a conference in Washington on naval arms control, to be attended by representatives of the major powers.

Hughes opened the conference in November 1921 with a startling proposal. He started by suggesting that for economic rehabilitation to take place worldwide, "competition in armaments must stop." He then argued that "if the present construction of capital ships goes forward other ships will inevitably be built to rival them and this will lead still to others. Thus the race will continue so long as ability to continue lasts." To stop the race without undermining the national security and defense of each state, he proposed that the major powers adhere to four general principles:

1. That all capital-ship building programs . . . be abandoned;
2. That further reduction should be made through the scrapping of certain of the older ships;

3. That in general, regard should be had to the existing naval strength of the Powers concerned;
4. That the capital ship tonnage should be used as the measurement of strength for navies . . .[2]

Based on these four principles, Hughes announced that the United States would limit its tonnage to 500,650 if Britain accepted a final tonnage limit of 604,450 for existing capital ships, Japan's navy adhered to a 299,700 tonnage limit, and the navies of France and Italy each limited its tonnage to 175,000. Agreement to this proposal, he added, would require that the United States scrap 846,740 tons of capital ships, Britain raze 583,375 tons, and Japan destroy 448,928 tons. Based on Hughes's 5:5:3:1.75:1.75 formula, the five entities signed the Five-Power Treaty. The formula limited the total capital ship replacement of the United States and Britain to 525,000 tons each, Japan to 315,000 tons, and France and Italy to 175,000 tons each. The treaty also stipulated that the United States, Japan, and Britain would not seek to alter the status quo by building new fortifications or naval bases on their territorial possessions in the Pacific Ocean. Participants at the conference also signed the Nine-Power Treaty. The new treaty, which also included Belgium, China, the Netherlands, and Portugal, legitimized the Open Door principle. It stipulated that China would adhere to the Open Door principle, and that all the major powers would recognize and respect China's sovereignty, independence, and territorial and administrative integrity.[3] Japan agreed to sign the treaty only after the adding of a "security clause" that accepted Tokyo's influence in Manchuria.[4]

During the rest of the 1920s, Japan and the United States developed a cordial relationship, based primarily on trade. The United States absorbed about 40 percent of Japan's total exports, including 90 percent of its raw silk products. Japan, in turn, bought most of its automobiles, machinery, building-construction materials, and oil from the United States. Furthermore, nearly 40 percent of the foreign investments in Japan came from U.S. banks. The prospect of further improvement in the overall relationship between Japan and the United States was believed to be very good, considering the type of trade association they had managed to build. This belief, however, was based on the often misguided assumption that trade relationships pave the road to better overall relations. The central weakness behind the trade relationship the United States and Japan developed was that while Japan's economic growth and development were highly dependent on the continued willingness of the United States to remain Japan's biggest customer and supplier of foreign investment, the United States did not have a symmetrical dependency on Japan.

Japan's domestic political system also faced a doubtful future. In the late 1920s, Japan was ruled by a very young and highly flawed "democratic" regime with imperial aspirations. Though its parliamentary system had some major imperfections, its two most important problems were the way its leaders were chosen and the relationship between the civil and military branches of government. Japan's prime ministers, rather than being selected by parliamentary majorities, were chosen by a few men who exercised an imperial prerogative. Under this system, parliamentary elections were held only after the selection of the prime ministers, who would then typically attain parliamentary majorities. The legitimacy of any democracy is profoundly dependent on the degree of control its civilian government has over the military. Although the Japanese Diet controlled the military budget, military ministers did not have to respond to party rules. More important, the armed forces were totally free of civilian control.[5]

A military, free of civilian control, will be inclined to subvert the authority of the government if the latter is unable to induce economic growth in a state besieged by a rapidly expanding population with limited access to arable and habitable land, mineral resources, and fossil fuels. Japan's economy plummeted after the fall of the New York stock market in 1929; the decision by the United States to cut down drastically on foreign lending and imports; the call by U.S. producers and labor organizations to boycott Japanese products in order to protect domestic earnings and jobs; the passage by Congress of the Smoot-Hawley Tariff Act in 1930, which raised duties on Japanese imports by an average of 23 percent; and the decision by most countries to adopt nationalistic economic policies.[6] Japanese silk exports, which made up 36 percent of exports in 1929 and contributed to 19 percent by value of total farm production, dropped from 781 million yen in 1929 to 417 million in 1930. During this same period, the price of raw silk fell by one-fourth. Both falls led to gold losses, which in November 1930 were estimated at $135 million. Japan might have weathered some of these problems more effectively if it had succeeded in encouraging emigration in the early 1920s in order to relieve domestic pressures on land, food, and natural resources. The United States, Canada, and Australia contributed to Japan's failure by opposing, on racial grounds, Japanese immigration. In 1924, Congress went so far as to enact a law that denied U.S. citizenship to Japanese immigrants.

Unable to continue exporting its manufactured products at the high rate necessary to finance the import of essential raw materials and foodstuff, and beset by inadequate natural resources and overpopulation, Japan had to search for a rapid cure. The answer, some Japanese military leaders believed, lay in Japan's weaker neighbors. Two developments persuaded them that conditions both at home and abroad called for the investiture of a radical policy change. In 1930, the five major powers met in London to reduce naval competition in categories of ships not covered by the earlier conference in Washington. The five-to-three ratio established earlier was extended to submarines, destroyers, and cruisers. Japan's naval officers opposed the agreement but were persuaded by Japan's civilian government to accept it. Their dissatisfaction was compounded by Washington's new aggressive policy toward China.

During the earlier part of the 1920s, Japan had attained substantial control over China's economy by exploiting the internal political divisions the latter had experienced. Nearly 25 percent of Japan's exports went to China, and about 90 percent of all new investments in China came from Japan. By the end of 1928, however, Chinese Nationalist forces, with extensive backing from the United States, had managed to suppress the Chinese Communist party, bring most of China under their control, and reunite China with Manchuria. Washington responded to these developments by unilaterally according tariff autonomy to China. In return, Washington and Beijing developed a most-favored-nation agreement. It did not take long for United States's businesses to reap the benefits of this new accord. By the end of 1931, the United States had become China's main supplier of foreign products. The United States's trade success in China came at a cost—Japan's. Between 1929 and 1931, Japanese exports to China had dropped by half.

These developments seemed to have reaffirmed the belief among members of Japan's military leadership that the West was opposed to Japan's becoming East Asia's hegemonic leader. However, they also estimated that Washington, London, and Paris were too immersed in their own country's economic woes to be distracted by an aggressive Japanese act that did not directly affect their national interests. More importantly, they assumed that Washington would not be able to initiate a credible deterrent response because the U.S. Congress had refused to appropriate funds to raise the U.S. naval strength to the levels delineated by the 1921 and 1930 naval agreements. Thus, on September 18, 1931, a group of Japanese army officers in Manchuria, with the tacit approval of their superiors in Tokyo, relied on a minor incident at a railway near the capital to launch an operation to take over Manchuria. By March 1932, Japan had established in Manchuria the puppet state of Manchukuo. Japan's initial assessment of Washington's likely response proved to be correct; Washington did little beyond stating that it deplored Japan's action.

These developments emboldened a faction of Japan's military leadership. Following the assassination of several prominent political leaders, including the prime minister who had forced the approval of the 1930 London Naval Treaty, parliamentary control over the cabinet, which had never been particularly strong, waned further. More importantly, the military became the principal foreign policy maker. But the military did not act immediately as a unified organization. The ultrarightists, with strong support from the impoverished peasants, who provided the bulk of the soldiers, denounced harshly the privileged classes of rich businessmen and powerful politicians for undermining Japan's world status. Leadership for this group was provided primarily by young officers who saw themselves as killers of "evil leaders" around the throne. Their commitment to cleansing the political system culminated in an attempted coup d'etat in February 1936. Moderate army and navy commanders responded by suppressing the attack and executing its leaders. Subsequently they reimposed sterner control over the officers and put an end to the factionalism among the higher officers.[7]

These actions by Japan's moderate military leaders, however, did not signal a decision on the part of Japan's leadership to forgo its imperial dreams. In fact, though the moderate faction of the military did not approve of the earlier excesses of their junior counterparts, they supported their foreign policy goals. One of the first steps taken by Tokyo after the failed military coup was to inform the West that Japan would no longer adhere to the terms of the 1930 naval disarmament treaty.[8] Next, Japan proceeded to revamp its economic system. Japan's policy makers believed that under an open market economy it would be nearly impossible to meet the requirements of a strong national defense. As an alternative, they opted for the creation of a state planning system. They also reasoned that to revive Japan's economy and create a strong national defense, Japan would need access to extensive oil reserves. Since such access would require protection, they proposed the creation of a powerful navy with the capability of extending its operations into Southeast Asia. These ideas were presented under the heading of "Fundamental Principles of National Policy" and were approved by the Japanese in August 1936.

Tokyo knew that its main rivals, especially Moscow, would not welcome its actions. Thus, to offset the possibility of an attempt on the part of the Soviets to move against Japan's northern flank as it expanded south, Tokyo signed with Berlin the Anti-Comintern Pact in November 1936. Washington was also displeased with Tokyo's more aggressive foreign policy stand, but it chose to wait. The wait did not last long. In early July 1937, Japanese forces, after engaging in a minor skirmish with Chinese troops, received orders from Tokyo to move against Beijing and topple the Nationalist Chinese government. The Japanese military, after marching into Beijing, won a series of victories as it pushed deep into China's northern and central sections and its southern coast.

This time Washington concluded that Tokyo had gone too far. Initially, however, President Roosevelt, determined not to elicit an outcry from those who opposed U.S. intervention abroad, opted for a stern verbal warning, which he issued on October 5, 1937, in a "Quarantine the Aggressor" speech. Roosevelt's measured response did not stop his domestic adversaries from mounting a major campaign against his implied policy. Thus, for nearly two years the Roosevelt administration watched as

Japan gained control over much of China. Finally, in the summer of 1939, after an intense debate among members of the Roosevelt cabinet as to whether the United States should or should not impose an economic embargo on Japan, Washington informed Tokyo of its intention to cancel the U.S.-Japan commercial treaty of 1911 by the end of the year.

The start of the war in Europe in September 1939 slammed the door on the formulation of an amicable solution to U.S.-Japanese differences in the Far East. As one European country after another found itself entangled with Germany's armed forces, Japan began to extract major economic and strategic concessions. The Netherlands removed restrictions on the export of petroleum from the Dutch East Indies to Japan. France had no choice but to acquiesce to Japan's occupation of the northern half of French Indochina. Roosevelt, convinced that he had to put a stop to Japan's bid for primacy in the Far East, imposed an embargo on Japan on aviation fuel and the highest grades of iron and scrap steel in the summer of 1940.

In early 1941, Tokyo and Washington agreed to meet to see whether they could resolve their differences without having to resort to war. Washington, however, interrupted the meetings when it learned that Tokyo was deploying Japanese troops into southern Indochina. On July 26, Roosevelt issued an executive order freezing Japanese assets in the United States and bringing under the control of the U.S. government all financial, import, and trade transactions in which Japanese interests were involved. Britain and the Netherlands followed the United States's lead by adopting similar measures. At the beginning of August, Washington tightened the economic squeeze by putting an embargo on the export of oil to Japan. These decisions shocked the Japanese policy makers. After extensive discussions, they agreed with Prime Minister Fumimaro Konoye that he should try to meet with President Roosevelt to see whether together they could break the impasse. However, the Japanese cabinet authorized the meeting between Roosevelt and Konoye only after they approved War Minister Hideki Tojo's recommendation that Japan begin preparations for war against the United States. On September 6 these same policy makers took another drastic step. They agreed that if negotiations between the United States and Japan did not bring about a solution to their differences by the last ten days of October, Japan would go to war. The rationale behind this decision was best explained by Japan's Navy Chief of Staff Osami Nogano, when he said:

> [In] the event that a peaceful solution is not attainable, and we have no alternative to resort to war, the Supreme Command believes, from the standpoint of operations, that we cannot avoid being finally reduced to a crippled condition if we delay for too long. A number of vital military supplies, including oil, are dwindling day by day. This will cause a gradual

weakening of our national status quo, the capacity of our Empire to act will be reduced in the days to come. . . . By the latter half of next year, America's military preparedness will have made great progress, and it will be difficult to cope with her. Therefore, it must be said that it would be very dangerous for our Empire to remain idle and let the days by.[9]

Three months later, Japanese planes that had been quietly transported by six aircraft carriers across the Pacific Ocean from Hitokappu Bay in the remote Kurile Islands, struck the U.S. vessels moored at Pearl Harbor. By 10:00 A.M. of December 7, 1941, two hours after the Japanese attack had started, Japanese aircraft had sunk eight U.S. battleships, thus depriving the United States Navy of the bulk of its Pacific fleet.

The Rise of Nazism in Germany and Its Drive for Hegemony in Europe

In light of what had been happening in Europe since late 1939, Japan's surprise attack on Pearl Harbor was not an anomalous act. In August 1939, almost exactly 25 years after the start of the First World War, German troops had marched into Poland. A few days later, on September 3, Britain and France announced the official start of the century's second major European armed conflict by declaring war on Germany. What provoked these developments?

At the start of the twentieth century, the citizens and leaders of the most advanced industrialized countries assumed that the rise of the values and institutions promoted by liberal democracy that had been unfolding since the middle of the nineteenth century would continue. This assumption lost its legitimacy shortly after the end of the First World War. In Europe, the only countries that were able to protect their democratic institutions without a break during the entire interwar period were Britain, Finland, Sweden, Switzerland, and the Irish Free States. In the Americas, the list of constitutional and nonauthoritarian states included only the United States, Canada, Uruguay, Colombia, and Costa Rica. In Asia, Africa, and Australasia, only New Zealand and Australia remained consistently democratic. In retrospect, the trend was dismal; in 1920 there were about 35 constitutionally elected governments, by 1938 the number had diminished to 17 states, and by 1944 it was barely higher than 12.[10]

During the interwar period, challenges to constitutionally elected governments came from both the Right and the Left. Though the Right shared a set of common attitudes, it was never shaped into a monolithic whole. The various groups that composed it were authoritarian, opposed to social revolution, hostile to liberal political institutions, approving of the military and the police, and highly nationalistic. But these similarities were accompanied by pertinent variances. Dictators, or *caudillos*, with no particular ideology other than hostility toward liberal political institutions, populated a great number of Latin American countries. A second group, the old-fashioned conservatives, also had no particular ideological agenda except to oppose communism and promote the interests of its own class. A third group directed its energy against both liberal individualism and the challenges of both labor and socialism. More specifically, it fostered the formation of an organic society defined by a social hierarchy in which the members of each social group willingly accepted their rank, value, and function in the collective entity. This group limited or abolished electoral democracy and relied on the rule of authoritarian regimes controlled mainly by bureaucrats and technocrats.[11]

None of these groups, however, ever gained the notoriety or power attained by the fourth group: the fascists. This dishonor must be bestowed on Adolf Hitler. "[W]ithout Hitler's triumph in Germany the idea of fascism as a *universal* movement, a sort of right-wing equivalent with Berlin as its Moscow, would not have developed."[12] Fascism had many sources, but as acknowledged by Hitler, its most important creator was Benito Mussolini. The Italian leader erected his fascist ideology on five interrelated foundations: i) the nation-state; ii) corporativism; iii) antiliberalism; iv) antibolshevism; and v) racism.[13] For Mussolini, the nation and the state served two indivisible and indispensable purposes. He proposed that since humans were by nature social animals, individuals could realize themselves only as members of a collectivity. The nation, with its history, culture, and cohesiveness, provided individuals the environment in which they could perform their functions and achieve fulfillment. The state, in turn, functioned as the "political, juridical, and economic organization of the nation. . . ."[14] For Mussolini, thus, the state was an organic unit that assumed responsibilities for Italy's political, economic, and social activities and well-being.

Mussolini was given the opportunity to put into practice his fascist doctrine when Italy's king invited him to join a coalition cabinet as prime minister close to the end of 1922. By that time, Italy was enduring the same pains many other democracies throughout Europe were suffering— a soaring rate of inflation that wiped out the salaries, pensions, and savings of the middle class, accompanied by mounting insurrectionist violence. By 1924, Mussolini had attained a clear majority in the Italian parliament and had moved forcefully to consolidate his power. He achieved these ends by stifling the opposition with the backing of a large number of armed gangs who roamed through both urban and rural Italy, and by promising the middle class that he would curb the freedom of the press, discipline opposition parties and labor, break strikes, end the widespread public disorder and, most importantly, provide Italy with a strong and efficient leader.

Italy's experience in the early 1920s had an indirect, but major, effect on the rest of Europe. Because of its limited military and economic power, Italy did not have a sound base from which Mussolini could launch fascism as a universal doctrine. The collapse of Italy's democracy during a period of tremendous economic and political turmoil, however, forced other European countries to give serious consideration to the tactics and policies adopted by Mussolini. While France and Britain managed to avoid Italy's fate, Germany and Spain did not. It would be Germany, with its expansive military and economic potential, that would attempt to promote its special form of fascism, Nazism, as a universal doctrine.

Nazism, though an outgrowth of fascism, was erected on a different foundation. Mussolini erected fascism on nationalism; Hitler built Nazism on racism. Nazism relied extensively on the racial theory posited by Count Joseph Arthur de Gobineau in his *Essay on the Inequality of Human Races,* published in 1854. Gobineau's central argument was that the only variable that could significantly explain human progress and decline was race. He divided the human species into three basic racial groups: white, yellow, and black. Blacks were endowed with a great sense of primitive sensuality but possessed the least intelligence of the three racial groups. Members of the yellow race were considered to have little imagination and creativity, and were inclined toward excessive materialism. Members of the white race were endowed with nobility, freedom, honor, and spirituality.[15] The white race, however, was not entirely "pure." It was divided into three categories, with the Semites presumably reflecting a combination of white and black races, the Slavs possibly entailing a mixture of yellow and white races, and the Aryans most likely symbolizing the pure white race. Based on this typology, Gobineau postulated that: "The basic organization and character of all civilizations are equal to the traits and spirit of the dominant race."[16]

Nazism carried Gobineau's proposition far beyond the author's original intent. First, Nazism advocated that since the black and yellow races were inferior to the white race, and within the white race the Semites and Slavs were inferior to the Aryans, the Aryans were justified in subjugating and even eliminating all those who were inferior to them. Second, Nazism fashioned the concept of the "folkish (völkish) state," which placed special emphasis on the unique racial qualities of the German people. However, because not all Germans were pure Aryans and many had been "infected" by members of lesser races, the task of the folkish state was to foster the fundamental traits of the Aryans. And third, it propounded that since a nation inhabited by Aryans was superior to non-Aryan nations, the former was justified in relying on war to subdue and conquer them.[17]

The rise of Nazism in Germany did not have a single cause. With the approval of the Dawes plan in 1924, Germany had hoped to begin its slow path toward economic recovery. Though the hyperinflation of 1923 brought about costly consequences in many spheres of German life, the loss of value of the currency enabled Germany to sell its exports cheaply and, thus, to start rebuilding and modernizing its industry. Germany's agriculture, however, did not undergo a similar revivification. The increase in overseas competition had weakened Europe's overall agricultural competitiveness, but especially in Germany. Prior to the war, Germany had concentrated on the production of grain and had not attempted to develop a more specialized production of marketable goods. After the war, the worldwide increase in agricultural competition forced German farmers to rely on protective tariffs and governmental support. In short time, this economic issue became a political problem. Farmers, on the one hand, demanded governmental support and protective tariffs in order to maintain the high price of domestic agricultural products; workers, on the other hand, were primarily interested in keeping food prices low.[18]

Germany's worries reached beyond agricultural productivity. Though by 1928 Germany's national income was 50 percent greater than it had been in 1913, and the per capita income had increased by the same proportion, these gains were being eroded by a major expansion in social expenditures. In 1927, a coalition government led by the Social Democratic Party expanded Germany's social security system substantially. By 1930, social expenditures consumed 40.3 percent of all of Germany's public expenditures, largely due to the rapid rise in unemployment. In September 1929, there were 1,320,000 unemployed people in Germany; one year later there were 3,000,000; by September 1931 the number had reached 4,350,000; and by 1932 it peaked at 6,000,000. In short, after 1929, successive German governments faced the dilemma of having to pay ever-rising unemployment benefits, just as their returns from taxation were diminishing because of business failures and decreasing income tax yields.[19]

Any country with a long-standing tradition of democratic rule and a political system that promoted governmental stability would have been able to manage the type of economic crisis experienced by Germany after 1929 without resorting to radical political measures. But in 1929, Germany's experience with democracy was only ten years old and was built on an exceptionally unstable foundation.

Democracy, in its simplest form, is a political system that is "completely or almost completely responsive to all its citizens."[20] Such a political system must extend to its citizens the opportunity to formulate their preferences unimpaired, and to manifest them to one another and to the government individually and collectively. Moreover, the system must guarantee that it will weigh the preferences of its citizens with no discrimination because of their content or source. For these opportunities to exist, the state must provide to its citizens the freedom to form and join organizations, the freedom of expression, the right to vote, the right to run for public office, the right of political leaders to compete for support and votes, the access to alternative sources of information, the holding of free and fair elections, and the establishment of institutions for making government policies depend on votes and other expressions of preference. Democracies are not equally democratic. A democratic regime's degree of democracy is determined by its level of public contestation—the broader the range of preferences the political party system can respond to, the more democratic the regime. Since preferences vary greatly and no single political party can represent all preferences at all times, political parties compete for the support of the electorate by delineating the preferences they represent. The extent to which political parties compete is dictated by constitutional design.[21] Certain constitutions dictate that elections use proportional representation and multimember electoral districts, while others decree that elections be based on a plurality system and single-member districts. Since in a proportional representation-type system the political parties are responsive, in the aggregate, to a broader set of preferences than in a plurality-type system, it follows from simple logic that the first system is more democratic than the second one.[22]

Greater political representation is not always desirable. The existence of a large number of parties, without the general acceptance of certain basic values and the presence of substantial political, economic, and social tranquillity, can have three closely related, negative effects. First, it can make it difficult for any one single party to gain a majority. This condition forces the political system to become highly dependent on rule by coalition governments. Second, it can enhance the likelihood that extremist groups, some of which may be antidemocratic, will become viable political parties. And third, it can force moderate parties struggling to create a coalition government, or to keep one alive, to reach irresponsible agreements with radical parties. The actualization of this last event can lead to the destruction of the same democratic political system that sanctioned the formation of both the moderate and radical political parties. It did so in Germany in 1933.[23]

At the end of the First World War, Hitler, embittered by its outcome and by the peace obligations imposed on Germany by the Treaty of Versailles, joined the German Workers' Party in Munich. In 1921, a year after the party had changed its appellation to National Socialist German Workers' Party, he became its new leader. Between 1925 and 1929, he helped increase membership in the Nazi Party from 27,000 members to 178,000, and he designed an effective and elaborate party structure, with himself as its head with the title of Supreme Leader of the Party. By the time 1929 moved in, Hitler and his party were prepared to play a major political role.

In March 1930, less than six months after the New York stock market had crashed, Germany's coalition government, unable to agree on measures that would put a stop to the accelerating economic crisis, fell. The Social Democratic Party, which dominated the coalition, had advocated maintaining unemployment benefits at existing levels by increasing contributions. The new coalition government, led by Heinrich Brüning and supported by Germany's army, sought to reduce government expenditures by cutting deep into unemployment insurance. When the proposal was rejected by the Reichstag, Brüning dissolved it, asked the president to grant him the authority to implement his financial plan, and called for new elections. Brüning received the president's backing, but not the support he had wanted from the people. In the new elections held on September 14, his party gained only six seats, while the Socialists, the Nationalists, and the People's Party all declined in strength. The big winners were the extremist parties, with the Communists increasing their Reichstag representation from 54 to 77 and the Nazis from 12 to 107.

After barely surviving a series of no-confidence votes, and battered by an economic crisis that showed no signs of wearing off, the Brüning government fell at the end of May 1932. Baron Franz von Papen became Germany's new chancellor. Support for the new Papen government never surfaced. At the elections held in July, the two main parties that supported him lost 44 seats, while the Communists gained 12 seats and the Nazis became the largest party with 230 seats. Papen dissolved the Reichstag immediately and called for new elections in November. The results proved to be disastrous. On December 2, the president named General Kurt von Schleicher as head of Germany's new government. When Schleicher assumed power, he was hopeful about his chances of gaining control over the Reichstag largely because during the November elections the Nazis had lost 34 seats. But his optimism proved to be unfounded. On January 30, 1933, the president asked the one political figure he despised most deeply, Adolf Hitler, to become Germany's new chancellor.

Hitler moved immediately to consolidate his domestic power. This involved dissolving the Weimar constitution and creating a new, all-encompassing state that would be responsible for coordinating the country's economy, society, and culture, all under the leadership of one party. To accomplish this end, he started by eliminating the historic rights of the separate German states, dismissing their governments, and appointing governors with extensive powers but answering directly to the chancellor. He then eliminated all potential political rivals within his own party and forced the passing of a law that declared that the NSDAP was the only legal party in Germany. Determined to make sure that the trade unions would not challenge his power and authority, Hitler replaced them with a Labor Front. This new organization had no genuine political or economic functions except to keep labor in an atomized and powerless condition and to eradicate the last marks of Marxism from its members.

To protect his regime from sabotage by the civil service, he decreed a law that called for the elimination from the service of all non-Aryans and individuals who were not ready to intervene at all times on behalf of the Nazi state. This law was then extended to cover members of Germany's judiciary and university systems. Finally, under an all-encompassing and domineering state, no church could reserve the right to regulate its own affairs.

Though Hitler relied extensively on highly restrictive measures to solidify his power base, he recognized that unless he transformed Germany's economy his success would be short-lived. Through deficit financing, which reflected a drastic departure from the deflationary fiscal policies of his predecessors, he stimulated employment and industrial production through an ambitious rearmament program. By 1936, Germany's unemployment had sunk to one million from a high of six million four years earlier, while during the same period both the national income and gross national product doubled. That same year he launched a four-year economic plan. The plan was designed to guarantee that Germany would become self-sufficient, so that it would not have to endure the hardships that it experienced during the First World War, when the Allies blockaded the country.

Hitler's four-year economic plan was tightly linked to the new direction he gave to Germany's foreign policy shortly after he assumed power. Germany's frontiers in 1914, he wrote, "were in reality neither complete with respect to the inclusion of people of German nationality, nor intelligent with respect to geo-military appropriateness." Germany, he added, must win land that "increases the area of the motherland itself and thereby not only keeps the new settlers in the most intimate community with the land of their origin but insures to the total area those advantages deriving from its united magnitude." Where should the new land come from? "When in Europe today we speak of new territory we cannot help thinking in the first instance of Russia and the border states that are subject to her."[24]

Almost every world leader understands that the difference between proffering a political doctrine while out of power and implementing such a doctrine while in power is considerable. If Hitler was aware of the difference, he did not allow his knowledge to prevent him from attempting to realize his objective. One of his first steps in implementing his "living space" doctrine was to pull Germany out of the disarmament talks that had been ensuing in Geneva since 1932. The Treaty of Versailles had restricted Germany's armed forces to a size no larger than 100,000 officers and men; dissolved its General Staff, the War Academy, and the cadet schools; denied its army the right to manufacture military aircraft, tanks, and other offensive weapons; and stipulated that the navy would be limited to a nominal force with no submarines and no vessels exceeding

10,000 tons. By 1932, Germany's former enemies, especially Britain, were willing to eliminate some of these military restrictions. Ramsay MacDonald, Britain's prime minister, drafted a plan whereby Germany would be granted equality of status in armaments. The plan stipulated that each European state would limit its armed forces to 200,000 men. Hitler rejected MacDonald's proposal, and on October 14, 1933, he withdrew Germany from the disarmament conference and the League of Nations.

As he rebuilt Germany's armed forces, Hitler made sure that his country would not be attacked prematurely, and that when it went to war it would be able to rely on the support of a few allies. On January 26, 1934, Germany and Poland, two traditional adversaries, shocked Europe by announcing the conclusion of a German-Polish nonaggression pact. Less than two months later, both countries revealed the signing of a trade concordat. With these agreements Hitler managed to weaken France's alliance system, which had depended substantially on the support of Europe's eastern countries, and to enhance the security of Germany's eastern flank. The German leader, however, had much more in store. One year later, he announced that Germany would not abide by any of the Treaty of Versailles's military clauses and would increase the size of its army from 100,000 soldiers to 550,000. France did not take Hitler's moves lightly. On May 2, 1935, it signed a mutual assistance pact with the Soviet Union. Two weeks later, one of France's principal allies in Eastern Europe, Czechoslovakia, signed a similar pact with the Soviet Union. Germany counteracted almost immediately. In June 1935, it announced the signing of a naval pact with Britain. The pact benefited Germany in two distinct ways. First, it enabled Germany to construct a fleet 35 percent as large as Britain's and build as many submarines as it wanted; and second, it legitimized Hitler's repudiation of the Treaty of Versailles's military clauses.

Events continued to unfold in the international arena in a manner that seemed to favor Germany. In early October 1935, Italy invaded Ethiopia. London and Paris immediately criticized the action and demanded that the League of Nations impose economic sanctions against Italy. Hitler chose to remain neutral but announced that Germany would supply Italy with iron, steel, coal, and other scarce assets. It did not take long for Germany's response to elicit Rome's gratitude. But another event surfaced on the European horizon before Italy and Germany would formulate a mutual accord. In February 1936, the French Chamber of Deputies formally ratified the Franco-Soviet Pact. Claiming that the pact increased the communist threat and violated the agreement signed at Locarno in 1925, Hitler ordered the deployment of three battalions of German infantry, along with antiaircraft guns and air force squadrons, into the Rhineland in early March.[25] French and British leaders met in London to discuss the possibility of a joint Anglo-French countermove, but Britain, determined not to become entangled in a new European war, made it clear that it would oppose such an action. Emboldened by Britain's and France's inaction, Hitler moved aggressively to consolidate new agreements. On October 26, 1936, Germany and Italy signed a cooperation agreement. A month later, Germany and Japan agreed by way of the Anti-Comintern Pact to work together to contain the spread of Soviet communist influence in both Asia and Europe. Germany and Japan's agreement became the basis of the Berlin-Rome-Tokyo Axis, which was formalized when Rome joined the Anti-Comintern Pact on November 6, 1937.

The year 1938 proved to be critical for Europe's major powers. By April, Hitler had forced Austria to unite with Germany. Though the Treaty of Versailles forbade the unification of both countries, neither Britain nor France was willing to enforce its provision and risk war. Their inaction further bolstered Hitler's temerity. That same summer, he demanded the separation of the Sudeten region, an area occupied principally by Germans located in the northwestern section of Czechoslovakia. Britain, under the leadership of Neville Chamberlain, feared that unless a suitable agreement was reached between the interested parties, the major European powers would be dragged into another major war. The British leader believed that Hitler's claim was justified. The Allies, reasoned Chamberlain, had mistreated Germany in 1919 by refusing to apply the principle of national self-determination when it decided to grant sovereignty over parts of its eastern frontier to Czechoslovakia. After extensive deliberations with the French and Czech governments, Chamberlain persuaded them to accept Hitler's demands. When faced with an agreement, Hitler, who seemed determined to attain his objective by war, rejected it and ordered Germany's armed forces to attack Czechoslovakia on September 30. At the last moment, however, Hitler agreed to meet with Chamberlain in Munich. In Munich, the two leaders, along with France's prime minister, agreed on the evacuation of Czechoslovakian troops from the Sudetenland between October 1 and 10, followed by its occupation by German forces and the redrawing of Czechoslovakia's borders. Prague, aware that it could no longer rely on the support of the West, accepted the Munich agreement. Chamberlain returned triumphantly to London proclaiming that they had just averted another major European war.

It took Hitler less than six months to wreck Chamberlain's hopes. On March 15, 1939, the German leader seized on the grievances of Czechoslovakia's Slovak minority as a pretext to order the military occupation of Prague. He then transformed the western part of Czechoslovakia into a German protectorate and converted the eastern side into the satellite state of Slovakia. With Hungary and Bulgaria already part of Germany's sphere of influence, it was not long before Rumania and Yugoslavia subordinated their diplomatic and economic activities to Berlin's decrees. At this point, Britain finally concluded that unless it acted forcefully, Germany would attempt to become Europe's hegemon. Convinced that Poland was Germany's next target, Britain publicly pledged on March 31 that it would guarantee the territorial integrity of Poland. The announcement did not deter Hitler. In a major display of ideological flexibility, he signed a neutrality act with the Soviet Union on August 23, 1939, thus guaranteeing that if his troops invaded Poland, Germany would not find itself fighting a two-front war as it did in 1914. Eight days later, German troops marched into Poland, and on September 3, Britain and France officially announced the continuation of the First World War by declaring war on Germany.

Democracy's Debilitating Effects on Foreign Policy

After the end of the First World War, it was not uncommon to assume that the world would be much less hostile if it were led by democratically ruled nation-states, where the public had a major voice in all political matters. Paradoxically, it was this assumption that freed aspiring political leaders to replace young and badly designed democratic regimes with fascist and military regimes committed to creating an international system that would meet their own needs and that impaired the ability of democratic leaders to preempt them with authoritative acts. Few leaders understood the quandary in which the principal democracies had inadvertently placed themselves better than those of Japan and Germany in the 1930s.

The foreign policy of the United States toward Japan was driven by a deep contradiction. While for most of the 1930s the United States had repeatedly voiced its determination not to become entangled in a major, distant war, its actions toward Japan helped intensify the likelihood that both countries would ultimately find themselves at war with one another. With the anchoring of U.S. vessels in Japanese waters in the mid-nineteenth century, Japan concluded that in order to compete effectively in an anarchical international system dominated by non-Asian powers, it would have to borrow many of their practices and adapt them to fit its own needs. Moreover, as a nation with a very large population but very few natural resources, Japan believed that in order to secure its access to raw materials and markets, it would have to dominate the political and economic life of Greater East Asia. For Japan, attaining hegemony in Asia was not an unreasonable expectation. This aspiration differed little from the actions initiated by the United States, near the end of the nineteenth century, in its drive to attain dominance of the political and economic life of the Caribbean Basin and Central America.[26]

It is not always possible for a state to ascertain whether or not an aggressive act initiated by a major rival against a third entity signals the start of a policy of imperialism. It is especially difficult for a democratic state to rely on force to prevent an aggressor from broadening the scope of its aggression if the democratic state itself has not been threatened by the aggressor. The United States faced this challenge in 1931, when Japan's armed forces, after taking over Mukden, gradually gained control over the rest of Manchuria. This action, claimed Secretary of State Henry L. Stimson, constituted a direct violation of the Kellogg-Briand Pact.[27] The pact, signed in August 1928 by all the main powers except the Soviet Union, stipulated that all signatories would renounce war as an instrument of national policy. Stimson argued that as the pact made the traditional concept of neutrality obsolete, its violators had to be denounced as lawbreakers and punished. His argument did not carry the day among members of the Hoover administration. Washington refused to recognize any territory conquered by Japan but did not impose economic sanctions.

The Manchurian crisis prompted different groups within the United States to advocate ways the government should respond to belligerent activities by other international entities. A group led by Hamilton Fish, a member of the House of Representatives, proposed that the U.S. government impose an impartial embargo on all belligerents in time of war. He based his recommendation on the assumption that such a response would reduce the risk of the United States's becoming involved in any foreign war. A second group contended that the United States's long-standing support for an Open Door policy had created a special bond between the United States and China, one which obligated Washington to rebuke Japan's action with an arms embargo. The immediate fate of this debate was to be decided by the incoming U.S. president.

Prior to taking office in 1933, Roosevelt had expressed support for a proposal that called for an embargo on arms against "aggressor nations." He continued to advocate his original recommendation during the early months of his administration. In April, for instance, he backed a resolution passed by the House of Representatives that granted the president discretionary authority to apply an arms embargo against aggressors. However, he reversed himself shortly afterward by supporting a Senate amendment to the arms embargo resolution that stipulated that the embargo had to apply not just to the aggressor but to all belligerents. Roosevelt's change of heart signaled the beginning of a major change in attitude by the American people regarding the United States's decision to enter the First World War.

Starting in the late 1920s, some intellectuals in both Britain and the United States began to claim that the Treaty of Versailles the Allies had imposed on Germany was unfair. It did not take long for analysts in the United States to move beyond the German issue and start questioning the United States's rationale for entering the war. In 1934, following the publication of H. C. Hengelbrecht's *Merchants of Death* and F. C. Hanighen's

Iron, Blood, and Profits, Senator Gerald Nye, a Republican from North Dakota, chaired a committee empowered to look into the charges that an alliance of bankers and munitions manufacturers had pressured President Wilson to enter the war. The Nye committee concluded that Wilson had been duped into war by a group of individuals whose sole rationale for the United States's going to war was "the sales and shipments of munitions and contraband, and the lure of profits in them."[28] The committee's conclusion was reinforced by Walter Mills's *Road to War, 1914–1917,* published in 1935. According to Mills, the shipment of arms and raw materials to the Allies between 1914 and 1917 brought great prosperity to certain Americans, who were effective in seeing that the United States would want to ensure an Allied victory. By 1935, many Americans, after having been exposed to a stream of denunciations against bankers and munitions and weapons makers, became convinced both that the United States's involvement in the war had been a mistake, and that had the United States adhered to a strict policy of neutrality prior to 1917, it would have altogether avoided becoming entangled in the war.[29]

President Roosevelt, always attuned to the mood of the country, asked Charles Warren, who had served as Assistant Attorney General under Wilson, to address the issue of neutrality. In a memorandum, Warren proposed that by imposing during a war an impartial embargo on all arms shipment, limiting all trade of nonwar materials to prewar averages, and banning the travel by U.S. citizens on belligerent ships, the United States would minimize significantly the likelihood of being drawn into it. Roosevelt was not happy with Warren's conclusion, nor with Congress's decision to consider an impartial arms embargo bill. At one point he went so far as to suggest that the impartial arms embargo "might have exactly the opposite effect from which it {is} intended. In other words, the inflexible provisions might drag us into war instead of keeping us out."[30] And yet, knowing that politically he could not afford to reject the bill, he signed the Neutrality Act on August 35, 1935.

It is rare that a president's foreign policy proves to be so wrong while his premonition about its effect turns out to be so accurate. Six months after the passage of the Neutrality Act, Hitler—convinced that the United States would do its best to remain clear of a European war, that Britain had concluded that the Treaty of Versailles had imposed an unjust peace on Germany, and that France had staked its security on the impotent concept of "collective security"—ordered German troops to retake the Rhineland. His assessment proved to be correct. The former allies, overtaken by guilt and fear of their constituents' wrath, gave in to Hitler's action. Thousands of miles away, the Japanese government realized that the future might not present Japan with a better opportunity to augment its power in East Asia. In July 1937, Japanese troops attacked Beijing, and the United States, along with its former allies, once again remained immobile. Both Roosevelt and Congress knew that the American public would not support any action designed to protect U.S. business interests in China that could result in war between Japan and the United States. Just a few months earlier, a Gallup poll had found that 94 percent of the American people favored a foreign policy directed toward keeping the United States out of war, rather than one aimed at preventing war abroad.[31] Shortly afterward, on April 30, Congress gave the Neutrality Act its permanent stamp of approval.

Washington continued to convey its determination to avert any action that might implicate the United States in another major war. As Germany prepared to take over the Sudetenland in Czechoslovakia in September 1938, Britain, the United States, and France strove to find a way to restrain Germany's drive without antagonizing the German leader. Roosevelt, in particular, recognized that, should hostilities break out in Europe, the United States, even if it did not become involved in the war, would not be able to escape "some measure of the consequences of such a world catastrophe."[32] In his attempt to persuade Hitler to meet with the British and French prime ministers to find a peaceful solution, Roosevelt wrote: "The Government of the United States has no political involvement in Europe, and will assume no obligations in the conduct of the present negotiations."[33] The Munich settlement, reached on September 30, 1938, convinced the British prime minister that Germany, Britain, and France had designed an agreement that would guarantee peace for Europe. Roosevelt and the American people were less sanguine. The U.S. president believed that world peace depended on Hitler's continued willingness to cooperate, which he felt was most unlikely. The American public agreed with Roosevelt. A Gallup poll conducted in the United States a month after the Munich agreement had been reached disclosed that 90 percent of those questioned were convinced that Hitler would attempt to seize more territory in Europe. More importantly, 86 percent of those interviewed believed that the United States should increase the size of its armed forces.[34]

Roosevelt decided not to shun the new public sentiment that seemed to be growing in the United States about its international role. In January 1939, in his annual address to Congress, he requested that it revise the Neutrality Act. "We have learned," he stated, "that when we deliberately try to legislate neutrality, our neutrality laws may operate unevenly and unfairly—may actually give aid to an aggressor and deny it to its victim."[35] Neutralists, however, were not yet ready to throw in the towel. Led by Senator Nye, they threatened to filibuster if a resolution authorizing the president to lift embargoes of arms and raw materials to victims of aggression was brought to a vote.

Roosevelt's next major opportunity came in March 1939 when German troops invaded the rest of Czechoslovakia. He once again publicly urged Congress to repeal the arms embargo. The chairman of the Foreign Relations Committee, Key Pittman, proposed a compromise that would permit the trading of arms and all other materials on a cash-and-carry basis and would ban U.S. loans to the belligerents. He then agreed with the Roosevelt administration on inserting a provision that empowered the president to punish with an embargo on all imports and exports any country that violated the Nine-Power Treaty. In July, Roosevelt learned once again that though Americans favored by 57 percent altering the Neutrality Act so that the United States could send materials to England and France, Congress was still not willing to revise it. It would take the invasion of Poland by Germany for Congress to finally redraft the Neutrality Act. In a speech delivered to a special session of Congress on September 21, 1939, three weeks after Germany had invaded Poland, Roosevelt left no doubt about his attitude toward neutrality: "I regret that the Congress passed the [Neutrality] act. I regret equally that I signed the act."[36] By this time, about 62 percent of the U.S. public seemed to share his sentiment.[37] Finally, on November 3, by a vote of 243 to 172 in the House, and 55 to 24 in the Senate, Congress revised the law. In its new form, the law stipulated that the United States could sell weapons to countries that were victims of aggression, but required that all trade with belligerent states be shipped on foreign vessels on a cash-and-carry basis, and kept the restrictions from the 1937 act on loans and passenger travel. In short, though by the end of 1939, Roosevelt, Congress, and the American public were still opposed to being drawn into another major war far from the United States, they recognized that it was no longer in its national interests to remain neutral as Germany sought to achieve hegemony in Europe.[38]

Developments in Europe did not stop the United States from keeping a close watch on developments in Asia. Shortly after Britain and France had declared war on Germany, and Japan had renewed its pressure on London and Paris to withdraw from China, Washington warned Tokyo that the United States would not tolerate further violations of American interests in China. This time, the Roosevelt administration had the strong support of Congress and 75 percent of the American public.[39] And yet, though Roosevelt felt strongly that the United States could not tolerate any attempt on the part of Japan to widen its control over East Asia, he remained reluctant to impose strict economic sanctions. Thus, toward the end of 1939, he told Secretary of State Hull to inform Tokyo that Washington would impose economic sanctions against Japan should the Roosevelt administration conclude that, because of Japan's intransigence, reaching a reasonable accord between the two countries was no longer feasible. On June 10, 1940, Roosevelt spoke to the graduates at the University of Virginia in Charlottesville. In a speech that would prove to be a decisive turn in his foreign policy, he condemned the concept of isolationism, arguing that if Germany were to succeed in Europe, the United States would become an island, with its people "lodged in prison, handcuffed, hungry, and fed through the bars from day to day by the contemptuous, unpitying masters of other continents." He announced that his administration would increase the United States's defense effort and would extend to England and France "the material resources of this nation."[40] The French, facing imminent defeat but heartened by Roosevelt's words, asked the American president to provide France with U.S. troops and supplies. Roosevelt agreed to increase the flow of arms and munitions to France, but he refused to commit U.S. forces. On June 17, 1940, the French government, headed by Marshall Henri Pétain, surrendered to the Germans. Britain, now led by Winston Churchill, stood alone.

Across the Atlantic, Roosevelt faced several challenges. He was committed to aiding Britain in its struggle against Germany and to hampering any attempt on the part of Japan to broaden its territorial empire. He recognized, however, that at that point the United States was not strong enough to act simultaneously on both fronts; therefore, he had to ensure that his decisions did not propel Japan to launch a major offensive that would force the United States to divert its resources from the Atlantic. Furthermore, he did not want to weaken his chances of being reelected in November for a third presidential term. He pursued these goals cautiously. Between October 1939 and April 1940, Roosevelt authorized the shipping of over $50 million in arms to Britain and France. After the fall of France, he informed Britain that the United States would give them 50 obsolete destroyers in exchange for U.S. Navy bases in British-controlled Caribbean islands. In August, he announced that he would support a bill designed to create a selective service system to draft young men into the military. With regard to Japan, Roosevelt decided to continue his middle-course policy. When Tokyo announced its decision to declare the regions of the South Seas part of Japan's Greater East Asia Co-Prosperity Sphere, following the Allied losses in Europe in June, Roosevelt responded by announcing a full embargo on all iron and steel scrap.

As these events ensued, Roosevelt kept a close watch on public opinion. Immediately after the fall of France, fewer than 40 percent of the American people believed that it was more important to help Britain than to stay out of war. By September, that number had increased to 60 percent. As these numbers changed, two committees, the Committee to Defend America by Aiding the Allies and the America First Committee, battled for the hearts and minds of the American people. The first committee claimed that a German victory over Britain would have a major negative effect on the overall economy of the United States, and lobbied for sending massive aid to Britain and strengthening America's defense. The second committee argued that the most effective way to protect the Western Hemisphere was by remaining noninterventionist.

During this period, the Republican candidate, Wendell Willkie, also found himself facing a political dilemma. Though he favored aiding Britain, he recognized that if he announced his willingness to help the British, even at the risk of leading the United States to war, he would weaken considerably his chances of defeating Roosevelt. Near the end of the presidential campaign, Willkie put aside his scruples and remarked that Roosevelt was a warmonger who would get the United States into war six months after the election. He then added: "If you elect me president, I will never send American boys to fight in any European war."[41] Roosevelt, no less determined to win, responded by saying: "I have said it before and I shall say it again and again: Your boys are not going to be sent into any foreign wars."[42] On November 5, 1940, the American public decided to keep Roosevelt at the White House for another term.

The presidential election freed Roosevelt to pursue a more vigorous foreign policy. As Congress convened in the first week of January 1941, he welcomed the senators and representatives by asking them to enact a "lend-lease" law. He claimed that this new policy, which would aid Britain and its allies in the battle against Germany, would enable the United States to protect its four fundamental freedoms: of speech, of worship, from want, and from fear. The following month, Japan initiated a series of new offensive actions against Southeast Asia. Under the impression that a strong response from his administration would threaten passage of Lend-Lease, Roosevelt decided against challenging Japan's new adventure. His belief was justified. An opinion survey conducted in February showed that though 59 percent of those interviewed favored U.S. action designed to keep Japan out of Singapore and the Dutch East Indies, only 39 percent favored risking war to achieve this end.[43] In March, the House and the Senate approved a bill that authorized the president to "lease, lend, or otherwise dispose of" arms and supplies to any country whose defense was vital to the interests of the United States. The next month, Congress appropriated $7 billion to aid Britain and its allies. Roosevelt did not stop with these measures. Convinced that the United States would find itself at war with Germany, and most likely Japan, in the near future, he ordered high-ranking U.S. military officials to meet secretly in Washington with some of their British counterparts to coordinate military strategies. By the end of March, negotiators had agreed that in the event of war against Japan and Germany, the United States and its allies would fight Germany first.

Throughout the remainder of 1941, while the United States and Britain continued to coordinate future military activities, the former slowly but steadily increased its naval presence in the Atlantic and overall involvement in the war. On August 14, after Roosevelt and Churchill had met for four days on two warships off the coast of Newfoundland, Canada, the two leaders issued a joint communiqué, called the Atlantic Charter. The document outlined the principles that would dictate the basis of a political settlement after the war.[44] In September, Washington underlined its commitment to helping defeat Germany when it announced that the United States would provide the Soviet Union one billion dollars' worth of aid.[45] Equally as significant, by this time Roosevelt no longer needed to concern himself with being out of step with the American people. During this time, another opinion survey showed that 67 percent of the American public agreed that the United States might have to risk war with Japan to keep the latter from augmenting further its power.[46]

Toward the end of November, after the latest series of negotiations between Washington and Tokyo had failed to elicit positive results, Roosevelt concluded that Japan and the United States would be at war with one another shortly. Roosevelt, however, was not going to "strike the first blow and prevent any sort of surprise." As "a democracy and a peaceful people," the United States had to protect its "good record."[47] Moreover, the Roosevelt administration had decided that "in order to have the full support of the American people it was desirable to make sure that the Japanese be the ones to do this [launch the attack] so that there should remain no doubt in anyone's mind as to who were the aggressors."[48] This sentiment also dictated Roosevelt's decision not to declare war on Germany, despite strong pressure that he do so from certain members of his cabinet. He believed that for many Americans a war with Japan did not necessarily mean a war with Germany. This "lingering distinction" became a mute issue when Germany and Italy declared war on the United States on December 11.

The First Requiem

The 1914 war erupted when the European balance-of-power system was no longer able to abate the tension that was generated by the power rivalry between some of its dominant members and was exacerbated by the rise in nationalism. The end of the war four years later provided the leaders of the dominant entities the opportunity to assuage the tension that had caused the war, and create a new international system void of perilous contradictory forces. They failed on both counts.

The United States sought to eliminate the tension generated by the pre-1914 balance-of-power system by replacing it with a different type of security system. This system would be guided by an international organization, which in turn would be directed by democratic states. To actualize this vision, the United States first had to succeed with two endeavors. To begin with, the newly formed international organization would be able to play an effective role only if the major international players were able to replace the old system with one that did not generate power rivalries.

Second, having fostered the creation of a new international organization, the United States had to agree to become one of its leading players. The United States and its allies failed on the first requirement. By giving in to France's and Britain's demand that they radically undermine Germany's power capabilities, the United States helped increase considerably the likelihood that at some point Germany would strive to regain its lost status and, consequently, that the system that they had hoped to end would resurface. Considering the type of international system the Allies created, it is not unreasonable to assume that had the United States broken with its past and become a member of the League of Nations, the world would have undergone a less traumatic experience during the 1919–1939 period. The United States's unwillingness to join the League all but doomed the organization's chances of becoming an effective agent of international cooperation.

The unintended consequences of an international entity's behavior are not always experienced immediately. The United States was eventually bedeviled by the consequences of two of its international initiatives. By imposing its own set of economic demands on Japan around the middle of the nineteenth century, the United States planted the seeds of a tension that would bloom in the twentieth century. It would be unrealistic to claim that had the United States not enmeshed itself in Japan's economic affairs, Japan would have refrained from developing imperial aspirations. It is credible to assert, however, that by following such a path, the United States increased measurably the likelihood that Japan would seek to design countervailing measures, and that these measures would provoke the United States to initiate its own set of retaliatory steps. Since neither party was prepared to back down, the only possible effect was an increase in the international system's tension.

The creation of an unsound international system did not automatically doom its members to war. It is quite possible that had the United States behaved differently during the two decades that followed the First World War, it would have been able to avert the war's recurrence in 1939. Its options differed immensely, depending on the decade. Though economic issues deeply affected the political agendas of the world's main players during both decades, it was in the 1920s that the United States could have played its most constructive role. Washington took too long to acknowledge that the system of reparations and loan payments imposed on Germany were crippling its ability to rebuild its economy and that, as a result, Europe's own opportunity to regain some of its lost economic strength was marred. The steps taken by Washington in 1924 and 1925 to eliminate some of the economic system's flaws helped Germany and Europe visualize a brighter economic future, but not for long. As the stock market plunged in 1929 and the world sought guidance from its most powerful member, the people of the United States demanded that their country be once again returned to its shell. This action forced the rest of the world to respond in form. By 1931, nearly every major state had decided to protect its domestic economy by closing most of its market to foreign economic rivals.

The costs of the economic depression and the closing of markets to external competition reverberated across the globe; the effects on Germany and Japan, however, proved to be the most consequential. Shamed by the peace agreement imposed on them by the Allies in 1919, and burdened by the economic ills that afflicted their country throughout much of the 1920s, the Germans sought leadership from those who advocated extremist solutions. The Japanese, in turn, knew that their country's economic growth was dependent on the uninterrupted access to foreign markets. The economic depression convinced their leaders that the only way to curtail the uncertainty generated by the global market economy was to gain direct control over vital foreign markets and resources. The ultimate goal of the leaders of both states was to create an international system that addressed their needs better than the existing one.

Washington recognized in a relatively short period that Germany's and Japan's power aspirations threatened the interests of the United States. Whereas in the 1920s the United States should have used its economic might to facilitate the rebuilding of Europe's economy, in the 1930s it should have utilized its potential for creating the world's most powerful military to warn both Germany and Japan decisively that it would not tolerate their aggressive moves. Just as in the 1920s, Washington's ability to respond effectively to a major international challenge was undercut by the unintended consequence of one of its earlier actions.

Though the prestige of the United States was very high at the end of the 1914 war, and though every state in the international system understood that its economic and military strength were unequaled, by the mid-1930s its reputation had experienced a peculiar collapse. Guided by the principle that in a democracy the sentiment of the people must dictate whether a state should initiate actions that could propel it to war, the United States in the 1930s repeatedly expressed its determination to avoid becoming entangled in any war that did not pose an immediate and direct threat to its national interest. It is not possible to contend with complete certainty that had the United States acted firmly against Germany and Japan in the 1930s, both parties would have forsaken their imperial aspirations. It is reasonable to propose, however, that because Washington did not move aggressively against Germany and Japan, Berlin and Tokyo assumed that their hands would be relatively free until their actions posed a direct and immediate threat to the United States. It is also credible to assume that had the United States taken the lead by threatening Germany and Japan with military action, other countries, particularly Britain and France, would have followed, and jointly they would have forced Berlin and Tokyo to reassess their policies. Germany and Japan were committed to aggrandizing their respective powers, regardless of what measures the United States or other international entities took. However, no two countries with imperial aspirations will recklessly pursue their goals without first estimating the types of responses their policies might elicit from their rivals, particularly if their opponents' joint relative war potential is three times greater than their own.[49]

Democracy induced more than one unintended consequence. During the second half of the 1930s, in Britain, just as in the United States, the people warned their leaders that they would not tolerate being drawn into another costly war. And the leaders listened. For Neville Chamberlain, the idea of becoming enmeshed in a quarrel in Europe, or in a distant country in Asia "between people of whom we know nothing," would have meant rejecting not only his ideals but also those of most of the British people. The new emphasis placed on popular involvement in international politics in the United States and throughout other democratic states, moreover, freed the people to pursue nationalistic economic policies during times of economic crisis, even when reason dictated that such a response would inflict major costs on everybody in the long run. And lastly, in states that had recently opted for the creation of open and competitive political regimes and that were also afflicted by major economic ills, such as Germany and Italy, democracy helped legitimize the voices of those who advocated extremist solutions to troublesome times, and who sought to destroy the very political system that had enabled them to come to power.

In sum, in politics, as in other physical and social domains, every major force spawns its own counterforce. At the end of the 1914 war, democracy was welcomed by many. It was not long before the international political and economic systems started to expose their drawbacks, and countries that had just started to experiment with this new political concept began to realize that the benefits a democracy induces do not always outpace the costs it engenders. Economic misery, accompanied by the vision of an uncertain future, might not be enough to impel the members of a well-founded democracy to sacrifice their form of government at the altar of expedience. But members of a younger and more fragile democracy are generally more predisposed to do so. The peoples of Germany and Japan capitulated to those who called for the creation of a political system that envisioned the state as a monolithic organization responsible for controlling and directing all functions of society. Under this system, the individual had no personal needs, except those decreed by the state, and was expected to work on its behalf. Thus, insofar as the war represented a power struggle between entities determined to structure the international system according to their own needs and interests, it also symbolized a power struggle between entities with opposing ideologies. The war would bring this rivalry to an end, but in the process it would also lay open one that had been dormant for years, and would bring human society to the verge of annihilation.

CHAPTER FOUR

A New Kind of War

A Second Try

By shifting the relative significance of productive technology and control of territory as factors in the uneven growth of wealth and power among world entities, the Industrial Revolution united military power and economic wealth.[1] Britain was the first state capable of building a bridge between its economic wealth and military power. Though it retained the remnants of a colonial empire, Britain derived most of its international might from naval supremacy and the control of a world market economy based on free trade, freedom of capital movements, and a unified international monetary system.[2] By the end of the First World War, the United States had surpassed Britain in military power and economic wealth. A few leaders in the United States recognized that the future growth of its economic wealth and military power depended heavily on its ability to replace Britain as the international system's new leader. Because of its limited international experience, however, the United States found itself bewildered by the challenges emanating from the international system and the extent to which its international actions would have to change if it hoped to succeed Britain.

The start of the Second World War convinced President Roosevelt that this time the United States could not fail to create viable international political and economic systems. As he studied the United States's past failures and the challenges it would face after the war, Roosevelt presupposed that to succeed, his administration would have to accomplish five objectives. First, it would have to commit the Allies to the full destruction of the political regimes and military structures of their main adversaries. The winning parties could not afford to be confronted, once again, with defeated enemies that remained ambivalent about their role during the war, and their status after the war. Second, it would have to convince the Allies that to avoid a new major war they would have to establish a world security system in which they would serve as the system's chief protectors. Third, it would have to persuade the American people that it would be in the United States's interests to assume the leadership role that it had failed to take upon itself during the interwar period. Fourth, it would have to prevail on the Soviet Union to take on the responsibilities of a superpower, and to understand that, even though the United States and the Soviet Union adhered to two conflicting ideologies, it was in their respective interests to collaborate in order to prevent the destabilization of the international system. And finally, it would have to create, with the collaboration of a wide range of international entities, the kind of international economic system that they had failed to create during the interwar period, one that would enable states to have access to trade and raw materials, and that would foster economic development, better labor standards, and social security.

An entity's ability to fulfill thoroughly its international objectives depends not only on the number and complexity of the tasks it must complete, but also on whether the tasks reinforce or contradict one another. The challenges confronting the Roosevelt administration at the start of the Second World War were daunting. The United States faced not one task, but five, each of which required the culmination of a series of highly elaborate steps. Ultimately, it succeeded by more than half. By the war's end, the United States and its allies had destroyed Germany's and Japan's political power and regimes, and had managed to keep their own bruised alliance intact. Five years after the war had come to an end, Washington was presiding over international security and economic systems that, though differing significantly from those originally envisioned by Roosevelt, served the United States's strategic and economic interests very well. Moreover, by then the American public had accepted, somewhat grudgingly, that the United States had no choice but to be the international system's central player.

The United States's major disappointment was instigated by its attempt to pursue contradictory policies. Specifically, the central members of the Roosevelt administration failed to comprehend the nature of two important problems. First, they failed to recognize that convincing the Soviet Union to work with the United States in the creation and implementation of a new international security system ultimately would have meant persuading the Soviet leaders to renounce the ideology that had guided them and their country to the pinnacle of power. Furthermore, they did not understand that their call for the establishment of a more open international market system posed a direct threat to both the security and the economic interests of the Soviet Union. In time the United States recognized that, because of its own interests and needs, there was little it could have done to eliminate these contradictions; but by then the "Cold War" was in full swing.[3]

Because the Cold War period lasted more than 40 years, wandered through different courses, and entailed much more than the rivalry between the United States and the Soviet Union, I rely on the next three chapters to discuss its evolution. Throughout the first phase of this chapter, I delineate the efforts initiated by the Roosevelt administration to create international security and economic systems that would both serve the United States's interests and maintain order and stability in the international arena, and I discuss the rationale it relied on to introduce them. I then describe the effects of these efforts, explain why in certain instances the original drives did not spawn the expected consequences, and depict the undertakings initiated by new administrations to rectify the adverse outcomes elicited by the earlier attempts. I conclude with a discussion of the events that elevated the tension generated by the rivalry between the two superpowers to a new plateau in the late 1950s.

The Steady Rise of a New World Tension

As they toil to design new foreign policies, leaders of democratic states consider the fears and aspirations of those whom they represent, and they look for direction to the lessons derived from consequential events. Prior to 1940, the U.S. Congress and public opposed the United States's becoming involved in international issues that could catapult it into another world war. Shortly afterward, 74 percent of the American public, convinced that the war could have been avoided had the United States not abrogated its leadership responsibilities after the end of the First World War, advocated a more active international role for the United States.[4] Encouraged by this change in attitude, Roosevelt launched his postwar initiative even before the United States was drawn into the war.

In August 1941, just a few months after Germany had attacked the Soviet Union, Roosevelt met with Britain's prime minister, Winston Churchill, off the coast of Newfoundland, Canada. During their meeting, the two leaders drafted the Atlantic Charter, a set of ambiguously worded principles designed to guide the international actions of their respective states at the end of the war and, as Roosevelt hoped, those of other states. The charter had a profoundly liberal quality. Its first two principles stipulated that neither the United States nor Britain would seek to enlarge its territory, and that they would not want to see any other state impose a territorial change on another state unless such a change corresponded "with the freely expressed wishes" of its people. The third principle strengthened the content of the first two by declaring that Britain and the United States advocated the right of all people to select their own form of government, and it supported the restoration of sovereign rights and self-government to those who had been forcibly deprived of them. The fourth and fifth principles sought to broaden the liberal nature of the charter. They underscored the United States's and Britain's commitments to help all states have access to trade and raw materials, and to foster greater economic collaboration in order to procure economic development, better labor standards, and social security.[5]

The United States's major allies did not immediately embrace the Charter. In fact, the first to dispute its presumed intent was one of its co-authors: Britain. From early on, Churchill feared that acquiescence to Roosevelt's demands would further undermine Britain's rapidly eroding international political and economic power. Still, after having fought one world war, and having become entangled in a second one that threatened to impose even greater material and human costs, Churchill reluctantly acknowledged that Britain could not challenge all the United States's terms. The major objection, however, came from the only state in the international system with the potential power to counter the United States's wants: the Soviet Union.

Events in 1941 did not seem to augur a promising future for the Soviet Union. Germany's attack in June had caught the Soviet leadership off-guard, and by the end of the year almost half of Russia's industrial resources and cultivated land were under German control, while over half of the Soviet army had been killed, wounded, or captured, and its tank force had been reduced from 15,000 to 700 tanks.[6] The steady flow of bad news about the status of the Soviet forces, however, did not abate Joseph Stalin's power quest, and for good reasons. In July 1941, less than a month after German troops had marched into Russian territory, London and Moscow completed a mutual assistance pact. Churchill made it clear that though he remained a strong opponent of communism, any "man or state who fights on against Nazism will have our aid. . . . [W]e shall give whatever help we can to Russia and the Russian people."[7] President Roosevelt followed suit immediately by announcing that the United States would grant the Soviet Union a one billion dollar lend-lease credit. He also noted that the "defense of the Union of Soviet Socialist Republics is vital to the defense of the United States."[8] By the middle of December, the United States was at war with both Japan and Germany. Each of these steps or events convinced Stalin that ultimately the joint Soviet, British, and American war effort would bring about Germany's defeat and enable the Soviet Union to emerge as continental Europe's undisputed power. Stalin, however, had not developed this conviction overnight.

The Russian Revolution of October 1917 had unnerved the United States and its two principal allies, Britain and France. As President Wilson approached the coast of France in 1919 armed with his Fourteen Points peace plan, he fretted about the effects Russia's domestic transformation would have on the new international system. He was alarmed by the Bolsheviks' call for a world revolution to dismantle the political and economic foundations on which France, Britain, and the United States were built. He was convinced that Russia's transformation from an autocratic, antirevolutionary institution committed to the European balance-of-power system, to a dogmatic, revolutionary regime determined to promote communism as the antidote to capitalism and democracy, would lessen the United States's chances of creating a new, stable international system. As one of Wilson's friends remarked: "Russia played a more vital role at Paris than [Germany]. For the Prussian idea had been utterly defeated, while the Russian idea was still rising."[9]

Wilson had good reason to be concerned. Uncertain whether he should use force to destroy the Bolsheviks or court them with a series of liberal promises, he had initially decided that his only option was to attempt to woo them. Shortly after the Bolsheviks had seized power in Russia, the U.S. president had proposed that other states yield to Russia's legitimate need to freely develop its own political system and national policy. He noted that this action would show their good will toward Russia and an understanding of its needs as distinguished from their own interests. He then added that it was the obligation of other states to extend to Russia "a sincere welcome into the society of free nations under institutions of [its] own choosing . . . and assistance also of every kind that [it] may need and [itself] desire."[10]

Wilson's initial conciliatory step misfired. Lenin dismissed the U.S. president's olive branch by signing the Treaty of Brest-Litovsk with Germany. For Lenin, terminating the war with Germany was the key to the success of the Bolshevik revolution. He justified the treaty by noting that the Bolsheviks would make "use of the respite . . . [to] heal the very severe wounds inflicted by the war upon the entire social organism of Russia and bring about an economic revival. . . ." Only then would Soviet Russia "be able to render effective assistance to the socialist revolution in the West which has been delayed for a number of reasons."[11]

Lenin's response, and the decision by the White Russian armies to launch a civil war to overthrow his regime, forced Wilson to reassess his own initial stand. His Fourteen Points peace plan recognized Russia's sovereign right to determine its own political future without external interference. Unwillingness on the part of the United States to intervene in Russia's domestic affairs, however, might enable the Bolsheviks to solidify their power at home and launch a major revolutionary campaign against the United States and its allies. Wilson momentarily extricated himself from the dilemma by concluding that the obligation to be faithful to one of his values was less important than the need to prevent the Bolsheviks from consolidating their power. In July 1918, he agreed to send U.S. troops to the eastern Russian port of Vladivostok and the northern Russian port of Murmansk. The intervention did not bring the

Bolsheviks down. By the end of 1921, after recognizing that their publics were against becoming involved in another major military campaign, the Allies ordered their forces home.[12]

The intervention by the Allies had momentous effects within Russia. First, it strengthened the Bolsheviks' conviction that communism and liberalism could not coexist and that the Soviet Union had to prepare itself to be involved in a lengthy and costly struggle. In Stalin's words, the world "was definitely and irrevocably split into two camps: the camp of imperialism and the camp of socialism." He added: "the earth is too small for both the Entente [Allies] and Russia, . . . one of them must perish if peace is to be established on earth."[13] More importantly, at least for the short term, the decision by the Allies to try to isolate Soviet Russia from the rest of the world convinced Lenin, and especially his successor, Stalin, that their first order of business would be to consolidate the Bolsheviks' power and rebuild the Soviet Union's military and economic foundations.

To achieve these two ends, Moscow sought to dispel any notion among Westerners that the Soviet Union was bent on undermining their power. As a result, Moscow instituted a temporary policy of "peaceful coexistence" with many of the European states, in which it pledged noninterference in their domestic affairs in exchange for both diplomatic recognition and economic agreements. Moscow lured the former Allies by signing a trade agreement with Britain in 1921 and a diplomatic and economic agreement with Germany in 1922. By 1924, France, Italy, and Japan had extended full diplomatic recognition to, and signed economic agreements with, the Soviet Union.[14] Within the Soviet Union, Lenin's successor, Stalin, moved rapidly on two fronts. He consolidated his political power by systematically eliminating his adversaries both inside and outside the Communist Party. On the economic front, he collectivized agriculture and started a major industrialization campaign.[15]

Throughout the remainder of the 1920s and during the early part of the 1930s, Stalin continued to claim that the very existence of the Soviet state was a "deadly menace to capitalism" and that the primary task of the Soviet and communist parties was to "utilize to the utmost all the contradictions in the camp of the bourgeoisie with the object of disintegrating and weakening its forces."[16] His claims were not accompanied by actions that posed a threat to Europe and the United States. Moreover, though the Western leaders were convinced that the Soviet Union possessed the potential for becoming a major threat to Western interests, they also believed that because its actual power had been so severely undermined by the war and the transformations imposed by the revolution, the threat was not imminent.[17]

The assessment was correct. Upon learning of Stalin's continued interest in developing a better relationship with the United States, President

Roosevelt granted the Soviet Union full diplomatic recognition in 1933. In exchange, the Soviet Union pledged to "respect scrupulously the indisputable right of the United States to order its own life within its own jurisdiction in its own way and to refrain from interfering in any manner in the internal affairs of the United States, its territories, and its possessions."[18] Through the rest of the 1930s, the Soviet Union's principal foreign policy objective paralleled that of the United States, Britain, and France: to avoid war. As the 1930s moved into its second half, however, Stalin began to doubt Britain's and France's intentions and capabilities, and to contemplate the possibility of reaching an agreement with Germany. The Soviet-German accord of August 1939 shocked the Western powers, but it had no major effect on the tension that had already been generated by Germany's earlier actions in Austria and Czechoslovakia. With Germany marching into Poland, and then Britain and France declaring war on Germany, Washington, London, and Paris assumed that Moscow would remain on the sidelines as long as possible to rebuild its military and consolidate its control over the territories it had recently appropriated in Eastern Europe with Germany.[19] Much of this became a moot issue in June 1941, following Germany's attack of the Soviet state.

Though the outbreak of the Second World War proved to be very costly for the Soviet Union, it also freed its leader to finally pursue the course he had long favored. Still convinced that the world was split into the imperialist and the socialist camps and that the globe was too small for the two to coexist, Stalin started to reveal why the United States and the Soviet Union would not be able to lessen their differences after the end of the war. In December 1941, during a visit to Moscow by Britain's Foreign Minister Anthony Eden, the Soviet leader informed the British representative that after the war the Soviet Union intended to regain control of the Baltic states, along with portions of Finland, Poland, and Rumania, and that he expected Britain and the United States to support his action.[20] Eden, aware that acquiescence to Stalin's request would make a mockery of the Atlantic Charter, refused to agree. Stalin did not accept Eden's response. A few months later, at the end of May 1942, Soviet Foreign Minister Vyacheslav Molotov traveled to Washington to reiterate Stalin's earlier demand and to request that Britain and the United States set up a second front in Western Europe to draw off 40 German divisions from the Soviet front. Roosevelt replied that the Soviet Union could "expect the formation of a second front this year [1942],"[21] proposed that the Soviet Union, China, Britain, and the United States work jointly after the war as the world's "four policemen," but opted not to commit himself with regard to the Baltic region.

The president's proposal underscored his commitment to bringing together two separate approaches to international order. As one who at an earlier time had firmly endorsed Wilson's League of Nations but had then been deeply disillusioned by its failure to prevent roguish states from disabling the international system, he was determined not to be blinded by his own dreams. "I dream dreams," he commented, "but am, at the same time, an intensely practical person."[22] Aware that Americans favored the creation of a similar type of international institution, he was willing to side with them. The new international organization, however, would have two parts: an assembly open to all nations, and a more restricted "executive committee." Persuaded that the new international security system had to be based on the realities of power, he anticipated that the executive committee would be dominated by four great powers, and that these entities would perform their peace-keeping functions outside the framework of the more encompassing international organization.

Stalin endorsed Roosevelt's "four policemen" framework, but at that moment the Soviet leader did not consider this issue to be the most important one. Of much greater concern to him was the future of the Baltic area and some of the adjacent states. Stalin calculated that he could force Britain and the United States to curb their objections. His trump card was the enormously costly land war in Europe. He understood that failure on the part of the Soviet Union to contain the German forces battling on the Eastern Front would impel the United States, which in the past had relied principally on its economic and industrial machinery to project its power, to assume a human burden it did not want to shoulder.

Stalin's negotiating stance was strengthened considerably by Roosevelt's failure to keep one of his promises. Shortly after the U.S. leader had informed Molotov that the United States and Britain would set up a second front in 1942, Churchill voiced his disapproval. He argued that the military forces of Britain and the United States were still too weak to mount a successful second front. After lengthy and heated arguments, the British and the Americans agreed to invade North Africa. The decision angered Stalin, but he immediately used it to his advantage. In February 1943, while the Western Allied forces were battling the Germans in North Africa, the Soviet army started to push back the German troops that had besieged Stalingrad for some 16 months. By the end of the year, the Soviets had regained nearly two-thirds of the territory they had lost to the Germans, and they had accomplished this feat without the assistance of Roosevelt's promised second front. Britain and the United States, which in the meantime had defeated the Germans in North Africa and were now fighting them in Italy, became concerned by this new development. On August 23, 1943, British and U.S. military leaders approved a plan designed to land troops in Germany at once if it seemed that the country was about to be overtaken by Soviet forces.

Though Roosevelt had no intention of letting Stalin win the race for Berlin, he remained committed to the belief that to build a less violent world system after the war, the United States had to be sympathetic to the security concerns of the Soviet Union. At a gathering in Tehran, the three leaders agreed that the United States and Britain would launch the second front in late spring 1944, and would divide Germany after the war. They were less successful with two other issues. First, they were not able to decide whether after the war the world would be run by regional committees controlled by "four policemen." Roosevelt, who had been the originator of the idea, was having difficulty justifying the creation of such a system when many in the United States were promoting the formation of an open international system, one not divided into "spheres of influence." Nevertheless, Roosevelt continued to emphasize that he had no intention of helping create an organization whose members did little but engage in sterile debates.

Of greater importance at Tehran was the future of Poland. Stalin reminded his counterparts that the last two major attacks on the Soviet Union had come through Poland, and left little doubt that he would do whatever was necessary to ensure that his country would not undergo a similar experience in the future. In an attempt to extract a reasonable compromise, Churchill suggested that the Soviet Union take part of Eastern Poland and that Poland, in turn, take part of Germany. Stalin accepted Churchill's proposal, but Roosevelt, who was planning to run for reelection eleven months hence, noted that he could not embrace the accord at the moment because of the disruptive effect it would have in the United States.

The Western leaders left the meeting in Tehran believing that though several important issues lingered, they had managed to outline Europe's and Asia's postwar political framework. Roosevelt remained determined to treat the Soviet Union not as a communist state committed to promoting an anticapitalist revolution, but as a traditional imperialist power concerned about its own security. He was also convinced that he understood the Soviet leader better than any of the foreign policy experts at the State Department. Churchill was equally buoyant about his prospects of developing a good working relationship with Stalin. As he remarked to a few of his British colleagues: "As long as Stalin lasted, Anglo-Russian friendship could be maintained. Poor Neville Chamberlain believed he could trust Hitler. He was wrong. But I don't think I am wrong about Stalin."[23] Time proved both Churchill and Roosevelt wrong.

On June 6, 1944, the Western Allied forces opened the second front in Europe. Two months later, they liberated Paris. As the prospects of defeating Germany improved, the discrepancies in interests between the Allies became more conspicuous. At a meeting in Quebec in September, Roosevelt sought to force Churchill to accept an economic plan designed by U.S. Secretary of Treasury Henry Morgenthau. The plan called not only for dividing Germany, as agreed in Tehran, but also for turning the country into an economic wasteland. Churchill opposed the project, claiming that neither Britain nor the rest of Europe could survive without a healthy German economy. He agreed to accept it only after Morgenthau offered Britain a $6.5 billion postwar credit. Fearful that he might not be able to count on the continued support of the United States after the war, Churchill traveled to Moscow in October to reach his own territorial agreement with Stalin. The two leaders worked out a pact whereby the Soviet Union and Britain would split their influences in Hungary and Yugoslavia 50–50; and while the Soviet Union would have 90 percent influence in Rumania and 75 percent in Bulgaria, Britain would have 90 percent influence in Greece.[24] Roosevelt did not welcome the accord and informed Stalin that it was merely preliminary, pending a new meeting between the three leaders. He also emphasized that in the war there was no issue, either military or political, that did not interest the United States.[25]

The final "point of separation, a time of endings and beginnings," came at the Yalta Conference, in early February 1945.[26] With regard to the war in Asia, Stalin informed Roosevelt and Churchill that his country would start fighting Japan some three months after the end of the war in Europe. The three leaders agreed to create a "United Nations" dominated by a Security Council, in which each of the four major powers would have veto power. Nations would be invited to attend a conference on the proposed organization, to be held in the United States in April 1945. With respect to Germany, Stalin made two demands. He first noted that at Tehran they had agreed to dismember Germany, and that he expected them to honor the understanding. He then remarked that he expected the Soviet Union to receive substantial reparations from Germany, because during the war his country had experienced the greatest human and material costs. Roosevelt and Churchill objected to Stalin's demand, but after extensive bargaining Roosevelt agreed to a plan whereby Germany would pay $20 billion in reparations, with 50 percent of it going to the Soviet Union. These reparations would be in the form of annual deliveries of goods from current productions in Germany; machine-tools; ships; rolling stock; German investments abroad; and shares of industrial, transport, and other enterprises in Germany. Churchill, convinced that the imposition of reparations would chain Britain "to a dead body of Germany," opposed mentioning any figure until a commission had considered the matter in some detail.[27]

Poland proved to be the thorniest issue. The three leaders agreed to accept Churchill's initial plan to move the Russian-Polish border westward and grant Poland control over some German territory. When it came time to decide what form of government Poland should have, however, Stalin and his western counterparts approached the matter from opposite perspectives. For Roosevelt, Poland symbolized his commitment to the Atlantic Charter, particularly the third principle, which called for the "right of all peoples to choose the form of government under which they will live; . . . and to see sovereign rights and self-government restored to those who have been forcibly deprived of them. . . ." Churchill, in an attempt to allay Stalin's fears, added that a free and sovereign Poland did not mean the creation of a Polish government with hostile designs against the Soviet Union. For Stalin, Poland was not only a question of honor but also of security. As he reminded the other two leaders, "Poland has always been a corridor for attack on Russia." [28] The Soviet leader finally agreed to broaden the composition of the Polish government, which the Red Army had set up after crossing into Polish territory, to include representatives of the government-in-exile and other important groups, and to hold timely and free democratic elections.

Stalin's concessions proved to be immaterial, and Roosevelt knew it. Prior to his departure for Yalta, Roosevelt told a group of senators that whoever occupied an area controlled it, and none of the other parties would be able to force matters to an issue. "[T]he Russians ha[ve] the power in Eastern Europe. . . ."[29] Believing that it would be imprudent for the United States to break its relationship with the Soviet Union, he added that the only practical course left to Washington was to use whatever influence it had "to ameliorate the situation."[30] The argument applied to Poland. Though Stalin had agreed to broaden the composition of the Polish government, the Red Army controlled Poland and there was nothing in the agreement reached by the three leaders that stipulated ways to ensure its implementation.

No Turning Back

The relationship between the three leaders suffered an unexpected blow on April 12, 1945. One day after he had written to Churchill recommending that they not make a major case out of Stalin's manipulations of the situation in Poland, Roosevelt died.[31] His death was followed by the realization on the part of Washington that the United States and the Soviet Union would not be able to eradicate the tension their radically dissimilar political, social, and economic systems were starting to spawn.

Though the Russian revolution had given birth to the rivalry between both systems, the discord generated very little tension during the 1920s and 1930s largely because the power of the Soviet Union was considerably smaller than that of the United States, and both entities, for very different reasons, limited their international involvement. These constraints disappeared the moment the Soviet Union was attacked by Germany, and the United States by Japan. As the war ensued and it became evident that no other international actor would be able to match their capabilities at its end, each entity began to foster the creation of a world system that would best serve its own interests. For the United States, a state that was about to emerge from the war comparatively untouched by its horrors and with the world's most powerful capitalist economy, the logical response was to create an international system with few national economic barriers. For the Soviet Union, the system sought by the United States spelled nothing but danger. First, Moscow recognized that though the Soviet Union possessed the potential to become one of the world's major economies, the costs it had absorbed during the war were so high that they precluded it from engaging in an open economic competition with the United States. Second, nature had not afforded the Soviet Union and its communist regime the luxury of being protected from external threats by two vast oceans, as had been the case with the United States and its democratic government. The opening of Eastern Europe would have meant competing for the "hearts and minds" of its people on terms that would have inevitably favored the United States. As he had demonstrated in the Soviet Union, Stalin did not believe that communism could defeat its rivals in an open and fair competition. For the Kremlin, "the mission of communism was primarily to consolidate the might of the Soviet state. Only military strength and domination of the countries on our borders could ensure us a superpower role."[32] In short, Roosevelt did not understand that so long as the Soviet Union remained a powerful entity and its political system continued under the control of a communist doctrine, there was little the United States could do to maintain the relationship that both entities had developed during the war. During the war the Soviet Union cooperated with the United States not because it shared Roosevelt's world order vision, but because it needed its military and economic assistance to defeat Germany. As noted by Molotov: "Our ideology stands for offensive operations when possible, and if not we wait."[33]

By the summer of 1945, there was no turning back for either the United States or the Soviet Union.[34] Stalin, who had moved quickly to implement the percentage agreement he had reached with Churchill by imposing Soviet predominance on Rumania, Bulgaria, and Hungary, continued to block attempts by his Western allies to broaden the composition of the Polish government. These actions elicited substantial criticism in the United States, particularly from certain members of the U.S. Congress. At the first United Nations conference, held in San Francisco in late April, Senator Arthur Vandenberg, one of the most powerful members of the U.S. delegation, denounced the Yalta agreement, especially with regards to Poland's future. The United States, he claimed, could not afford to turn San Francisco into another Munich; it had to end "the appeasement of the Reds before it is too late."[35] A couple of weeks later, Germany surrendered. By this time, the United States had already started to reevaluate its postwar policy toward Germany. Analysts began to revive the argument posited, at the end of the First World War, by the likes of John Maynard Keynes, who had contended that the only way to avert economic chaos in Western and Central Europe was by rebuilding Germany's economy. To achieve this end, the United States considered giving precedence to the welfare of Western Europe's and Germany's economy over reparations to the Soviet Union. At the same time, Washington began to reassess its lend-lease policy toward the Soviet Union. Some of Truman's advisers endorsed the idea of using this policy, along with reparations, to force Moscow to conform to the agreements reached at Yalta.

The extent to which the policies advocated by both powers had moved in opposite directions became clearer during a meeting held by the leaders of Britain, the United States, and the Soviet Union at Potsdam, outside Berlin, between July 17 and August 2. By then, the members of the new U.S. administration had become convinced that Roosevelt had built his hopes on establishing a long-term association with the Soviet Union on unsound assumptions. Secretary of State James Byrnes fittingly summarized the change in attitude when he remarked: "There is too much difference in the ideologies of the U.S. and Russia to work out a long term program of cooperation."[36] As Truman traveled to Potsdam, he wondered how he might resolve the strain generated by two contradictory objectives. Though on the one hand he wanted to impel Stalin to be more acquiescent about U.S. goals for Germany, Poland, and Eastern Europe, on the other hand he also needed the support of the Soviet Union to bring the war against Japan to an end. Some U.S. military planners feared that the war against Japan might take another five years and require the actual invasion of the islands. Soviet participation in the war against Japan would help shorten the war and reduce the number of American casualties. The two issues, however, never really clashed.

Without much ado, Stalin informed the U.S. president that the Soviet Union would declare war on Japan on August 8, and then went on to delineate the concessions he hoped to draw from his Western partners with regard to Europe. In very short time, the leaders settled that for economic purposes Germany would be treated as a single unit, and that a council composed of the Allied occupation commanders of Britain, the Soviet Union, France, and the United States would administer it.[37] But that was as far as they got during the early stages of the negotiations. Upon learning that the United States wanted Germany to use the revenues it derived from its economy to pay for German imports before it paid reparations, the Soviet Union objected to giving priority to the "Wall Street bankers." The United States raised its own objection when it refused to recognize the governments of Rumania, Hungary, and Bulgaria, claiming that their citizens had not freely chosen them. The Soviet Union interjected by claiming that Britain and the United States had no right to reach a separate peace agreement with Italy without Soviet involvement. The two parties had a third issue to contend with—the amount of territory taken away from Germany and given to Poland by the

Soviet Union. Washington opposed the action on two grounds. First, it believed that Moscow could not make the decision unilaterally. And second, it feared that the loss of territory would radically undermine Germany's ability to resurrect its economy and build a stable political system. After lengthy negotiations, the three parties agreed to a compromise devised by the United States. Each state, they decided, would take reparations from its own zone, with the Russians and the Poles getting an additional 15 percent of capital equipment from the Western areas, in exchange for food and raw materials. In return, the West agreed to extend Poland's southwestern boundary up to Naysa. With regard to Italy, Rumania, Bulgaria, and Hungary, they decided to confer the responsibility for reaching an agreement to their respective foreign ministers, who would meet at a later time.

The tone of the Potsdam conference took a dramatic turn a few days after it had started. On June 16, Truman learned that the test of the first atomic bomb in Alamogordo, New Mexico, had been successful. Five days later, the U.S. president was informed that the destructive power of the weapon was far greater than originally assumed, and that it would be ready for use in a very short time. On July 22, in an attempt to use "atomic diplomacy" to force the Soviets to accept some of his demands, Truman informed Stalin that the United States possessed a new weapon of "awesome destructiveness."[38] Stalin, who already knew about the nuclear project, refused to be awed by the news and wished Truman good luck in the struggle against Japan. Truman and Byrnes decided that the United States, with the bomb in its possession, no longer needed assistance from the Soviet Union to defeat Japan. In fact, they now hoped to end the conference as soon as possible, and use the bomb against Japan to preempt the Soviet move in East Asia.

On July 22, President Truman wrote a letter ordering the use of the atomic bomb against Japan. Three days later, General Carl Spaatz, the commander of the United States Army Strategic Air Forces, received a letter from the Office of the Chief of Staff at the War Department, ordering the 509 Composite Group, 20th Air Force to drop the first "special bomb" on Hiroshima, Kokura, Niigata, or Nagasaki, sometime after August 3, 1945. On August 6, 1945, a U.S. Army Air Force B-29 airplane dropped an atomic bomb on the Japanese industrial city of Hiroshima, killing some 80,000 people. Three days later, the same day Stalin declared war on Japan and Soviet troops crossed the border between Siberia and Manchuria, another U.S. B-29 detonated a plutonium-based bomb on Nagasaki, killing more than 60,000 inhabitants.[39] The following day, Japan announced its intent to surrender. On September 3, less than four years after it had launched its surprise attack on Pearl Harbor, Japan formally surrendered and placed itself under the rulership of the allied forces headed by General Douglas MacArthur.

Into Uncharted Waters

As the war in Europe and Asia came to an end in 1945, the U.S. government came under intense pressure to abolish universal military conscription and reduce drastically the size of the armed forces. By the end of 1947, the United States's armed forces, which just two years earlier had exceeded 12 million members, had been reduced to 1.4 million. Military expenditures, which had been $81.6 billion in the 1945 fiscal year, had been lowered to $13.1 billion for the 1947 fiscal year. These actions did not go unnoticed.

In late 1945, the Soviet government, which had controlled the northern part of Iran since the start of 1942, sent a letter to the Iranian government demanding that it agree to the indefinite posting of Soviet troops in northern Iran, and that it recognize the autonomy of the northwestern province of Azerbaijan.[40] In February 1946, Britain and the United States made it clear that they would not tolerate any further Soviet advances in the region. By May, the Soviet army had evacuated from Iran's northern region. This outcome did not inhibit the Soviet Union. Since 1943, Moscow had been attempting to regain control over the strategic straits connecting the Mediterranean Sea to the Black Sea, which had been given back to Turkey in 1936. Having been promised by Churchill in 1943 and in 1944 that Moscow would gain access to the straits, Stalin demanded that the Turkish government relinquish control over territory in the Caucasus, agree to a joint control of the Turkish straits, and authorize the leasing of Soviet bases on Turkish shores. For Truman, the Soviet claim represented the resurgence of Russia's attempt to gain access to the Mediterranean Sea at Turkey's expense. As he remarked in a January 1946 letter to Secretary of State James Byrnes: "There isn't a doubt in my mind that Russia intends an invasion of Turkey and the seizure of the Black Sea Straits to the Mediterranean. Unless Russia is faced with an iron fist and strong language another war is in the making. . . ."[41] He then ordered the Department of State to inform Turkey that it could count on U.S. support. Close to the end of 1946, about a month after Turkey had turned down Stalin's demand, the U.S. Navy announced that a fleet, led by an aircraft carrier, was to stay permanently in the eastern region of the Mediterranean Sea.

Though these Soviet activities troubled the Truman administration, its leader was not yet ready to articulate publicly a policy designed to neutralize them. Truman recognized that without additional evidence of Soviet offensive intent, the Republicans, who had recently gained control of Congress, would oppose him. Truman's concern was justified, particularly since he knew that he could not rely on his own popularity to compel Congress to support him. At the start of 1946, the president's approval rating was above 60 percent; by September of that same year, however, it had plummeted to 32 percent. The one thing that he had in his favor was that the U.S. public had become increasingly displeased about Moscow's actions. While in early 1945, 55 percent of the U.S. public believed that Moscow could be trusted to cooperate with Washington after the end of the Second World War, by May 1946, some 58 percent had become convinced that Moscow was determined to control the world.[42]

For Truman, the turning point came in February 1947, when the British Foreign Office informed the U.S. Department of State that the weak state of Britain's economy was forcing its government to terminate its financial assistance to Greece and Turkey and to remove its 40,000 troops from Greece. Dean Acheson, who was now serving as undersecretary of state, warned Truman and congressional leaders that if the United States did not stand up to the challenge occasioned by Britain's retreat, then "like apples in a barrel infected by one rotten one, the corruption of Greece would infect Iran and all of the east."[43] Cognizant that Britain's decision had granted him the justification he needed to launch formally the policy of "containment" his administration had been implementing since 1946, Truman presented his "doctrine" to the U.S. Congress in March 1947:

> The foreign policy and the national security of this country are involved. One aspect of the present situation . . . concerns Greece and Turkey. . . . One of the primary objectives of the foreign policy of the United States is the creation of conditions in which we and other nations will be able to work out a way of life free from coercion. This was a fundamental issue in the war with Germany and Japan. . . . The peoples of a number of countries of the world have recently had totalitarian regimes forced upon them against their will. The Government of the United States has made frequent protests against coercion and intimidation in violation of the Yalta agreement in Poland, Rumania, and Bulgaria. . . . It is necessary only to glance at a map to realize that the survival and integrity of the Greek nation are of grave importance in a much wider situation. If Greece should fall under the control of an armed minority, the effect upon its neighbor, Turkey, would be immediate and serious. Confusion and disorder might well spread throughout the entire Middle East. . . . I therefore ask the Congress to provide authority for assistance to Greece and Turkey in the amount of $400,000,000. . . . In addition to funds, I ask the Congress to authorize the detail of American civilian and military personnel to Greece and Turkey. . . .[44]

The Truman Doctrine

The doctrine's theoretical core had been proposed by a U.S. Department of State official. In February 1946, George Kennan, while serving as the chargé d'affaires in the U.S. Embassy in Moscow, sent a telegram to Washington delineating what he thought were the underlying sources of Soviet behavior. Kennan, who was an authority on classic nineteenth century Russian literature and an expert on twentieth century Soviet politics, noted that:

1. Soviet power . . . does not work by fixed plans. It does not take unnecessary risks. Impervious to logic of reason, and it is highly sensitive to logic of force. For this reason it can easily withdraw—and usually does—when strong resistance is encountered at any point.
2. Gauged against Western World as a whole, Soviets are still by far the weaker force. Thus, their success will really depend on degree of cohesion, firmness and vigor which Western world can muster.
3. . . . In Russia, [Communist] party has now become a great and—for the moment—highly successful apparatus of dictatorial administration, but it has ceased to be a source of emotional inspiration. Thus, internal soundness and permanence of movement need not yet be regarded as assured.[45]

Kennan then added a series of policy recommendations. He proposed that the United States government: i) study the Soviet problem objectively; ii) educate the American public to the realities of the Russian situation; iii) address U.S. internal problems in order to deny Moscow the chance of using them to its advantage; iv) assist other nations, but especially the European nations, to gain greater security; and v) not sacrifice its methods and conceptions of human society as it struggled to cope with Soviet communism.[46]

Kennan's initial argument was well received by several members of the Washington community, who were beginning to accept that the United States's quid pro quo strategy vis-à-vis the Soviet Union was not working. Encouraged by Kennan's analysis, the Department of State proposed that the United States: i) no longer conceal its disagreements with the Soviets; ii) "draw the line" against future attempts by the Soviet Union to expand; iii) reconstitute its military strength and give favorable consideration to requests from allies for economic and military aid; and iv) continue negotiating with the Soviets, but for the intent of ensuring that Moscow understood Washington's position or of publicizing Soviet obstinacy in order to gain support abroad and at home.[47] The strategy was used to induce the Soviet government to remove its troops from Iran and relinquish its demands for boundary concessions and base rights from Turkey. It was also employed to support the Greek government against Communist attempts to gain power, and to prevent the Soviet Union from playing a meaningful role in the occupation of Japan.[48] Truman's request to

Congress in 1947 became an attempt to formalize a policy that his administration had been implementing for a year, but without the congressional endorsement and financial means it needed to be effective. Within weeks, the Truman administration received approval to aid Greece with $250 million and Turkey with $150 million. The U.S. public's response to the situations in Greece and Turkey was mixed. Though about 56 percent of those who knew about Truman's aid program to Greece supported his bill, 63 percent believed that the United Nations should assume responsibility for addressing the problems in Greece and Turkey. This public sentiment was not surprising, considering that in 1947 about 85 percent of the U.S. public endorsed the United Nations.[49]

A New Arms Race

In 1939, just after Britain and France had declared war on Germany and Italy, Alexander Sachs, a man with strong political connections in Washington, met with Roosevelt. During the meeting, Sachs presented the president a letter from Albert Einstein, but drafted by fellow physicist Leo Szilard. The letter noted that some scientists were studying the possibility of emitting neutrons in the splitting apart of uranium. It also pointed out that this fission could result in a chain reaction that would lead to the generation of vast amounts of energy. "This new phenomenon would also lend to the construction of bombs, and it is conceivable—though much less certain—that extremely powerful bombs of a new type may thus be constructed."[50] Einstein recommended that Roosevelt appoint a person who had the president's confidence to serve as liaison between his administration and the group of physicists working on chain reactions. Roosevelt agreed, and asked Lyman Briggs of the Bureau of Standards to create and head a small committee responsible for maintaining communication with interested scientists.

The appointment proved to be inconsequential. Between the meeting with Roosevelt and the spring of 1940, Briggs's committee did little. But as the war in Europe unfolded, a group of scientists and engineers, led by Vannever Bush, had concluded that the U.S. government had to start financing chain reaction research. Bush, who was serving as the president of the Carnegie Institution in Washington, met with Roosevelt in June 1940. At the meeting, Bush stressed the need to put together a group that would spearhead new research and would report directly to the president. Roosevelt agreed, and asked Bush to head a new organization called the National Defense Research Committee (NDRC).

Bush and his committee went to work immediately. A year later, he submitted to the president a report in which he remarked that recent studies, particularly in England, indicated that "the production of a super-explosive may not be as remote a matter as previously appeared."[51]

Bush met again with Roosevelt in October 1941, and requested permission to push his work to a much higher level of intensity. Bush pointed out that for the new operation to succeed, he would require the commitment of millions of dollars and the concerted effort of the best physicists in the country. Roosevelt immediately extended his authorization. In November, just a month before the Japanese attack on Pearl Harbor, Bush received a report from a review committee of the National Academy of Science stating that by bringing quickly together a sufficient mass of element U-235 it would be possible to produce a fission bomb of superlative destructive power. It added that if enough effort was put into the program, it was reasonable to expect "fission bombs to be available in significant quantity within three or four years."[52] With the report in hand, Bush reorganized the entire technological and scientific effort. One of the most difficult tasks fell on the shoulders of Robert Oppenheimer, who assumed responsibility for turning fissionable material into weapons. In the spring of 1943, Oppenheimer, accompanied by some of the world's best scientists and their families, opened the Los Alamos Scientific Laboratory in a rugged, mountainous area in New Mexico. Just a little over two years later, in the summer of 1945, they successfully tested the first implosion bomb near Alamogordo, New Mexico.

With its first successful nuclear test completed, the United States's government faced two new decisions. The immediate aftermath of the first decision was the destruction of Hiroshima and Nagasaki. The initial effect of the second decision did not become evident until later in 1945, but the issue around which the decision revolved began to take root as early as 1942. In June of that year, Roosevelt and Churchill agreed that the United States and Britain would jointly undertake the development of nuclear weapons and would share equally the results. By early 1943, however, disagreements and mutual distrust between lower level officials from both governments put an end to almost all forms of cooperation. Faced with this obstacle, Churchill repeatedly demanded that Roosevelt live up to his earlier commitment. Finally, Roosevelt agreed to authorize British scientists to participate in the American project.

The difficulty the two allies encountered paled when compared to the problem Washington experienced in its dealings with Moscow. The central question Washington faced immediately after dropping the two atomic bombs on Japan was: Should the United States disclose information regarding the construction of nuclear weapons to the Soviet Union? The Navy and the Army immediately opposed revealing the secret to any state but those that had participated in the development of the bomb. The responses by the civilian leaders varied. Initially, Truman emphasized that the bomb was "too dangerous to be loose in a lawless world" and that Britain, Canada, and the United States would not divulge the secret of its production until they had found the means to "control the bomb so as to protect ourselves and the rest of the world from the danger of total destruction."[53] The U.S. public sided with Truman and the Army and Navy, with 73 percent contending that the United States should keep control of atomic weapons and only 14 percent recommending that it delegate such responsibility to the United Nations Security Council.[54] Secretary of War Henry L. Stimson, on the other hand, believed that the United States should try to control and limit the use of the atomic bomb by working with Britain and the Soviet Union. His concerns were twofold. First, he feared that unless the three powers developed an instrument designed to control the development of nuclear energy, the future of civilization would be severely jeopardized. Second, he was convinced that if the United States tried to use its knowledge about the weapon as a means of winning concessions from the Soviet leaders, rather than discussing with them its development and ways of controlling future production, the relations between both states would be "irretrievably embittered." Acheson agreed with Stimson's assessment. He remarked that "a government as powerful and power conscious as the Soviet Government" would "exert every energy to restore the loss of power which this discovery has produced." He then added that if the United States declared itself "the trustee of the development [of the weapon] for the benefits of the world," the Soviet leaders would view the action as an "outright policy of exclusion."[55] However, Acheson emphasized that before the United States disclosed any of its secrets to the Soviet Union, the Truman administration had to discuss the matter with both Congress and Britain. Congressional leaders made it clear that they believed that the United States should maintain complete secrecy regarding the production of atomic bombs.

Truman's strategy involved more than protecting the secret. He shared with the Joint Chiefs of Staff the belief that because other states might succeed in developing nuclear weapons in the very near future, the United States should take the lead in the search for political control. In March 1946, Acheson and David Lilienthal, the chairman of the Tennessee Valley Authority, proposed a means for attaining such control. Cognizant that it would be ineffective to outlaw the production of atomic weapons, they suggested that the best alternative would be to establish an Atomic Development Authority. This agency would have total control over all the dangerous elements of the field of atomic energy, from mining through manufacturing, and would be responsible for staying at the forefront of all types of nuclear research and development. It soon became evident that the proposal had a major flaw. An organization with a worldwide monopoly over the whole field of atomic energy would be effective only if it had the backing of a strict system of enforcement. The Acheson-Lilienthal report had purposely chosen not to address the issue because its principal members recognized that the inclusion of a system of enforcement would imply mistrust of the Soviet Union. Truman supported the idea of imposing sanctions on those parties that violated the agreed-upon rules of enforcement and denying them, or any other entity, the power to veto a ruling against a violator. On June 16, 1946, Bernard Baruch set forth the U.S. plan at the opening session of the Atomic Energy Commission of the United Nations in New York. A week later, Andrei Gromyko denounced the U.S. proposal, rejected the no-veto principle, and made it clear that the Soviet Union would not accept the plan as a whole or in its separate parts. Acceptance of the plan would have placed "the Soviet Union in a position of permanent inferiority."[56]

In short, having attained nuclear superiority, the United States was not about to give up the knowledge it had worked so hard to gain, even though it knew that eventually other states would be able to produce their own nuclear weapons. As Truman remarked during a press interview: "If they catch up with us on that [the development of nuclear bombs], they will have to do it on their own hook, just as we did."[57] Furthermore, the United States hoped that by creating an international organization with the power to sanction violators, it would be able to impose a major control on the ability of other states to produce nuclear weapons. However, Acheson and Lilienthal recognized that this hope was unfounded; as they correctly predicted, the Soviet Union would use its own veto power in the United Nations to derail any attempt to insert the no-veto principle.

There was little the United States could have done, after dropping the atomic bombs on Hiroshima and Nagasaki, to persuade the Soviet Union not to start its own major atomic research project. In August 1945, Stalin gathered some of the most prominent Soviet scientists and told them:

[P]rovide us with atomic weapons in the shortest possible time. You know that Hiroshima has shaken the whole world. The equilibrium has been destroyed. Provide the bomb—it will remove a great danger from us."[58]

Aware that if they failed to produce a nuclear bomb they would be heavily punished, the Soviet scientists embarked on a race to catch up with the United States.

It did not take long for the world to learn that the two superpowers had unleashed a nuclear arms race. On September 23, 1949, President Truman announced that in late August the Soviet Union had conducted its first successful nuclear test. A few months later, he ordered the Atomic Energy Commission to initiate, with the Department of Defense, a program designed to build a thermonuclear weapon.[59] Shortly before the end of 1952, the United States successfully tested its first full-scale thermonuclear device. Less than a year later, the Soviet Union accomplished the same result. The new arms race, like all previous arms races, was the product of an international system that produced insecurity and as a result placed a premium on military strength.[60] As time would tell, the international nuclear program proposed by the United States and the response by the Soviet Union became part of a ritual that would extend to other issues, and from which neither party seemed able, or willing, to retreat.

The Marshall Plan, Gatt, and the New International Economic Order

The Truman Doctrine reflected only one side of the challenge the United States faced in the 1946–1947 period. As the war with Germany approached its final days, the Western Allied leaders began to erect the second pillar on which they hoped to build the new international system. Though they remained committed to bridging their differences with the Soviet Union, they were also aware that their problems were very broad in scope. As already conveyed by the nature of the Atlantic Charter, the trauma of the Great Depression had persuaded them that their governments could not remain aloof to the ruinous effect market forces sometimes have on domestic economies. U.S. policymakers, in particular, had become convinced that had the United States played the leadership role decreed by its world economic standing, the economic ordeal experienced by most states during the 1930s would have been less intense. These leaders hoped to bring about economic growth and full employment, and they assumed that to realize these goals they would have to create a world economic system with the capacity to prevent a return to the economic nationalism of the 1920s and 1930s. With this intent in mind, the United States and Britain invited representatives of 43 other countries to meet at Bretton Woods, New Hampshire, in July 1944.

At Bretton Woods, the representatives tried to find a compromise between domestic autonomy and international norms. Their intent was to create a system that would not hold domestic economic activities captive to the stability of the exchange rate, as had been the case with the gold standard system, and would not sacrifice the stability of the international economic system to the domestic policy autonomy characteristic of the interwar period. "[U]nlike the economic nationalism of the thirties, it would be multilateral in character; unlike the liberalism of the gold standard and free trade, its multilateralism would be predicated upon domestic interventionism."[61] They believed they found a compromise solution in a system of fixed exchange rates among currencies, relying on the dollar as the new key currency. In this type of system, balance-of-payments deficits and surpluses—that is, reductions or increases in international reserves—were expected to be temporary. Each country pledged to maintain a par value for its currency in gold or in dollars at a rate of $35 per ounce, and the exchange rate of its currency within 1 percent of this par value. A country that developed a deficit would use its international reserves to help weather the storm until it secured a surplus balance of payment. If this measure did not reverse the deficit and the country found itself facing a "fundamental disequilibrium," it would receive authorization from the international community to devalue its currency. Conversely, a country with a fundamental surplus would be allowed to revalue its currency. The United States, which in 1944 held most of the world's gold reserves, was approved to serve as the converter of foreign holdings of dollars into gold.

Two public international organizations, the International Monetary Fund (IMF) and the International Bank for Reconstruction and Development (known as the World Bank), were set up to serve as the international system's banks. The IMF was to function as the keeper of the rules for maintaining the fixed exchange rates, and as the provider of short-term loans to countries with balance-of-payments problems. These loans would come from contributions made by each IMF member, whose quota was to be determined by its trade and national income. The IMF was to be composed of a professional staff overseen by a board of governors, an executive board, and a managing director. The board of governors, which was to serve as the Fund's highest authority, was to be made up of a representative and alternate from each member country. Since the quotas would be determining the distribution of the members' voting rights, the United States was expected to become the Fund's most influential entity.[62] The World Bank was established to complement the functions of the IMF. With access to $10 billion (and the authority to lend twice that amount), it would help deficit countries develop those productive resources with a good potential for spawning dependable foreign exchange earnings. It would promote foreign investment for development through loan guarantees and participation, and it would complement private investment in projects it judged suitable, particularly when other sources of funds were not sufficient. Since the voting power of each member was to be determined by the country's capital subscription to the Bank, the United States was expected to become its dominant member.[63]

By 1947, it had become evident that the measures designed at Bretton Woods would not help resolve the economic problems Europe faced at that moment. Washington reasoned that the costs absorbed by the major industrial European states during the war had been so great that the financial goals it had helped design two years earlier could not be realized without substantial United States economic involvement. By the war's end, for instance, Britain had been forced to liquidate its foreign reserves and much of its overseas investments to pay for imports from the United States, while France and Germany each had lost 8 and 13 percent, respectively, of the prewar stock. Moreover, by 1947 the total European balance-of-payments deficit had risen to $7.6 billion, which was nearly one billion dollars over the reserves available to pay for them.

Washington's apprehension reached beyond the weak state of Europe's economy and the negative effect it would have on the United States's own economy. Though the Truman administration was convinced that the Soviet Union would not seek to overtake Europe by force, it feared that the European communist parties might rely on the economic and social dislocation engendered by Europe's economic woes to gain power. Of particular concern to Washington's foreign policy makers was the fate of the governments in France and Italy, where the communist parties had considerable popular backing. Mindful that the credit resources controlled by the IMF would not be large enough to help the European states cope with their huge deficits and that its articles of agreement prohibited the extension of loans for capital and reconstruction purposes, Washington concluded that the United States would have to assume many of the initial financial responsibilities for helping them rebuild their economies. Backed by a $10.1 billion U.S. trade surplus and U.S. reserves that totaled some $25.8 billion, Secretary of State George C. Marshall, during a speech he delivered at Harvard University in June 1947, invited the European states, including the Soviet Union and its satellites, to design a plan for European recovery. The United States, added Marshall, would utilize its own extensive financial resources to foster their economic betterment.

On June 26, Molotov, accompanied by a large entourage of Russian economic specialists, arrived in Paris to discuss Marshall's proposal. Their stay was short. Convinced that acceptance of the plan would further solidify the hegemonic status of the United States and relegate the Soviet Union to the standing of a supplicatory state, the Soviet government condemned the proposal and prohibited its Eastern European dependencies from accepting Washington's offer. Moscow's objection was grounded in two conditions demanded by Washington. First, Washington required that most of the aid provided by the United States be used to buy U.S. exports. This proviso persuaded Moscow that Washington was using the plan to prop up the United States's economy. Moreover, Moscow was unwilling to tolerate Washington's requirement that the recipient states open their internal budgets to external inspection to ensure that the funds disbursed were spent appropriately.[64] If ever there was a hope that the United States and the Soviet Union would be able to resolve their economic differences amicably, the Marshall Plan and Moscow's reply swiftly erased it.

Europe, on the other hand, welcomed Washington's proposal. On July 12, representatives from 16 European states met in Paris to design the structure of the new plan. On April 3, 1948, the U.S. Congress approved a four-year European recovery plan and appropriated $6 billion to cover the combined deficits of the 16 European states for the first year. With this action, the United States became the manager of the international monetary system. With neither the gold nor the pound serving as the world's money, the dollar was the only currency strong enough to meet the increasing demands for international liquidity. The United States reversed the existing economic process by running balance-of-payments deficits through the various U.S. aid programs, thus providing the much-needed liquidity for the international economy.[65]

The Truman administration's international economic plan reached beyond the creation of a new international monetary system. During the early 1940s, the Department of State, under the leadership of Secretary of State Cordell Hull, had argued that in order to prevent future wars, preserve private enterprise, and attain full and effective domestic employment in the United States, the volume of international trade would have to undergo a substantial expansion. The Department of State also remarked that because of its relatively great economic strength and its favorable balance-of-payment position, the United States was the "only nation capable of taking the initiative in promoting a worldwide movement toward the relaxation of trade barriers. . . ."[66] In 1945, the United States proposed a plan designed to regulate and reduce restrictions on international trade. The following year, it called for an international conference to consider the plan and put in place a new trading system. In March 1948, some 50 countries signed the Havana Charter for the International Trade Organization (ITO). The charter included a set of rules designed to regulate the policies of states on a wide range of trade-related issues. Because trade policy, more than any other international economic issue, "is the stuff of domestic politics," the Truman administration was not successful in creating the system it had wanted.[67] First, many of the negotiating parties, facing major domestic constraints, demanded the inclusion of provisions that would protect and foster their own domestic economic interests. The Havana Charter was an agreement that expressed in one way or another the interests of everyone, but that in the end satisfied few.[68] Second, the U.S. Congress, coming under intense pressure from a wide range of domestic interest groups, made it clear to the Truman administration that it would not support the Havana Charter if submitted for consideration. Aware that it did not have the support it needed, the Truman administration decided in 1950 to accept the advice from the U.S. Congress.

Not all the trade negotiations came to naught. In October 1947, delegates from 23 countries signed the General Agreement on Tariffs and Trade (GATT). Though originally designed to be replaced by ITO, GATT was transformed into an institutional framework used by governments to consider trade policies the moment it became evident that ITO would not work out.[69] The agreement consisted of tariff concessions and trade barrier rules. Three principles were to guide GATT's operation: i) nondiscrimination, multilateralism, and the application of the Most-Favored-Nation (MFN) to all members; ii) expansion of trade through the reduction of trade barriers; and iii) complete reciprocity among all members.[70] GATT's objective was not to end all national controls over trade barriers, for it contained numerous provisions designed to protect states from the harmful effects of international trade.[71] Its intent, instead, was to bring about greater economic stability in order to encourage states to become more receptive to trade liberalization.

Germany, Japan, and Other Disconcerting Issues

The worthiness of a foreign policy strategy is partly determined by whether it enables foreign policy leaders to respond effectively to unforeseen international challenges. By April 1948, Congress had approved the military and economic plans submitted by the Truman administration. These plans had the support of the U.S. public.[72] By then, however, several U.S. foreign policy makers were beginning to realize that the military and economic strategies they had persuaded Congress to approve would have to be used to protect two of the United States's most formidable former enemies: Germany and Japan.

Notwithstanding the fears a strong Germany would animate among its European neighbors, U.S. foreign policy makers concluded that if they hoped to rebuild Europe's economy they would also have to overhaul Germany's economy. As Kennan noted, Germany was the center of the region's industrial complex, and its recovery was essential to the restoration of stability in Europe.[73] In January 1947, Britain and the United States took the first step to help rebuild Germany's economy, by merging the German zones that each one ruled into a single economic unit. France, though unwilling to fuse its zone with the Anglo-American zone until June 1948, agreed in the summer of 1947 to allow its own zone to participate in a common economic policy with those controlled by the United States and Britain. The process of integrating the economies of the three zones entailed setting up a central bank, establishing a common currency, forming German-directed economic bodies with extensive decision-making powers, and removing all restrictions on the internal circulation of labor, capital, and products.[74]

Events in Germany were not the sole concern of those whose attentions were centered on Europe. By the start of 1948, the French government, which had been heavily hampered by Communist-inspired labor strikes, sought some sort of political reassurance from Britain and the United States. On January 22, the British Foreign Minister Ernest Bevin delivered a major speech in the House of Commons in which he called for the creation of a union between Britain, France, and the Benelux countries

(Belgium, the Netherlands, and Luxembourg). In the meantime, conditions in Czechoslovakia were giving rise to a mixture of hope and uneasiness in the West. By 1946, the Communist Party had emerged as Czechoslovakia's dominant party, and the West had virtually conceded the country to the Soviet sphere. By the beginning of 1948, however, the popularity of the Communist Party had faded noticeably, and many observers believed that the elections scheduled for May might force it to relinquish control over the coalition government it headed. After intense political maneuvering from both sides, the Soviet Union forced the country's president to entrust the leader of the Communist Party, Clement Gottwald, with the creation of a new government. Gottwald, after forming a government that became a coalition only in name, replaced the president with one who had demonstrated his firm allegiance to Moscow.[75]

Events in Czechoslovakia elicited strong views. In March, John Foster Dulles, who had been serving as Marshall's representative in Europe as some of its leaders discussed the creation of a union, wrote: "Today there is hardly anyone in Europe or Asia who does not feel that if he asserts himself in a manner displeasing to the Soviet Communist Party, he will be, or shortly may be, liquidated."[76] That same month the Department of State produced a report noting that the Soviet Union's ultimate objective was "the domination of the world."[77] And on March 16, the Central Intelligence Agency, upon assuring Truman that the Soviet Union was unlikely to resort to war for the next 60 days, added that it felt much less confident about Moscow's intention after that period.[78] Resolute steps followed these conclusions. On March 17, during a meeting in Brussels, representatives of Britain, France, and the Benelux countries signed a 50-year military defense alliance. The alliance, which was referred to as the Brussels Pact, committed the five countries to repel an armed attack against any one of the signatories. That same day, during a speech to a joint session of Congress, Truman hailed the Brussels agreement and made it clear that "the United States will, by appropriate means, extend to the free nations the support which the situation requires."[79] The concern generated by Moscow's behavior and by the signing of the Brussels Pact provided Truman the stimulus he needed to persuade Congress to authorize his administration to create a new security system with the Europeans. On June 11, the Senate authorized the Truman administration to discuss the creation of a North Atlantic security system with members of the Brussels Pact and other pertinent parties.[80]

The Soviet Union did not remain idle during this period. Fearful of the economic power that might be spawned by a region that contained three-fourths of Germany's population and the core of Europe's industry, and determined to test the West's resolve, Moscow ordered on June 24 the halting of all surface traffic from Germany's western zone through the zone controlled by the Soviet Union to West Berlin. The United States and Britain responded by mounting a major airlift. Truman was pleased by the support his decision received from the U.S. public. When asked whether the United States and its European allies should stay in Berlin even if it meant war with the Soviet Union, 80 percent replied yes.[81] Truman knew that this attitude was backed by a strong anti-Soviet sentiment. A series of Gallup polls conducted during this period disclosed that 77 percent of the U.S. public was convinced that the Soviet Union was attempting to become the ruling power of the world; 73 percent believed that it would start a war to get something it wanted; and 73 percent maintained that the policy of the United States toward the Soviet Union was too soft.[82] Thus, after an 11–month Anglo-American airlift that kept Berlin's besieged citizens supplied with basic commodities, Stalin acquiesced and ended the blockade. His decision came a little over a month after the United States, Canada, and ten European states signed the North Atlantic Treaty, a regional security arrangement that compelled each member to provide assistance to any of the others that experienced an armed attack.[83]

Events in the Far East were no less unsettling. By early 1949, the Truman administration had resigned itself to the fact that Mao Tse-tung's Communist forces were about to trounce Chiang Kai-shek and his Nationalist forces, and gain full control over mainland China. The outcome did not surprise the Department of State. As early as 1944, some of its officials had questioned the notion that it was in the interest of the United States to side with the Nationalists. Two years later, George Marshall, after a year-long effort to construct a compromise and coalition between the Nationalists and Communists, informed Truman that he saw no possibility of compromise between the two sides, and that he believed that Mao's forces would eventually win. Shortly after his return to the United States, Marshall was named secretary of state and was immediately pressured by Congress to investigate whether the United States might still be able to save Chiang Kai-shek and his Nationalist forces. A report by General Albert Wedemeyer recommended that the United States send to China massive economic aid and some 10,000 U.S. advisers to work with the Nationalist forces. Marshall, convinced that such help would not be enough to save Chiang and his followers, rejected the advice.

Marshall's decision did not signify that the Department of State believed that the fall of China to the Communists would automatically strengthen the Soviet Union's hand, nor that the Department of State was ready to surrender the Far East to the Communists. In May 1947, Kennan, who by then was serving as director of the Policy Planning Staff at the Department of State, remarked during a lecture at the War College that there was a good chance that if China came under the control of the Chinese Communists it would take "an independent line vis-à-vis Moscow."[84] Moreover, he and his colleagues did not view the deterioration of the situation in China as particularly detrimental to U.S. interests. They assumed that China could become neither a strong military power nor a major industrial power in a short space of time. Japan, on the other hand, he considered to be "more important than China as a potential factor in world-political developments."[85] This belief did not reflect a late conversion on his part. It was fully consistent with his contention that to attain a balance of power on the Eurasian land mass it was imperative to make sure that neither Germany nor Japan remained power vacuums for long.

Guided by the conviction that the rebuilding of Japan was as important to the national interest of the United States as was the rehabilitation of Germany, Kennan and a few members of his policy planning staff turned their attention to the situation in the Asian state. The principal objectives of the occupation forces in Japan had been to demilitarize the country and collect reparations. Originally, it had been assumed that the signing of a peace treaty with Japan would follow the completion of these tasks. Kennan and his associates immediately concluded that leaving Japan to its own devices after the signing of the peace agreement made very little sense. First, they learned that nobody had given much thought to providing Japan the means to defend itself after the occupational forces had departed. Second, they agreed that it was imperative for the United States to focus on ways to rehabilitate Japan's economy. In October 1947, Kennan met with Marshall and delineated the dangers the United States would generate were it to relinquish its control over Japan early. Kennan emphasized that an early U.S. exit would render Japan vulnerable to Communist political pressures and pave the way for a Communist takeover.

Kennan traveled to Japan at the end of February 1948 to discuss the situation with the commander of the occupation forces, General Douglas MacArthur. During his meeting with MacArthur, Kennan remarked that the United States had greatly overextended itself and would have to show greater restraint in the Far East. He then noted that Japan and the Philippines would have to constitute the cornerstones of the United States's Pacific security system. After declaring that Washington would have to end the United States's "unsound commitments in China," he observed that Washington would also have to:

devise policies toward Japan which would assure the security of the country from Communist penetration and domination as well as from military attack by the Soviet Union and would permit Japan's economic potential to become once again an important force in the affairs of the area, conducive to peace and stability; and permit Philippine independence, but in such a way as to assure that the archipelago remained a bulwark of American security in the Pacific region.[86]

Kennan returned to the United States convinced that his meeting with MacArthur had been fruitful. His assessment proved to be correct. He submitted his recommendations to his superiors, and by the end of 1948 and start of 1949, the United States was ready to commence in earnest the transformation of Japan's economy. The most forceful impetus to this transformation, however, came from a totally unexpected source, and not until 1950.

How Much Containment?

The start of the new decade brought a new set of challenges for the United States. As the American public and Congress struggled to accept that the United States no longer held a monopoly over nuclear weapons and that China was now being led by a Communist regime, the Truman administration concluded that its policy of containment lacked a carefully designed framework. The responsibility for designing one fell on the shoulders of Kennan's successor as director of Policy Planning at the Department of State, Paul H. Nitze. Nitze and his associates drafted a document that came to be known as NSC-68. Though they never intended to negate the essence of the policy of containment presented by Kennan in a series of papers and lectures, they broadened its scope considerably.

Since his final days in Moscow, Kennan had consistently argued that Washington had to devise a policy of containment mindful that the United States did not possess unlimited resources. As he stressed at the end of 1947, the United States's opposition "to communist expansion is not an absolute factor. . . . We are not necessarily always against the expansion of communism, and certainly not always against it to the same degree in every area. It all depends on the circumstances."[87] A year later he drew up a list of the countries and regions the United States could not afford to lose to communism. Aside from the states and territories of the Atlantic community (all Latin American states and African states bordering the Atlantic Ocean were also on the list), he added Japan and the Philippines, and the countries of the Mediterranean and the Middle East, including Iran. For the drafters of NSC-68, Kennan's strategy of protecting selected areas was no longer sufficient. The United States, they believed, had to design a perimeter and place equal value on the defense of each point in the perimeter.

The implications of this contention were monumental. Essentially, the document argued that insecurities manifested themselves in both physical and psychological terms. Though the United States had to remain vigilant about Soviet attempts to alter existing military and economic distributions of power, it also had to be alert about Soviet worldwide efforts to humiliate, intimidate, or undermine the credibility of the United States. World order, in other words, depended as "much on perceptions of the balance of power as on what that balance actually was."[88] By vastly increasing the number and variety of interests considered relevant to the security of United States, the document was alerting foreign policymakers to the need of revising the amount of resources they would require to be effectual. The creators of the document assumed that such a goal could be attained by augmenting the efficiency of the American economy. They posited that the American economy, when "it operates at a level approaching full efficiency, can provide enormous resources for purposes other than civilian consumption while simultaneously providing a higher standard of living."[89]

Initially unsure as to whether NSC-68 would be backed by the administration's top officials and Congress, its drafters learned on June 25, 1950, that their concerns were no longer pertinent. On that date, North Korean troops moved across the 38th parallel, which had been dividing North Korea from South Korea since 1945. At the end of the Second World War, the Soviet Union and the United States had disarmed the Japanese armies occupying Korea. The Soviet Union assumed responsibility for disarming the Japanese forces stationed north of the 38th parallel, and the United States for the Japanese troops posted south of the line. Stalin, having failed to unify Korea under the rulership of a Communist regime, and concerned about the effect Washington's decision to grant Japan independence and set up U.S. bases on Japanese soils might have on the distribution of power in the Far East, decided to test the United States's resolve once again. The risk of spurring Washington to assist South Korea might not have seemed particularly high to Stalin. The United States had recalled its troops from South Korea in 1949, and in early 1950, Secretary of State Acheson, in a poorly worded speech, excluded both South Korea and Taiwan from the United States's defense perimeter in the Western Pacific.

Five days after North Korean troops had crossed into South Korea, Washington once again reminded Stalin that it had no intention of being the first to blink. On June 30, Truman, believing that if North Korea were allowed to succeed, the Soviets would interpret the occurrence as an open invitation to initiate acts of aggression elsewhere in the world, ordered U.S. ground troops to intervene. Shortly after the decision, Truman approved NSC-68.

A war that could have ended in a status quo before the end of 1950, with North Korea and South Korea still divided by the 38th parallel, continued into the next administration, until the middle of 1953. By mid-July 1950, General MacArthur's United Nations forces had stopped the North Korean invasion. With MacArthur claiming that his forces could take over North Korea, and with nearly two-thirds of the American public wanting to drive the Communists out of both Koreas, Truman authorized the general in September to cross the 38th parallel.[90] By mid-October, MacArthur and his forces were moving rapidly toward the Chinese-Korean border, determined to rid Korea of all Communists. It was not to be. Mao's government decided it would pay almost any price to prevent the United States from gaining control over China's northeast border. With this objective in mind, hundreds of thousands of Chinese troops attacked MacArthur's forces. MacArthur's forces paid dearly for his daring, enduring some 11,000 casualties in just two days. His forces were finally able to stabilize the battlefront in the spring of 1951, with a successful offensive.

By then, however, support in the United States for the Korean War had dwindled. Sixty-six percent of the U.S. public, though convinced that China had entered the war in Korea on orders from the Soviet Union, maintained that the United States should not fight Communist China and should pull out its troops from Korea.[91] Truman did not think that it was possible for the United States to simply pull out, but did decide that the time had come to commence truce talks with North Korea. Concerned that his new efforts were being undermined by MacArthur's public assertions that negotiations were not a substitute for victory, he discharged the general from his command. The action did not help Truman's standing among U.S. voters, nor did it expedite negotiations. By May, support for his performance as president had faded to 24 percent and would barely rise above 30 percent by the start of 1952.[92] Shortly afterward, he announced that he would not seek the presidency for another term. Thus, it took the arrival of Dwight Eisenhower to the White House to bring the Korean War to an end on July 27, 1953.[93] The parties involved in the negotiations agreed that the same parallel that had divided Korea into two parts prior to 1950 would continue to separate them in the future.

The Significance of the Korean War

Every so often there is an event in history that renders clarity to the foreign policy expectations and objectives of the international system's principal members for an extended period. The Korean War was not such an event. In a "rational" world, the war would have forced the Soviet Union to recognize that in the future it would have to engage in a judicious analysis of the United States's strategic interests before moving into an area that was, or had been until quite recently, part of its strategic domain. From 1945 until 1949, Moscow repeatedly tested Washington's commitment to Europe and the Middle East. With the Truman Doctrine, the Marshall Plan, the Berlin airlift, and NATO, Washington tried to signal that it would not tolerate any Soviet attempt to raise the communist banner in Western Europe, the Mediterranean region, or the Middle East. In the Far East, initially Washington was not as lucid about its intentions as it could have been. In 1949 it openly expressed a strong desire to sign a peace treaty with Tokyo and help Japan rebuild its economy in order to help strengthen the United States's ability to protect its interests in the Pacific. Within a year's time, however, Washington inadvertently conveyed the impression that it was not prepared to include South Korea and Taiwan within its defense perimeter. This action might have convinced Moscow that testing the United States's will and commitment in South Korea would not elicit unreasonable risks. Washington's response to North Korea's invasion should have been the proof Moscow needed to accept that its initial expectations might have been based more on wishful thinking than on prudent analysis. But as a later event would show, Moscow did not take the lesson to heart.

Likewise, the Korean War should have pressed Washington to concede that the magnitude of the United States's power would not automatically propel rivals to acquiesce to its dictates. As events in Southeast Asia would eventually tell, this acknowledgment did not fully materialize. Prior to the beginning of the Korean War, Truman had expected to request $13.5 billion for defense for the fiscal year 1951. Within six months after the start of the war, Congress had approved a defense budget of $48.2 billion and continued to increase it for the next two years. The defense budget experienced its first drop following the July 1953 armistice, but the annual numbers continued to be nearly three times higher, until 1960, than they had been just prior to the start of the war. Washington used these additional funds primarily to strengthen the United States's presence in Europe. Access to these funds, however, also had a negative effect. Washington became less concerned about systematically prioritizing the strategic significance of different regions of the world and examining the real nature of the problems that afflicted some of them, and more interested in solidifying its reputation as the world's leading anti-Communist crusader.

Latin America, Southeast Asia, the Middle East, and Africa

As political and economic conditions in Europe and Japan began to stabilize during the 1950s, and as Washington demonstrated its determination to obstruct any attempt on the part of the Communists to undermine the United States's interests in Korea, the Cold War rivalry moved to new battlegrounds. The ideological and power discord of the two superpowers afflicted Latin America, Southeast Asia, the Middle East, and Africa, even when Moscow did not have the interest or means to champion the cause of those who might have shared its world perspective.

Latin America

In June 1954, a small number of paramilitary forces funded by the Central Intelligence Agency (CIA), and led by Castillo Armas, a Guatemalan national, entered Guatemala hoping to topple its president, Jacobo Arbenz, for his failure to free his government from communist influence.[94] Ten days later, Armas was sworn in as Guatemala's new provisional president. The decision to overthrow Arbenz was not made in haste; it was carefully weighed by the Truman and Eisenhower administrations for nearly two years. More importantly, the decision did not reflect a unique attitude toward Latin America. To understand the roots of the action, one must go back to the early 1900s, and then reflect on decisions made by different U.S. administrations until shortly after the end of the Second World War.[95]

Following the decision in the early 1900s to force Cuba's first free government to add the Platt Amendment to its newly drafted constitution, Washington launched a series of steps designed to situate the United States as the Caribbean Basin's hegemonic leader. In 1906, Theodore Roosevelt dispatched U.S. troops to Cuba to bring to an end a civil strife that threatened the economic interests of North Americans and Europeans. In 1913, Woodrow Wilson announced his own "doctrine." As he informed Congress, the United States was "the friend of constitutional government in America; we are more than its friends, we are its champions. . . ." He then added: "I am going to teach South American Republics to elect good men."[96] Determined to keep his promise, Wilson ordered U.S. troops to land in Veracruz, Mexico, in 1914 to compel the government of General Victoriano Huerta, who had used force to gain power, to hold new elections in which he, Huerta, would not be a candidate. Wilson succeeded, but not in the manner he had hoped. In August 1914, Venustiano Carranza became Mexico's new president and immediately turned against the United States. In late 1915, after Carranza had launched a radical agrarian reform and declared Mexico's legal rights to all its subsoil minerals, thus threatening the substantial interests of U.S. companies in the region, Wilson reluctantly recognized Carranza's government.

Wilson's 1914 decision against Mexico was not an isolated event. He resorted to similar steps against Haiti in 1915; Cuba, the Dominican Republic, and Nicaragua in 1916; and Honduras in 1919. By the start of the 1920s, the leaders of the Central American countries recognized that unless they stopped toppling their own governments by force, they risked becoming the perennial hosts of U.S. military forces. At a conference held in Washington in 1921, they agreed to prohibit the recognition of any government established by force. The United States tried to enforce the rule, but after other Latin American countries denounced the agreement as interventionist, Washington resigned itself to accepting any type of political regime, so long as it was stable and did not threaten U.S. strategic and economic interests in the region.[97] Finally, in 1933, the White House's new occupant recognized that the United States's interests were not being served by its continued intervention in Latin America's affairs. At his inaugural speech, Roosevelt remarked that he would dedicate the United States "to the policy of the good neighbor who resolutely respects himself, and, because he does so, respects the rights of others."[98] Later that same year, at a conference of American states in Montevideo, Uruguay, Secretary of State Cordell Hull translated Roosevelt's rhetoric into governmental policy by supporting a resolution that prohibited any state in the Western Hemisphere from intervening "in the internal or external affairs of another."[99] As a result of this new commitment, the United States withdrew its forces from Haiti and Nicaragua and abrogated the 1901 Platt Amendment. The decision did not indicate a willingness on the part of Washington to authorize Latin American governments to pursue whatever policies they wanted. Instead, it meant that Washington recognized that it had a major public relations problem on its hands and that it could address the matter more effectively by using less stentorian and visible forms of control. It began to help friendly, autocratic governments balance their budgets and stabilize their currencies, and it began to rely on its control over international loans to compel other governments to protect U.S. interests. In addition, the U.S. military started to participate in the suppression of domestic insurrection by playing an active role in the training of the national police forces of many Latin American governments.[100]

The Second World War opened new opportunities for the United States in Latin America. As conditions in Europe deteriorated, Washington began to pressure Latin American states to institutionalize its principle of hemispheric security, whereby each country would pledge to cooperate in the defense of any Latin American state threatened by the actions of a nonhemispheric entity. In July 1940, less than a year after the start of the war in Europe, foreign ministers of the American states met in Havana to approve the Declaration of Reciprocal Assistance and Cooperation for the Defense of the Americas. The declaration stipulated that an act of aggression against any American state signified an act of aggression against all of them. The declaration, which in fact was aimed against the Axis powers, formally replaced Washington's unilateral prerogative to obstruct any foreign intervention in the Western hemisphere, as dictated by its Monroe Doctrine, with a regional collective security system.[101]

The end of the Second World War did not annul the Declaration of Reciprocal Assistance. Two years after the Axis powers had been defeated, six months after Truman had informed Congress about his new doctrine, and four months after George Marshall had invited the Europeans to meet to discuss a new U.S. economic assistance plan, representatives of the American states met in Brazil to discuss the signing of a new inter-American pact. In September 1947 they signed the Inter-American Treaty of Reciprocal Assistance, generally known as the Rio Treaty. The treaty, crafted by Washington, committed all its signatories to come to the defense of any other signatory in the event of an attack by an outside entity.[102] This time, the Soviet Union, not Germany nor Japan, was the outside threat. Only one Latin American state refused to sign the treaty: Guatemala.[103] Seven years later, the United States bestowed on Guatemala the doubtful privilege of becoming the first Latin American country to be invaded after the end of the Second World War by paramilitary forces financed by the CIA. The Cold War had finally secured its first Latin American victim.

Southeast Asia

Eisenhower took little joy from his administration's latest triumph in Guatemala. In early May 1954, he had learned that France, which had been struggling to regain control over Vietnam since the end of the Second World War, had been defeated by the Communists at Dien Bien Phu. France and its adversary, the Vietnamese Communists led by Ho Chi Minh, agreed to keep Vietnam divided in two at the 17th parallel pending free unifying elections in the North and South to be held in July 1956. The Eisenhower administration became convinced that without substantial external support, South Vietnam, which had been devastated by the war, would collapse into the hands of the Communists. However, this was not the first U.S. administration to be alarmed by developments in Vietnam. In March 1950, the Truman administration had concluded that Vietnam was strategically important because it provided "a natural invasion route into the rice bowl of Southeast Asia should the Communists adopt this form of aggression. Moreover, it [had] great political significance, because of its potential influence, should it fall to the Communists, on Thailand, Burma, Malaya, and perhaps Indonesia."[104] Aware that France lacked the economic means to pay for the war, the Truman administration decided that the United States would act as its principal financier. Eisenhower, though conscious that a very high percentage of the U.S. public opposed sending war materials to help France fight the Communists in Indochina, kept Truman's Indochina policy in place.[105] In 1954, as he conceded that the Vietnamese would defeat France, Eisenhower expanded on Truman's domino theory by noting that if South Vietnam were captured by the Communists, the other "countries in Southeast

Asia would be menaced by a great flanking movement. The freedom of 12 million people would be lost immediately and that of 150 million others in adjacent lands would be seriously endangered."[106] In August, Eisenhower and his foreign policy advisers agreed that the United States had to replace France and become the direct supplier of financial and military assistance to South Vietnam. Two years later, in 1956, as it became evident that if elections were held as scheduled the Communists would win, the South Vietnamese government, with strong encouragement from the Eisenhower administration, refused to hold them.

The Middle East

Just as the Eisenhower administration was laboring to figure out how to contain the expansion of communism in Southeast Asia, it was reminded by new developments in the Middle East that U.S. governments rarely have the freedom to address one major international problem at a time. In September 1955, after a lengthy and futile attempt to persuade the Eisenhower administration to sell Egypt U.S. weapons, Egyptian President Gamal Abdel Nasser signed an arms deal with Moscow. With the signing of the pact, the Egyptian president not only broke the Western monopoly of arms supply in the Middle East, but also increased considerably the ability of the Soviet Union to exert influence in this region. Within a year's time, this event would lead to a major crisis that would involve Egypt, Israel, Britain, France, the United States, and the Soviet Union, and would transform the Middle East into another Cold War battleground.[107]

Throughout history, the Middle East had been one of the most burdened regions in the world. The end of the Second World War, along with the birth of Israel three years later, ensured that the pattern would continue, but in a markedly more complex form. During its early years the Cold War had little effect on the Middle East. After being forced out of northern Iran by the United States in late 1946, Moscow decided not to expend its energies in the region until conditions became more suitable to Soviet interests. The first seed for change was planted in Egypt in 1952. In July of that year, a group called the Free Officers Movement overthrew Egypt's monarch during a military coup and assumed power. In 1955, Nasser, after emerging as the group's dominant figure, began to center his attention on foreign policy. His central objective was to ensure that Egypt and other Middle Eastern states would remain free from foreign control. He believed that they could attain this end by maintaining a united front and not joining either of the two great power blocs.[108] For Nasser, his commitment had a more specific, and better defined, purpose—that of forcing Britain to withdraw its forces from the strategically important Suez Canal base.

Nasser believed that he had taken the first major step toward removing a major vestige of colonialism in Egypt when he wrested from Britain, in October 1954, a pledge to relinquish its right over the Suez Canal base. In February 1955, however, Nasser was struck by bad news. First, he learned that Iraq, Turkey, and Iran, with substantial prodding from Britain, had signed a defense treaty known as the Baghdad Pact.[109] The pact, concluded Nasser, undermined not only his long-term goal of creating a vast Pan-Arab empire from the Atlantic to the Persian Gulf under Egypt's leadership, but also his reputation. His prestige suffered another setback at the end of February when Israeli forces launched a raid on Gaza and killed several Egyptian soldiers. These events pushed Nasser to try to counterbalance the Baghdad Pact with his own pact and to increase considerably Egypt's military strength. One of Nasser's gravest concerns was that if Iraq persuaded Syria to sign the Baghdad Pact, Jordan and Lebanon would feel compelled to do the same, and Egypt would find itself completely isolated.[110] By March, Nasser had managed to put this fear to rest by convincing Syria and Saudi Arabia to form an alliance with Egypt.

The alliance, however, did not increase Egypt's military strength significantly. Hoping to finally solve this problem, Nasser once again asked the United States to sell weapons to Egypt. Washington, which had rejected a similar Egyptian petition in 1953, proposed that it might now be willing to authorize the sale if Egypt agreed to a peace treaty with Israel. The Eisenhower administration believed that a peace treaty between Egypt and Israel would reduce considerably the likelihood of instability in the region and as a result diminish the Soviet Union's chances of becoming one of the area's key players. Concerned that if he acquiesced to Washington's demand he would lose the support of his army officers and harm his prestige in the region, Nasser decided that he had no choice but to appeal to the Soviet Union. Moscow, which just a few years earlier had characterized the 1952 military coup as "just another one of those military take-overs which [they also] had become accustomed to in South America," capitalized on the new opportunity. The Soviet Union's new leader, Nikita Khrushchev, not only agreed to sell weapons to Egypt, but also offered to accept deferred payment in Egyptian cotton and rice, and to help Egypt with an industrial project. The accord was completed in September.[111]

The Cairo-Moscow pact worried Washington. A few days after it was completed, Kermit Roosevelt, the head of the Middle East section of the CIA, met with Nasser and warned him that the arrangement signaled a willingness on the part of Egypt to challenge the United States's role in the Middle East, and that Washington might have to respond with severe diplomatic or economic measures. Specifically, the Eisenhower administration considered rescinding its original offer to help Egypt finance the construction of a new dam at Aswan on the Nile River. The dam, which according to its planners would increase Egypt's cultivable land by one-third and its electrical power by one-half, was one of Nasser's favorite economic development projects. By the end of 1955, however, the Eisenhower administration had concluded that the best way to prevent Egypt from falling into the Communist camp was by helping finance the construction of the Aswan Dam. This decision did not indicate that Washington had given up hope of achieving a rapprochement between Egypt and Israel. In early 1956, Washington sent emissaries to Cairo to pressure Nasser to make peace with Israel. Presuming that if he gave in to Washington's pressure he would sacrifice his and his country's independence, Nasser rejected the request. Finally, after Nasser once again tried to signal his independence by extending diplomatic recognition to China's Communist government in May 1956, Washington decided to punish Nasser by going back on its agreement to help Egypt construct the dam. According to Dulles, the decision, which he announced on July 20, would impede Egypt's attempt to build the dam and as a result bring Nasser's demise as the country's central political figure.[112]

Dulles underestimated Nasser's resolve. Though conscious that Moscow was willing to help Egypt finance the construction of the dam, Nasser opted for a course of action that would not tie him to either superpower. On July 26, he announced that Egypt was nationalizing the Suez Canal Company. The action, declared Nasser, indicated that Egypt would not surrender to the "domination of force and the dollar."[113] Britain and France welcomed Nasser's decision with silent glee. For some time, Prime Minister Anthony Eden had been upset at Nasser for hampering Britain's attempt to organize the defense of the region. Premier Guy Mollet, in turn, resented Nasser's continued support of the Algerian nationalists fighting for Algeria's independence from France. Washington, however, was not ready to resort to force to overthrow Nasser. Such an act, feared Eisenhower and Dulles, could undercut the United States's standing in the Middle East. Consequently, on July 28, the Department of State declared that it was within Egypt's right to nationalize the Suez Canal. During private conversations, Dulles warned the British prime minister that though Washington also wanted to get rid of Nasser, it would not associate itself with any type of military undertaking. These remarks did not deter France and Britain. On October 22, representatives of Britain, France, and Israel met in secret in France to plan a joint attack on Egypt. A week later, Israeli forces attacked Egypt, and within a few days they had routed the Egyptian army on the Sinai peninsula.

Nasser, fearful that the Israeli attack might bring about his political demise, asked Washington for immediate military assistance. On October 30, the Eisenhower administration took the matter to the United Nations and requested a cease-fire and the withdrawal from Egypt by Israel.

Britain and France vetoed Washington's proposed resolution, and for the first time since the end of the 1940s, doubt arose in Washington about the worthiness of NATO. The following day, Anglo-French forces landed in Egypt. Believing that the United States's standing in the Middle East would be severely crippled if it chose to ally itself with the aggressors, Washington threatened Israel with economic and military sanctions, and Britain and France with oil embargoes. For the next few days, Washington continued to pressure the three aggressors to withdraw from Egypt. On November 5, Moscow raised the stakes by sending letters to Israel, Britain, and France warning them that unless they pulled out of Egypt the Soviet Union would use force to restore peace in the area. Finally, on the next day the three invaders bowed to the pressure and agreed to stop the fighting.

By the time the last shots had been fired, political leaders across the international spectrum were acknowledging that conditions in the Middle East had been conspicuously altered in at least two ways. First, they noted that the war had fully exposed France's and Britain's economic and military weaknesses and their considerable dependence on the United States.[114] Second, they conceded that the conflict had empowered the Soviet Union to claim that as one of the world's two strongest entities, its standing on matters that affected the distribution of power in the Middle East could not be taken lightly. In short, by the end of 1956, Middle Eastern leaders no longer had to ponder what type of response their actions would elicit from Washington and London. Instead, they had to consider what type of reply their policies would evoke from Washington and Moscow.

Africa

By 1956 it seemed as if every corner of the world was being contaminated, directly or indirectly, by the tension generated by the rivalry between the United States and the Soviet Union. This perception was not entirely accurate. Africa, a continent that in the 1970s became a platform for the proxy conflicts financed and sanctioned by Washington and Moscow, seemed, in the 1950s, ready to design and follow a course entirely different from that endorsed by either superpower.[115]

With the end of the Second World War in sight, Washington had increased its pressure on Britain and France to break up their empires. Roosevelt had recognized that he could not demand that every state shape its political system according to democratic tenets. He believed, however, that the United States could not tolerate the continued existence of colonialism from its own allies so long as it called for the restoration of sovereign rights and self-government to those who had been forcibly deprived of them. This belief was shared by his successor. Their efforts proved futile, at least initially. Both Paris and London vehemently opposed Washington's appeals by contending that without their respective empires they would not be able to rebuild their badly damaged economies. As the Cold War gained intensity, and Washington concluded that the containment of communism in Southeast Asia was heavily dependent on whether France kept Indochina within its domain, the United States abated its pressure.

Washington's inclination to soften its anticolonial stand did not signify that in Africa Britain and France faced futures devoid of obstacles. Both states had launched their imperialist activities in earnest in 1870, and by 1914 they had resolved most of their territorial conflicts. Britain had attained control over Egypt, Sudan, Uganda, Kenya, Zanzibar, Nigeria, Gold Coast, Sierra Leone, Gambia, Northern and Southern Rhodesia, Swaziland, Basutoland, Nyasaland, and Bechuanaland. France's empire, in turn, extended over Algeria, Morocco, French West Africa, French Equatorial Africa, French Somaliland, and Madagascar.[116] By the end of the 1930s, the limited economic gains spawned by their colonial holdings in Africa forced London and Paris to reevaluate the costs and benefits of preserving them. However, with the war at an end, and the Soviet Union and the United States emerging as the world's new titans, British and French leaders concluded that their countries' abilities to regain some of their past political and economic status were in part dependent on whether they could generate ancillary profits from their colonies. Britain, with the largest colonial holdings in Africa, focused on constructing stronger and more viable colonial states. This aim, for instance, led to the creation, under the control of white settlers, of the Central African Confederation (now Zimbabwe, Zambia, and Malawi) in 1953. France, on the other hand, used its 1946 constitution to integrate its colonies as members of the French Union. This approach enabled France to claim that although its African subjects were not members of independent African states, they could aspire to be citizens of French Overseas. In addition, France sought greater economic integration by establishing a fund for economic development designed to develop its colonies' potential as suppliers and markets, and to connect them more closely to the metropolis. Portugal, which was the third largest holder of colonies in Africa, imposed closer political and economic controls, and promoted Portuguese settlement.[117]

These actions by the European states did not result in the establishment of closer partnerships with their African subjects. As time went by, loosely coordinated African resistance to the postwar colonial policies of the Europeans began to surface. The responses to these challenges varied considerably. Portugal, which was the smallest of the European colonial powers, refused to surrender its colonial domain until the 1970s. Belgium simply decided in 1960 that the costs of protecting its interests in the Congo were too high and left without even attempting to establish a successor government. Britain's responses varied depending on the territory; while it granted independence to Nigeria in 1960 even before Nigerians started to demand it, it considered delaying self-government to East Africa for another 15 years. France's responses also fluctuated. It granted independence to French West Africa without first having to face the wrath of its inhabitants, but it surrendered control over Madagascar only after Madagascarians had mounted an insurrection against colonial rule.

By the beginning of the 1960s, many political leaders in Africa had become convinced that their continent's movement toward independence would give shape to a unique international political situation. At a meeting held in Addis Ababa, Ethiopia, in 1963, representatives of the newly created African states founded the Organization of African Unity (OAU). Inspired by the ideology of Pan-Africanism, its members proposed that the OAU operate to help fulfill four major goals. Its first major task would be to prevent territorial conflict between the newly created African states. Its second function would be to assist in the creation of a united Africa under the protection of a single sovereign ruler. Its third responsibility would be to avoid a fate that very few countries in the third world had been able to elude—being drawn into the camp of either superpower. And its fourth obligation would be to assist in the design of a continent-wide program of economic development that would be closely tied to the international economic order dominated by the United States, Western Europe, and Japan.[118]

Ideals authored by inexperienced political leaders seldom materialize. Starting with the second half of the 1960s and throughout the 1970s, Africa witnessed the perdition provoked by a multitude of factors, with the Cold War rivalry once again playing a central role. During the 1950s and early years of the 1960s, however, Africa was spared the ill effects of such friction. As different African entities labored to break their colonial ties, neither Washington nor Moscow expressed much interest in their fate. For them, Africa was still not a region with immense political potential. The challenges they faced in other parts of the world were perilous enough to thwart any longing they might have had about broadening the scope of their respective political agendas.

A Precarious Moment

Each international system is saturated with contradictions, but not all of them induce immoderate tensions. Cognizant that an international system's survival is dependent on the tensions generated by its predominant contradictions, its leader strives to curb them. It is not unusual, however, for an international entity, in its drive to repress existing contradictions, to unintentionally help generate a new set of contradictions.

Determined to create an international system less treacherous than its progenitor, Roosevelt sought to ensure that the new one would not be afflicted by the contradictions that had plagued the old one. He channeled his country's efforts to guarantee that the power and regimes of the culprit states would be razed, that the major powers would monitor and police international activities, that the United States and the Soviet Union would work together as the international security system's principal entities, that the economies of the states would adhere to the tenets of a world market economy, and that Americans would accept that the United States could no longer renege on its responsibility as the world's most powerful entity. In his haste to carry out these tasks, however, Roosevelt chose to ignore two important matters. First, he disregarded the fact that the United States and the Soviet Union had erected their respective powers on inherently contradictory political and economic structures. And second, he overlooked that some of the foreign policies initiated by his administration, though well intended, threatened to undermine the same political and economic structures that the Communist Party had created to become sovereign in the Soviet Union, and that had enabled the Soviet Union to obtain its superpower status.

Though each international system is affected by numerous contradictions, with one or two governing the foreign policy agendas of its most consequential entities, it is rare that one single contradiction completely eclipses the various contradictions that affect all states. In its drive to ensure it would win the nuclear arms race against Germany and would be able to limit the length and cost of the war, Washington helped conceive the most perilous contradiction the world had ever witnessed. The United States brought the Second World War to an early end by becoming the first international entity to develop nuclear bombs. The Soviet Union, convinced that its capacity to act and preserve its status as a world superpower rested largely on its ability to shoulder the vicissitudes and costs engendered by entering a nuclear arms race, fully committed itself to the challenge. It was not long before the threat evoked by the nuclear arms race, and the weapons that framed it, became so prodigious that the two superpowers were forced to accept that the political applicability of a nuclear arsenal was limited, and to search for alternative instruments. However, because neither superpower dared to drop from the race for fear that the other would try to use its superiority to impose its political will, the nuclear arms race proceeded.

An entity's competence to respond firmly to international threats is in no small measure a function of its ability to prevent the tension at home from rising to an intolerable level. Though the American Congress and public had vehemently opposed the United States's entering the war in Europe and assisting China in its struggle against Japan in the late 1930s, Japan's attack on Pearl Harbor erased the opposition. By the end of the war, the American Congress and public understood that the United States would not be able to relive its past and return to its earlier policy of splendid detachment. The Berlin crisis seemed to convince the American public that on certain occasions the United States might have to risk war to prevent the Soviet Union from becoming the world's sole ruler. This willingness on the part of the American public to support aggressive actions by the United States was reinforced by the initial success of General MacArthur's forces against North Korea. The strength and commitment revealed by the Chinese Communists in late 1950, however, exposed a much starker reality—that though the United States was the most powerful military entity in the international system, its victories against resolute adversaries would not come about cheaply.

Two states, each striving to attain full dominance of the international system, consistently reassess each other's strength and resolve. After a series of bouts in which each party demonstrates its unwillingness to abandon the challenge, each entity must decide whether or not to intensify and expand the rivalry, and how to respond if the other chooses to do so. By brutally thwarting Hungary's attempt to claim its independence from the Soviet Union, Moscow had strengthened its grip over Eastern Europe. This success freed the leaders of the Soviet Union to venture into the Suez Canal crisis to help Nasser elude the snare that Israel, France, and Britain had erected. As the year 1956 moved into its final days, thus, the world was forced to concede once again that the Soviet Union was not a historical aberration prone to retreat at the first sign of a major international provocation. The reputation of the United States at the end of 1956 was no less noteworthy. After having almost single-handedly pressured Japan to accept an unconditional surrender, and having played a critical role in Germany's defeat, the United States assumed the burden of helping Europe and Japan rebuild their economies. As if to warn the world that its power was limitless, the United States became a member of NATO to strengthen Europe's strategic stance, committed its armed forces to a three-year war to avert the military takeover of South Korea by its northern counterpart, and enlarged its nuclear arsenal and tested the world's first hydrogen bomb. Disinclined to stop there, it organized and directed the overthrow of Guatemala's president to hamper the flourishing of communism in that country, threatened Britain and France with an economic embargo to prevent the demise of Egypt's leader, and shored up the armed forces of South Vietnam to protect it and contiguous states from the communist menace.

The raising of stakes in a major struggle can elicit unexpected consequences, primarily because its most immediate effect is an increase in uncertainty, which in turn fosters greater tension. By the start of 1957, the United States and the Soviet Union were poised to elevate their rivalry to a new plateau. The Soviet Union was the first to up the ante by launching, on October 5, 1957, the world's first man-made satellite. From that moment on, and for a long period, both superpowers were caught in a whirl of events from which they seemed unable to escape. The consequences of their actions, as I explain in the next chapter, proved to be exceedingly costly to both superpowers. But only one entity began to recognize, after some 17 years, that in its drive to attain supremacy it might destroy itself. This recognition, and its willingness to deal with the new peril, are what ultimately enabled the United States to exit the Cold War as the only surviving superpower.

CHAPTER FIVE

Exuberance Hindered

How Far to Expand

It has been noted that a state will seek to alter the international system "through territorial, political, and economic expansion until the marginal costs of further change are equal to or greater than the marginal benefits."[1] It has also been proposed that once "an equilibrium between the costs and benefits of further change and expansion is reached, the tendency is for the economic costs of maintaining the status quo to rise faster than the economic capacity to support the status quo."[2] The last proposition is critical. From it, one could infer that a hegemon augments considerably the chance of its own downfall by remaining committed to increasing its power after the costs and benefits of further change and expansion have reached an equilibrium.

In 1987, six years after the above propositions were offered, Paul Kennedy wrote: "[T]he United States now runs the risk, so familiar to historians of the rise and fall of previous Great Powers, of what might roughly be called 'imperial overstretch': that is to say, decision-makers in Washington must face the awkward and enduring fact that the sum total of the United States's global interests and obligations is nowadays far larger than the country's power to defend them all simultaneously." Kennedy concluded his analysis on a hopeful note. He stated that given "the considerable array of strengths still possessed by the United States, it ought not, in theory, to be beyond the talents of successive administrations to arrange the diplomacy and strategy of this readjustment so that it can . . . bring into balance . . . the nation's commitments and the nation's power."[3] That same year, Walter Russell Mead, in a highly critical analysis of the United States's domestic and foreign policies, concluded that the tides of history were flowing against the American Empire and "that no president and no Congress could stop them" from bringing about its demise. He also claimed that the United States had become powerful not because of its intelligence nor because it overpowered the rest of the world, but because of its wealth and the exhaustion of the rest of the world.[4]

As I intend to demonstrate in the next two chapters, some of these arguments do not accurately depict the United States's international experience. Before a major power decides whether to continue its expansion beyond the point of equilibrium, it must ascertain whether it is the sole leader of the international system, or whether it shares the leadership with other bona fide rivals. If a state dominates the international system and estimates that its power is unlikely to be contested by an upcoming rival for some time, then the hegemon will simply attempt to protect the status quo. A state that shares control of the international system with one or more powerful rivals, however, encounters a very different situation. Theoretically, such a state faces three choices: i) to relinquish its role as the international system's protector, ii) to try to maintain the status quo in the international system, or iii) to try to change the structure of the international system. The common denominator for all three cases is each state's relative economic capacity.

A state will relinquish its role as one of the international system's protectors only after it recognizes and accepts that it no longer possesses the economic means to carry out its responsibilities. Historically, most international leaders have been reluctant to concede that they were incapable of sustaining their roles. Those that have finally accepted their new fates have done so only after imposing on themselves exceedingly high costs. Britain is a prime example. Though by the end of the First World War Britain was already too weak to retain its function as the international system's principal guardian, it did not yield to this fact until the start of the Cold War and after having absorbed immense losses. More complex are the conditions that dictate whether an international leader will actively strive to preserve an international system or attempt to alter it. A leader will keep on safeguarding an international system so long as it believes that the system serves its interests.[5] That same leader will try to change the system if it concludes that protecting the system has become too burdensome and has weakened its own capacity to tackle ponderous domestic economic and social problems. Which option the leader will choose depends on whether it: i) believes that it still possesses the economic potential to raise the international stakes substantially and that its rival is not strong enough to meet the challenge; and ii) assumes that its adversary, upon recognizing that it is being outbid, will not opt for a drastic solution to avert the altering of the international system.

One of my central arguments has been that the past constantly informs leaders about the types of policies they should, and should not, implement. I also claimed that one of the major advantages of a state having open and competitive domestic political and economic systems is that they force its leaders to continually reassess their policies and to try to amend errors. In this chapter and the next one, I propose that the United States proceeded along the last two policy paths I just delineated, and that its willingness to experiment with such disparate alternatives can be attributed to the nature of its political and economic systems. In this chapter I argue that during the late 1960s and early 1970s, the Nixon administration came under intense domestic pressure to reduce the burden the United States had been shouldering for serving as one of the two guardians of the international system. Mindful that the United States's economic capacity to maintain the international status quo was increasing slower than the economic costs it was accruing in its effort to achieve such an end, the Nixon administration sought to persuade the United States's allies, the Soviet Union, and the People's Republic of China that it would also be in their interests to replace the bipolar system with a multipolar one. By the early 1980s, the direction of the domestic pressure had changed. Fearful that the power and image of the United States had been harmed by a series of foreign policy failures and convinced that the Soviet Union was determined to alter the international system, the American public and Congress embraced the claim that Washington had to launch a new drive to offset both developments. In chapter 6, I focus on the attempts by the Carter administration to expand on the Nixon administration's foreign policy initiatives, and on the negative effects of its policies on the United States's international reputation and domestic political, economic, and social agendas. I then propose that the Reagan administration, enthused by the latest domestic political winds, decided to replace the foreign policy doctrine initiated by the Nixon administration with a more daring one. Believing that the Soviet Union had relied on a policy of deception to increase its nuclear and political power, the Reagan administration strove to remove the Soviet Union from its lead ership role by raising the costs both would have to bear to remain co-leaders of the international system. The Reagan administration estimated that the Soviet Union lacked the economic capability to match the raising of the ante, and assumed that Moscow would not rely on violent means to prevent the United States from attempting to alter the international system.

A Race to the Edge of the Abyss

In international politics, the way a state's power is perceived does not always correspond with its actual military or economic capabilities. This kind of dissonance can wreak havoc in the affairs of competing states. Between 1957 and 1961, the common perception among the uninformed public was that there was a missile gap between the United States and the

Soviet Union, and that the United States was trailing. At the end of 1961, the Kennedy administration revealed that the gap favored the United States, not the Soviet Union. Less than a year later, Moscow tried to revive the illusion by deploying some of its nuclear missiles in Cuba. For 13 days the leaders of the two superpowers watched one another intently, each trying to force its foe to blink first. Moscow finally yielded; but its acquiescence was followed by the most costly arms race ever experienced in the history of the world.

In late October 1953, President Eisenhower approved a statement that altered the national security policy of the United States. He ordered that: "In the event of hostilities, the United States will consider nuclear weapons to be available for use as other munitions."[6] Two factors shaped Eisenhower's new strategic policy. First, after leading the Allied forces in Europe during the Second World War and then learning about the devastation caused by the dropping of two atomic bombs on Japan, he had concluded that the United States would never engage again in another full-scale conventional war. Second, he was determined to reduce the size of the federal budget and believed that the most effective way to achieve this goal was by contracting the military budget. As he noted on several occasions, military budgets should never expand beyond what a prosperous economy could support.[7] He believed that the United States's military could help accomplish this end by increasing its reliance on nuclear weapons.

This change in policy raised the question: Under what circumstances would the United States employ its nuclear weapons? Eisenhower rejected the idea of using them for preventive purposes. "A preventive war," he remarked during a press conference, ". . . is an impossibility today . . . I don't believe there is such a thing; and frankly, I wouldn't even listen to anyone seriously that came in and talked about such a thing."[8] But his answer failed to address the issue fully. This responsibility fell, initially, on the shoulders of Secretary of State John Foster Dulles. In early 1954, while speaking at the Council of Foreign Relations in New York, he observed that the "way to deter aggression is for the free community to be willing and able to respond vigorously at places and with means of its own choosing."[9] Though Dulles made it clear that the Eisenhower administration had no intention of turning every local war into a world war, he also emphasized that it was ready to use air and naval power and a wide range of atomic weapons for strategic and tactical purposes. He deliberately chose not to disclose in what regions and under what circumstances the administration would use the United States's great nuclear capacity to retaliate. This form of uncertainty, he argued, would force a potential aggressor to think carefully before it decided to initiate an offensive act.

In early October 1957, the Soviet Union announced that it had launched the first man-made satellite. This statement came on the heels of an earlier communiqué in which Moscow revealed that the Soviet Union had successfully tested an intercontinental ballistic missile (ICBM). The events marred the United States's image as the world's most technologically advanced state.[10] Eisenhower, who for years had sharply separated the problem of satellites in space from that of ballistic missiles with warheads, appointed a special assistant for the president for science. In his new post, James Killian organized programs that in a three-year period solidified the United States's leadership in land-based and submarine-based strategic missiles. But Eisenhower also concluded that the Soviet challenge required a more immediate response. He found his answer on the other side of the Atlantic.

In 1949, Germans approved two different constitutions, one for West Germany and the other for East Germany. Both constitutions laid claim to Berlin. The constitution for the western side, formally referred to as the Federal Republic of Germany (FRG), declared Berlin to be a land under its jurisdiction. The other Germany, known as the German Democratic Republic (GDR), proclaimed Berlin its capital city. In 1955, the Western allies formally agreed to end the occupation of the FRG. A few months later, the Soviet Union reached a similar agreement with the GDR. During this period, one issue that consistently troubled the western side was the civilian traffic to and from the western sectors of Berlin, which was regulated by the GDR. The GDR did not always make it easy for West Germans to access Berlin. But since the Soviets had lifted the blockade on Berlin in 1949, the two sides had been able to control the strain incited by this matter. In late November 1958, it became evident that the Berlin issue had been elevated to a much higher plateau.

About two months after the Soviet Union had announced the launching of Sputnik, the NATO Council announced that it had accepted the Eisenhower administration's offer to deploy U.S. medium-range Thor and Jupiter ballistic missiles in Europe. The new U.S. missiles would be stationed in different parts of Europe, including the FRG. The decision did not surprise Moscow. Aware that by deploying medium-range missiles in Europe, Washington would be able to strike Soviet territory more rapidly than Moscow would be able to hit the United States, Nikita Khrushchev had proposed, prior to NATO's decision, the establishment of a zone in Central Europe free of nuclear weapons.[11] After his proposal had failed to elicit the response he had hoped, Khrushchev raised the stakes. In November 1958, he demanded the termination of the occupation of Berlin, either by the GDR's assuming full control of the city or by converting West Berlin into a demilitarized zone. He warned that if an acceptable solution were not reached, the Soviet Union would withdraw from Berlin and transfer all of its responsibilities to the GDR.

Washington paid careful attention to the threat. It recognized that if the Soviets passed on all of their obligations to the GDR, the West might not be successful at negotiating a new agreement regarding transit to West Berlin. Washington, however, refused to cave in and, with its allies, rejected Moscow's ultimatum. Moscow responded in March 1959 by revoking its demands and calling for a meeting to resolve once and for all the Berlin issue. Khrushchev traveled to the United States in September, and after a series of meetings, he and Eisenhower agreed to put aside the Berlin problem until 1960, at which time representatives of the major powers would gather in Paris to try to settle the matter. At first glance, thus, it would seem as if Moscow had once again decided to retreat after realizing that it lacked the means to confront a united West. This verdict, however, would be premature.

The year 1959 opened with a new government in Cuba. After two years of battling the government of Fulgencio Batista, thousands of guerrillas, led by Fidel Castro, marched victoriously into Cuba's capital, Havana. Unsure about Castro's ideological creed and political intentions, Washington decided to play it safe by granting diplomatic recognition to the new government. It was not long before Castro's government disclosed that it had no intention of kowtowing to the United States. In just a few months Castro's government redesigned Cuba's military by replacing elements loyal to Batista with a peasant force committed to the revolution, and ordered the termination of the U.S. military mission in Cuba. In the political arena, the new Cuban government granted all political parties, including the Communist Party, the right to organize. More importantly, it ordered the concentration of executive and legislative powers in the hands of a cabinet led by Castro. It took equally radical steps in the economic field. It started by nationalizing the telephone company, a subsidiary of the International Telephone and Telegraph Company, and soon followed this action by announcing a major agrarian reform. By November, Secretary of State Christian Herter had concluded that the United States could not count on Castro's voluntarily adopting "policies and attitudes consistent with minimum Washington security requirements and policy interests. . . ." He then recommended that the United States help build within Cuba a "coherent opposition" made up of parties interested in achieving "political and economic progress within a framework of good United States–Cuban relations. . . ."[12]

After being warned by the U.S. ambassador to Cuba that a blockade of the island would only reinforce Castro's power, Eisenhower ordered the Department of State to announce that the administration would observe a policy of nonintervention. However, Eisenhower's willingness to tolerate the presence of a Cuban government that consistently scorned the United States eroded rapidly. It came to an end in March 1960, a month after a large Soviet delegation had finalized a major trade and financial agreement with Cuba during an official visit to the island. Upon learning about the event, the U.S. president ordered the CIA to design a plan to overthrow Castro's government. Though relations between the United States and Cuba continued to deteriorate, the CIA could not persuade Eisenhower that its anti-Castro plan would succeed in overthrowing Castro and replacing him with a moderate government capable of maintaining internal stability. To make matters worse, Moscow decided to engage in some saber rattling by warning Washington that it was ready to use its Soviet military arsenal to protect Cuba against U. S. aggression. As 1960 came to an end and the Cuban government continued to voice its independence from Washington and to develop closer ties with the world's second superpower, the United States prepared itself to welcome a new president.

John F. Kennedy moved into the White House backed by a sparse résumé. As a congressman and a senator, he had gained notoriety more for his appearance and his family's wealth than for his legislative acumen. His modest accomplishments did not prevent him from claiming that under his leadership the United States would embark on a "New Frontier," and that a different foreign policy would define a substantial part of it. He proposed that the United States's central objective should be to ensure not that the world become a reflection of the United States, but that neither the Soviet Union nor the People's Republic of China become the world's dominant force. This declaration forced members of his administration to reflect on a series of related issues. Since the days of the Truman administration, Washington had stressed that though it reluctantly accepted Moscow's domination of Eastern Europe, it would not tolerate any attempt on the part of Moscow to usurp the sovereignty of Western European states. Any doubts that might have lingered in Khrushchev's mind about Washington's resolve should have been abated by Eisenhower, when he underscored that he would not remove U.S. forces from West Berlin. With regard to Latin America, Washington had been equally forceful, until Castro came to power. It would be for the Kennedy administration to decide whether the United States could continue to tolerate the presence of a Communist regime less than 100 miles south of Florida. More importantly, the presence of the Castro government forced Kennedy and his administration to ask: What measures was the United States prepared to take to keep Latin America free of communist regimes?

The matter became more complicated as Washington pondered the United States's relationship with Asia. By the start of 1951, Washington had left very little doubt that it would oppose any Soviet or Chinese efforts to violate Japan's, the Philippines', or South Korea's sovereign rights. Likewise, by assisting France in its failed attempt to regain control over Indochina, and by siding with South Vietnam after France had been forced to retreat from the region, Washington seemed to warn that it was prepared to broaden the scope of its involvement in Asia. The United

States's decision to assist South Vietnam, however, begged answers to two questions: Which other Asian countries, besides those already under its shield, would the United States help if they were to come under the threat of a communist takeover? And assuming that one or more of the Asian countries that the United States had decided to protect found themselves threatened by a communist takeover, what measures would the United States take to prevent such an outcome? The problem became markedly more complex with regard to Africa. Until the start of the 1960s, both superpowers had paid little attention to developments in Africa. This did not mean, however, that if either the Soviet Union or China opted to broaden its sphere of influence by moving into Africa, Washington would tolerate a change in the status quo.

The Kennedy administration recognized some of these problems. Like his predecessor, Kennedy believed that the power of the United States depended primarily on its material capabilities. However, he also emphasized that these capabilities were of little value unless the United States proved that it was prepared to use them, and did so effectively. The combination of material power and resolve was at the heart of the Kennedy administration's foreign policy in two areas. First, it meant that failure on the part of the United States to respond to a Soviet threat in an area that the United States considered to be central to its interests "would free their hands for almost any kind of intervention that they might want to try in other parts of the world."[13] It also signified that Washington could not afford to disregard areas that in the past it had considered to be part of the United States's periphery. "If you don't pay attention to the periphery," remarked Secretary of State Dean Rusk, "the periphery changes. And the first thing you know the periphery is the center. . . . [W]hat happens in one place cannot help but affect what happens in another."[14] Walt Rostow, who became the administration's principal foreign policy theorist, expanded on Rusk's comments by noting that "major losses of territory or resources would make it harder for the U.S. to create the kind of world environment it desires, [and] might generate defeatism among governments and peoples in the non-Communist world."[15]

The second assumption generated a new set of issues. The premise should have pressed the Kennedy administration to decide which governments it was prepared to assist in the periphery, how it would assist them and to what extent, and how it would pay for the additional expenses the new policy would generate. With respect to which political regimes it was ready to help, the Kennedy administration remarked that its principal objective was to support "progressive" elements, and that it was not too concerned with whether they favored the U.S. position in the Cold War, private enterprise, or democratic institutions. So long as these governments remained autonomous, noted the administration, the United States should have no difficulty developing peaceful relationships with them. The Kennedy administration, however, never meant to suggest that the United States was prepared to accept the creation of just any kind of government. On the contrary, it concluded that the United States had to be ready to intervene in the domestic affairs of states anywhere in the periphery to ensure that they developed "along lines broadly consistent with our concepts of individual liberty and government based on consent."[16] Regarding the type of assistance that it was prepared to provide, the Kennedy administration contended that the United States's standard approach to warfare would not enable its forces to win wars against unconventional adversaries. To fight guerrillas, the United States had to learn and employ the same tactics they employed. This meant training special forces who would be versed in the "techniques of political, social, and economic action as well as irregular warfare. . . ."[17] The Kennedy administration also concluded that to immunize countries at the periphery against communism, the United States would have to help them create more equitable domestic environments.

Any state that considers broadening the scope of its national interest must first assess whether its economy can withstand the expansion. The Eisenhower administration had believed that the increase in the allocation of resources to defense could be achieved only at the expense of other priorities. The Kennedy administration was less concerned than its predecessor about deficits and inflation, and assumed that the U.S. economy could bear the extra burdens of expanding its defense commitments. As its leader claimed shortly after becoming president: "Our arms must be adequate to meet our commitments and ensure our security, without being bound by arbitrary budget ceilings."[18] Kennedy's comment reveals his inability to grasp the types of tensions that his expansionist foreign policy doctrine would begin to generate and that would severely weaken the United States's power by the decade's end. To explain the evolution of these tensions, I must focus on the economic challenges and opportunities the United States faced as Kennedy entered the White House in early 1961.

By 1958, the United States's efforts to help reconstruct Europe and Japan had paid off. The European states gained the financial strength to close their payments gap and accumulate the reserves necessary to support their respective currencies at fixed prices against the dollar. In March 1957, France, the FRG, Belgium, Italy, the Netherlands, and Luxembourg agreed, with the backing of the United States, to create the European Economic Community (EEC). By the end of 1958, these states and Britain had moved to accept full convertibility of their currencies, and had started to cut off tariffs and eliminate trade quotas. In the Far East, Japan was starting its own impressive economic growth.[19]

But not all was well in 1958. The United States's balance of payments had dropped sharply into deficit, and gold began to leave the U.S. Treasury in substantial quantities.[20] Though the United States still held a surplus in its goods and services and in investment income accounts, they were offset by foreign aid, military expenditures, and private overseas investments.[21] The continued presence of a substantial deficit and gold drain in 1960 persuaded some economic analysts to question whether the United States should reconsider its financial policy. Possibly the most detailed analysis of the international monetary situation was presented by Robert Triffin, an economist at Yale University.

According to Triffin, there was a fundamental contradiction between the mechanism of liquidity creation and confidence in the system.[22] In order to finance imbalances and to have capital in case of war, every country needed international reserves. Though since the end of the Second World War many countries had increased their reserves by accumulating gold and foreign exchange, they had done so without first agreeing on a set of rules that would regulate the world's official money supply. Instead, they had relied on the unwritten rule that the United States would provide liquidity with its balance-of-payments deficits. Triffin warned that a costly contradiction would ensue if this dependency were not ended. As the United States accumulated more debts or was required to pay more from its reserves in response to the decisions by other governments, foreign depositors would lose confidence in its ability to continue redeeming its commitments. If foreign depositors stopped having faith in the system, they would resort to financial speculation. The end result of this process, cautioned Triffin, could be a debacle similar to that experienced in the early 1930s. He then added that though the United States could stop the outflow of gold by bringing to an end its balance-of-payments deficits, this action could lead to a decrease in the rate of liquidity and as a result slow down world economic growth. As an alternative, he proposed replacing the decentralized financial regime with one managed by the IMF. He believed that by placing the control of the financial system in the hands of the IMF, the world supply would no longer risk becoming a "casualty of decisions taken unilaterally in reserve-currency countries or of instabilities due to shifts in confidence in national currencies and gold."[23]

Not every economist agreed with Triffin's recommendation. Milton Friedman, for instance, presented a simpler alternative. "The single and most effective way to make a crisis of this kind impossible," he remarked during a Congressional hearing, "is to introduce a system of free market exchange rates. That would provide an automatic and effective adjustment mechanism for changes in international trade. . . ."[24] Friedman's contention that the United States had an international payments deficit because the dollar was overvalued was supported by Hendrik Houthakker's comparative analysis of the purchasing power of the dollar and the German deutschmark. Houthakker established that in terms of purchasing power, the value of the dollar should be 22 percent lower.[25]

The Kennedy administration was not prepared either to relinquish the United States's role as the world's financier or to promote the adoption of a system of free market exchange rates. Guided by C. Douglas Dillon, who was at the helm of the Department of Treasury, the Kennedy administration held fast to three beliefs. First, it remained convinced that the international economic system designed and directed by the United States had brought about major benefits to the free world. Second, convinced that there was no grave liquidity shortage in the world and that the dollar was not seriously overvalued, it opposed going off gold or devaluing the dollar. These actions, it noted, would destroy the international monetary system, and the world would once again risk being afflicted by trade wars and disastrous levels of inflation. And finally, though it acknowledged that the United States was assuming a major burden for serving as the world banker, it was convinced that the costs were more than offset by the benefits.[26] Guided by these beliefs, the Kennedy administration assumed that it could ameliorate the costs of broadening the United States's international involvement by inducing rapid economic growth. It also reasoned that the increase in productivity, coupled with the speeding up of the liberalization of world trade, would help solve the balance-of-payment problem.

Kennedy began to broaden the scope of the United States's international commitments immediately after he assumed power. Persuaded by Rostow's contention that the struggle between capitalism and communism would be substantially defined by each faction's ability to generate political and economic development in the Third World, the new president immediately set his sights on Africa. Though the Soviet Union's involvement in the region had been limited, Kennedy feared that Khrushchev would turn Africa into the new battleground for his "wars of national liberation."

The United States faced several challenges in Africa; its most pressing one, however, was the turmoil in the Congo.[27] Within hours after attaining independence on June 30, 1960, Congolese troops rebelled against their white officers. In short time, sustained violence and random brutality ravaged the country. Its leader, Patrice Lumumba, traveled to Washington to lobby for support from the United States, but after Eisenhower refused to meet him, the Congolese leader accepted Moscow's offer of military aid and advisers. By the fall, however, a new Congolese leader had placed Lumumba under house arrest, and expelled the Soviets. Two weeks after taking office, Kennedy proposed the release of all political prisoners and the reconvening of the Congolese parliament to choose a coalition government. The CIA, afraid that after his release from prison Lumumba would quickly regain power and turn the Congo into a Communist state, ordered that its plot to assassinate the Congolese leader be carried out. On February 13, the world learned of Lumumba's death, and Kennedy, who had not been informed of the assassination plan, was publicly accused by African leaders of orchestrating the act.[28]

Kennedy's fortunes did not improve as he sought to address an international problem closer to home. In March 1961, he announced the establishment of a major financial aid program. Through the Alliance for Progress program, he pledged some $20 million to assist the economies of Latin American states. To ensure that no one would misread the intent of the new program, he noted that tyrannies, such as the governments ruling Cuba and the Dominican Republic, would not qualify as recipients of financial aid.[29] He soon learned that a leader's worth is measured not by his promises but by the effect of his actions. While campaigning against Richard Nixon in 1960, Kennedy had accused the Eisenhower administration of allowing Castro to come to power, and had promised that if elected he would return Cuba to the "Cubans." In mid-April 1961, just two years after Castro and his guerrillas had toppled the Batista government, and two months after Kennedy had been publicly labeled a murderer by many Africans, 1,400 Cuban exiles, trained by the CIA, disembarked on the island, at the Bay of Pigs, with the intent of mounting a revolt against the new political regime. A few days later the world learned that the Cuban government had defeated the invaders.[30]

Sometimes the failures of a new leader tempt rivals to engage in perilous activities. The Bay of Pigs event did not undermine Kennedy's reputation in the United States.[31] Abroad, however, Kennedy's blunder gave Khrushchev the break he had been eagerly awaiting. For some time, East Germany had been losing some of its best-educated professionals and trained workers to West Berlin. Fearful that unless he helped stop the talent drain, East Germany's economy would be severely harmed, Khrushchev decided to settle the matter on his terms. At a summit conference held in Vienna in June 1961, Khrushchev demanded that Kennedy assent to a German peace treaty, an end to the occupation regime, and the transformation of West Berlin into a free city.[32] The Soviet leader made it clear that unless the Western powers agreed to his terms, the Soviet Union was prepared to sign a peace treaty with the GDR that would transfer full responsibility for developing new agreements with the West regarding the city to the GDR. Khrushchev, aware that the West feared that the GDR might not agree to share responsibility for the ruling of Berlin, warned that if the Allied forces were to violate East Germany's borders after the signing of the Soviet-GDR treaty, Moscow would meet force with force. "[I]f the United States wanted war," he admonished, "that is your problem."[33] As if to underscore his resolve to oust the Allied forces from Berlin, Khrushchev increased the Soviet military budget by one-third shortly after he returned to Moscow from Vienna.

Kennedy immediately recognized that he could not afford politically to cave in to Khrushchev. On July 25, he reaffirmed the United States's commitment to West Berlin by stating that "an attack upon the city will be regarded as an attack upon us all. . . ."[34] He also requested authorization from Congress to increase the military budget by $3 billion and to double the draft. The U.S. public strongly endorsed Kennedy's decision.[35] Less than three weeks later, the Soviet Union and the GDR cut off the two Berlins with barbed wire fences and started to build the Berlin Wall. Though Washington and its allies responded with a barrage of diplomatic protests, they ultimately decided that they had no choice but to accept the wall.

The strain generated by the Congo crisis, the Bay of Pigs fiasco, and the Berlin Wall proved to be minor compared to the international tension two very different events were about to spawn. Presidents abhor being entangled in their predecessor's plight. In matters of foreign affairs, however, they rarely have the freedom to discard them as unsolicited nuisances. Kennedy walked into the White House convinced that the Eisenhower administration had overextended the United States in Southeast Asia. It did not matter. Following France's retreat in 1954, the United States had committed itself to protecting South Vietnam, and the new administration could not rescind the pledge.[36] To do so would raise doubts about the new president's will to stand against a communist threat. [37] The day before the presidential inauguration, Eisenhower warned Kennedy that Communist China and North Vietnam were determined to destroy Laos's independence. Should Laos fall to the Communists, added the departing president, it would be just a question of time before South Vietnam, Cambodia, Thailand, and Burma would experience a similar fate.[38] Initially, Kennedy concurred with Eisenhower's advice. In March he called for an end to the hostilities in Laos and the beginning of negotiations. Just as he was focusing on Laos, however, he realized that though Eisenhower had not uttered a word about Vietnam during their last meeting, that was the country in which the United States was likely to face its major challenge. In late January, Kennedy had received a report indicating that the South Vietnamese government risked being toppled by the Communists unless the United States expanded its support of Diem. In April, Rostow wrote a confidential memorandum to the president stressing that if the United States had to commit its forces in Southeast Asia, it should "do so in Vietnam rather than Laos."[39] In May, Kennedy approved National Security Action Memorandum 52. This decision marked the first time he would have a chance to test his claim that to win wars against guerrilla forces, the United States had to employ the means used by its adversary. The memorandum called for the sending of 400 Special Forces to Vietnam to engage in covert warfare against North Vietnam in order to prevent Communist domination of South Vietnam.

By the end of 1961, as he realized that he would need to send additional

U.S. troops to save South Vietnam, Kennedy began to recognize the burden his earlier rhetoric was starting to impose on his administration. During his inaugural speech he had stated that the United States had to be prepared to pay any price and bear any burden in the defense of freedom. Now, the Pentagon was telling him that the only way the United States would be able to protect South Vietnam was by sending large numbers of U.S. forces. Kennedy vetoed the request but authorized significant increases in military equipment such as helicopters, transport aircraft, and light aviation. He also asked the Diem government to accept an American "share in the decision-making process in the political, economic, and military fields as they affect the security situation."[40]

Kennedy's decision did not stop the thrust toward greater involvement. In July 1962, as the United States and North Vietnam were getting ready to end their negotiations regarding Laos, the U.S. negotiator, Averell W. Harriman, offered a neutrality agreement concerning Vietnam. North Vietnam replied that it would accept a cease-fire, form a coalition government with the South, conduct talks to reunify the country, and hold new elections if the United States agreed to withdraw its advisers and if the great powers guaranteed Vietnam's neutrality and independence. The Kennedy administration, which by then had deployed 11,000 U.S. military personnel, 300 military aircraft, 120 helicopters, and additional heavy weapons in South Vietnam, rejected the offer. It had concluded that if the United States left, the Communists, because of their strength in the countryside, would win the elections and consolidate their power throughout the entire country.[41]

By the fall of 1962, Kennedy was no longer an unseasoned leader. The crisis in the Congo, the Bay of Pigs fiasco, the dispute over Berlin, and the conflict in Vietnam had turned him into a more deliberate and thoughtful decision-maker. However, the international hazards he had encountered during the first 20 months of his presidency would pale when compared with the challenge he was about to face. On October 14, 1962, the president was informed that U.S. analysts had concluded that the Soviet Union was installing in Cuba nuclear missiles that could reach parts of the eastern and southern sections of the United States. For seven days Kennedy and his advisers evaluated options ranging from surprise air strikes against the missiles in Cuba, to direct negotiations with the Soviets. For Kennedy, the central challenge was to design a response that would enable his administration to protect both the political and strategic interests of the United States without sparking a major confrontation with the Soviet Union elsewhere in the world. His predicament is aptly illustrated by a conversation he had with General Maxwell D. Taylor, the chairman of the Joint Chiefs of Staff, a few days after the Soviet missiles had been detected. Taylor began the discussion by summarizing his colleagues' recommendations.

From the outset I would say that we found we were united on the military requirement: we could not accept Cuba as a missile base; that we should either eliminate or neutralize the missiles there and prevent any others coming in. From a military point of view that meant three things. First, attack with the benefit of surprise those known missiles and offensive weapons that we knew about. Second, we continue surveillance then to see what the effect would be. And third, a blockade to prevent the others from coming in. [42]

The general then added that he and the chiefs recognized that the actions they were proposing could generate political problems, and he acknowledged that they did not know how to address them. Before the other chiefs were able to express their own views, Kennedy presented his interpretation of the problem.

If we attack Cuban missiles, or Cuba, in any way, it gives them a clear line to take Berlin. . . . We would be regarded as the trigger-happy Americans who lost Berlin. We would have no support among our allies. We would affect the West German's attitude toward us. And [people would believe] that we lost Berlin because we didn't have the guts to endure a situation in Cuba. After all, Cuba is 5[,000] or 6,000 miles from them. They don't give a damn about Cuba. But they do care about Berlin and about their own security. So they would say that we endangered their interests and security. . . . If we go and take them out on a quick air strike, we neutralize the chance of danger to the United States of these missiles being used, and we prevent a situation from arising, at least within Cuba, where the Cubans themselves have the means of exercising some degree of authority in this hemisphere. On the other hand, we increase the chance greatly. . . . [of] a reprisal from the Soviet Union, there always is—[of] their just going in and taking Berlin by force. Which leaves me only one alternative, which is to fire nuclear weapons— which is a hell an alternative—and begin a nuclear exchange, with all this happening. [43]

After presenting the pros and cons of a blockade, Kennedy, in frustration, acknowledged that the United States did not have any satisfactory alternatives.

[O]ur problem is not merely Cuba but it is also Berlin. And when we recognize the importance of Berlin to Europe and recognize the importance of our allies to us, that's what has made this thing be a dilemma for 3 days. Otherwise, our answer would be quite easy. [44]

On the evening of October 22, Kennedy announced that the United States was imposing a naval quarantine on Cuba to prevent the delivery of additional Soviet offensive weapons, and was demanding that the Soviets remove the missiles they had already deployed. He started his address by noting that the "secret, swift, and extraordinary build-up of Communist missiles—in an area well known to have a special and historical relationship to the United States and the nations of the Western Hemisphere, in violation of Soviet assurances, and in defiance of American and hemispheric policy—this sudden, clandestine decision to station strategic weapons for the first time outside of Soviet soil—is a deliberately provocative and unjustified change in the status quo which cannot be accepted by this country if our courage and our commitment are ever to be trusted again by either friend or foe." To remove any doubts about the United States's resolve, he added: "I have directed the Armed Forces to prepare for any eventualities." He then warned Moscow that the United States would "regard any nuclear missile launched from Cuba against any nation in the Western Hemisphere as an attack by the Soviet Union on the United States, requiring a full retaliatory response upon the Soviet Union." Finally, in an attempt to ensure that Cuba would not pose any future threats to the United States, he noted that his administration would ask the United Nations to supervise "the prompt dismantling and withdrawal of all offensive weapons in Cuba. . . ."[45] That same day, a U.S. emissary delivered to the Soviet leader a copy of the speech and a personal letter from Kennedy.

For the next few days, as the world waited wondering whether it would witness the first nuclear showdown, Washington and Moscow engaged in a test of wills. In one message to Kennedy, the Soviet leader warned that "the Soviet Government cannot give instructions to the captains of the Soviet vessels bound to Cuba to observe the instructions of the American naval forces blockading the island. Our instructions to Soviet mariners are strictly to observe the generally recognized norms of navigation in international waters and not to retreat from them by even one step. . . . [I]f the American side violates these rules . . . [w]e will then be forced for our part to take the measures which we deem necessary and adequate in order to protect our rights. For this we have all that is necessary."[46] Finally, following a series of private threats and counterthreats between the leaders of the two superpowers, the world was able to take a deep breath of relief. Early on the morning of October 28, a Soviet ship en route to the interception zone stopped. A few hours later Khrushchev broadcasted to the world over Radio Moscow his message to Kennedy. The Soviet leader informed the U.S. president that the Soviet government, "in addition to previously issued instructions on the cessation of further work at building sites for the weapons, has issued a new order on the dismantling of the weapons which you describe as 'offensive,' and their crating and return to the Soviet Union." Kennedy replied that same afternoon. In his letter, he both welcomed Khrushchev's decision and proposed that representatives of the two governments meet in Geneva or elsewhere to discuss questions relating to the proliferation of nuclear weapons, efforts for a new nuclear test ban, and whether wider measures of disarmament could be agreed upon and put into operation as soon as possible.[47]

The Cuban missile crisis reminded leaders in Moscow and Washington that the nuclear age had reduced dramatically their margin for error. They had averted the start of a nuclear war, but there was no guarantee that they would be as fortunate the next time. The crisis had two additional interrelated effects. Its first effect was on the Soviet Union's nuclear strategic doctrine, which in turn affected the nuclear arms race between the two superpowers.

By the end of 1962, the United States possessed a total of 294 ICBMs, 144 submarine-launched ballistic missiles (SLBMs), and 600 long-range bombers. The Soviet Union, on the other hand, had only 75 ICBMs, just a few SLBMs, and 190 long-range bombers. The Cuban missile crisis convinced Moscow that it could not continue to tolerate the imbalance. As noted by a top Soviet diplomat, the "Americans will never be able to do this to us again."[48] Still, it would be two more years before Moscow's central leaders would able to agree on a common strategy. To give way to the new era, Khrushchev, who according to one of his domestic rivals had "provoked the deepest crisis [and] carried the world to the brink of nuclear war" by ordering the deployment of Soviet missiles in Cuba, was ousted in October 1964. [49] The change that followed was dramatic. In 1964, the United States and the Soviet Union allocated $47.8 billion and $43.6 billion, respectively, for defense; five years later, Washington allotted $81.4 billion, while Moscow earmarked $89.8 billion for defense.[50] During that same period, the number of U.S. ICBMs increased from 834 to 1,054, while the number of Soviet ICBMs went from 200 to 1,050.[51] But this was not the only challenge confronting the United States in 1969. With a new administration occupying the White House, Washington was beginning to recognize that the future of the United States as the international system's hegemon would also be affected by how effective it was at resolving two other critical problems: the Vietnam War and the diminishing potency of the United States economy.

The Costs of Intemperance

In February 1965, the United States found itself at a crossroad in Vietnam. As reported by Lyndon Johnson's national security adviser, McGeorge Bundy, conditions in Vietnam were grim. The Viet Cong had proven to be astonishingly energetic and persistent, and seemed convinced that the United States did "not have the will and force and patience and determination" to gain the upper hand. Bundy added that the international prestige of the United States would be severely undermined if it withdrew from Vietnam. He concluded by noting that though the struggle in Vietnam would be long, the United States had no choice but to follow a policy of "sustained reprisal."[52]

During the early days of the Johnson administration, its central foreign policy makers assumed that by bombing North Vietnam the United States would be able to stop the infiltration of supplies to the Viet Cong, harden the resolve of the South Vietnamese forces, and demonstrate that the United States was determined to contain communism. On August 10, 1964, the U.S. Senate passed the Southeast Asia Resolution, giving the president the power to use whatever amount of force he needed to protect South Vietnam and other Southeast Asian states. However, by the end of the year, after the United States had conducted several bombing raids against North Vietnam, many members within the administration were beginning to accept that the war could not be won from the air alone. In February 1965, the commander of the U.S. forces in Vietnam, General William Westmoreland, requested that he be given two battalions of marines to protect the U.S. air base at Danang. In early March, 3,500 U.S. Marines arrived in Danang.

By June, the evidence that the bombing of North Vietnam had not reduced the country's overall military capability and had not weakened the morale of its population had become nearly incontestable. Faced with this evidence, U.S. analysts proposed that unless the United States increased its military presence in Vietnam considerably, it would no longer be a question of whether the North Vietnamese would win the war, but when. To reinforce their claim, General Westmoreland made it clear that to continue with his mission he needed an additional 150,000 U.S. troops. The general emphasized that the increase in U.S. forces would not convince North Vietnam and the Viet Cong that they would not be able to win the war. But he believed that the additional forces would help establish a favorable balance of power by the end of the year. Westmoreland then warned that if the United States hoped to seize the initiative from the enemy, he would need additional forces in the future.[53] Johnson agreed to send a 95,000–man force to South Vietnam. But as predicted by Westmoreland, it was not long before the president had to enlarge the numbers. By the end of 1966, the United States had 385,000 military personnel stationed in Vietnam; a year later the number had increased to 535,000. The costs of the war also increased quickly. In 1966, McNamara calculated the price of the war for that fiscal year at $9.4 billion, and estimated that it would increase to $19.7 for the next fiscal year, and to $22.4 billion for the year after. In short, the war was becoming "an albatross around the Administration's neck. . . ."[54]

Vietnam was not the only issue troubling the Johnson administration. In 1961, the Kennedy administration, in addition to believing it could contain communism on a global scale, assumed it could initiate major reforms designed to both reduce poverty and end racial injustice in the United States. Guided by Keynesian principles, it reasoned that the federal government would be able to afford these new international and domestic activities by activating the economy and tolerating short-term budget deficits until tax revenues from increased economic activity started to flow in. The Kennedy administration wasted little time in trying to realize its economic and social goals. It immediately forwarded to Congress a housing bill, a rise in the minimum wage, an extension of unemployment insurance, and an area development bill. By 1962, Congress had liberalized social security benefits, enacted a Housing Act that provided funds for urban renewal and area redevelopment to create about half a million more jobs in construction, raised the minimum wage, and enacted a Manpower Retraining Act designed to provide matching grants to train the unemployed in new skills. In the social arena, the administration was very careful during its early days in the way it used its executive power to enforce the protection of civil rights. It followed in the footsteps of its predecessor by sending troops to Mississippi in 1962 to enforce a court order directing the University of Mississippi to admit an African American student; and to Birmingham, Alabama in 1963 to restore order after the police had used brutal force against African American demonstrators. But finally, in June 1963, the administration submitted to Congress a proposal designed to ban discrimination in all places of public accommodation and to strengthen the authority of the attorney general to accelerate the desegregation of public schools.[55]

The Kennedy administration's early attempts to stimulate the economy did not succeed. Consequently, in January 1963 it asked Congress to reduce personal and corporate income taxes as a way of stimulating consumer expenditures and new plant investment. Because the tax reduction plan did not include proposals for reducing federal expenditures, Congress rejected it. Kennedy did not witness the enactment of all of his administration's proposals before his death in November 1963. This burden fell on the shoulders of his successor, Lyndon Johnson.

Using the knowledge and experience he had gained first in the House of Representatives and then as floor leader in the Senate, Johnson was able to push his predecessor's legislation and promote enactment of far-reaching social programs. In March 1964, in a speech at the University of Michigan, he proposed that Americans should become "more concerned with the quality of their goals than the quantity of their goods." To enrich and elevate life in the United States, he added, its people must end "poverty and racial injustice."[56] A few months later, he signed the Economic Opportunity Act and the most comprehensive civil rights act since Reconstruction. The Civil Rights Act of 1964 prohibited public discrimination in public facilities such as hotels, theaters, and restaurants, and authorized the withholding of federal funds from any state-administered agencies that practiced discrimination on the basis of race, color, or creed. The second act was designed to inaugurate Johnson's war on poverty by appropriating nearly a billion dollars for education and training programs. In addition, the administration launched the Community Action Program, which sought to increase the limited power of the poor and revive neighborhood life. As if these achievements were not enough to embellish his national status, Johnson persuaded Congress to enact a revised version of Kennedy's proposed tax reduction. [57]

Johnson's initial success can be attributed, in no small measure, to the health of the United States's economy. By the time the tax plan was approved in February 1964, the economy had already been growing strongly for seven months and unemployment had been going down steadily.[58] Moreover, when the economic upswing started in 1963, the consumer price index rose slowly at an annual rate of 1.2 percent, and the rate increased to 1.3 percent during 1964. By 1966, however, the economy of the United States had started to experience the ill effects of its domestic and international overreach. The costs of the war in Vietnam, along with the costs generated by the inauguration of the "Great Society" programs, forced Johnson to evaluate his fiscal policy. He initially rejected his advisers' recommendation that he increase taxes. Such a measure, he argued, would lead congressional conservatives to cut expenditures for his "Great Society" and congressional liberals to cut funds for the war in Vietnam. This decision forced the Federal Reserve Board to raise the discount rate from 4 percent to 4.5 percent. Tight money slowed the economy considerably, leading Congress to question the board's decision. Finally, at the start of 1967, Johnson asked Congress to place a 6 percent surtax on incomes. With a recession in place, Congress was hesitant to approve Johnson's request. In the meantime, the Federal Reserve Board reversed its earlier decision and launched a highly expansive monetary policy. The economy resumed its expansion in 1967, while spending on defense and the Great Society welfare programs continued to climb rapidly. With unemployment below 4 percent, wages rose at inflationary rates, reaching 6.2 percent in 1968. Finally, after a lengthy struggle with the administration, Congress agreed in June 1968 to impose a 10 percent income tax surcharge, in exchange for a $6 billion cut in federal expenditures, most of which came from Johnson's social programs.[59]

Johnson's policies had additional repercussions. To begin with, they provoked his personal political downfall. Public approval of his presidency in January 1965 was slightly higher than 71 percent. This support came on the heels of his recent election to the presidency and of Congressional approval of the various social and economic programs he had advocated. The support reflected satisfaction with an economy that had been growing steadily since late 1963 and the hope that the United States would be able to resolve the Vietnam problem without amassing unreasonably high costs. His popularity, however, languished rapidly. By May 1966, only 50 percent of the American public believed Johnson was doing a good job as president; and by March 1968 the number had dropped to 36 percent, with 52 percent remarking that they disapproved of his performance.[60] Aware that he was caught in a predicament much of his own making, Johnson announced at the end of March that he would not seek reelection.

The above numbers may help capture the American public's growing discontent with Johnson's presidency, but not the range of contradictory reactions his policies spawned. The policies widened the gulf separating liberals from conservatives in two nearly irreconcilable ways: while liberals favored his social policies and conservatives opposed them, conservatives defended his actions against North Vietnam and liberals challenged them. In a sense, both sides demanded greater governmental restraint— liberals abroad, conservatives at home. The tension generated by these opposite forces reached new heights in the summer of 1968, as the Democrats and the Republicans gathered in Chicago and Miami, respectively, to select the candidates who would seek the presidency. In November, the majority of the American voters decided to forego idealism in favor of pragmatism. Disillusioned by the costs imposed by the ideals of yesteryears, they favored the candidate that offered them, however vaguely, a way out from the costly impasse.

In Search of an Exit

Every hegemon overextends itself at some point in its existence. A hegemon's character is determined not by its ability to prevent this outcome, but by its capacity to discern the result before accumulating intolerable costs. A hegemon will not detect that it has reached beyond its means until it has endured major losses. Washington concluded in early 1969 that the economic costs of maintaining the international system were rising faster than the United States's economic capacity to support it. The United States's struggle to institute a new one lasted nearly a quarter of a century and induced tangible internal and external discord and uncertainty. The responsibility for conceding that the United States was living beyond its means, and for proposing a way out without undermining its status, fell on the shoulders of Richard Nixon. Nixon, however, did not develop a full understanding of the extent to which he would have to remodel the foreign policy of the United States until the fall of 1971.

Nixon assumed the presidency in 1969, determined to restructure the foreign policy framework of the United States. To assist him in this effort, he chose as his national security adviser Henry Kissinger, a German immigrant who had studied and taught at Harvard University. Though different in background and temperament, Nixon and Kissinger shared many beliefs about the United States and the hazards and opportunities it faced in the international arena. They were both deeply convinced that the Kennedy and Johnson administrations had to be blamed for overextending the United States. "In the life of nations, as of human beings," wrote Kissinger, "a point is often reached when the seemingly limitless possibilities of youth suddenly narrow and one must come to grips with the fact that not every option is open any longer." He added that the United States was "becoming like other nations in the need to recognize that [its] power, while vast, had limits. [Its] resources were no longer infinite in relation to [its] problems; instead [it] had to set priorities, both intellectual and material."[61]

The challenge encountered by the Nixon administration was to ensure that as it abridged the United States's commitments, it did not undermine the United States's credibility.[62] To attain both objectives simultaneously, the president and his national security adviser concluded that they needed to alter the power relationships between the United States and the Soviet Union and China on the one hand, and the United States and its allies on the other. Like other U.S. foreign policy makers since the dawn of the nuclear age, Kissinger was intrigued by the effect that nuclear weapons had on the relationship between the United States and the Soviet Union. He believed that during the early years of the Cold War, when the United States had a nuclear weapons monopoly, Washington had failed to use this advantage intelligently, largely because its leaders viewed "power and diplomacy as distinct and successive phases of foreign policy. . . ." Treating nuclear power and diplomacy as discrete phenomena while the power of the Soviet Union was a fraction of that of the United States caused the power of the latter to lack purpose and its negotiations to lack force. By the late 1960s, nuclear parity had robbed the United States of the opportunity to use its nuclear arsenal for purposes other than deterrence in core areas. Or, as noted by Kissinger, "[n]uclear weapons were so cataclysmic that as the arsenals grew they proved less and less useful to repel every conceivable aggression."[63] Faced with this new reality, the Nixon administration decided that the United States should shift the emphasis from nuclear superiority to nuclear sufficiency. Nuclear sufficiency would help reduce costs and convince the Soviets that it was in their best interest to adopt the same strategy.[64]

Kissinger's assessment of the United States's future nuclear strategy was steered by his and Nixon's analysis of the structure of the international system, and the way it could be altered by changing the United States's relationship with its allies, on the one hand, and the United States's power relationship with the Soviet Union and China, on the other hand. Kissinger was convinced that in order to reduce the tension in the international system it was imperative to undo the bipolar world that had emerged at the end of the Second World War. In a bipolar world, he wrote, each "of the superpowers is beset by the desire to maintain its pre-eminence among its allies, to increase its influence among the uncommit-ted, and to enhance its security vis-à-vis its opponent."[65] He noted that although a multipolar world is harder to manage than a bipolar one, a multipolar system distributes responsibilities for maintaining order in a more equitable fashion than a bipolar system.

The United States could not expect to create a multipolar system unless the Europeans were ready to assume greater responsibilities. Europe had become heavily dependent on the United States during the second half of the 1940s and throughout most of the 1950s. By the start of the 1960s, Europe had regained much of its economic health, and the major European states were finally able to retrieve some of their lost inde-pendence. However, because none of the Western European powers pos-sessed the strength it had commanded in the nineteenth century, it was imperative that they integrate on a supranational basis. Europeans under-stood this reality well, but feared that the United States might be foster-ing greater European integration solely for the purpose of distancing itself from the responsibility of helping to protect Europe in case of a major threat. The United States's North Atlantic allies, wrote Kissinger, "never had an incentive to contribute to a real capacity for regional defense. . . . Periodic attempts to rationalize the defense structure in Europe were bound to run into resistance. Any American initiative to strengthen local defense raised questions whether it was a device to reduce our nuclear commitment." Kissinger added that the Europeans would not be willing to assume greater responsibilities until they developed their own perception of what role they wanted to play in the international arena, and until they became convinced that the United States could not continue to carry the load alone.[66]

Like the leaders of the four previous administrations, Nixon and Kissinger shared the belief that the Soviet Union would never restrain itself from exploiting circumstances it considered to be favorable. Thus, the primary task of the United States would continue to be to foreclose Soviet opportunities. It was up to the United States to determine the lim-its of Soviet Union's objectives. This did not mean, however, that the United States could not modify some of its policies toward the Soviet Union. The Soviet Union, argued the new president, might want to reduce the tension with the West because of fear that Nixon might begin a new round of weapons procurement, which would strain the Soviet economy. This pressure, added Kissinger, would not be welcomed by those within the Soviet Union who had been claiming for some time that Moscow had to tend more to the needs of the Soviet consumers.

Nixon and Kissinger decided that the new administration's foreign policy toward the Soviet Union would be erected on three principles. First, after having acknowledged that there were incompatible interests between the United States and the Soviet Union in many areas, they proposed that the United States had to be prepared "to explore areas of common concern and to make precise agreements based on strict reciprocity." Based on the principle of concreteness, the Nixon administration was determined to insist that any negotiations between the two powers deal with "specific causes of tension. . . ." Second, they emphasized that both powers had to agree to restrain attempts to pursue unilateral advantages and exploit crises. Past unwillingness to avert adventurism had generated too much tension between both powers, which neither could survive much longer if left uncontrolled. To force Moscow to restrain itself, Kissinger asserted, the United States had to pursue a "carrot-and-stick approach, ready to impose penalties for adventurism, willing to expand relations in the context of responsible behavior." Finally, to ensure that both parties addressed concrete issues, it was imperative to establish linkages between issues in different parts of the world. In the past, by placing issues in distinct compartments, the United States government had encouraged the Soviets to assume that while they were cooperating in one area, they were free to strive for unilateral advantages in other areas. Linkage, added Kissinger, was a way of responding to the realities of a new interdependent world, one in which "the actions of a major power are inevitably related and have consequences beyond the issue or region immediately concerned."[67]

Though deeply committed to easing the tension between the United States and the Soviet Union, both Nixon and Kissinger were convinced that such an outcome would still leave in place another major source of strain in the international system. Since 1949, China and the United States had treated one another as piranhas. During the early years, Washington had assumed that because China and the Soviet Union shared the same ideology, the United States should treat them as one and the same rival. As it became evident that a major Sino-Soviet rift had ensued, Washington began to consider ways of exploiting it. By the second half of the 1960s, there were several signs indicating that Beijing saw the United States as a less formidable threat than the Soviet Union. Nixon and Kissinger were encouraged by these signals. Nixon made it clear in October 1967 that the international system could not afford to allow a state with a billion people to live "in angry isolation." Kissinger, with his commitment to creating a multipolar international system, believed that by establishing "a subtle triangle of relations between Washington, Beijing, and Moscow," the United States would improve the possibilities of accommodations with each as it increased its options toward both. Nixon, moreover, was hopeful that as the United States developed a closer relationship with China, he would be able to pressure the Soviet Union to provide him with some help in Vietnam.[68]

By 1969, there were few leaders in Washington who did not believe that the United States was caught in a quagmire in Vietnam. Nixon and Kissinger were no exceptions. Since late 1965, Kissinger had been claiming that the United States's principal error had been to become involved in a war without first determining and synchronizing its military and political objectives. This omission in judgment, he claimed, had freed the North Vietnamese and Viet Cong to control the military operations and the political context in which they were conducted. In late 1968, before Nixon named him national security adviser, Kissinger delineated the steps the United States would have to take to end the Vietnam War. He proposed that:

i)   the military operations be geared to clearly defined negotiating objectives;
ii) the South Vietnamese government develop a political program which non-Communist South Vietnamese could support;
iii) the United States cede increasing responsibility for the conduct of the war to the South Vietnamese;
iv) the United States seek to achieve as many of its objectives unilaterally as possible if in negotiations Hanoi proves intransigent and the war continues;
v)   in negotiations the United States concentrate on military issues such as a cease-fire, while leaving the distribution of political power to the Vietnamese parties.[69]

Every individual who finally manages to play a defining role in government learns that it is simpler to propound a strategy when out of power than to carry it out while in power. Nixon and Kissinger proved to be no different. Both were aware that public support for the war was ebbing. And yet, both were also convinced that if the United States walked away from a war that had involved two administrations and had caused the death of 31,000 U.S. soldiers, the credibility of the United States would suffer. "A nation cannot remain great," noted Nixon during a speech in late 1969, "if it betrays its allies and lets down its friends. Our defeat and humiliation in South Vietnam without question would promote recklessness in the councils of those great powers that have not yet abandoned their goals of world conquest."[70] Kissinger, wholly committed to the notion that for major powers everything in the world arena was linked, delineated his concern in much more specific terms. For Washington to abandon Vietnam to obtain "a respite from [its] own travails would mean" that the United States would not be able to revitalize the Atlantic Alliance, to move the Soviet Union toward the imperative of mutual restraint, to achieve an opening with China, and to convince its allies in the Middle East and their adversaries that the United States was impervious to threats of military pressure or blackmail.[71]

Nixon unveiled his Vietnam plan in June 1969, following a talk with

South Vietnam's president, Nguyen Van Thieu, in Midway Island. During the meeting, Nixon made it clear that the United States would withdraw 25,000 troops from South Vietnam and that removal of additional troops would most likely follow. Nixon recommended that Thieu undertake major political reforms to enhance his legitimacy as a nationalist leader, and that South Vietnam start adjusting its own defense structure so as to be able to cope with the removal of U.S. troops. Finally, Nixon warned that the United States was preparing to initiate negotiations with North Vietnam at the highest governmental level. After the meeting, Nixon jubilantly announced the first withdrawal of U.S. troops.

This announcement was followed by another troop-withdrawal declaration in August, and was accompanied by secret attempts on the part of Kissinger to meet with top North Vietnamese officials with the authority to engage in serious negotiations. Unable to generate fruitful negotiations, and fearful that Hanoi was capitalizing on his decision to withdraw U.S. troops to broaden North Vietnam's dominion, Nixon widened the Vietnam War by invading Cambodia. In April 1970, U.S. forces moved into Cambodia with the intent of interdicting the supply routes from North Vietnam to South Vietnam and driving out the North Vietnamese soldiers from their Cambodian sanctuaries. The Cambodian campaign triggered mass demonstrations in the United States and led Senators Frank Church and John Sherman Cooper to propose an amendment prohibiting U.S. military activities in Cambodia after June 30. On that date, the Senate approved the Cooper-Church amendment by a vote of 58 to 37, and U.S. forces left Cambodia.

The war continued to drag on, with the Nixon administration attempting to reach a negotiated agreement with Hanoi and the Pentagon proceeding with its removal of U.S. troops from South Vietnam. By 1971, however, while Washington and the rest of the United States remained attentive to the war in Vietnam, a few officials in the Nixon administration were struggling to persuade the president and his national security adviser to attend to another major problem that had been brewing steadily for some time.

Political leaders envision the future by analyzing past problems. Nixon and Kissinger recognized that the United States's nuclear policy had severe shortcomings, that its Vietnam policy was dividing the country and undermining its international reputation, that its policies toward China and the Soviet Union were too rigid and did not take into consideration new important developments, that its association with its Western European allies did not take into account their increased ability to assume greater responsibility for their own security, and that it had overextended its commitment toward peripheral entities and interests. What made Nixon and Kissinger notable, however, was their initial inclination to disregard economic problems. For a couple of years they remained oblivious to the fact that in an interdependent economic system the economic ills of a powerful state can have major economic and political repercussions on other states.

In retrospect, this attitude was not surprising. Like George Kennan before him, Kissinger believed that because the United States did not possess boundless capabilities, it had to establish priorities of interests. During his early years at the White House, however, Kissinger viewed the capabilities of the United States from a perspective significantly different from that proposed by Kennan. The former Department of State official had repeatedly emphasized that because the material resources the United States could afford to devote to outside affairs were limited, its leaders had to apply them where they would "do the most good." Kissinger, on the other hand, though aware that the power of the United States was not limitless, feared above all that its leaders would fail to recognize its psychological frailty. "If the United States insisted on being the trustee of all the non-Communist areas," he wrote, "we would exhaust ourselves psychologically long before we did so physically."[72] Kissinger's emphasis on the psychological dimension of power rather than on its economic component was not accidental. As a trained historian interested in the relationships between the leaders of the dominant European states during the early part of the nineteenth century, and in the post–Second World War foreign policy of the United States, Kissinger had never asked himself what effects economics had on politics, or vice versa. As Kissinger acknowledged in a moment of unusual candor, when he assumed his post as national security adviser he did not expect to play a major role in international economics because "it had not been a central field of study for me . . . ," and because he had not yet learned "that the key economic policy decisions are not technical but political."[73] Nixon seemed to share a similar lack of interest in the economic dimension of politics. Like many other Republicans, he was hostile to government intervention in the economy. But more specifically, Nixon initially did not show much interest in wrestling with the international economic challenges faced by his administration. He, like Kissinger, regarded most international economic problems as "quartermaster corps stuff."[74]

In 1971, Nixon was finally forced to concede that he could no longer neglect the political implications of international economics. As I remarked earlier, the Johnson administration's decision to launch its Great Society program, to escalate radically the United States's involvement in the Vietnam War, and to refuse, for a brief period, to increase taxes to pay for both, led to immoderate demand and inflation. In earlier periods, inflation had been considered primarily a national problem, conceived by policies that had pursued unreasonably high levels of employment. The economic policies promoted by the United States since the end of the Second World War, however, had brought about a major expansion of interdependence in the international economic system. Consequently, as the Federal Reserve Bank created additional money to cover the United States's deficits, the excess money began to flow into economies that encountered little inflation. The immediate effects of the monetary policies of the United States were to increase monetary instability and speculative attacks on the dollar worldwide.[75] Cognizant that the monetary policies of the United States were distorting currency values and undermining economic stability both at home and abroad, the United States's closest economic partners launched measures designed to increase confidence in the dollar and reduce monetary speculation, and to solve the liquidity-creation problem. Europe and Japan had good reasons for assisting the United States. By holding inflated dollars in the form of interest-bearing U.S. securities, Japan and Europe were paying for the United States's commitment to their security, and for Washington's willingness to tolerate their aggressive export expansion strategies and discriminatory policies against U.S. exports. Their support also helped pay for the United States's foreign aid, increased involvement in the Vietnam War, and its new Great Society program, without Washington's having to raise taxes.

Upon taking office in 1969, the new administration was confronted with an economy emitting mixed signals. Manufacturing costs in the United States had been rising faster since 1965 than in West Germany, Japan, and Britain. A decrease in U.S. exports and an increase in U.S. imports had accompanied this trend. In the late 1960s, however, aggregate unemployment declined, while short-term capital inflows helped generate overall payment surpluses. Moreover, in 1970 the U.S. trade balance showed a recovery.[76] Faced with these ambiguous signals, the Nixon administration decided to adopt conventional economic measures. It reduced the investment tax credit, cut the federal spending, and continued the tax surcharge adopted by Congress in 1968. These steps did not have the intended effect. In 1970, the Nixon administration faced the first recession experienced by the United States in 11 years, along with an inflation level that was still too high.[77] The U.S. public let Nixon know that it did not approve of the way he was handling the economy. The Republican Party, which had been unable to take control of either chamber of Congress, failed to increase substantially its strength during the midterm congressional elections. Moreover, the Democratic Party was finally able to gain control over the majority of the nation's governorships. Determined to improve his domestic political position, Nixon appointed John Connally as Treasury secretary immediately after the elections. Connally, a highly respected and powerful member of the Democratic Party, wasted no time in letting everybody know that he was determined to defend U.S. economic interests, that he would run the United States's international economic policy, and that he had no intention of altering the United States's exchange-rate policy.

His claims were followed by mixed results. In May 1971, after West Germany had abandoned its peg and allowed the mark to float upward as a result of exchange-market pressure, Connally delivered a powerful message that had at least two objectives. While speaking in Munich, he made it clear that in his own mind "[t]o revert to the use of exchange rates as supplementary tools of domestic policy is fraught with danger to the essential stability and sustainability of the system as a whole."[78] Though committed to protecting the existing exchange-rate system, at the same time he was determined to force the United States's major partners to assume additional responsibilities for the burden it had been carrying since the end of the Second World War.

We today spend nearly 9 percent of our Gross National Product on defense—nearly $5 billion of that overseas, much of it in western Europe and Japan. Financing a military shield is part of the burden of leadership; the responsibilities cannot and should not be cast off. But 25 years after World War II, legitimate questions arise over how the cost of these responsibilities should be allocated among the free world allies who benefit from that shield. No longer does the U.S. economy dominate the world . . . , no longer will the American people permit their government to engage in international actions in which the true long-run interests of the U.S. are not just as clearly recognized as those of the nations with which we deal.[79]

Connally's strong words did not help alter the domestic and international economic threats faced by the United States. In the United States, inflation, which had started to go down during the first four months of 1971, began to go up again after April. The GNP did not grow as fast as expected, and consequently the unemployment rate remained at 6.2 percent. Moreover, the balance-of-payments deficit, which had experienced its highest level in 1970, was doomed to surpass that mark in 1971 by a considerable margin.[80] To make matters worse, on August 9 the dollar fell to its lowest level vis-à-vis the mark since the Second World War. This development finally forced Nixon to accept that his policy of "benign neglect" of the dollar was undermining his political standing both in the United States and abroad.

In the middle of August, the president went on national television to announce his new economic policy. On the domestic side, he proposed a repeal of the excise tax on automobiles, acceleration of income tax exemptions, a $4.7 billion cut in federal spending, postponement of government pay raises, a 90–day freeze on wages and prices, and investment tax credits. On the international side, he announced a 10 percent surcharge on all imports, a 10 percent reduction in foreign aid, and the suspension of the convertibility of the dollar into gold.[81]

Nixon's decision to let the dollar depreciate has been seen by some analysts as an attempt to save his administration. The president and Connally recognized that the administration was caught in a predicament. They believed it would not be able to remain in power past the next election in 1972 unless it altered the state of the domestic economy; but they also acknowledged that an attempt to promote rapid domestic prosperity would undermine the Bretton Woods monetary regime. High and escalating inflation had consistently weakened the dollar. If the Nixon administration attempted to save the dollar's parity, it would have to impose deflationary restraints that would forestall prosperity and reduce inflation only gradually and up to a point. On the other hand, if it tried to bring near full employment by encouraging rapid economic growth, it would also spawn a high and accelerating rate of inflation. [82]

The year 1972 proved to be a highly deceptive period for both the Nixon administration and the United States. By the end of December 1971, the major states, except Canada, returned to pegged exchange rates. Japan revalued the yen against the dollar 16.9 percent, West Germany revalued the mark against the dollar 13.6 percent, and Britain and France revalued their respective currencies against the dollar 8.6 percent. Moreover, Japan accepted Connally's demands for restrictions on its export of textiles, and both Japan and Western Europe agreed to tighten their restraints on their exports of steel to the United States. [83] Two months later, on February 21, 1972, Nixon broke the 23–year impasse between the United States and China when he shook hands with China's premier, Chou En-lai, at Beijing's airport. By the time Nixon boarded Air Force One six days later to return to the United States, he and the Chinese leadership had discussed the long-term trends of world politics, the new international order, and the type of power balance the new order would necessitate. Mindful of his administration's negotiations with Japan and the major Western European states in 1971, Nixon suggested to the Chinese leaders that a new world order was emerging, one in which economic power would serve as the key to other forms of power. This new world would have the United States, the Soviet Union, China, Japan, and Western Europe at its center. [84] In turn, the Chinese repeatedly voiced disquiet about the Soviet Union. They were critical of the United States's failure to obstruct Soviet expansionism and insinuated, by noting that neither China nor the United States had any aggressive intentions, that they considered the Soviet Union the greater threat to world order. [85] Nixon, happy to hear the Chinese buttress his decision to eliminate ideology as the chief criterion by which to identify threats, emphasized that the United States had no territorial aspirations in Asia, that its alliance with Japan and its presence in South Korea and the Philippines contributed to China's security and economic interests, and that it hoped to reach a negotiated settlement in Vietnam.

Nixon left China with many issues unresolved. [86] There was little doubt, however, that he had accomplished his two main objectives. He and the Chinese ended the stalemate that had divided the United States and China for more than 20 years. Moreover, by remarking that the United States would judge other countries on the basis of their actions and not their ideologies, and by reaching a series of agreements with China, Nixon signaled to Moscow that it was in the Soviet Union's interest to be more flexible in its negotiations with the United States. Moscow did not ignore the message.

From the outset, Nixon had assumed that the Soviets would recognize that it would be in their interest to meet with him because the rivalry between the Soviet Union and the United States had become too intense and too costly. He argued that, because the two superpowers had reached nuclear arms parity, it made little sense for them to continue the arms race at the rate they had until then. He assumed that the Soviets shared his belief that the "objective condition" of deterrence precluded "meaningful superiority," and that unless they did something to constrain the arms race, it would continue to induce more uncertainty and greater costs.[87] Nixon delineated the rationale for an arms control in his first Annual Foreign Policy report to Congress as follows:

> Modern technology makes any balance precarious and promotes new efforts at higher levels of complexity. Such an arms race absorbs resources, talents and energies. The more intense the competition, the greater the uncertainty about the other side's intentions. The higher the level of armaments the greater violence and devastation should deterrence fail.[88]

After several days of intensive negotiations in the latter part of May between members of the Nixon administration and top Soviet officials, including the Secretary General of the Communist Party Leonid Brezhnev, the Soviet President Nikolai Podgorny, and the Soviet Premier Alexei Kosygin, they produced four major agreements. The most relevant one was SALT I (Strategic Arms Limitations Talk). SALT I was erected on the assumption that security would not require numeric equality, let alone superiority. It established some quantitative limitations, but very few qualitative constraints. For instance, it limited the number of launchers, but not the number of warheads or reentry vehicles that could be placed on a single missile. Thus, though initially the United States ended with fewer land-based missiles and submarine-launched missiles than the Soviet Union, the United States more than made up for the gap with its multiple independent reentry vehicles.[89] Moreover, it placed no restraints on the testing or upgrading of reentry vehicles.

The second agreement (which in fact was part of SALT I), was designed to limit the United States's and the Soviet Union's defensive capabilities against a nuclear attack. Ever since it had assumed power, the Nixon administration had attempted to persuade the Soviets that their strategy of deploying defensive antiballistic missile systems (ABMs) was counter-productive, because if not halted it would force the United States to design more and larger nuclear weapons to overcome Soviet defenses. The Soviets accepted the U.S. rationale, and both parties agreed to establish a defense perimeter involving no more than 100 ABMs each, at two different sites: one to protect the state's capital, the other to defend an ICBM field. The third agreement was not a treaty. It simply stipulated that both parties would attempt to coexist peacefully and would set up rules designed to make their competition less risky. The fourth agreement was erected on the concept of linkage. The Soviet economy was in horrible shape; consumer goods were still in short supply, and foreign assistance was desperately needed. Aware of the economic challenges that lay ahead for the Soviet Union, Nixon and Kissinger hoped to entice Moscow to become part of a network of economic relationships and to use the promise of closer and broader economic relations as "a carrot for restrained Soviet political behavior."[90]

The good news kept rolling on through much of 1972. On the economic front, though the trade imbalance increased from $2.7 billion in 1971 to $6.9 billion in 1972, unit costs in the United States remained constant, and the inflation rate went down. The news on the international political front was also more obliging. In the last week of October, just a few days prior to the presidential elections, Kissinger announced that peace with North Vietnam was at hand. On national television, he remarked that despite the fact that there were still some issues that needed to be resolved, what stood in the way of a peace agreement between North Vietnam and the United States were issues that were less important than those that had already been resolved. His announcement was disingenuous. Having reached an agreement with Le Duc Tho, the North Vietnamese negotiator, Kissinger traveled to Saigon determined to persuade South Vietnam's President Thieu to accept the peace settlement. The settlement separated the military from the political issues. The United States agreed to withdraw the last of its troops in South Vietnam, while North Vietnam agreed not to introduce any new forces in the South. With regard to the political issues, North Vietnam accepted the United States's refusal to depose Thieu. The United States, in turn, acquiesced to North Vietnam's claim that the political issues had to be resolved through negotiations between the North Vietnamese government and the Provisional Revolutionary Government on the one hand, and the Thieu government on the other hand. Thieu, who was convinced that after an adequate interval following the departure of the last U.S. troops the Communists would launch a major offensive designed to take over the entire country, rejected the agreement.

Following his unsuccessful trip to Saigon, Kissinger returned to Paris in early December to meet with Le Duc Tho.[91] The two representatives failed to design a new accord. The North Vietnamese representative rejected every one of the 69 changes requested by Kissinger on behalf of Nguyen Van Thieu, and submitted his own new set of demands. Tho, however, made it clear that he would be willing to sign the October agreement, so long as it did not incorporate any of the newly proposed changes. Kissinger and Nixon concluded that failure on their part to insert some of the changes demanded by Thieu would both impair considerably South Vietnam's ability to survive the United States's troop withdrawal, and impart the image that Washington lacked the nerve to stand by one of its weak allies in its greatest moment of need. Upon Kissinger's return from Paris, Nixon decided to force a conclusion to the negotiations by ordering the resumption of heavy bombing over North Vietnam. The decision elicited strong criticism from both within the United States and abroad. Nonetheless, on December 28, two days after the United States had launched one of its biggest B-52 raids over North Vietnam, Hanoi agreed to another meeting between Kissinger and Le Duc Tho. On January 13, negotiators on both sides completed the draft agreement that the United States would submit to Thieu for his final approval. Three days later, Kissinger's assistant, Alexander Haig, delivered the provisional agreement to the South Vietnamese president, along with a letter from Nixon. In the letter, Nixon informed Thieu in no uncertain terms that the United States would sign the accord and would "do so, if necessary, alone." [92] Nixon warned that failure on Thieu's part to approve the agreement would impel him (Nixon) to make public that the South Vietnamese government was obstructing the peace process, and that the United States would immediately terminate all its military and economic assistance to South Vietnam. After one last attempt to persuade Nixon that the United States should pressure North Vietnam to accept some additional changes, Thieu relented and accepted the peace treaty. For all practical purposes, this decision brought the United States's involvement in Vietnam's civil war to an end.

Burdened by Contradictions

Adolescence is the season of hope and impetuousness. The Japanese attack on Pearl Harbor in late 1941 forced Americans to accept that the United States, as the youngest, most powerful state, could not continue to regard itself as a state separate from, and unencumbered by, the international system. Mindful of the United States's past mistakes, Roosevelt viewed the Second World War as a chance to create an international system that would no longer be besieged by the contradictions that had tormented it during the interwar period. Convinced that his vision was not the result of an inexperienced and idealistic mind, Roosevelt tried to conceive an international system that would be guided by the United States, the

Soviet Union, and two other powerful international entities. The American president was neither foolish nor idealistic; but he was also not exceptionally perspicacious about international power politics, or about the nature of the Soviet Union's leadership and political system. His nescience proved to be costly. Upon his death, his successor assumed the reins of a government unclear as to what path to follow as it recognized that the one that had been originally chosen was no longer suitable.

Every state that strives to reduce domestic and international tensions faces the laborious task of gauging whether its attempt will in the long run bring about unintended and unwanted effects and, as a result, new tensions. For hegemonic states, particularly youthful ones, this is an exceptionally onerous responsibility. Their policies ordinarily bear consequences, both intended and unintended, of greater import than those generated by other states. During the second half of the 1940s, Washington endeavored to devise an international strategic system and an international economic system that would safeguard and advance the strategic and economic needs of the United States. Though the two systems would be very different, Washington calculated that together they would help contain Soviet expansion and promote economic prosperity in the United States. Washington succeeded in both endeavors, but thereafter its actions spawned new contradictory forces, which in turn gave rise to new tensions.

During the early years of the Cold War, the United States assumed it would be able to rely primarily on its nuclear superiority to contain the Soviet Union. Determined not to be surpassed militarily, the Soviet Union responded to the challenge by developing its own nuclear arsenal. Their unwavering commitment to nuclear weapons propelled both states into a nuclear arms race. During the 1950s, they multiplied the number, accuracy, range, and speed with which they could deliver their nuclear weapons. In the early 1960s, the Cuban Missile Crisis compelled them to acknowledge that a nuclear war could literally obliterate civilization, and to start gauging more carefully the manner and extent to which they challenged each other's interests. The crisis, however, did not abate the arms race. Instead, the event forced the Soviet Union to recognize that its nuclear power was inferior to that of the United States, and to reason that to retain its superpower status it had to, at minimum, match the nuclear capacity of its more powerful rival. This inference pressed the Soviet Union to commit additional resources to the development of its nuclear arsenal. When the Soviet Union finally attained nuclear parity in the late 1960s, Washington sought to persuade Moscow that it would be impossible for either party to achieve meaningful superiority, and that it would be in their mutual interests to slow down the nuclear arms race.

In short, a quarter of a century after having dropped its first atomic bomb on enemy territory, the United States accepted the contradiction it had unintentionally helped induce. It recognized that its technical ability and that of the Soviet Union to perfect nuclear weapons had grown at a pace considerably faster than their ability to understand and accept the shortfalls of their own nuclear policies. The power rivalry, along with modern technology, consistently forced each actor to try to attain nuclear superiority. This drive made it nearly impossible for either party to accept a balance of power. Finally the United States concluded that unless they both controlled the competition, they would continue to accumulate greater costs and foster more uncertainty about each other's intentions. SALT I, which was erected on the premise that security did not require numeric equality, let alone superiority, was the first major attempt designed to, if not eliminate, at least constrain the contradiction and tension the arms race had generated.

Nuclear weapons were not the only instrument used by the United States to contain the Soviet Union, nor the only one that produced contradictions. The Cold War was defined by one of the most atypical international systems ever devised. Since the birth of the global market economy, the entities with the strongest economies and the most stalwart militaries had dictated the nature of the international system. The emphasis placed by the United States and the Soviet Union on augmenting their military capabilities concealed, but did not devalue, the pertinence of the other half of the power equation—economics. The United States and the Soviet Union sought to shape two very different types of economic systems. Washington focused on creating a liberal international economic system that would help foster domestic economic prosperity in the United States in the form of economic growth, full employment, and a sufficiently stable price level, and would provide a secure and stable basis for the development of global economic relations. As its rivalry with the Soviet Union grew, the United States reasoned that by helping its main Western European allies and Japan rebuild their economies, it would strengthen their ability to protect themselves from attempts by the Soviet Union and communist parties outside the Soviet realm to subvert their regimes.

At the end of the Second World War, the Soviet Union faced a challenge very different from the one confronting the United States. While the United States was trying to create an international economic system that would keep its own economy bustling after the war, the Soviet Union encountered the more burdensome task of not only rebuilding a devastated economy, but also designing one that could compete with that of the United States. Convinced that if it became part of the international economic system the United States was striving to create, the Soviet Union would lose not just its freedom but also its reputation as the only viable ideological alternative to capitalism, Moscow responded by relying on the same strategy it had used to bring about rapid industrial growth during the 1930s: central planning. The first step the Soviet Union took when it switched to a centrally planned economy was to replace the drive to accumulate capital with specific state-proposed social goals. These goals did not remain constant, but varied according to circumstances and were placed in descending order of significance as conditions changed. Second, the Soviets reasoned that short-term profit calculations in planning investments, which capitalist economies relied on, placed severe burdens on long-term planning. They acknowledged that capitalist economies could plan for winning a major war or restoring their strength thereafter. But in their minds, states committed to growing fast had to be able to design goals that required long-term plans. Aware that conditions never remained constant, they opted for the establishment of five-year strategy plans. Finally, for the state to dictate social priorities and to rely on long-term planning to fulfill them, it also had to decree the inputs and outputs of each industry and enterprise, of imports and exports, of supply and money demand and, accordingly, prices and wages, jobs and available labor, and credit.

Inordinate amounts of power often afford a hegemonic state the freedom to act impulsively. It frees a hegemonic state from having to assess carefully the internal and external contradictions its policies may generate.[93] On the other hand, the rise of costly contradictions can force a hegemonic state to seek an equilibrium between its goals and means. The liberal international economic system the United States created was markedly more effective and encircled many more entities than the closed economic system created and dominated by the Soviet Union. In the early 1950s, the United States, with only 6 percent of the total world population, accounted for approximately 40 percent of the gross world product. Between 1947 and 1958, the United States used its economic might to help Europe and Japan rebuild their economies by providing aid and using its purchasing power. By 1964, the United States, Europe, and Japan had undergone major economic growth, and had established liberal international arrangements for trade and international finance, each bound by a series of rules, norms, principles, and decision-making procedures. By the time the 1960s had moved to the second half and given way to the next decade, however, several contradictory forces had started to converge on the United States. These contradictions forced the United States to recognize that its power, though of titanic proportions, was not boundless.

It is commonly contended that competition in the market economy uproots inefficiency. This assertion is based on the assumption that competition in the market is determined solely by economic activities. In the international arena this is rarely the case, largely because any one state typically has political interests contending with economic needs. Between 1945 and the late 1960s, though the United States did not compete in the international market to the level afforded by its actual economic capabilities, its actions were based on calculations of both its economic and political interests. The United States initially estimated that it would not be in its interest to compete against its major industrialized allies to the extent facilitated by its capabilities. Such behavior would undermine the ability of the economies of the major industrialized states to grow, and consequently impair attempts on the part of the United States to ensure that its own economy continued to grow and to contain the Soviet Union.

Hegemonic states with market-oriented economies can disguise their overcommitment and "irrational" economic acts for an extended period if their leaders do not exercise their functions under the threat of the ruinous forces of the electorate. Viewed from a purely economic standpoint, the United States should have considered adopting a more cost-conscious foreign policy course during the first half of the 1960s. And yet, while the advanced industrialized European states and Japan were finally competing in earnest with the United States in the economic field, Washington kept pace with the Soviet Union's nuclear arsenal, started to conduct a major war in Southeast Asia, began to foster economic development in destitute regions, and struggled to create a new "Great Society" at home. This reluctance to maintain an equilibrium between the benefits and costs of its commitments remained unchallenged until the costs evoked considerable negative political repercussions domestically. By the late 1960s, these costs had become intolerable, and the United States's leadership began the search for a way to restore the lost equilibrium.[94]

The quest for a lost equilibrium by a hegemon bound by a bipolar system abroad and a democratic political order at home is a momentous responsibility. To illustrate the hazards faced in the international and domestic arenas by the party attempting to reestablish the equilibrium, I will assume that the bipolar system is dominated by states A and B, that the former is the originator of the actions, and that it is constrained by a democratic political order at home. If A channels its efforts to replace the bipolar system with a multipolar one, then the effects of its actions could differ significantly, depending on B's calculations. Such actions might result in lower costs for A if B agrees that it would also be in its interest to replace the bipolar system with a multipolar one, and is prepared to openly cooperate in its creation. However, such actions could bring greater costs to A if B feigns to agree with A, but decides that because A no longer possesses the power and will to co-rule the bipolar system, it will strive to further increase its own power underhandedly while A endeavors to create the multipolar system.

The effects of these actions on A's domestic environment will also vary. From the outset, A's major domestic challenge will be to coalesce the competing perspectives and concerns of a wide range of interest groups into a rational set of foreign policies. If B agrees that it would be in its interest to create a multipolar system and demonstrates its willingness to cooperate by not engaging in any type of deceitful activity, then the leaders of A will eventually be able to lessen the concerns and fears of those at home who initially questioned the endeavor. However, if B strives to surreptitiously increase its power and A learns about B's actions, then the leaders of A will come under intense domestic pressure to abandon their original scheme and pursue a more aggressive foreign policy course against B. If we assume that A is the United States and B the Soviet Union, then the worst-case scenarios I have just delineated were the ones Washington encountered following the collapse of the Nixon administration. In the next chapter I describe the new challenges and contradictions faced by the United States, and how it devised a way to extricate itself from their grip.

CHAPTER SIX

Audacious Titan

The Challenge

A hegemon that experiences a decline in its economic capacity to protect the international system, and as a result tries to restructure it, must contend with the tension and uncertainty these developments generate both abroad and at home. Other states in the international arena, both allies and adversaries, unsure as to the intentions and capabilities of the hegemonic state, will increasingly contest its authority. If the hegemonic state is bound by domestic political and economic systems that are open and competitive, its leaders will be forced to cope with the contradictory demands and proposals emanating from competing domestic groups. For a number of years after the end of the Vietnam War, U.S. leaders were unable to persuade the American people, and its allies and adversaries, that the United States possessed the capability and the will both to create a less tense and costly international system and to lead it. In 1981, however, the United States altered its course. Troubled by several foreign policy mishaps and by the belief that the Soviet Union had reneged on many of its international accords, the American people elected as president in late 1980 an individual who promised that he would reinvigorate the United States's economy and reclaim its standing as the world's leader.

The concurrent achievement of both objectives is exacting, especially for the co-leader of a bipolar system that had recently declared that it no longer possessed the economic capacity to perform its expected international functions, and faced an adversary that seemed determined to continue enlarging its own military power. With the United States's economy suffering from its leaders' earlier decisions to simultaneously address its needs at home and fulfill its obligations abroad, many Americans wondered how the new president would be able to outmatch the power of the

Soviet Union as he sought to help revitalize the American economy. For Ronald Reagan, who came to power in 1981, the two goals did not stand in conflict. Convinced that major cuts in taxes and social spending would help reawaken the economy and, as a result, generate the financial resources the United States would need to outbid the Soviet Union's power aspirations, the new president put forth the efforts to commence both initiatives.

In a democracy, presidents often envisage lofty futures, but the prospects of realizing them are always dependent on whether they win the support of the legislature. The Reagan administration persuaded the U.S. Congress to reduce taxes and increase military expenditures, but the administration was successful only after acquiescing to Congress's demands that social spending be cut scantily. This decision proved to be both rewarding and costly. In very short time the United States threatened to surpass by a significant margin the military might of the Soviet Union, but in the process it built the largest economic deficit in its entire history.

The structure of a bipolar system will remain unaltered until one or more states join the two superpowers at the top of the system, the two superpowers go to war against one another, or one of the two superpowers reneges because it is no longer able to absorb the costs necessary to co-lead the system. By the start of the 1980s, there were no other international entities that could match the military power and economic capacity of the United States and the Soviet Union. China possessed great potential, but its realization lay decades away. The economies of Germany and Japan had grown considerably, but they were still substantially inferior to those of the United States and the Soviet Union, and militarily both were much weaker than a great number of other states. Furthermore, the likelihood of a nuclear confrontation between the two superpowers had been almost effaced by the enormity of their respective nuclear arsenals. Though each state continued to augment its nuclear capacity and refine its ability to engage in a "limited" nuclear war, each party also comprehended that such a war was unfathomable. A nuclear war could end without a victor only if both states agreed at the same time to end it and not claim victory, or both states destroyed one another. Neither scenario made sense. The bipolar system could come to an end only if one of the two superpowers conceded that it no longer possessed the economic vigor to continue playing its role as co-leader.

Convinced that the economy of the Soviet Union was in shambles, the Reagan administration gambled that if it raised the stakes in the nuclear arms race it would outlast its communist adversary. The risk paid off. By the end of the 1980s, the Cold War had come to an end and the United States stood alone at the pinnacle of the international security system. Free of the Cold War tension, the United States diverted a major portion of its energy and resources away from the military into the revitalization of its economy. Ten years after the end of the Cold War, the United States had once again become the envy of those who just a few years earlier had written its obituary. In this chapter I delineate the manner in which these two changes came about.

Morality, Money, War, and Oil

The war in Vietnam forced the United States to examine the moral implications of its foreign policies. For a while after the war, some forceful American voices argued that it was immoral for the United States, as a democracy, to support undemocratic regimes and to rely on inhumane actions to protect and advance its interests. The war also helped instigate criticism against any attempt on the part of foreign policy makers to rely on duplicity, secrecy, and deceit to fulfill the United States's foreign policy objectives.[1] The criticism intensified after it was uncovered that the Nixon administration had played a major role in the 1973 overthrow of Salvador Allende, an avowed socialist who, with the help of the Communist Party, had been elected president of Chile in 1970. Discontent with the "imperial presidency" became singularly evident in early November 1973, when the U.S. Congress passed the War Powers Act and overrode Nixon's veto. Under the terms of the act, the president would have to inform Congress of his decision to commit troops abroad, and Congress would have to grant its own formal approval for the troops to remain longer than 60 days. Antipathy toward the White House's occupant reached its peak in August 1974, when the world learned that Nixon had ordered one of his assistants to force the Central Intelligence Agency to stop the Federal Bureau of Investigation's inquiry into the Watergate break-in. Americans, who through the years had grown suspicious of their president and were beginning to demand of him greater moral accountability, made it clear that Nixon should either resign or be impeached. On August 8 Nixon announced his decision to resign, and on the following day Vice President Gerald Ford became the new chief executive.

The domestic turmoil could not have arisen at a worse time. As questions about the "imperial presidency" continued to mount throughout 1973, the Nixon administration was compelled to focus on three very important and interrelated issues: i) the January currency crisis, ii) the Yom Kippur War, and iii) the October oil crisis. Though the second issue was defined primarily by strategic and political factors, the interrelated effects of the three issues had a profound impact on the nature of the international economic system and, as a result, on the new role the United States would play for the next 15 years.

By the early 1970s, the international monetary system had become highly interdependent and pluralistic. Both developments undermined radically the United States's ability to manage it. Three factors contributed to the system's increased interdependence. First, between 1960 and the early 1970s, the number of multinational banks with the ability to make large international transfers of capital, for both lending purposes and hedging and speculating against rate exchanges, rose rapidly. Second, production became more international. Large multinational corporations, controlling enormous liquid assets, moved vast sums of money from one country to another in order to take advantage of interest rate spread or possible exchange rate adjustments. And third, Eurodollars, which are dollars in the form of bank deposits held and traded primarily in Europe and lent in the form of dollars, increased to large proportions. Because the market for Eurodollars was controlled neither by state regulations nor by constraints of domestic money markets, and because it consisted largely of short-term funds, it became highly mobile and volatile. In addition to growing more interdependent, the international monetary system became more pluralistic. By the mid-1960s, Europe's and Japan's per capita income each approached the United States's, their total reserves exceeded the United States's, and their growth and trade reached higher levels than the United States's.[2]

This increase in interdependence and pluralism had several major effects on the United States. Its first significant effect was on U.S. trade. By the 1960s, expenditures on the arms race, the Vietnam War, and Johnson's "Great Society" had induced inflation and distorted the real value of the dollar. The overvalued dollar brought about a decrease in U.S. exports, along with growth in imports, and increased the pressure to send dollars abroad for investment purposes. This activity, in turn, had an adverse effect on employment in the United States and provoked labor unions to demand that steps be taken to limit the outflow of dollars. Finally, because the inflationary forces emanating from the United States began to move from one country to another throughout the entire world economy, the shift toward a more pluralistic distribution of economic power enabled Europe and Japan to demand that Washington adopt a deflationary policy.

Between 1968 and 1971, the United States did little to alter the management of the international monetary system. However, following Nixon's unilateral decision to stop the convertibility of the dollar into gold in August 1971, the United States sought to devise a new international monetary system. Initially, its efforts did not bring about considerable changes. The Smithsonian Agreement reached in December 1971 reflected an attempt to control the crisis rather than to reform the system. The signatories devalued the dollar in relation to gold, realigned the exchange rates of several countries, and agreed on greater exchange rate flexibility by allowing currencies to float within plus or minus 2.25 percent of parity, which was twice the range tolerated by the Bretton Woods agreement.[3] The new monetary agreement lasted a little over a year, in spite of continuing U.S. trade deficits. In March 1973, however, the new system of fixed rates collapsed following a renewed selling of the dollar, after which the United States decided to devalue the dollar by 10 percent and demanded that Western Europe and Japan float their currencies. These events marked the formal end of the Bretton Woods agreement and the dawning of an international monetary system managed almost entirely by the market.

The system experienced an unexpected jolt in the last quarter of 1973. In early October 1973, Egypt and Syria attacked Israel. The genesis of this decision can be traced to the war won by Israel against Syria and Egypt in 1967. The 1967 war ended with Israel's seizing vast pieces of territory from Egypt and Syria. For several years thereafter, the United States and the Soviet Union tried to persuade Egypt, Syria, and Israel to reach a peace agreement. The principal obstacle to the formulation of an accord was disagreement about how much territory Israel would return to its two adversaries. Though prepared to return some territory, Israel held fast to the contention that, for security reasons, it would not withdraw all the way to its former borders. After accepting that Israel had no intention of receding to its pre-1967 borders, Egypt's new president, Anwar Sadat, concluded that his country would once again have to wage war to regain its lost territory and prestige.

Sadat was a realist. He understood that, alone, Egypt could not match Israel's military strength. He sought to abridge the military gap by persuading his Syrian counterpart, Hafez Asad, to join him in a military attack against Israel. The Egyptian leader, however, was not convinced that, even together, Egypt and Syria would be able to defeat Israel. This concern led him to propose to Asad that they attack Israel with the intent not of attaining a military victory, but of destabilizing the Middle East to the point that it would become a threat to U.S.-Soviet détente. Washington, reasoned Sadat, had invested too much in détente to allow a war in the Middle East to threaten the new relationship the United States was attempting to forge with the Soviet Union. Faced with such a prospect, Washington would most likely pressure Israel to accept some of Egypt's and Syria's claims.[4] Sadat's plan did not develop exactly as he had hoped. On October 6, his troops and Asad's forces launched a surprise attack on Israel. During the initial days, Israel's military seemed unable to mount a creditable counterattack. However, as the war progressed, the tide of conflict changed course. In Syria, Israeli forces advanced beyond the territory they had captured in 1967 and moved closer to Damascus than ever before; in Egypt, they crossed to the Cairo side of the Suez Canal and began to entrap the Egyptian forces. Moscow, mindful that if it were to allow Israel to defeat Egypt and Syria the Soviet Union would lose its influence in the Middle East, proposed a meeting with Nixon's recently appointed secretary of state, Henry Kissinger. Kissinger traveled to Moscow, and in short time he reached an agreement with his hosts. The accord stipulated that both sides would stop fighting, that Israel would not be required to withdraw immediately from the new territory it had conquered, and that the combatants would continue to negotiate. The United Nations Security Council approved the proposal under Resolution 338.

The agreement did not end the war immediately. Israel took advantage of Egypt's cease-fire violations to surround the Egyptian forces in the Sinai. These actions once again threatened U.S.-Soviet relations. Moscow, fearing that Israel would impose a humiliating defeat on Egypt, threatened to intervene militarily. Washington responded immediately with a nuclear alert designed to signal that it would not tolerate Soviet intervention. After a "shuttle diplomacy" that lasted until January 1974, Kissinger convinced Egypt and Israel to approve a disengagement agreement. According to the treaty, Israel would retreat to its side of the Suez Canal and return a small portion of the Sinai along the canal to Egypt. In return, Egypt would reduce its military presence in the Sinai. Both entities agreed to have their forces separated by a United Nations military contingency. By May, Kissinger had persuaded Israel and Syria to sign a separate disengagement accord.[5]

It is not unusual for international relations analysts to assume that the effects of war are considerably more discordant than the consequences yielded by economic issues. The Yom Kippur War had a major effect on the relationships among states in the Middle East, and between the United States and the Soviet Union, but it paled when compared to the worldwide effect spawned by the oil crisis that erupted in October. The price of crude oil had varied very little between 1950 and 1970, mainly because the international oil companies controlled the market. Starting in 1970, however, as states began to nationalize their oil industries, prices began to increase. Initially, the jump, though significant, was not radical. Between 1970 and the start of October 1973, the price of oil rose from about $2 per barrel to about $3 per barrel. During the 1970–1973 period, an institution that played a critical role, and would continue to do so during and after the October war, was the Organization of Petroleum Exporting Countries (OPEC). On October 16, six Persian Gulf states decided to abandon the slow increase of oil prices by unilaterally raising the posted price by 70 percent. The next day, Arab members of OPEC announced that they would reduce their oil production by 5 percent and would repeat the procedure every month until Israel agreed to withdraw from all occupied territory. On October 18, Saudi Arabia decided to go a step further by announcing that it would cut its production by 10 percent until Israel fulfilled all the Arab terms. Finally, on October 20, a day after

Nixon had asked Congress to approve a $2.2 billion assistance package to Israel to pay for the military equipment it was purchasing from the United States, Saudi Arabia and other Arab states imposed a complete embargo on oil exports to the United States. By the end of 1973, worldwide supplies of oil had fallen by 7 percent, and the price had quadrupled from about $3 per barrel in October to almost $12 per barrel by the end of December.[6] The oil crisis became a financial crisis almost immediately. In Kissinger's own words: "The seemingly inexorable rise in prosperity was abruptly reversed. Simultaneously, inflation ran like a forest fire through the industrialized countries, and recession left millions unemployed. The poorer countries without oil plunged into deeper depression and unredeemable debt, while the oil producers had more money than they could possibly spend. Their vast, mobile cash balances played havoc with currencies as they moved among capitals for reasons economic or political."[7]

As if the labor of designing two new international regimes, one oil and the other financial, were not formidable enough, the United States was also forced to revisit détente and to cope with the aftermath of the Vietnam War. Nixon and Kissinger had built détente on the assumption that the United States could resist Soviet expansionism while it negotiated on concrete issues. In other words, they sought to practice deterrence and coexistence concurrently. By 1974, the policy was encountering strong criticism from the conservative corner of the Republican Party. The common sentiment among members of this group was that since the introduction of détente, the United States had fallen behind the Soviet Union militarily. The Soviets, argued conservatives, could never be trusted; the only way to deal with them was confrontationally. Liberals, who for years had criticized Nixon, were forced to accept that détente brought the United States closer to the kind of relationship with the Soviet Union that they had been advocating for years. Still, they were not yet ready to disregard the legacies of some of his other foreign policies. Driven by a strong antimilitarist sentiment, liberals continued to oppose large-scale defense spending, military aid, military intervention, and covert activities by the CIA.[8]

These events and issues cast long shadows on the 1976 U.S. presidential election. Gerald Ford, hoping to win the presidency on his own terms, was keenly aware that his chances of remaining at the White House would be determined by his ability to overcome the political and economic burdens he had inherited from his predecessor. His nemesis from the Right was Ronald Reagan, who throughout the primaries castigated him for not battling the Communists vigorously enough. Ford tried to cope with this challenge by dropping détente from his political vocabulary and using "peace through strength" instead, by delaying ongoing arms negotiations with the Soviets, and by accepting an amendment to the Republican

Platform that for all practical purposes opposed the relationship with the Soviet Union that Nixon had initiated.[9] Ford's success against Reagan during the primaries proved to be fleeting; in November he was defeated by Jimmy Carter, a farmer from Georgia who had also served as that state's governor.

The Costs of Righteousness

One of the major consequences of Jimmy Carter's presidency was to expose the dangers of relying on righteousness to erect a foreign policy without first giving serious consideration to the contradictions it may generate. Foreign policy entails more than identifying objectives. It demands the creation of a strategy that explains the interconnection between objectives, and between objectives and policies.[10] For foreign policy objectives to be mutually consistent, they must be ranked and ordered in terms of importance to the state selecting them. The state that is ranking and ordering them must place the objectives in the context of an "overall conception," that is, a "generalized future state of affairs toward which" the objectives hope to lead the state and the international system.[11]

Carter assumed the presidency convinced that in order for the United States to regain its strength and respect, it had to design a foreign policy that emphasized the same values it stressed at home: morality and a commitment to freedom and democracy.[12] During his inaugural address in early 1977, he claimed that: "Our Nation can be strong abroad only if it is strong at home. And we know that the best way to enhance freedom in other lands is to demonstrate here that our democratic system is worthy of emulation."[13] Shortly after assuming office, he praised the activities of Soviet dissident Andrei Sakharov, criticized Czechoslovakia for badgering dissidents, expressed concern over the arrests of Soviet dissidents Alexander Ginsburg and Yuri Orlov, and welcomed Soviet exile Vladimir Bukovsky to the White House.[14] Carter sought to impose a structure on his foreign policy objectives during a commencement address at the University of Notre Dame, where he noted that:

> First, we have reaffirmed America's commitment to human rights as a fundamental tenet of our foreign policy. . . . This does not mean that we can conduct our foreign policy by rigid moral maxims. . . . I understand fully the limits of moral suasion. We have no illusion that changes will come easily or soon. . . .
>
> Second, we've moved deliberately to reinforce the bonds among our democracies. In our recent meetings in London, we agreed to widen our economic cooperation, to promote free trade, to strengthen the world's monetary system, to seek ways of avoiding nuclear proliferation. We prepared constructive proposals for the forthcoming meetings on North-

South problems of poverty, development, and global well-being, and we agreed on efforts to reinforce and to modernize our common defense.

Third, we've moved to engage the Soviet Union in a joint effort to halt the strategic arms race. . . . We desire a freeze on further modernization and production of weapons and a continuing, substantial reduction of strategic nuclear weapons as well. . . . We hope that we can take joint steps with all nations toward a final agreement eliminating nuclear weapons completely from our arsenals of death. . . . We hope that the Soviet Union will join us and other nations in playing a larger role in aiding the developing world, for common aid efforts will help us build a bridge of mutual confidence in one another.

Fourth, we are taking deliberate steps to improve the chances of lasting peace in the Middle East.[15]

One ought not to infer from the above actions and comments that Carter was incapable of recognizing that in its relationship with the Soviet Union, the United States would have to give priority to a much more tangible value: arms control. The relationship between arms control and human rights was best expressed by Carter's Secretary of State, Cyrus Vance. "[T]he most pressing issue in U.S.-Soviet relations," noted Vance, "was how to proceed in the SALT II negotiations." He added that though the United States was determined to "speak frankly about injustice both at home and abroad . . . ," it did "not intend to be strident or polemic. . . ." The shape and substance of the Carter administration's human rights policy, he concluded, "was universal in application, yet flexible enough to be adapted to individual situations."[16]

One of the first foreign policy challenges faced by the Carter administration was reviving SALT II. In late 1974, the Ford administration and the Soviet leaders had agreed at Vladivostok that in the next round of negotiations they would focus on imposing on both sides a limit of 2,400 strategic launchers and a sublimit of 1,320 missiles with multiple, independently targeted warheads (MIRVs). But just a week after his presidential inaugural, Carter learned that the U.S. intelligence had recently discovered that the Soviet Union had perfected the guidance technology that would enable it, theoretically, to destroy most of the United States's ICBMs in their concrete silos. This piece of information elicited immediate reactions from Carter's principal foreign policy makers. Zbigniew Brzezinski, Carter's national security adviser, contended that though he had no difficulty acknowledging that at a "certain point strategic weaponry ceases to exercise military significance in terms of marginal differences and consequences," the United States could not afford to disregard the political consequences of such superiority.[17] Vance, in turn, retorted that the theoretical vulnerability of the United States's ICBMs would not inevitably expose it to nuclear coercion, because its nuclear capability was erected on a triad of land-based missiles, sea-based missiles, and bombers.

"[T]h̄e vulnerability of any one leg would not undermine nuclear deterrence."[18] However, he acknowledged that because the development of the SS-18 gave the Soviets a political advantage, the United States would be forced to take countermeasures. He then warned that unless Washington reached a new agreement with Moscow that eliminated the theoretical vulnerability of the United States's silo-based ICBMs, both countries would find themselves caught in a new arms race cycle.[19] After extensive debate about whether the United States should try to finalize the tentative agreement reached at Vladivostok or should try to persuade Moscow that it would be in their mutual interests to negotiate deeper cuts, Carter opted for the second approach.

Two factors seem to have persuaded Carter to decide on deeper cuts. First, he was convinced that it was irrational to continue piling up thousands upon thousands of destructive nuclear weapons in both sides' arsenals. He remained convinced that 200 nuclear weapons on each side would be enough to deter war. Second, he came under intensive pressure from those who believed that the agreement reached at Vladivostok favored the Soviet Union too much. Senator Henry Jackson, a Democrat who would play a leading role in determining whether Congress would approve SALT II, asked Carter to demand deep cuts in Soviet heavy missiles. In late March, Vance traveled to Moscow, ready to present Carter's deep-cuts proposal. In the first meeting, Leonid Brezhnev launched a stinging critique of human rights abuses in the United States. Vance responded by making it clear that he was there to engage not in polemics but in concrete discussions. At their second meeting, Foreign Minister Andrei Gromyko proposed that they design an agreement based on Vladivostok. Vance immediately suggested that instead they consider designing a fully comprehensive agreement. He offered that they both reduce the Vladivostok ceiling from 2,400 to between 1,800 and 2,000 launchers; the Soviets cut their number of heavy missiles from 308 to 150; they both limit the number of land-based missiles with MIRVs to 550; they place severe restrictions on testing; they ban mobile land-based ICBMs; and they prohibit the development and deployment of a new ICBM.[20] Since the recommended reductions would be absorbed primarily by the Soviets, Moscow not only rejected the proposal but criticized Washington for assuming that it could "outplay" Moscow. Moscow's criticism, however, seems to have been based on the belief that Washington had yet to learn that the Soviet Union had perfected the guidance technology for the SS-18.[21]

Vance returned to the United States almost empty-handed. Both parties agreed to continue meeting, but neither side assumed that they would be able to reach a new accord prior to the expiration of SALT I in October 1977. More importantly, Vance's failure to make significant headway forced Carter to accept two major Pentagon policy recommendations. He approved the production and deployment of the MX, a new and much more accurate ICBM with 10 warheads, and a plan that called for the construction of 200 racetracks and 4,600 launch sites that would enable the Pentagon to move some 200 missiles from one hiding place to another and to launch each one of them from any one of 23 hiding places. Pentagon analysts contended that with this arrangement they would be able to reduce the Soviet Union's ability to detect the exact location of the new MXs.[22]

Success in the international realm eluded the Carter administration in many other areas. Determined to anoint his foreign policy with human rights activism, Carter viewed Africa and Latin America as two regions where his administration could display its deep commitment to social justice. From a pragmatic standpoint, it meant that the Carter administration would have to assess carefully the manner in which its other foreign policy interests might be linked to human rights. It was not long before the contradictions began to surface. Until around 1974, the Nixon administration had tried to balance the United States's "economic, scientific, and strategic interests in the white states [in Africa] with the political interest of dissociating [itself] from the white minority regimes and their repressive racial policies."[23] In 1970, the Nixon administration vetoed a United Nations resolution designed to condemn Britain for failing to overthrow by force the illegal white-minority regime in Rhodesia; two years later it voted against a UN resolution that called on all states to implement an arms embargo against South Africa; and in 1973 it opposed a UN resolution that reaffirmed the legitimacy of the struggle by colonial peoples for self-determination and independence "by all necessary means at their disposal."[24] In 1974, however, the political tide in Africa changed radically. After enduring its own military coup in April, Portugal finally accepted that 170,000 whites could not rule a population of 4.6 million blacks, and thus relinquished its control over Angola. Portugal's departure was followed by a civil war between the three factions that had struggled to expel the Portuguese. Each of these entities had its own foreign backer(s). The Soviet Union and Cuba supported the Popular Movement for the Liberation of Angola (MPLA); South Africa backed the National Union for the Total Independence of Angola (UNITA), and the United States and China endorsed the National Liberation Front of Angola (FNLA). By September 1975, the United States had decided to join forces with South Africa, and the battle for Angola raged. But not for long. Three months later, the U.S. Senate approved an amendment that authorized the Ford administration to use funds for intelligence-gathering operations in Angola, but not to supply military equipment or trained military personnel. In January 1976, the House voted 323 to 99 to ban covert military aid to Angola. Shortly thereafter, the Soviet-Cuban backed MPLA won the war.[25]

No longer able to rely on covert operations to offset the Soviet-Cuban push in Africa and aware that this confrontational approach was not winning the United States any major friends in Africa, Kissinger concluded that he would have to move toward a policy of conciliation. "The radicalization of the Third World and its consolidation into an antagonistic bloc," noted Kissinger, "is neither in our political nor economic interest." [26] In April 1976, he offered his new approach toward Africa. His proposal had little effect, for it was not long before he and his boss, President Ford, found themselves replaced by a new set of foreign policy makers.

The first challenge faced in Africa by the Carter administration came from Ethiopia. In late February 1977, Vance went before the Senate Appropriations Subcommittee on Foreign Operations determined to show that the new administration was prepared to carry out its promises. He announced that the United States would reduce foreign aid to Ethiopia because of its government's dismal human rights record. Conditions in Ethiopia had deteriorated rapidly since the middle of 1974, when its emperor, Haile Selassie, after failing to quell the outbreak of rebellion in the coastal province of Eritrea, relinquished power to a military council known as the Dergue. By early 1976, the Dergue had declared Ethiopia a communist state and began receiving substantial quantities of military equipment from Moscow. This new development alarmed neighboring Somalia, which had been a Soviet client since 1969. Somalia's leader, General Siad Barre, who for some time had been attempting to gain control over Ogaden, an Ethiopian province inhabited primarily by Somalians, intensified his efforts. Siad Barre traveled to Washington to ask the Carter administration that the United States become Somalia's new supplier of military equipment. Carter, after being advised by Vance that it would be unwise for the United States or any of its allies to provide Somalia with U.S. weapons, informed Somalia's ambassador to the United States that in principle his administration was prepared "to help other countries to meet Somalia's needs for defensive equipment." [27] In July, convinced that the United States would furnish him the weapons, Siad Barre launched a full scale invasion of Ogaden. In early August, the U.S. Department of State informed the Somalian leader that his decision to attack the Ogaden province in Ethiopia would prevent the United States from providing the defensive weapons it had promised. This decision did not stop Siad Barre. His forces continued their move inside Ethiopia, and by the end of November both sides were ready to engage in a decisive battle. During this period, Washington asked Moscow not to assist Ethiopia. Moscow, conscious that failure on its part to assist Ethiopia would enable Somalia to gain complete control of the province of Ogaden, mounted a massive airlift to prevent Ethiopia's defeat. By January 1978, the Soviets, with the aid of more than 15,000 Cuban troops, began to turn the tide of the battle for the Ogaden province. [28]

The Carter administration's policy regarding the Horn of Africa was the outgrowth of the conflicting counsel the president received from his two most influential foreign policy advisers. Vance believed that it would not be in the interest of the United States to become involved in the struggle between Somalia and Ethiopia, or to criticize the Soviet Union for its overt support of Ethiopia. If Washington supported Somalia while Somalian forces invaded the Ogaden province, the United States would find itself "on the wrong side of Africa's most cherished principles—the territorial integrity of the postcolonial states."[29] Second, any action by the United States to support Somalia would be used by the Soviet Union and Cuba as a justification to support Ethiopia. And third, in the long run, Soviet influence in the region would diminish in the face of nationalistic feelings, just as it had in Egypt.[30] Brzezinski objected to Vance's analysis. The national security adviser argued that the local conflict between Somalia and Ethiopia was not particularly relevant. What was important, he added, was that the Soviet Union was using the conflict as part of a grand strategy in Africa designed to attain some specific goals. As it became evident that the Soviets and the Cubans were helping Ethiopia in its war against Somalia, Brzezinski proposed that the United States send a naval force to the region and provide air cover for the Somalian troops. Moreover, in early March 1978, he released a public statement in which he noted that failure on the part of the Soviets and Cubans to withdraw their forces from Ethiopia would have a negative effect on SALT negotiations. Vance immediately asked the president to rebut publicly Brzezinski's claim. He warned that any attempt on the part of the United States to link the trouble in the Horn of Africa to SALT negotiations would adversely affect U.S. interests. Carter opted for a middle ground. He noted that he had no intention of linking SALT negotiations to other issues, but then added that failure on the part of Moscow and Havana to withdraw their troops from Ethiopia "would make it more difficult [for Congress] to ratify the SALT agreement or comprehensive test-ban agreement if concluded. . . ."[31] By March 14, the Ethiopian forces, with Soviet and Cuban support, had managed to push the Somalian troops out of Ethiopia. Addis Ababa, Moscow, and Havana kept their promise; their forces did not cross into Somalian territory.

The hazards faced by the Carter administration in southern Africa were no less ponderous. Upon assuming office, Carter and Vance agreed that the United States would not be able to develop a solid working relationship with black Africa and block the spread of communism unless it helped push South Africa away from apartheid, helped secure independence for the South African–controlled territory of Namibia, and persuaded the white government of Rhodesia to acquiesce to majority rule. If success were to be measured according to present conditions, it would be appropriate to contend that Carter's initiatives were effective. By the end of his tenure as president, however, his record with regard to southern Africa was mixed. On the positive side, Rhodesia had become Zimbabwe, had held its first free election, and had chosen its first black prime minister on the basis of majority rule. On the negative side, Namibia remained under South Africa's control; and South Africa's white government, rather than moving away from apartheid, intensified its oppression of blacks and moved against whites who called for the government to alter its policies.

As if the problems the United States faced in Africa were not enough, the Carter administration was embarrassed by a major event closer to home. By the end of 1976, the leader of Nicaragua, Anastasio Somoza, found himself facing an uncertain future. Following the 1972 Managua earthquake, which killed some 10,000 people and destroyed homes, commercial businesses, and small industries, opposition against the Somoza family mounted steadily. Initially, the challengers argued that the Somoza family, which had been ruling Nicaragua for nearly 40 years, was using the economic package provided by the United States to help rebuild Managua to further enlarge its own personal wealth. In time, these critics, in unison with the Catholic Church, also drew attention to the human rights violations committed by the government and called for the establishment of a democratic political system. They were not the only domestic groups challenging the regime. The Nationalist Sandinista Liberation Front (FSLN), an organization created in 1961 by veteran leftists with various backgrounds, had been mounting sporadic attacks against Somoza's military, the National Guard.[32] When Carter became president, he instructed his administration to pressure the Somozas to open Nicaragua's political system. In March and April, members of his administration pledged to cut military aid to, and not sign a security act pact with, the Somoza regime unless it improved the human rights situation in Nicaragua. For a brief while, however, not every member of the Carter administration believed it would be wise to bring to an end the Somoza dynasty. Assistant Secretary of State for Inter-American Affairs Terrence Todman, for instance, cautioned that it would be imprudent for the United States to assume that it could deal with the issue of human rights without considering other aspects of the United States's relationship with Nicaragua. In September, Carter approved a $2.5 million arms credit to Nicaragua. But within a month's time, his administration was taken by surprise by a series of successful attacks launched by the Terceristas, one of the FSLN's three factions. The attacks, though small in scale, for the first time brought the war from the mountains to the cities, and gave the insurrection a popular component.

Unable to decide how to respond to the latest development, the Carter administration opted for a "wait and see" policy. It did not have to wait long. In January 1978, Pedro Chamorro, the editor of the opposition paper *La Prensa,* was assassinated. His death was followed by an outbreak of spontaneous demonstrations and general strikes, all aimed at weakening the Somoza regime. Nicaraguan businessmen approached the U.S. ambassador and requested that he pressure Somoza to resign. For the remainder of 1978, the Carter administration dealt with the Nicaragua situation without a clear sense of what it hoped to accomplish. Initially, it condemned Chamorro's assassination and asked Somoza to start negotiations with his political adversaries. In May, however, Carter approved the release of a $12 million package in economic aid to Nicaragua, and a month later he praised the Nicaraguan dictator for his latest political reforms. In the meantime, pressure against Somoza within Nicaragua continued to mount. Political moderates announced in August a 16–point program calling for, among other things, Somoza's resignation, the establishment of a government of national unity, and the scheduling of elections for December 1981. More importantly, the three factions of the FSLN agreed to unite with the Nicaraguan Socialist Party to form the United People's Movement. Shortly afterward, the Terceristas seized the National Palace and took 1,500 captives. After two days of negotiations, Somoza agreed to release 50 political prisoners, publish a FSLN communiqué, and give safe passage out of Nicaragua to the guerrillas and the released political prisoners.

This event finally convinced a few members of the Carter administration that it would be in the United States's interest to persuade Somoza to exit honorably from his post. A negotiating team made up of representatives from Guatemala, the United States, and the Dominican Republic met with Somoza and his political rivals in early October. Negotiations dragged on until early February 1979, when the U.S. Department of State, after deciding that Somoza had no intention of abdicating, reduced its diplomatic staff in Managua, withdrew the United States's military mission and all Peace Corps volunteers from Nicaragua, and stopped considering new Agency for International Developments (AID) projects. Somoza was not intimidated by these steps and continued to oppose any proposal that stipulated his ceding power. By the end of June, however, he recognized that he could no longer endure the pressure that was being exerted on his regime. The governments of Venezuela, Colombia, Ecuador, Bolivia, and Peru had released a joint statement calling for the formation of a "truly democratic regime" and the recognition of the FSLN as a legitimate organization. Moreover, the FSLN had announced the creation of a provisional government that included leaders of Nicaragua's moderate faction, and was preparing its forces for the launching of a final attack on Somoza's National Guards.

The Carter administration once again had difficulty deciding what course of action to take. Initially, Brzezinski proposed that the Organization of American States (OAS) move into Nicaragua with its own military force to prevent the FSLN from gaining power. After his recommendation was voted down by the OAS, the Carter administration wondered whether it should recognize the provisional government or create a separate "pillar of power," independent of Somoza, which could then negotiate with the provisional government. The Carter administration decided to play it safe, and chose both options. Its decision had no significant effect. On July 20, three days after Somoza had left the country, the provisional government, led by FSLN representatives, assumed power. During the next three months, the FSLN moved swiftly to consolidate its internal power, establish close relationships with Castro's government in Cuba, and oppose any U.S. effort to influence Nicaragua's domestic and foreign policies.

The political signals emanating from the Persian Gulf were also highly disquieting. Iran had been governed by the regime of Shah Mohammed Reza Pahlevi for most of the Cold War. In the early 1950s, the shah had been deposed by a nationalist group, but had been returned to power by the CIA after a very brief interval. Since then, he had maintained closed military and economic relationships with the United States, even through the first part of the 1970s, when Iran became one of the principal forces behind the rapid increase in oil prices.[33] Starting in the 1960s, but especially after 1973, as Iran began to harvest the benefits from the windfall of high oil prices, the shah encouraged Iranians to adopt Western values, fostered rapid industrial development, and launched a major military buildup.[34] Fundamentalist Shi'ite Muslims, led by their religious leaders, denounced the shah's actions. The shah responded by strengthening his military and using his secret police, Savak, to imprison fundamentalists and send them into exile. This action did not prevent religious leaders from mobilizing supporters in Iran. From abroad, and under the leadership of Shi'ite clerical leader Ayatollah Ruhollah Khomeini, they carefully monitored and nurtured discontent toward the shah's regime and its economic and social policies.

Carter, mindful that because of Iran's economic and strategic value to the United States his administration could not rely on the same standard it used to judge other dictatorial regimes, eventually agreed to continue the practice of selling highly sophisticated military equipment to Iran. Congress, afraid that Iran's increasing military power might offset the balance of power in the Middle East, initially opposed Carter's decision.[35] Though Congress eventually gave in to Carter's request, the battle led the shah to question whether his country would be able to count on the continued support of the United States. Believing that the shah needed some reassurance, Carter agreed to visit Iran during his scheduled foreign travel to eight countries in Europe and Asia. During a brief stop in Tehran at the end of December 1977, Carter referred to Iran as an island of stability.[36]

Little did Carter realize that his latest claim would only fuel stronger opposition within Iran. By October 1978, strikes and demonstrations, instigated by the left and fundamentalists, had paralyzed the country. Oil production had dropped from six million barrels a day to little over one million barrels a day. The Carter administration was caught totally unprepared.[37] After intensive debate between its principal foreign policy advisers as to whether it should advise the shah to authorize the military to move aggressively against his political adversaries or install a moderate civilian government, the Carter administration once again opted for a compromise. It recommended the creation of a civilian government, but with the understanding that if the Iranian army faced the "danger of becoming more fragmented, then a military government under the shah may be unavoidable."[38] The advice arrived too late. In early February 1979, after months of exhorting his followers to strike, disrupt, riot, and create chaos, Khomeini returned triumphantly to Tehran. By then, the shah had already left the country on an extended vacation. Thus, almost overnight, Iran, a state that for a quarter of a century had maintained a close relationship with the United States, began to depict its former associate as "the great Satan." Adding insult to injury, in early November Americans woke up to the news that a huge mob of Iranian youths had taken over the U.S. embassy in Tehran and held 76 American hostages.

The Triumph of Economics

After nearly a year and a half of attempting to cope with the inflation, recession, and recycling problem spawned by the oil shock, the leaders of the United States, France, Britain, Japan, Italy, and West Germany met in France to create the framework of a new monetary system. In early 1976, they finalized an agreement at an IMF meeting in Kingston, Jamaica. The agreement, with its final details outlined in the Second Amendment to the Articles of Agreement of the International Monetary Fund, dealt with both liquidity and adjustment. In 1968, the ten major financial powers had agreed to create Special Drawing Rights (SDRs). The IMF created SDR as a reserve asset to complement the dollar as a reserve currency. SDRs were allocated to IMF's members according to their quotas, in order to solve the liquidity creation problem. The rationale behind this action was that a deficit country in need of international reserves could transfer its SDR balance to other countries. Nine years later, in 1976, the six major financial powers agreed to reduce the world's dependency on the dollar by making SDR the principal reserve asset of the international monetary system, eliminating its link with gold, increasing its interest rate, and liberalizing the conditions under which it could be used. With regard to the problem of adjustment, the Second Amendment authorized each country to adopt whatever exchange-rate system it wanted—fixed or floating. The appropriate authorities in each country could buy or sell foreign exchange in order to "prevent or moderate sharp and disruptive fluctuations from day to day and from week to week" but not to suppress or to reverse long-run exchange-rate movement.[39]

The Carter administration welcomed the new monetary arrangement but still wanted greater multilateral management of international economic relations. The United States's economy had experienced some disconcerting swings just before Carter assumed power in early 1977. Unemployment had risen from 5.5 percent in the third quarter of 1974 to 9.9 percent by the following May, and then had gone down to 7.7 percent by the second quarter of 1976. The inflation rate had fluctuated from 9.1 percent in 1975, to 5 percent by 1976. By the start of the third quarter, however, the U.S. economy once again began to slow down. Congress sought to stimulate the economy by adopting measures similar to those it took in 1974, when it passed the largest tax reduction in history and increased federal spending by 19 percent. However, the Ford administration, afraid that such measures might result in an increase in the rate of inflation, refused to approve them.[40] Nobody benefited more from these decisions than Jimmy Carter in his election campaign.

Like previous administrations, the Carter administration came to power convinced that the effective implementation of its own economic theory would help ease the economic problems afflicting both the United States and the world in general. Its "locomotive theory" proposed that countries with a balance-of-payments surplus, such as Germany and Japan, could, by coordinating their expansionary policies, serve as engines of growth for the rest of the world. The Carter administration was not entirely successful in its first attempt to coordinate the domestic economic policies of the United States with those of Japan and West Germany. At the London summit meeting held in London in May 1977, Tokyo and Bonn agreed to secure during that same year a growth rate of 6.7 percent and 5 percent, respectively, for 1977. Neither Japan nor West Germany, however, fulfilled its pledge. In the meantime, the Carter administration had begun to put into practice its economic theory by sending to Congress an amended budget, with tax reductions, rebates, and increased expenditures, and by unveiling its first energy program designed to cut down on excessive oil consumption.[41] The domestic and international economic consequences of these decisions were mixed. In the United States, real GNP and per capita income increased by 4.9 percent; industrial productivity rose by 5.6 percent and corporate profits by 9.5 percent; employment went up by 4.1 million workers; and unemployment dropped from 7.7 percent in 1976 to 6.4 percent. The economic boom continued through 1978.[42]

Still, with the expansion came a backlash. According to Under Secretary of State for Economic Affairs Richard Cooper, the Carter administration launched its policy of economic expansion conscious that if Germany and Japan did not initiate compatible policies, the United States's trade position would worsen and the dollar would depreciate relative to some other currencies. Failure by the United States to pursue this course, added Cooper, would "have courted far graver dangers for the world economy—extreme financial difficulties for a number of countries and protectionist actions in most of the industrialized countries."[43] Neither Bonn nor Tokyo followed Washington's lead. With Bonn contending that the United States's economic policies were "naïve" and Tokyo refusing to reduce Japan's current account surplus, they criticized Washington's unwillingness to use external methods to prevent the continued fall of the dollar, or to slow down the domestic growth rate in order to bring down inflation and reduce deficits. Bonn, however, decided to do more than just criticize. Mindful that West Germany's economic power was considerably greater than that of its Western European counterparts, Bonn decided to start behaving according to its status. Troubled by the disruptive effects of unstable exchange markets, by the problems generated by the weak dollar, and by Washington's persistent pressure on Germany to reflate its economy, Bonn, with strong support from Paris, urged the other members of the European Economic Community in early 1978 to agree to the formation of a zone of monetary stability within Western Europe.[44]

The United States did not outright object to Bonn's initiative. Still, the Carter administration voiced its concerns in May 1978. Specifically, it sought to ensure that the new European Monetary System (EMS) would not consistently overvalue the dollar vis-à-vis European currencies, would not restrict capital movements, would not set up rigid exchange rates, would not strive to undermine IMF, and would have neither a low-growth nor an inflationary bias. In July, representatives of the major financial powers met in Bonn. Those representing Germany, France, and Japan agreed to push for more expansionary policies, while those acting on behalf of the United States agreed to curb inflation and energy consumption. The future of EMS, however, was barely discussed.[45] In spite of that, by the end of the year the EEC members had agreed to create their zone of monetary stability by establishing a system of fixed exchange rates among EEC members and a floating rate for non-members, a basket of EEC currencies that would serve as a basis for fixing exchange rates, and a network of credit arrangements.[46]

In the meantime, the Carter administration tried to adhere to the economic terms it had agreed upon in July in Bonn with the other major financial powers. In August, the Federal Reserve Board tightened domestic credit. In mid-October, Congress approved a watered-down energy package. Some nine days later, the Carter administration announced that it would limit federal spending and reduce the deficit from its current level of 23 percent of GNP to 21 percent by 1980, institute voluntary policies designed to control increases in wages and prices, and adjust government wage and procurement policies correspondingly. In early November, the Carter administration, for the first time in the postwar era, altered the United States's domestic economic policy for international monetary reasons. Its new financial package consisted of a policy of active intervention in foreign exchange markets, backed by $30 billion in foreign currencies for possible intervention in the financial markets to strengthen the position of the dollar.[47]

These measures introduced much-needed stability to the dollar and the exchange markets, but not for long. During the first half of 1978, oil companies reduced their oil stocks after concluding that there was no international adversity burgeoning over the horizon that could disrupt oil productions. In October 1978, however, as the shah's regime became the target of major domestic demonstrations and strikes, Iran's oil production dropped considerably. The United States and the other major industrial powers were not entirely unprepared for this kind of event. In 1974, Washington, conscious that the United States was the only entity with the power and status to help create an international regime capable of coordinating responses to the consequences spawned by the 1973–1974 oil crisis, organized an international energy conference. By the end of the year, the principal economic powers had established the International Energy Agency (IEA), which was responsible for: i) initiating joint energy research and development activities, ii) developing an emergency system for sharing oil, iii) setting up an information system to monitor the oil market, and iv) designing new long-term measures to reduce net demand for oil.[48] The new agency failed to pass its first test in 1978–1979. Iran's oil exports virtually ceased during the first two months of 1979, as the shah relinquished control of Iran's government to the Khomeini regime. While the IEA was reluctant to take strong formal action, spot oil prices doubled almost immediately, and the major oil-consuming countries, rather than coordinating their responses, put pressure on the oil companies to grant them preferential treatment.

The nature of the 1979 oil crisis was not as simple as I have just depicted it. By the start of 1979 there was no real shortage of petroleum. As it became evident that the exports of Iranian oil were declining, Saudi Arabia increased its production. Nigeria, Iraq, and Mexico took similar measures at the start of 1979, and by March, Iran's own oil exports were up to the 60 percent level from a year earlier. In the meantime, the price of oil had not yet sustained a major increase. OPEC members met in late December and agreed to raise the price of oil immediately from $12.70 a barrel to $13.34 a barrel.[49] They also agreed to add new increases until they reached the price of $14.54 per barrel by October 1979. But then, in late March 1979, a new event disrupted their plans. The Carter administration had been trying for some time to persuade Israeli Prime Minister Menachem Begin and Egyptian President Anwar Sadat to reach a peace agreement. As evidence that their efforts might pay off mounted, Arab states began to warn Egypt that they would not endorse an agreement with Israel. Arab states feared that in order to secure a promise for greater economic assistance from the United States, Egypt would capitulate on the issue of granting the West Bank self-governing authority.[50] At the end of March, after Begin and Sadat had signed the peace treaty at the White House, Riyadh agreed with other OPEC members to advance the price of $14.54 per oil barrel, scheduled to go into effect in October, to April 1. In early May, Saudi Arabia, along with Kuwait and other Arab states, decided to express their discontent with the Israeli-Egypt pact more vigorously. They approached several European leaders and suggested that they would be willing to guarantee the flow of Arab oil to the members of the EEC in return for their support for a Palestinian state in the Middle East. The Carter administration tried to mend its relationships with some of the Arab states, but to little avail. To compound the problem, OPEC met again in Geneva in late June and agreed with Saudi Arabia's initiative to raise the price of crude oil by 60 percent, from $14.54 to $23.50 per barrel.

From then on, there was little the Carter administration could do to alter the growing perception that it was not able to handle competently the challenges faced by the United States. In June, Carter traveled to Tokyo hoping to convince the United States's allies to agree on specific oil-import reductions, and to start shifting away from oil to greater use of coal and nuclear energy. At their first meeting, Germany's Chancellor Helmut Schmidt rebuked Carter by remarking that the president's attempt to negotiate a peace treaty in the Middle East had brought about the oil crisis. Schmidt and the other leaders had good reason to be upset. By June, the dollar had recovered significantly against both the yen and the deutsche mark, and the United States was the only country to report an improvement in its current account balance. On the other hand, West Germany's current account balance had experienced a drop from a surplus of $8.9 billion in 1978 to a deficit of $5.8 billion a year later, while Japan's current account balance had taken a dip from a $16.5 billion surplus to an $8.6 billion deficit during the same period. Finally, after several highly acrimonious exchanges, the leaders agreed on oil import targets, none of which was likely to affect domestic consumption in a major way. This small victory paid no major dividends. Soon after his return to the United States, Carter learned that the domestic expansion of the previous three years, along with high oil prices, had generated a major increase in inflation, that the dollar was showing signs of weakness in the international markets, and that his popularity had dipped further.[51]

Carter's Last Friendly Embrace

One of Carter's initial goals had been to set up the groundwork for the eventual elimination of nuclear weapons. He recognized that his chances of realizing such a goal were nonexistent. Still, he was determined, at minimum, to halt the strategic arms race by putting a freeze on the further modernization and production of weapons and, at maximum, to reduce the number of strategic nuclear weapons considerably. He failed on both counts.

At his meeting with the Soviet leaders in Moscow in 1977, Vance had proposed that both parties reduce the Vladivostok ceiling from 2,400 to between 1,800 and 2,000 launchers, limit the number of land-based missiles with MIRVs to 550, accept severe restrictions on testing; and refrain from developing a new ICBM and mobile land-based ICBMs. He had also suggested that the Soviets cut their number of heavy missiles from 308 to 150. The meeting did not elicit the results hoped by Carter. Still, both parties agreed to continue negotiating. Finally, after lengthy and tortuous discussions, the leaders of the Soviet Union and the United States met in Vienna on June 18, 1979, to sign SALT II. The agreement was a far cry from the one Carter had proposed some two years earlier. The treaty capped strategic nuclear launchers of all types at 2,400, with the understanding that they would be further reduced to 2,250 by the end of 1981; and land-, air-, and sea-based MIRVed ICBMs were limited to 1,320.

The Carter administration submitted the treaty to the Senate for ratification four days after it had been signed, and it immediately came under intense criticism from both outside and inside the Senate. The Committee on the Present Danger, a group that was formed in 1975 to lobby against détente, and that had the backing of Harvard history professor Richard Pipes, maintained that the agreement should not be ratified, because the Soviet Union had launched an unprecedented military buildup that threatened the United States, world peace, and the cause of human freedom.[52] Another major critic of SALT II was Paul Nitze, the former head of the Arms Control and Disarmament Agency. In 1976, while commenting on SALT I, Nitze remarked that under the terms of the agreement "the Soviet Union will continue to pursue a nuclear superiority that is not merely quantitative, but designed to produce a theoretical winning-capability." He then added that only if the United States decided "to redress the impending strategic imbalance, can the Soviet Union be persuaded to abandon its quest for superiority and to resume the path of meaningful limitations and reductions through negotiations."[53] In 1979, after the new SALT treaty had been signed, Nitze spoke before the Senate Foreign Relations Committee and noted that the new agreement was weighted in favor of the Soviet Union by permitting it to retain its 308 launchers of heavy land-based missiles while banning them for the United States, and by not counting the Backfire medium bomber under the 2,400 aggregate ceiling. In late July, former Secretary of State Henry Kissinger went before the Senate and expressed his support for the treaty under the condition that the United States increase its defense spending, adopt a new strategy designed to strengthen its capability to attack Soviet strategic forces, and demand Soviet international restraint. A few days later, Senator Henry Jackson, a Democrat from the state of Washington, informed Carter that his support for the agreement would most likely be contingent on whether the Pentagon increased its budget by at least 4 to 5 percent after inflation.

These challenges, though significant, did not automatically doom the agreement. In August, in an attempt to defuse criticism that the United States was relinquishing nuclear superiority to the Soviet Union, the Carter administration approved the deployment of 108 Pershing II intermediate missiles and 464 cruise missiles in Western Europe. In October, the NATO High Level Group welcomed the decision. Shortly afterward, Moscow warned that the deployment of the Pershing IIs and cruise missiles could imperil arms control.[54] By this time, however, the Carter administration, particularly Carter and Vance, were questioning their original assumption that they could persuade the Soviet leaders that it was in the interests of the United States and the Soviet Union to broaden détente. Of significant concern to Carter and Vance (and Brzezinski), was the discovery by U.S. intelligence that Soviet activity in Cuba had increased considerably. In late August, Vance learned that there was enough information to conclude that the Soviet Union had established a Soviet motorized rifle brigade in Cuba consisting of some 2,000 to 3,000 men, and that it had been in the island since at least 1975 or 1976. The Carter administration provided this information to the Senate. Almost immediately, Frank Church, who was the chair of the Senate Foreign Relations Committee and was being accused by conservatives of being soft on defense, released the news to the media and called on Carter to demand that the Soviets remove the brigade immediately. A few days later, Church warned that the Senate would most likely not ratify SALT II if the Soviet Union refused to remove its brigade from Cuba.[55]

In late September, the Soviet leaders told the Carter administration that they had no intention of removing the brigade. Carter then decided that it would be counterproductive to link the brigade issue to SALT II. On October 1, the president informed the American public that though the United States would set up a Caribbean military task force to prevent any possible unfriendly activities by the Soviet brigade, the issue was not grave enough to justify a return to the cold war.[56] Little did he realize that Moscow was getting ready to provide him with a more compelling rationale for rekindling the Cold War. On Christmas Eve, 200 troop-transports began to unload Soviet troops in Afghanistan. Three days later, some

6,000 Soviet troops were on Afghanistanian territory, with five divisions standing at the border ready to enter.

During the next month, the world witnessed a radical change in the foreign policy of the United States. On January 3, 1980, Carter asked that the Senate to delay consideration of the SALT II Treaty because of Soviet action against Afghanistan. The following day, he announced an array of sanctions against the Soviet Union. Some of the more notable ones were an embargo on the exports of grain, the prohibition of sales of high technology, and the cancellation of U.S. participation in the 1980 Summer Olympics in Moscow. The coup de grâce, however, came on January 23, during Carter's State of the Union address before a joint session of Congress. During the speech, which came to be referred to as the "Carter Doctrine," the president remarked that the Soviet invasion of Afghanistan "could pose the most serious threat to the peace since the Second World War," and that the Soviet Union had to pay a concrete price for its aggression. He also noted that he was determined to keep the United States "the strongest of all nations," and emphasized that any "attempt by an outside force to gain control of the Persian Gulf will be regarded as an assault on the vital interests of the United States of America, and that such an assault will be repelled by any means necessary, including military force."[57] The new foreign policy represented an attempt by Carter to save his failing presidency. It was not to be. In late April, the world learned that an U.S. attempt to rescue the hostages held by Iran had ended in disaster. The news on the domestic front was no less bleak. By July, unemployment in the United States had risen to 7.8 percent; by August, the inflation rate was touching 11 percent; and on election day the prime rate hit 20.5 percent. With Carter's foreign and economic policies in shambles, the U.S. public decided to give the presidency to his most vociferous critic: Ronald Reagan. On January 20, 1981, Carter sustained his last humiliation as president. As Reagan was being sworn in as president of the United States, Iran released the remaining 52 hostages.

The Death of Innocence

It is doubtful that the United States experienced more foreign policy failures in one year than it did in 1979. In that 12–month period, Iran and Nicaragua came under the control of regimes that not only questioned the authority of the United States but also made a point of acting against the interests of the United States; oil prices took a quantum leap; the signing of SALT II abetted further the division in the United States between supporters and opponents of arms control; Moscow informed Washington that it had no intention of removing Soviet troops from Cuba; and Moscow thumbed its nose at Washington's attempt to diminish the tension between the United States and the Soviet Union following the Soviet invasion of Afghanistan.

It is tempting to contend that the United States would have encountered fewer international troubles had it been led by a president with a clearer understanding of the nature of power, and less driven by the need to imbed his foreign policies with moral norms. It also seems sensible to propose that the United States might have found its foreign policy compass had Carter chosen as his advisers individuals with less disparate goals. But before concurring with these assertions, one should develop a better understanding of the challenges confronting the United States, both at home and abroad, during the second half of the 1970s.

The tension between the Soviet Union and the United States had not lessened since the early 1970s. Notwithstanding SALT I and détente, both entities were still engaged in an arms race, and their rivalry in many regions of the developing world had gained considerable intensity. On the international economic front, the picture had become noticeably more complex. The United States's economic allies, conscious of their new power, were much more inclined to challenge Washington's leadership and to question its domestic and international economic policies. Moreover, the two oil crises had muddled further the international economic system by adding new international actors, increasing the interdependence between the system's dominant entities, and enlarging the economic disparity between the developed and developing worlds. With these perils binding the international system, the United States needed a leader with the competence to understand them and the mettle to act on them intelligently. Those with the authority to select the leader who must contend with the international system's most critical hazards, however, often have other priorities or are unable to anticipate the effect that failure by their leader to alleviate the international system's problems could have on their own lives.

Carter was elected, in part, because he campaigned as a Washington outsider who promised to inculcate in politics a new sense of moral integrity. In the United States, however, morality wore different masks. Those who rebuked Nixon's policy of détente and claimed that the Soviets could not be trusted were as persuaded about the righteousness of their moral claim as those who demanded that the United States adopt an antimilitary stand and stop bolstering dictatorial regimes that violated human rights. Members of the first group viewed communism, and any state that adhered to a communist ideology, as the gravest imaginable political evil. They did not condone noncommunist dictatorial regimes, but considered them less immoral than communist regimes. They argued that noncommunist regimes had shorter life spans than communist regimes, and that their political tentacles did not extend across the entire domestic social body as did those of communist regimes. Members of the second group, in turn, did not necessarily approve of communists, but maintained that it was less baneful living with them than promoting an arms race that held the world hostage to terror. They added that an excessive fear of communism had led the United States to disregard those values that defined its identity, to tolerate ruthless dictatorial regimes, and to ignore the woes of those who, because they were left with no other choices, viewed communism as the only way out of their misery.

Brzezinski and Vance represented, respectively, each moral stand. The national security adviser, though willing to acknowledge that not all of the world's ills could be ascribed to communist activities, invariably recommended that the United States take a tough stand when he believed that the national interest of the United States was threatened by the conduct of the Soviet Union or one of its allies. Vance, on the other hand, without fail opposed a rigid stance against the Soviet Union and always called for moderation, especially if he feared that the response by the United States might undermine its ability to finalize the SALT II negotiations. A perusal of the foreign policy cases dealt with by the Carter administration supports this contention. When Brzezinski argued that the United States should send a naval force to the Red Sea, near Somalia and Ethiopia, to provide air cover for the Somalian troops who were at war with Soviet-backed Ethiopian troops, Vance contravened by contending that it would be unwise for the United States to become involved in a regional conflict that could throw off track SALT II negotiations with the Soviet Union. When Brzezinski proposed that the Carter administration recommend to the shah that he use his military force to neutralize the antigovernment actions by the fundamentalists, Vance objected and urged that it recommend the formation of a civilian government. When Brzezinski argued that the OAS should intervene militarily in Nicaragua to prevent the Sandinistas from gaining power, Vance advised against such a policy. When Brzezinski suggested that the United States should use the Soviet brigade incident in Cuba to step up its condemnation of Soviet-Cuban involvement in the developing world, Vance, fearing that the broader approach would undermine SALT II, asked that the issue be confined to Cuba itself. And finally, when Brzezinski recommended that the United States use the Soviet invasion of Afghanistan to restart its policy of containment, Vance, though appreciative that the event enfeebled his repeated calls for moderate responses, once again asked for restraint.

Secretary of State Vance resigned in late April 1980, after learning that Carter had approved a rescue mission of the hostages held by Iran. For all practical purposes, however, his role as secretary of state had come to an end following the Soviet invasion of Afghanistan. After the event, and aware that most of the strategic decisions he had favored had not brought about the results he had wanted, Vance distanced himself from the day-to-day policy process. But his decision, and the renewed attempts by the Carter administration to convey a new aura of competence, proved to be unconvincing. In November 1980, the American voters placed their hopes on a new leader: Ronald Reagan.

Simplifying the Problem

On June 5, 1989, during the first freely contested election held in Poland since the end of the Second World War, Solidarity, an independent union that had been granted legal status only a couple of months earlier, ousted the Communist Party from power. On October 7, Hungary's Communist Party disavowed marxism. On November 9, a caretaker government in East Germany that had replaced the Communist leadership, authorized the opening of the gates to West Berlin. Immediately, jubilant demonstrators began the destruction of the 28–year-old Berlin Wall. On November 10, Bulgaria's Communist leader resigned. On November 24, Czechoslovakia's Communist regime surrendered its power, and the new government began to draft a new constitution. On December 25, a violent revolution brought to an end the 24–year rule of Romania's Communist dictator. Exactly two years later, Moscow formally agreed to replace the multinational Soviet state with a loose federation of republics known as the Commonwealth of Independent States (CIS). And finally, in early October 1993, Russia's president, Boris Yeltsin, disbanded Russia's Communist Party.

Some political analysts have questioned the claim, typically voiced by conservatives, that Ronald Reagan's foreign policies must be credited for provoking these changes. Other skeptics have suggested that though his foreign policies played a very important role, it is unlikely that they were initiated with the intent of ending the Cold War. And finally, a third group of critics has contended, with unmasked envy, that the end of the Cold War has proven only that Reagan was blessed by an unusual amount of good luck. Major international changes can rarely be attributed to a single cause. To understand the transformation the international system experienced starting during the second half of the 1980s, one must also focus on the domestic and international challenges the Soviet Union faced during that same period. This is another way of saying that the changes the international system withstood in the late 1980s and early 1990s could not have taken place during the Nixon era. In spite of these qualifiers, it is also fair to contend that had Reagan chosen not to initiate the foreign policies his administration started, it is highly doubtful that the world would have witnessed the dramatic transformation it sustained in such a brief period of time.

The media and many political analysts have portrayed Reagan as a leader either unwilling or unable to grasp the complexity of the problems faced by the United States. The evidence seems to back their contention. Reagan, unlike Carter, was not a leader endowed with superior intelligence who tried to understand the full nature of each issue he had to address or who attempted to monitor carefully the implementation of his policies. But as one compares the achievements of both presidents, it is useful to keep in mind that though: "[C]omplexity, sophistication, and nuance may be prerequisites for intellectual leadership, they are not necessarily so for political leadership, and can at times actually get in the way."[58] During his campaign for the presidency, Reagan emphasized three political themes. He repeatedly stated that under his administration national defense would be increased to ensure that the United States possessed the strength necessary to meet the growing Soviet threat, taxes would be cut, and government spending and involvement in private affairs would be reduced. Though his strategic and economic agendas did not exist independently of one another, I will keep them separate during the early phase of my discussion.

Students of international politics have long acknowledged the value of using game theory to explicate in very simple terms different types of political confrontations between two or more entities, and possible outcomes. One of the models used most frequently is the Chicken Game. The model focuses on the basic strategic choices faced by two rival international entities, and excludes details such as the tactics relied on by each party, the communications that ensue within and between them, and changes of tactics. The advantage of relying on this approach to delineate the relationship between the United States and the Soviet Union is that it brings out the essential structure of their problem and the basic options that were available to them. In this section, I will first describe the Chicken Game and then apply it to a particular period in the relationship between the United States and the Soviet Union. I will end the section by discussing in some detail what led Reagan to choose the strategy he opted for, what persuaded the Soviet leadership to respond as it did, and the kinds of negotiations that ensued and agreements that were reached between the leaders of both entities.

In a 2 × 2 game matrix, each party has two choices and faces four possible outcomes. The two essential strategic possibilities are to hold firm to one's original demands (D), or to concede or accommodate to the opponent's demands (C). An entity that intends to hold firm to its original demands typically uses one or more coercive tactics to force the opponent to accommodate or concede. The four possible payoffs are: both parties agree on a compromise (R); neither party is willing to concede (P); only one party concedes (S); and only one party gets its way (T). The worst possible strategy for both entities would be to hold firm to their original demands. The second worst possible strategy for either entity would be to concede to the other entity's demands, while the other entity holds firm to its own demands. The third worst possible strategy (or second most attractive strategy) would be for both entities to compromise simultaneously. The most desirable strategy for either entity would be to hold firm to its original demands while the other entity concedes or accommodates. In other words: $T > R > S > P$.[59]

When Nixon became president in 1969, he and Kissinger sought to persuade Moscow that it would be in the interests of both the United States and the Soviet Union to control the pace of the arms race and to ensure that neither party would erect a nuclear defense system. Initially, Moscow seemed willing to accept Washington's rationale that an attempt to develop such a defensive system would be prohibitively costly, would be destabilizing, and would not be able to achieve its driving objective. Reagan never accepted this rationale and challenged it publicly in 1983 by announcing that the United States would start investing heavily in research aimed at creating a defensive system capable of intercepting and destroying strategic ballistic missiles before they reached the soil of the United States or its allies. Using a game-theory approach, one could propose that the announcement compelled the Soviet Union to consider whether it would counteract Reagan's decision by: launching a surprise nuclear strike, announcing its own strategic defense initiative (or some other arms development initiative), seeking a compromise with Washington that would require the United States to agree not to go ahead with the development of its strategic defense system, or acquiescing.

The first option was out of the question, for Moscow knew that a nuclear attack on the United States would result in a nuclear war that would impose insupportable human and material costs on the two superpowers and the rest of the world. An analysis of its own earlier behavior, moreover, would have led Moscow to conclude that its only viable alternative was to announce the start of its own strategic defense initiative. In 1945, upon learning that the United States had dropped two atomic bombs on Japan, Moscow launched its own nuclear initiative and rejected Washington's plan to create an international organization responsible for overseeing and controlling the development of atomic energy. Based on this action and the policies initiated by the Nixon administration nearly a quarter-century later, Moscow could have calculated that if it counteracted with its own defense initiative, it would eventually force the United States to try to negotiate an agreement designed to bridle the new type of competition. In short, experience had taught Moscow that Washington would seek some form of arms control agreement only if the Soviet Union demonstrated that it was capable of competing with the United States in an arms race. And yet, in December 1987, the leaders of both countries agreed on an accord that stipulated that the two sides would eliminate both their intermediate missiles (600 to 3,400 miles) and short-range missiles (300 to 600 miles), but that Washington would not be constrained from developing a defense system against a nuclear attack.[60] Moscow's acquiescence illustrated, more than any other past or future decision, its admission that the Soviet Union could no longer compete with the United States militarily. Moscow's capitulation epitomized the end of the Cold War and the emergence of the United States as the undisputed victor.

The story behind the end of the Cold War is quite simple. In 1969, Nixon and Kissinger, after concluding that the costs of maintaining the United States's power status and international commitments for nearly a quarter of a century were beginning to exceed the benefits, sought to find a new equilibrium. One of the ways they attempted to create a new balance between costs and benefits was by developing a different type of relationship between the United States and the Soviet Union. Détente was devised in order to reduce the pace of the nuclear arms race between the two superpowers and to abate their global competition. By 1980, even before Reagan's election, a great number of political leaders and analysts had concluded that détente had failed. The Soviet Union, they argued, had attained nuclear superiority over the United States and, as illustrated by the Soviet invasion of Afghanistan, had not moderated its global goals. Reagan moved into the White House with an elementary foreign policy agenda. For the new president, the most important lesson of détente was that the Soviet Union had exploited the United States's attempt to ease the tension between the two, and had given little in return. He also believed that the Soviet Union was the cause behind almost every major problem ensuing in the international arena. As he noted just a few months before he was elected president, "the Soviet Union underlies all the unrest that is going on. If they weren't engaged in this game of dominoes, there wouldn't be any hot spots in the world."[61] The only way to respond to this form of behavior, proposed Reagan, was by containing, and over time reversing, "Soviet expansionism by competing effectively on a sustained basis with the Soviet Union in all international arenas, particularly in the overall military balance and in geographical regions of priority concern to the United States."[62]

Did Reagan and his associates expect their policies to intensify the tension generated by the Cold War? The evidence suggests that they believed that their policies would not heat up the Cold War. Their belief was built on the conviction that the Soviet Union no longer possessed the strength to continue competing with the United States. In June 8, 1982, during an address to members of the British Parliament, Reagan noted:

> We are witnessing today a great revolutionary crisis, a crisis where the demands of the economic order are conflicting directly with those of the political order. . . . [T]he crisis is happening . . . in the home of Marxist-Leninism, the Soviet Union. . . . [The Soviet Union] is in deep economic

difficulty. The rate of growth in the national product has been steadily declining since the fifties and is less than half of what it was then.

The dimensions of this failure are outstanding: A country that employs one-fifth of its population in agriculture is unable to feed its own people. . . . Overcentralized, with little or no incentives, year after year the Soviet system pours its best resources into the making of instruments of destruction. The constant shrinkage of economic growth combined with the growth of military production is putting a heavy strain on the Soviet people. What we see here is a political structure that no longer corresponds to its economic base, a society where productive forces are hampered by political ones.[63]

Reagan was not alone in this belief. Though his foreign policy advisers often differed about the specific steps the United States should initiate to counteract Moscow's actions, they shared the conviction that the Soviet Union had overextended itself. By increasing the United States's overall military budget and by backing with "money and political muscle" the various movements throughout the world battling communism, the United States would create fissures in the Soviet system and force Moscow to curtail its foreign activities.

The Reagan administration wasted little time in launching its new foreign policy. In 1981, the budget for the Department of Defense accounted for 24.1 percent of the total budget; by 1984 it had risen to 32.4 percent.[64] Moreover, during that three-year period, the Reagan administration approved two very important national security directives. The first directive, NSDD 32, proposed providing funds to anti-Communist movements as a way of putting pressure on the periphery of the "Soviet empire." By the "periphery," the directive meant principally Eastern Europe. The second directive, NSDD 75, went beyond the intent of NSDD 32; for the first time since the Truman days an administration made the argument that the United States would not accept the existing Soviet sphere of influence beyond its own borders and claimed that it was determined to roll it back.[65]

These directives codified policies that the Reagan administration had been implementing since 1981. In July, it had asked authorization from Congress to launch a covert intelligence operation against Grenada, with the intent of toppling its Communist regime.[66] Also, at about this time it pressured the Caribbean Development Bank to exclude Grenada from the countries receiving aid for domestic programs. With regard to Nicaragua, it approved an increase of subversive activities inside the country, support for paramilitary operations against the Sandinistas from the outside, and the design of a contingency plan for direct military intervention. Moreover, in a major drive to "arrest the spread of communism" in Honduras and El Salvador, it funneled, respectively, $95.1 million and $230.0 million in military aid between 1981 and 1983.[67] And in Afghanistan, it steadily increased funding levels to the Afghan rebels battling the Soviet forces. The central intent behind this action was to "keep maximum pressure on Moscow for withdrawal" and to "ensure that the Soviets' political, military, and other costs remain high."[68] These actions, though central to Reagan's foreign policy, were merely a prologue to the project he had in store.

In July 1979, Reagan visited the North American Defense Command (NORAD) at Cheyenne Mountain, Colorado, which amounted to an underground city carved out of the mountain, protected by massive steel doors several feet thick. During the tour, Reagan learned that if a Soviet SS-18 were to hit within a few hundred yards of the massive steel front doors, everybody inside would be killed. The future president asked whether there was anything the United States could do to prevent such an outcome. Upon learning that the United States could track the missile but not stop it, he said: "There must be something better than this."[69] A few days later, Martin Anderson, an economist working as an adviser to Reagan, drafted a policy memorandum in which he noted that perhaps the time had come to reconsider whether the United States should build an anti-ballistic missile system. He then added that the idea "is probably fundamentally far more appealing to the American people than the questionable satisfaction of knowing that those who initiated the attack against us were also blown away."[70] A year later, the Republican national convention, controlled by Reagan's supporters, pledged in its platform to proceed with "vigorous research and development of an effective anti-ballistic missile system. . . ."[71]

For Reagan this pledge was more than a promise proclaimed for the purpose of gaining some additional political leverage. Encouraged by Edward Teller, who had pushed for the creation of the hydrogen bomb in the early 1950s and had noted in 1980 that "particle beams could aid in defense against incoming missiles that are as close as a few miles," a small group started to work secretly in the White House in September 1981 on a new strategy that would switch the emphasis from offense to defense.[72] Until March 1983, Reagan advisers discussed quietly the merits of altering the nuclear strategy of the United States in such a dramatic fashion. Some argued that it would demolish the foundation of the Western alliance, while others contended that the whole notion was a pipe dream, because the United States did not possess the technology to design such a system. A third group emphasized that though the United States lacked the technology to create an effective defensive system, the mere announcement that it intended to launch a major research initiative would force the Soviet Union to be more responsive to Washington's proposals during future nuclear arms negotiations. On March 23, 1983, Reagan announced his new Strategic Defense Initiative during a televised address to the nation. Two days later, he issued an executive order instructing his national security adviser, William Clark, to supervise an intensive effort to define a long-term research and development program of the system.

The Reagan administration's aggressive policy in the area of nuclear weapons did not stop with SDI. In October 1983, Moscow warned Washington and its NATO partners that the Soviet Union would walk out of the Geneva talks over intermediate nuclear forces (INF), if they went ahead with the deployment of Pershing-2 intermediate range ballistic missiles in West Germany and grounded-launched cruise missiles (GLCMs) in Britain and Italy. The threat did not have the effect hoped by Moscow. Americans and Europeans mounted massive demonstrations against the planned deployments throughout the months of November and December. Leaders in the United States, Britain, West Germany, and Italy, however, argued that they needed to deploy their own intermediate range missiles both to counterbalance the SS-20 mobile missiles with multiple warheads the Soviets deployed in East Germany and Czechoslovakia and to pressure Moscow to sign an INF agreement.[73]

Reagan's new defense strategy was not without risks. To begin with, a great number of scientists and political analysts questioned the feasibility of the program and the effect its development would have on the relationships both between the superpowers and between the United States and its major allies. Compounding the problem was the fact that Reagan's anti-Communist rhetoric frightened many people. As the United States began to spend more on defense, and the American public began to feel more secure militarily, Reagan's image as a man of peace grew somewhat. But concern about his intentions never vanished fully. For instance, in 1980, 43 percent of the people interviewed believed that the United States lagged behind the Soviet Union in nuclear strength, and 56 percent thought the United States was not spending enough on defense. In 1984, when asked the same questions, the numbers fell down to 27 percent and 17 percent, respectively. Moreover, in 1980 Carter showed a 24-point favorable margin over Reagan when people were asked who they believed would be more effective at keeping the United States out of war; by 1984, however, when Reagan ran against Walter Mondale, the margin had decreased to 12 points.[74] It is evident, thus, that though by the time Reagan announced his Strategic Defense Initiative the American public was less inclined than in 1980 to assume that he would involve the United States in another major war, its comfort level was not solid. This ambivalence was reflected in the public's response to his March 1983 announcement. Americans were willing to support the Strategic Defense Initiative (SDI), preferred it over a mutually assured destruction strategy, believed it could work, and thought it would improve the chances for arms control. At the same time, they did not like the idea of putting nuclear weapons in space, suspected that SDI would make the arms race more dangerous, and were worried about its cost.[75] Though his reelection in 1984 did not stop the criticism, from both specialists and many of the United States's allies, it freed Reagan from the pressure of public opinion to pursue the course he believed appropriate.

Nevertheless, there was one major risk still looming over the international horizon: the Soviet Union. Was the Reagan administration's policy toward the Soviet Union based on wishful thinking, driven essentially by a blind anti-Communist ideology, or was it erected on concrete evidence? In other words, was the Soviet Union facing such a deep economic crisis, brought about both by its imperial overextension and the nature of its political and economic system, that the prospect of a new "heating" of the Cold War would force it to concede that it was no longer able to compete with the United States? There is no evidence to suggest that members of the Reagan administration envisioned the Soviet Union's collapsing as rapidly and dramatically as it did. There is no question, however, that their assessments of the burdens afflicting its system were right on target.

Until the early 1990s, the Soviet economy was a gigantic economic conglomerate. The 1977 Soviet Constitution (Article 16) defined it as "a single public economic complex embracing all sectors of social production, distribution and exchange on the country's territory." This meant that the Soviet Constitution prohibited, with very few exceptions, individuals or groups from owning the means of production or from engaging independently in entrepreneurial activities.[76] Like market-oriented economies, the Soviet Union accumulated and invested capital for economic return and development. Unlike market-oriented economies, the Soviet state owned the capital and allocated it among the various sectors of the economy based on priorities determined by government officials.[77] Centralized planning by the state enabled the Soviet Union to develop many of its industries at a very rapid pace. Its success was so formidable that just eight years after the end of the Second World War, the Soviet Union was outproducing the United States in steel, oil, cement, and textiles.[78] This success, however, was accompanied by failures that, in time, overwhelmed it.

Between 1958 and 1989, GNP growth rates in the Soviet Union declined from 9.9 percent to -1.0 percent. The Soviet leadership recognized this economic downturn relatively early. In 1962, a Soviet economist proposed that factory managers be granted greater freedom to decide what style, assortment, quality, and quantity of goods to produce, and that the performance of factories be evaluated in terms of profits. This approach, he added, would stimulate market forces. After three years of extensive debate, the Soviet leadership opted for a compromise that afforded factory managers some degree of freedom over production decisions, and included profitability as one among several indicators that would be used to evaluate factories and enterprises. The economic system, however, remained highly centralized.[79]

Khrushchev, who was removed from power in late 1964, was succeeded by a group of leaders, with Leonid Brezhnev at the head, whose main interest was to restore stability to the Soviet political system and who became highly dependent on the opinion of "specialists." Its unwillingness to consider alternative economic approaches proved to be very costly. During the eighth five-year plan, implemented between 1966 and 1970, the Soviet GNP increased at an annual rate of 5.0 percent; during the eleventh five-year plan, implemented between 1981 and 1985, it grew by only 2.0 percent. Growth rates for specific sectors during those two same periods, were as follows: i) industrial production went from 8.3 percent to 3.7 percent; ii) agricultural production went from 4.3 percent to 2.1 percent; iii) labor production went from 6.8 percent to 3.1 percent; iv) total investment went from 7.5 percent to 3.5 percent; and v) per capita income went from 5.9 percent to 2.1 percent. Still, the Soviet Union continued to invest an estimated 15 to 17 percent of its GNP on defense, compared to approximately 7 percent by the United States.[80]

Brezhnev died in November 1982 and was replaced by Yuri Andropov. During his brief tenure as Soviet leader, Andropov called for greater independence for factories, enterprises, and state and collective farms, and launched a massive crackdown on absenteeism, alcoholism, shoddy work, and black market activities. His death in early 1984, however, prevented the Soviet Union from undergoing more sweeping economic reforms. Konstantin Chernenko became the new Soviet leader. At the outset it became clear that his driving goal would be to return to the stability of the Brezhnev era, especially the policy of "stability of cadres." Chernenko's role as leader lasted only until March 11, 1985. Upon his death Mikhail Gorbachev replaced him.

Gorbachev moved swiftly to reinvigorate the economy and to alter the makeup of the ruling party. He did not envision creating a political and economic system that would deviate significantly from the one established by Joseph Stalin in the 1920s and 1930s. This expectation, however, was soon discredited by his own actions. One of his major earlier decisions was to promote greater openness in discussing the wide range of problems afflicting the Soviet Union. His policy of openness (*glasnost*) was used to apply pressure on ministers, factory managers, and economic officials. As the idea gained momentum, Gorbachev and his closest associates began to use the term "crisis" to describe the Soviet Union's social and economic predicaments, to speak forcefully in favor of decentralizing the planning of the economy by granting greater decision-making authority to factory managers, and to demand that greater attention be paid to housing, health care, education, and consumer needs.[81] As he implemented these measures, he also took steps to consolidate his power in the Politburo. By September 1989, he had succeeded in removing from the Politburo the last member of the "old guard."

These changes were not the only ones Gorbachev sought to introduce. He recognized that unless the Soviet Union also altered its foreign policy, his new domestic economic and political economic measures would not be enough to bring about the results he hoped. Hostility with the United States was as intense as it had been during the early days of the Cold War; Washington was now daring Moscow to engage in a highly costly new type of technological competition; the war in Afghanistan was becoming exceedingly expensive and there were no signs that victory was at hand; the economies of the Eastern European states were depleting the Soviet economy; and the protection of the 4,000 mile Soviet border with China was tying up as much as 25 percent of its entire military budget. In 1984, Georgii Shaknazarov, a close associate of Gorbachev, published an article titled: "The Logic of Political Thinking in the Nuclear Era." In the piece, Shaknazarov noted that because a formal interdependence of security had arisen in the nuclear age, security could be viewed only collectively. Two years later, in his formal address to the Twenty-Seventh Party Congress, Gorbachev remarked that the changes in the international arena were so profound and significant that the Soviet Union had to rethink, and conduct a comprehensive analysis of, all its factors. "The situation of nuclear confrontation calls for new approaches, methods, and forms of relations between different social systems, states, and regions." He then added that war "had ceased to be the continuation of state policy by other means," that the Soviet Union could not continue to advocate the export of violent revolutions, that states, even socialist ones, had to determine their own fate without Soviet direction, and that the rapid decline of the Soviet economy compelled it to bring to an end its isolation from the rest of the global economy.[82] In short, after more than 40 years of competing with the United States in the international arena, a Soviet leader acknowledged that the economy of the Soviet Union was no longer able to continue absorbing the costs induced by the rivalry.[83]

There was real commitment behind these words. In 1988, Reagan and Gorbachev signed the INF Treaty in Moscow. By then, the Eastern European dominoes were already falling, beginning with the election of Solidarity candidates in Poland in the June 1988 elections. By the end of 1989, the Berlin Wall had been crushed and so had the Communist regimes of Czechoslovakia, Hungary, Bulgaria, and Romania. Equally significant, in 1989 Gorbachev admitted that the invasion of Afghanistan had proven to be a dismal failure. He recognized not only that the intervention had been costly and had undermined the Soviet Union's reputation, but also that it had further deepened its hostility with China and moved its Asian rival closer to the United States. He followed his avowal with the withdrawal of the Soviet forces from Afghanistan. Finally, as if to underscore his commitment to improve his country's relationship with the United States, Gorbachev informed Washington that same year that he had ordered the suspension of all military aid to Nicaragua and that he would not provide its Sandinista government the emergency economic funding it had requested.[84]

Titan Undaunted

In a bipolar nuclear system, the entity that wins is the one with the economic capacity to sustain longer a negative imbalance between the benefits and costs of further change and expansion. The United States and the Soviet Union emerged from the end of the Second World War as the two states with the most powerful military and the greatest economic potential. In 1959, the growth rate of the Soviet economy began to slow down. Its leader, concerned with the effect this development could have on the Soviet Union's stand in the international arena, opted for a two-pronged policy. Hoping to limit the costs to the Soviet economy provoked by the arms race with the United States, Moscow sought to project the image that the nuclear capability of the Soviet Union was superior to that of the United States. In addition, it tried to bring about major domestic reforms that would help revitalize the Soviet economy. Both strategies failed. By the end of 1961, it became known that Soviet claims about its nuclear strength were false, and by the end of the Cuban Missile Crisis the following year, the United States had made it abundantly clear that it was prepared, if necessary, to use its nuclear arsenal to protect its vital national interests. The second shoe fell in 1964, when Nikita Khrushchev, who had advocated the implementation of new Soviet economic policies, was replaced by a leadership determined to offset the United States's nuclear superiority and to ensure that the Soviet economy not undergo major changes.

The United States faced similar concerns in the late 1960s. Its leaders feared that the United States had unduly committed itself in the international arena, and that the international economic system it had put in place toward the end of the Second World War was no longer serving the United States's interests. Washington created détente in an attempt to ameliorate the tension between the United States and the Soviet Union. Had it worked, it would have slowed down the arms race and reduced the superpower rivalry in the periphery. By 1980, however, few U.S. leaders supported détente. Instead, they contended that the Soviet Union had used détente to strengthen its nuclear arsenal and bolster revolutionary regimes in the developing world. Convinced that Moscow would not discontinue its policy of expansion unless the United States demonstrated its resolve, Washington decided not just to match Moscow's actions but also to challenge it to a new type of race: a strategic defensive race. Notwithstanding the conviction among a great number of scientists and political analysts that neither side possessed the technology necessary to create a foolproof strategic defensive system, it was conceded that Washington's decision threatened to provoke a new and exceedingly costly arms race. Already burdened by a number of costly travails, and convinced that the Soviet economy could not absorb a new major increase in military expenditure, Moscow chose not to meet the new challenge.

In short, though each state discerned that its struggle for hegemony threatened to incapacitate its standing as a superpower, only the United States, with a more developed and sophisticated economy, was ultimately able to overcome the threat. What is more, after conceding that the Soviet economy could no longer compete with that of its most powerful rival, Moscow was compelled to forsake its economic system and create a new one. This decision, if nothing else, symbolized Moscow's acknowledgment that its political, economic, and social experiment had failed. Moscow's allies, which for years had yielded to its demands, were forced by their own people to accept that the course of history would not move along the path they had proclaimed. The tumbling of the Communist house of cards brought to an end the contradiction that had dominated international affairs for almost half a century. The United States stood alone as the undaunted military titan.

The Economic Renaissance of the United States

As analysts witnessed the demise of the Soviet Union and its Communist empire, many pondered whether the United States would be able to regain its economic strength. Walter Russell Mead, a major critic of the United States's foreign policy, doubted that it possessed the capability to stop its downward spiral. As he noted, the United States's principal sources of economic strength had been agriculture, manufacturing, and energy extraction. All three sectors had been experiencing a continuous decline since the late 1960s. Moreover, the new high-tech industries that were once hailed as the replacement for the dying industries of the past had also been experiencing a slump.[85] Mead then predicted that the negative effects of these developments would not be confined to the United States. In an attempt to save jobs and keep wages high, the United States would adopt protectionist measures, which would bring about a reduction in world trade. The reduced trade, in turn, would reduce the exports of capital, technology, and finished material from the developed world to the developing world. This set of interconnected events would seriously compromise the ability of developing countries to repay their loans and, thus, to narrow the economic gap that separates them from countries in the upper echelon.[86]

Paul Kennedy and David Calleo also voiced concern about the future of the United States, but neither assumed that the country lacked the capability to regain its economic health. Kennedy proposed that the United States had to recognize that nations that built their military power to protect their expanding economic interests eventually found their strength undermined by the cost of projecting military power. He noted that the "difficulties experienced by contemporary societies which are militarily top-heavy merely repeat those which in their time affected Phillip II's Spain, Nicholas II's Russia, and Hitler's Germany."[87] Washington, he added, could not afford to dismiss the lessons from these cases and had to understand that if the United States wanted to avert the costs they had experienced, it had to reduce its overcommitments in foreign policy.[88] He concluded that though the United States was in the midst of experiencing a decline in power, it would remain a significant power in a multipolar system because of its size.[89] David Calleo, in turn, propounded that the United States could not maintain its power status without first alleviating its fiscal deficit, which he attributed to its comparatively large military expenditure. Present international conditions, in Calleo's opinion, should enable the United States to reduce military costs by withdrawing troops from Europe and selectively enhancing the nuclear capability of its allies.[90] By the second half of the 1990s, however, even pessimists were forced to acknowledge that the economy of the United States had regained its vitality. To delineate the economic transformation experienced by the United States following the end of the Cold War, I will first focus on the economic policies initiated by the Reagan administration and then discuss those implemented by the Clinton administration.

Reagan's approach to economic issues was influenced by his own self-confidence and optimism, his belief in individualism, his aversion to governmental interference in the economy, his attuned sense of populist politics, and his conviction that the United States's economy was stronger than, and superior in nature to, the economies of other international entities. In 1980 he noted that, historically, the United States's economy had been revitalized not by "government but by people free of government interference, needless regulations, crippling inflation [and] high taxes. . . ." A year later he added that "[t]he production of America is the possession of those who build, serve, create and produce. For too long, we've removed from our people the decision on how to dispose of what they've created. We have strayed from first principles. We must alter our course."[91] With regard to the international economic system, he viewed it not as being made up of interdependent entities, but of entities dependent on the health and strength of, and the economic policies initiated by, the United States. As his Council of Economic Advisors remarked: "The successful implementation of policies to control inflation and restore vigorous real growth in the United States will have a profound and favorable impact on the rest of the world. . . ."[92] It is also significant to note that though time and again he spoke about balancing the budget, he never made it his primary goal. He favored balancing the budget, but not if it threatened to constrain some of his choices or to undermine his popular support.

Students of international politics often avoid discussing elusive concepts such as faith in government, credibility, and confidence. Despite the fact that they use these terms almost daily, they are reluctant to apply them to their studies because they have great difficulty figuring out how to gauge them. Still, it is wrong to disregard them when focusing on the Reagan presidency. Reagan believed that his most important function as president was to restore the United States's self-respect and confidence. He did not have a fixed plan for accomplishing these ends, beyond his conviction that government should interfere less in the economy, that taxes should be reduced, that the military power of the United States should be increased, and that the revitalization of the United States's economy would help energize the economies of other international entities. But these creeds were backed by the belief that, above anything else, he had "to lead the way in restoring a sense of hope and national pride."[93]

In my earlier analysis of the Carter administration, particularly of its foreign policy, I noted that one of its dominant problems was that the two principal advisers to the president held conflicting views about the Soviet Union and the manner in which the United States should respond to its international activities. I also remarked that Carter, though attentive to details, did not seem willing to choose sides and instead almost always tried to find a compromise. When President Reagan moved into the White House, he was accompanied by advisers who championed at least three different, and often contradictory, approaches to economic recovery. The "supply-siders," represented by Arthur Laffer, looked into microeconomics to explain where the incentives for greater productivity could be found. They contended that because work involves disutility, particularly in the form of taxes, an economic agent works only so long as it is able to provide income sufficient to meet its demands for goods. An economic agent would not want to work beyond a certain point if a significant portion of the additional income is bound to be taken away by taxes.[94] Laffer sought to demonstrate that tax revenues rise with the tax rate only until they have reached some optimal point, after which the continued increase in tax rates would be accompanied by a decrease in tax revenues. He then argued that if tax rates were higher than the optimal point, the only logical response would be to reduce them. Reductions in tax rates, he added, would stimulate productive activity and, as a result, increase tax revenues. The second group, the monetarists, proposed that the Federal Reserve Board could bring down inflation by gradually, but persistently, reducing the growth of money. A restraint in monetary growth rates would also help bring about the decline of inflationary expectations. This result was considered to be critical, because interest rate movements were considered to be mostly a reflection of price expectations—a reduction in the latter would induce a decrease in the former. In short, by restricting the growth of the money supply, the economy would be able to grow unburdened by inflation. The third group, the budget balancers, represented the traditional branch of the Republican Party. This group had for years been at odds with Keynesians, who argued that an annually balanced budget would actually destabilize the economy. Keynesians were concerned with the short-term contradictions that the balanced budget criteria would most likely generate. Adherence to the balanced budget criteria would require that the government increase spending during an economic boom, since it would have access to higher tax revenues, and that it curtail expenditure when the economy was in a downswing, because it would collect fewer tax receipts. The government, in other words, would pour money into the economy when it did not need a stimulus, and would decrease spending when the economy needed a stimulus. Failure to stimulate the economy during a downturn, added Keynesians, would simply worsen the recession and extend the downturn. Budget balancers did not deny the existence of the business cycle, but argued that in the long run it was preferable to brave the swings in economic activity than to rely on governmental intervention. Governmental officials, added budget balancers, lacked discipline and could not be trusted. They tended to tax excessively and to invent new programs that were supposed to bolster the economy but instead typically incurred higher deficits.[95]

Unwilling to take sides, Reagan proposed to his economic advisers that they find a compromise. It did not take long for contradictions to surface and to provoke the first set of undesirable effects. In 1981, Congress agreed to reduce personal income tax rates by 25 percent over three years, and to cut $95 billion in spending from the next two fiscal years while still increasing military expenditures. By the second half of 1981, the Federal Reserve Bank had slowed down monetary growth to under 4 percent from an annual rate of 13 percent in the last quarter of 1980. As these changes were being implemented, the Reagan administration augured a GNP growth of 11.1 percent for 1981, 12.5 percent for 1982, 12.4 percent for 1983, and 10.8 percent for 1984. By the end of 1981, however, it became evident that the Federal Reserve Board's monetary plans were inconsistent with the forecasted GNP growths. Real GNP fell at a rate of over 5 percent in the last and first quarters of 1981 and 1982, respectively, and unemployment rose to 8.6 percent and then reached 9.5 percent by the start of the summer of 1982. The public outcry was strong enough to convince the Federal Reserve to permit the money supply to grow faster, from an annual rate of 2.2 percent in the second quarter of 1982, to 16.2 in the fourth quarter. From then on until the last quarter of 1984, the Federal Reserve steadily decreased the growth of the money supply as the GNP grew at an annual rate of approximately 4 percent in 1983 and 6.5 percent in 1984. In 1985 and 1986, as the economy once again became sluggish, the Federal Reserve allowed the money supply to grow faster; in the fourth quarter of 1986 it grew at an annual rate of 19.1 percent.

By 1988, as Reagan's term as president was reaching its end and Vice President George Bush was vying to replace him, the departing leader could claim that under his administration productivity had risen at an annual rate of 4 percent, unemployment had gone down to 5.5 percent, inflation had been lowered to about 4.4 percent, and exports had increased at an annual pace of 20 to 30 percent since 1987.[96] But these improvements came at a cost. The budget deficit in FY 1980 was $74 billion (2.7 percent of the GNP), but by FY 1988 it had ballooned to some $155 billion (3.2 percent of the GNP). Measured in constant 1990 dollars, total federal spending for the 1981–1990 period was $1.9 trillion higher than it would have been had the 1980 spending level remained the same.[97] The most noticeable increases came in the form of military expenditures and the interest paid on the deficit. National defense spending, corrected for inflation, rose from 4.4 percent of the GNP in 1980 to 5.7 percent in 1989, while the interest paid on the deficit went up from 1.7 percent of the GNP in 1980 to 3.2 percent in 1989. Moreover, though prior to becoming president Reagan had hoped to cut down considerably on education, training, and social services, he understood that had he attempted to do so, Congress would have forced him to forgo the military buildup and tax cuts. As a result, by the end of his two terms the percent of change in these areas was not as large as originally feared by many of his political adversaries, while expenditures for health and Medicare actually increased. As Republican Congressman Willis Gradison of Ohio noted: "Reagan was enthusiastic about financing defense and foreign aid, and Congress was enthusiastic about financing domestic spending. They reached a compromise that only a politician could love."[98]

The United States's economic picture, however, did not look as dim as conveyed by the above figures. First, though the United States's federal debt was serious, as a percentage of the GDP or on a per capita basis it was not as large as that carried by many other developed states, including Canada. Second, the United States alone still accounted for more than 20 percent of the world's total production, with Japan a distant second. Third, U.S. citizens and corporations had invested abroad $450 billion, more than the citizens of any other country. Fourth, the purchasing power of the U.S. consumers continued to rank number one in terms of the goods and services they could buy with their average paychecks. And fifth, the United States was still considered the world's major breadbasket.[99] The concerns, moreover, were voiced without a clear understanding of the monumental effects that the demise of the Soviet Union could have on the United States. Little attention was given to the fact that the collapse of communism would free the new White House occupant to reduce military expenditures and foreign aid,[100] and that the disappearance of this threat would reduce dramatically the bargaining power of those members of Congress who in the past had used the threat to cut down on military expenditures as a way of preventing the government from trimming down welfare and social programs. In the new era, a president committed to lowering the budget deficit would find himself in an enviable position.

Under the guidance of his first Secretary of the Treasury, Lloyd Bentsen, and his successor, Robert Rubin, and with the backing of the chairman of the Federal Reserve Board, Alan Greenspan, President Clinton decided that the best way to promote economic growth would be by reducing the deficit. All four agreed that a reduction of the deficit would bring down long-term interest rates. Lower interest rates, in turn, were expected to act as a forceful stimulus to investment-led growth. In 1993, the Congress approved Clinton's deficit reduction program after a lengthy and acrimonious battle. The largest cut came in defense, which in 1989 had accounted for 27 percent of the federal budget but nine years later had been reduced to 16 percent. Almost immediately, long-term rates began to move down, and the United States's economy began to grow at a reasonable pace without spawning inflation. By the start of 1999, the United States's unemployment hovered at 4.3 percent, its annual inflation rate stood at 1.7 percent, and its economy was ranked first in the world's competitiveness index. Also, in 1998 the Clinton administration projected that the United States would experience its largest federal budget surplus, as a share of its economy, in 40 years. With an estimated surplus of $39 billion, the Clinton administration and the U.S. Congress found themselves in the unusual position of having to decide how to spend money they actually had.

The rapid economic turnaround experienced by the United States in the 1990s was not an anomalous event. As in the past, it was brought about by the United States's extraordinary economic power and diversity, and by the openness and competitiveness of its political and economic subsystems. It reinforced the sentiment of earlier eras that the United States was like a gambler who could play simultaneously at each and every table that mattered, and with more chips than anyone else.[101]

CHAPTER SEVEN

Made by the U.S.A.

The world which is rising into existence is still half encumbered by the remains of the world which is waning into decay; amidst the vast perplexity of human affairs, none can say how much of ancient institutions and former manners will remain, or how much will completely disappear.

—Alexis de Tocqueville[1]

An Old Road Map to the Future

On April 2, 1917, President Woodrow Wilson went before a joint session of Congress to propose that the United States enter the war that had engulfed Europe for nearly three years. His rationale was simple. The United States, he noted, had to enter the war "for democracy, for the right of those who submit to authority to have a choice in their own government, for the rights and liberties of small nations . . . and to make the world itself at least free."[2] The protection and advancement of democracy were not Wilson's sole motives. As he remarked during his Fourteen Points speech to Congress on January 8, 1918, U.S. participation in the war would assist in the "removal . . . of all economic barriers and the establishment of an equality of trade conditions among all the nations consenting to the peace and associating themselves for its maintenance."[3] By the start of the next decade, however, Americans were no longer willing to shoulder the responsibilities the fulfillment of Wilson's international goals would have demanded.

Three-quarters of a century later, after having eliminated the communist threat, Americans were once again asked by their president to believe that for the United States there was no national interest "more urgent than securing democracy's triumph around the world."[4] They were told by William Clinton that the globe had become their theater, and that in the ideological realm there was no longer an adversary capable of challenging the moral authority claimed by democracy. They were also urged to believe that the United States should push for the globalization of market economies. As explained by Anthony Lake, Clinton's first national security advisor, during a speech at Johns Hopkins University in September 1993:

The expansion of market-based economics abroad helps expand our exports and create American jobs, while it also improves living conditions and fuels demands for political liberalization abroad. The addition of new democracies makes us more secure because democracies tend not to wage war on each other or sponsor terrorism. . . .

These dynamics lay at the heart of Woodrow Wilson's most profound insights; although his moralism sometimes weakened his argument, he understood that our own security is shaped by the character of foreign regimes. . . .

Throughout the Cold War, we contained a global threat to market democracies; now we seek to enlarge their reach, particularly in places of special significance to us.

The successor to a doctrine of containment must be a strategy of enlargement—enlargement of the world's free community of market democracies.[5]

Every major international force galvanizes one or more counterforces. The counteractions are generally a function of the predicaments the original impetus generates or intensifies in a state or region. Because states or regions are afflicted by various sets of internal problems, the counterforces that emerge from them can vary considerably in both form and intensity.

Widespread political, economic, and social tensions besieged the global arena in the late 1990s, but the United States reacted to few of them. During most of the Cold War, Washington was guided by the principle that even the appearance of a change in power relationship with the Soviet Union could imperil the national interest of the United States. Washington reasoned that assessments based on economic capacity, military potential, or geography always had to be weighed against considerations of prestige. The effect of this reasoning was to increase noticeably the number of regions the United States judged relevant to its own national security.[6] The end of the Cold War did not free the United States's leaders to neglect the effects an international crisis might have on their country's prestige; it did enable them, however, to be more selective about which problems to address. In the 1990s, for instance, war and civil discord spread rapidly through many parts of Africa, inducing appalling levels of death and destruction. The United States, after calling for a return to reason and voicing its profound discontent and sorrow, did very little else.[7] Conversely, as Yugoslavia's Serbs moved to eradicate Kosovo of its Albanian population, the United States and its NATO allies launched a major air campaign on the perpetrators. The responses by the United States in both cases were prescribed by the impact the rise in instability in each region was expected to have on the security and economic interests of the international system's core units.[8] By the late 1990s, Africa had once again been relegated to the periphery, while the Balkan region, because of its proximity to Western Europe, was deemed too important to be left to its own devices.[9]

As one might expect, the foreign policy strategy of the Clinton administration has generated a plethora of interpretations. These interpretations have often been accompanied by foreign policy recommendations. My intent in these last pages is not to posit my own set of suggestions, but to identify the major contradictions and tensions the United States is likely to face both in the international environment and in its own domestic arena in the next quarter of a century. To provide context to my projections, I revisit the past with a comprehensive summary of the evolution of the United States's foreign policy. I then examine the forms assumed by the wave to liberalize the international economic system, and the United States's rationale for committing itself to the creation and protection of new democracies. Third, I review the tensions these two processes generated, and are likely to generate. I begin this discussion with a brief analysis of the effects the United States's drive to globalize the market has had on the sovereignty of states. I then focus on the globe's regions and try to explain which ones will generate the greatest contradictions and tensions, and to ascertain whether the United States will be effective at coping with them. I close this aspect of my analysis with a short discussion of terrorism, and the foreign policy challenges it will spawn for the United States. In the very last section I identify the two major domestic obstacles the United States must overcome if it hopes to retain its world leadership role.

The United States: The Past

I built this study on four ideas. I contended that history is framed by the presence of conflicting forces that originate within the international system itself, and within different states. These contradictory forces create tensions that eventually compel the principal international entities to implement policies designed, at minimum, to alleviate their costly effects and, at maximum, to replace the system with a more effective one. I then claimed that a hegemon that steadily grasps the nature of the tensions afflicting the international system, and diminishes those that affect its own national interests, is more likely to retain its position in the international structure than one that repeatedly fails in both endeavors. Third, I proposed that the ability of the major entity to lessen the tensions dominating the international system at any one time is a function of both its military and economic capabilities and the attributes of its domestic political and economic systems. And finally, I stated that leaders are prisoners of history. Specifically, I noted that most foreign policy decisions are anchored to lessons inferred from previous occurrences.

The openness and competitiveness of the United States's domestic political and economic systems contributed notably to its international successes and failures. Always attentive to the domestic repercussions of its foreign policies, Washington confronted the future by gauging the costs the United States had encountered in its immediate past. A troublesome past experience generally elicited responses designed to avert its recurrence. On such occasions, it was not unusual for Washington to opt for the path of less domestic resistance; but that path, in turn, often generated new, unexpected, costs. When such an outcome resulted, Washington, always attuned to the U.S. public's disposition, drew up new policies designed to revert it. In short, possession of an open and competitive domestic system did not prevent the United States from committing grave foreign policy errors; it did, however, enhance its ability to unveil them before they became unbearably costly.

Since its conception, the United States committed itself to becoming a powerful international state. Cognizant of its own military and economic weaknesses, the United States initially endeavored to augment its power by enlarging its territory. This policy generated few risks. Typically, the United States moved against states that were considerably weaker or that were too preoccupied with their own political affairs thousands of miles away to become unduly concerned with Washington's expansionary actions. During much of the second half of the nineteenth century, after having nearly tripled its territorial power, the United States strove to accelerate the pace of its economic growth. By the end of the century, most members of the international system agreed that the United States had become one of its most powerful and wealthy actors. Still, the United States feared that unless it built new bridges with, and modified the structure of, the international economic system, its domestic economy would not be able to sustain the rate of growth it had enjoyed for nearly three decades.

The United States faced its first critical test as a major power when the international system that had been created by the dominant European entities was no longer able to handle the tensions that beset it. The 1815 balance-of-power system had been designed to restrain the excessive power aspirations of its strongest states. By the start of the twentieth century, Germany's rapid emergence as continental Europe's most powerful member, and the swift rise of an inflexible form of nationalism, had nullified the system's rationale. If the 1914 war served any purpose, it was to inform leaders that they needed to invent an international system that would not be afflicted by the forces and tensions endured by the one that had preceded it. By the end of the First World War, the United States was the only international actor with the power to do so.

The United States sought to replace the pre-1914 balance-of-power system with a "liberal" security system. As envisioned by President

Woodrow Wilson, the new international system would be guided by an international organization, directed by democratic states, and committed to the expansion of the world's community of market democracies. The United States's decision not to join the League all but doomed the organization's chances of becoming an effective agent of international cooperation. What is more, by consenting to the weakening of Germany's power, the United States, along with Britain and France, reinforced the belief that a country's status was still measured by its relative power. These problems were not the only ones bedeviling the United States after the end of the First World War. By enmeshing itself in Japan's economic affairs around the middle of the nineteenth century, the United States unwittingly invited Japan to design countervailing measures. Since Japan aspired to become the dominant state in the Far East, and the United States feared that such a development would encroach on its own economic interests, the only possible consequence of this rivalry was an increase in the international system's tension.

The United States might have been able to avert the recurrence of a world war had it responded differently to the challenges that emanated from the international system after the end of the First World War. During the 1920s, the United States could have acknowledged earlier than it did that the conditions of reparations imposed on Germany, and of loan payments decreed principally on France and Britain, were impairing Europe's opportunity to regain much of its lost economic strength. Washington's measures in 1924 and 1925 to eliminate some of the economic system's flaws helped Europe envision a brighter economic future, but not for long. As the stock market plunged in 1929 and the world sought guidance from its leaders, the United States retreated into its shell. The international effect of this action followed quickly. By the start of the 1930s, the United States and much of the rest of the world had independently decided to protect their domestic economies by closing most of their markets to foreign rivals.

The costs of the economic depression and the closing of markets to external competition reverberated around the globe; the effects on Germany and Japan, however, proved to be the most consequential. Shamed by the 1919 peace agreement, and burdened by the economic ills that besieged their country throughout much of the 1920s and early part of the 1930s, the Germans sought new leadership among those who prophesied a return to the glories of yesteryears. In the Far East, Japan's leaders, convinced that its economic growth was heavily dependent on ceaseless access to foreign markets, endeavored to curtail the uncertainty generated by the global market economy by gaining direct control over vital foreign markets and resources. Washington recognized that Germany's and Japan's power aspirations threatened the interests of the United States, and yet it did little to stop them. Afraid of being rebuked by the American public, U.S. leaders repeatedly expressed their determination to avoid becoming entangled in any war that did not pose an immediate and direct threat to the United States's national interest. By 1941, when it was too late, some of these same leaders acknowledged that their fear of the public's wrath might have propelled the United States into the war that they had been admonished to avoid.

As Roosevelt prepared the United States to fight another major war in 1941, he set his sights on the future that would supervene the war. The United States's failure to prevent another major international war had convinced him, and the American public, that the country would have to become intensely involved in helping direct the affairs of the world. As envisioned by Roosevelt, the relationships between states in this new world would be monitored and guided by an international organization, similar to that yearned for by Wilson, but created and controlled by the United States, the Soviet Union, Britain, and China. Under this new arrangement, the United States and the Soviet Union would not allow their competing ideologies and very different political and economic systems to obstruct the design of a less conflict-prone international system. Furthermore, it would be a world in which the economic system would be regulated by the tenets of the open market, and thus free of high tariff walls and regional trading blocs.

By the end of 1945, the United States was once again beholding the demise of one of its ideals. The power rivalry and the ideological barrier between the United States and the Soviet Union had proven to be too intense for the two entities to create the international political system originally envisioned by Roosevelt. For the next 40 years, the affairs between the two superpowers were defined by what came to be known as the Cold War. During the early years of the Cold War, one of the main instruments relied on by Washington to contain the Soviet Union was the United States's nuclear superiority. Determined not to be surpassed militarily, the Soviet Union developed its own nuclear arsenal. Through the years, their unwavering commitment to nuclear weapons propelled both states into a fierce arms race. When the Soviet Union finally attained nuclear parity in the late 1960s, the United States understood the contradiction the two powers had spawned. The United States recognized that its power rivalry with the Soviet Union, along with modern technology, had consistently forced each to try to attain nuclear superiority. Washington sought to persuade Moscow that unless they both controlled the competition, they would continue to provoke more uncertainty about each other's intentions. SALT I was the first major attempt designed to constrain the contradictions and tensions the arms race had generated.

Not all of Roosevelt's initial efforts came to naught. In the international economy arena, the United States succeeded at creating a system that helped sustain its own economic growth, revitalize the economies of

Western Europe and Japan, and contain the Soviet Union. By the 1960s, the United States had created an economic order framed by a series of international regimes, each disciplined by a series of rules, norms, principles, and decision-making procedures. But by the start of the next decade, the United States could no longer disregard its domestic economic woes induced by the arms race with the Soviet Union, a war in Vietnam that seemed to be raging out of control, and a major war on poverty at home. These costs forced Washington to restructure its role in the international economic system it had so scrupulously helped create and nourish.

Throughout the 1970s, the United States struggled to attenuate some of these tensions, but with little success. By the end of the decade, though the United States's involvement in the war in Vietnam had come to an end, its rivalry with the Soviet Union had increased in intensity, and so had the dissension with its counterparts in the international economic system. Ten years later, however, one of these tensions had eased completely. Convinced that the economy of the Soviet Union was in shambles, Washington gambled that if it challenged Moscow in areas where its authority was fragile and raised the stakes in the nuclear arms race, the United States would outlast its communist adversary. The gamble paid off. Mindful that the Soviet Union's economic and political systems had assumed an unconscionable burden in the drive to deny the United States world hegemony, Moscow finally pulled out of the competition. With the thawing of the Cold War came the dissolution of the Soviet empire and the demise of communism in Eastern Europe and throughout most of the world.

The United States and the International Economic System

For much of the twentieth century, the United States has been guided by the principle that the market is the most efficient form of human organization, and the knowledge that though through specialization in the division of labor everyone can benefit from international exchange, the more capable and more technologically advanced economies generally benefit the most. During the Cold War, Washington never lost sight of the fact that its success at fostering the liberalization of the market worldwide depended on the United States's ability to contain the Soviet Union. This ability, in turn, rested not only on the United States's military strength and that of its allies, but also on whether it kept its allies united and prosperous. To achieve the latter objective, the United States often depreciated its own economic and commercial interests. After the demise of the Soviet Union, however, Washington decided that it would be sensible for the United States to reduce its relative dependency on the military and to place greater emphasis on the further globalization of the free market. By the middle of the 1990s, the United States seemed closer than ever to realizing its ideal of creating a world economy organized in terms of a self-regulating market. The speedy expansion of international trade, the exorbitant growth in the international flow of capital, the rapid integration of national economies in the form of organized monetary and trade unions, exceptional advances in technology, and increasing deregulation convinced many analysts that the world was well on its way to becoming an open market system.[10]

Since Adam Smith argued that trade vents a surplus of productive capacity that would otherwise go unused, the promulgators of free trade have cited its alleged advantages with great aplomb. Free trade, they emphasize, advances specialization, prompts efficiency, induces innovation, increases productivity, widens the extent of the market, transfers technology, stimulates savings and capital accumulation, and provides for a higher standard of living and greater welfare in the future. Countries in the developing world, moreover, have the greatest potential for relative gain from an increase in trade. According to the IMF, the benefits "for developing countries include increased efficiency in the use of domestic resources as tariffs and nontariff barriers are reduced or removed, economies of scale in production are realized, and technology transfers resulting from increased openness and global cooperation are increased. In addition, higher growth in the world economy and increased access to industrial country markets for developing countries will improve the external environment for developing countries."[11] These benefits will result only if developing countries effectively implement a series of structural adjustments such as privatization of public enterprises, price and market liberalization, and the elimination of restrictions in the trade sector. It was reasoned that since private investment is generally more productive than public sector investment, the expansion of the private sector and open market activity would spur economic growth.[12] Perhaps the most important aspect of structural adjustment programs was the emphasis placed on export-led growth. The expansion of an economy through an increase in the volume of trade is professed to expedite two important developments. To begin with, it facilitates access to foreign exchange— and thus the convertible currency—necessary to pay for the additional imported capital and technical inputs required for expansion.[13] Moreover, export-led growth can help increase an economy's competition and international exposure. Access to foreign markets provides a means of permitting more rapid growth than would otherwise be feasible "through the promotion of comparative advantage, by forcing an economy to specialize for a wider export market in goods that it produced most efficiently, and through the spread of new skills and technology."[14]

While highly significant, the burgeoning volumes of international trade among both industrialized and developing countries was not the most consequential aspect of the globalization phenomenon. In terms of absolute numbers as well as their rate of increase in the past two decades, global capital flows far outweighed world trade. In recent years, the world witnessed a remarkable shift away from the employment of capital controls. Capital moved so freely that "the financial markets of industrialized countries [became] subsets of one global market."[15] There was a progressive liberalization of policy toward private foreign capital, and a number of investment incentive measures were adopted in many countries. In fact, open international capital markets were almost universal among the industrialized countries, and they were being instituted in an increasing number of developing countries. While annual average net flows of capital to developing countries, excluding foreign aid, fell from over $30 billion during the 1977 to 1982 period to under $9 billion during the rest of the 1980s, they subsequently rose conspicuously to an average of almost $92 billion during the 1990 to 1993 period, peaking at $130 billion in 1993.[16] The rationale behind this increase of private capital flows worldwide was based on the assumption that foreign capital could provide an important basis for successful economic expansion by injecting investment and technology into sectors that were not receiving these inputs from domestic sources. The result was said to be not only a more efficient national economy, but also a more efficient and productive world economy.

The most visible manifestation of this capital revolution was the proliferation of foreign direct investment (FDI) on the part of multinational enterprises (MNEs). Compared to only a few hundred multinationals two decades earlier, mostly from the United States and Britain, there were more than 1,000 large MNEs in 1990 from the five largest economies (United States, Germany, France, Britain, and Japan), as well as dozens of smaller MNEs from other countries. During the second half of the 1980s, the global flows of new FDI rose by 29 percent annually—nearly three times the growth of international trade.[17] This investment was not only being exported from the major industrialized economies; it was also being received.[18]

This transnational spread of firms and proliferation of FDI became "one of the most striking international phenomena" of the past decade.[19] The description was fitting not just in light of the sheer volume of FDI and its effect on national economies, but also in consideration of the significant bearing the phenomenon had on transforming the way in which international business was conducted and on altering the very conceptual foundations of international political economy. Companies that wanted to become major competitors had to transcend their "home base, with regard both to production facilities and to management philosophy and style." Only firms that adopted this doctrine were able to build "a truly successful global strategy."[20] The result of this global strategic approach was the blurring of national designations for these corporations.[21]

"[C]ompetitive firms [were] competitive everywhere; their advantage [was] not necessarily tied to any specific geographical location. As Japanese firms [proved] in the U.S., and as U.S. firms [proved] in Europe, what [counted was] a competitive product and world-class production and delivery process, rather than the geographical location of production."[22]

Although multinationals were sometimes seen as a sort of malevolent foreign encroachment, they have also benefited many of the recipient economies. As some successful firms expanded into a national economy, they increased that economy's productivity both by spurring competition and by necessitating improvements in the quality and efficiency of input production by local companies. It is for these reasons that direct investment was often billed as an engine for development. FDI constituted one of the largest components of private capital flows to developing countries and also accounted for almost half of all their external finance. For a developing country, this inflow of foreign capital usually generated a considerable number of employment opportunities and increased the productivity of the labor involved. In addition, the introduction by MNEs of more modern factors of production (capital, skills, technology, management), in conjunction with their increased research and development and marketing capacities, made them "a unit of real international integration" for developing world economies.[23] In short, FDI magnified the ability of many economies to compete in the world economy.

MNE activities, however, did not prove to be the most significant form of capital globalization. Indeed, direct investment was "dwarfed by other, more arms-length, forms of cross-border capital movements."[24] "The globalization of financial markets [was] one of the most critical, though least understood, developments in the international economy in recent years. World financial flows [dwarfed in the 1990s] goods flows by a factor of 50 to 1."[25] An increase in transnational activity in the realm of finance occurred almost universally, as countries around the world moved to remove exchange controls, eliminate interest rate regulations, and open domestic financial markets to foreigners. The daily turnover on the world's exchange markets rose tremendously after the 1970s, multiplying more than sixfold during the 1980s alone.[26] The stock market crash of October 1987 was a very good indication of just how integrated global finance had become. The crash demonstrated the significance of swift flows of information and panic around the globe made possible by new global information systems, the availability of large pools of funds that could and did move around the world at the push of a button in response to troubling information, and the integration of formerly isolated national economies into one increasingly seamless global market.[27] In such a world, "purely domestic financial markets had become a thing of the past."[28]

At the apex of economic globalization stood the regional integration of economies in the form of trading blocks and monetary unions. International economic integration was defined as the elimination of economic frontiers between two or more economies, a frontier being "a demarcation across which the mobility of goods, services and factors is relatively low."[29] Formal integration entailed not only the discriminatory removal of all trade impediments between participating nations but also the establishment of certain elements of coordination among the governments involved, such as the equalization of the prices of all similar goods and the establishment of a common division of labor among the integrated national economies.

For many, regional integration became the only road to economic survival, or prosperity, amid rapidly globalizing international markets. It was decided that the lowering of barriers among member countries in a regional agreement, and the increased trade that it fostered, would lead to the replacing of relatively inefficient domestic production by more efficient partner-country production, which, according to the IMF, raised "the welfare of the members and of the world as a whole."[30] While the European Economic Community (EEC)—in which the process of "unbundling territoriality" had gone further than anywhere else—was the most profound example of this harmonization of national economies, there were dozens of other cases involving both industrialized and nonindustrialized countries—and sometimes even a combination of the two.[31] The North American Free Trade Agreement (NAFTA), for instance, called for the eventual, complete elimination of tariffs among Canada, Mexico, the United States, and possibly Chile. In fact, some economists pointed to such integration pacts as a form of economic development for low- and medium-income countries. This strategy was recommended for countries trying to industrialize or make the transformation to a market economy. "A policy recommendation for small and medium-sized countries is that in a world of continuous technological and market changes, integration may expand and secure markets for the greatest variety of a country's goods and services in the future and, hence, mitigate the possible costs of adjustment."[32] In apparent agreement with this contention, many developing countries sought to pool their resources and productive capacities in the form of regional trade agreements.

The advent of more sophisticated communication, computer, and transportation technology revolutionized financial management and transnational economic practices in the 1980s and 1990s. These innovations were largely responsible for the exchange of information, goods, and financial products worldwide, often on a 24–hour basis. They served to link markets and their players with an intimacy and immediacy unimaginable in the 1970s. Closely linked to the global nature of the financial markets was their dependence on technology. The widespread application of new technologies in communications and computers reduced transaction costs and stimulated the creation of new, complex financial instruments.

Information became cheaper and easier to obtain. Even with markets in different time zones, investors and borrowers worldwide gained competitive equality and were able to react instantaneously. They traded around the clock and around the world. Because technology enabled financial transactions to take place more frequently and more rapidly, there was a sharp increase in the velocity of money, in the liquidity of markets, and in the magnitude of international capital flows. Various trading exchanges established links across national boundaries.[33]

While technology's most profound effect was in the realm of finance, by diminishing the relative importance of location it altered the dimensions of markets with respect to all aspects of economic activity. Stated more bluntly, the transformation of technology was responsible for permanently changing relations between national economies. These innovations toppled spatially grounded economic paradigms by "destroying those barriers around markets that hitherto have been synonymous with specific geographical coordinates."[34]

Finally, governments and their policies also played a fundamental role in the transformation of the global economy. Along with the information and computer technology revolution, the globe was swept by a regulatory revolution. Deregulation ended many controls around the world on foreign investment and international trade, thus liberating capital and goods to move freely among previously distinct markets. In conjunction with modern technology, a situation of fewer restrictions vastly enhanced the mobility and fungibility of money.[35] This fungibility drove markets toward more openness and dramatically increased the amount of market activity around the world.

The Globalization of Democracy

Since Woodrow Wilson proposed that democracies would help reduce conflict in the international system, analysts have debated the merit of his contention. For years, particularly immediately after the end of the Second World War and after the end of the Cold War, many maintained not only that history challenged the argument but also that it was dangerous to advocate it. Lately, however, a number of scholars have both argued and demonstrated that there was some truth to Wilson's original claim. As one of them put it, there was solid evidence that "established" democracies have not fought one another since the start of the century. Based on a thorough and extensive empirical analysis, the same analyst hypothesized that the "more democratic each state is, the more peaceful their relations are likely to be."[36]

This last belief was shared by the Clinton administration.[37] As Deputy Secretary of State Strobe Talbott noted in late 1996, in an increasingly economically interdependent world, democracy reduces the likelihood that other entities will be badly governed, that they will engage in terrorism or wreak environmental damage, and that they will go to war against one another. Cognizant that in the world of politics, generalizations rarely apply to every case, Talbott cautioned that the United States should not view support for democracy as an absolute imperative that had to always take precedence over competing goals. He also warned that democracy was no panacea, especially among states going from authoritarian to democratic politics and from centralized to market economies. New democracies that do not gain full legitimacy often fall prey to ethnic and national passions and use them as pretexts to initiate aggressive measures against foreign entities.[38]

The Doctrine of Enlargement and the Future of the State

For nearly four centuries political leaders and analysts have claimed that sovereignty is a state's most precious right. The new drive by the United States to further liberalize the world economy, however, persuaded many analysts that it was taking "place against a backdrop of retreating governments and diminished social obligations."[39] By the middle of the 1990s, it seemed as though the state was destined to become little more than a bit actor in the international arena.[40] As an increasing number of states acquiesced to the imperatives of the global market while they failed to abate economic inequality, bring down unemployment, enhance job security, and provide better retirement pensions and disability insurance, the belief that they would soon be replaced by another form of human organization became stronger. This belief, however, experienced a shock in 1997 and 1998, when some of Asia's major economies experienced firsthand some of the maladies of the global market.

International politics has always been about who rules. In the modern system of international rule, the state has been the central feature.[41] Asia's economic malady in 1997 and 1998, along with the Russian and Brazilian crises, reminded many global leaders, first, that a global market economy left to its own devices would eventually elicit substantial domestic political, economic, and social losses and, second, that the state remained the only human organization capable of finding a balance between two sets of conflicting needs and expectations—those generated by a global market economy and those spawned by different domestic environments.

To propose that the state is the only organization capable of finding a balance between competing sets of needs and expectations is not to contend that all states are equally capable. The only states capable of consistently exercising their sovereign rights successfully have been the powerful ones. The relationship between a state's power and its ability to contain the pressures exerted by the global economy can be unraveled by analyzing the way entities with varying strengths responded to the imperatives of the global economy when their own economies were performing poorly. During the 1980s, the United States's economy was consuming at a pace faster than its ability to pay. As its trade deficits expanded, its major military buildup helped bring about a rapid increase in budget deficits. Washington did not respond to these economic hazards by implementing structural adjustments. Instead, it persuaded other states' political leaders, central bankers, and corporate investors to accept its IOUs. In the meantime, developing states enduring their own economic ailments were forced by the IMF to undergo costly structural adjustments as an exchange for financial credit. Everyone knew that domestic austerity programs would further aggrieve the weaker segments of the populations; however, developing states, because of their inherent internal political and economic weaknesses, had little choice but to abide by the dictates of the entities at the core of the system.[42]

If the role of powerful states has not been handicapped by the globalization of the market economy, then how does one explain the decision by 11 European states that, beginning in 1999, their respective banks and stock exchanges would start using a single European currency, and would adhere to a fixed exchange rate for each of their individual currencies? Clearly, the joint action by Austria, Belgium, Finland, France, Germany, Ireland, Italy, Luxembourg, Spain, Portugal, and Netherlands denoted a willingness on their part to sacrifice an important component of their sovereignty: that of designing their own individual monetary policies. To understand the effect of the action on the nature of sovereignty, one must first comprehend the rationale behind the action. The 11 signatories estimated that by forsaking the right to create their own individual monetary policies, they would arrest Europe's relative decline in a world market economy dominated by the United States. At the signing of the accord the European states acknowledged not the power of the global market per se, but the realization that separately they could not match the competitive power of the United States in the global market.

The state encompasses more than a country's economic arena. It still retains the final authority for addressing, without external interference, a wide gamut of non-economic issues. Nevertheless, in a world bounded by power, a state's sovereignty remains dependent on its capacity to cope effectively with domestic and external pressures.[43] The United States's drive to liberalize the international economy might have further lessened the ability of weaker states to function as viable sovereign institutions.

The Doctrine of Enlargement and Its Effects on Advanced Market Democracies

During the Cold War, the United States and its principal European and Asian partners did not agree on a number of economic and security issues, but the existence of a common external threat served as a powerful incentive for compromise. The inducement to cooperate retained much of its strength for a number of years after the Cold War; in 1997, however, it experienced a major jolt when several Asian economies tumbled.

By the late 1980s, much of the world had become convinced that the East Asian economies, led by Japan, had created a new political economic model, one that guaranteed political stability and rapid economic growth with relative equity. With Japan's economy at the forefront, the success of the East Asian economies had been based on a relatively simple formula. To become effective competitors in the global market, the states had to shield their domestic markets from foreign competition and help their domestic firms become powerful and effective international competitors. The state intervened in the domestic economy not by attempting to roll the market back or by replacing it, but by erecting trade barriers, facilitating credit and investment, ensuring high saving rates, keeping inflation low, promoting exports, and fostering education attentive to the skills required by industrialization. Moreover, in each instance the state fostered political stability by relying on varying degrees of regulated politics, from dictatorship to a one-party system, and by rewarding their citizens' commitment to the common cause with relatively equitable economic returns from the proceeds of economic growth.[44]

This approach enabled the East Asian economies to catch up with the more advanced economies. However, in 1989, as Japan's "bubble" economy burst, the dominoes started to waver. It was not long before the United States and the IMF started to pressure Japan to revive its economy by: i) reducing the role of the "iron triangle" of power controlled by bureaucrats, business leaders, and politicians, ii) bringing down market barriers and stimulating trends already underway, iii) permitting foreign ownership of domestic companies, including the banking sector, iv) granting loans and making financial deals based on economic criteria rather than favoritism, v) deregulating capital and product markets, vi) persuading firms to focus on maximizing profits rather than on market shares, and vii) pressing companies to replace their seniority and lifetime employment with a Western-style merit system. By the middle of 1998 it became evident that Japan was not the only Asian country misguided by a distorted sense of economic security. Afflicted by fragile banking systems loaded with bad loans, the stock market indexes of Indonesia, Malaysia, the Philippines, Singapore, South Korea, Taiwan, and Thailand started to drop in 1997. Shortly afterward, each economy was forced to devalue its currency and to dig deep into its reserves in an attempt to stop the economic plunge. It was not long before some of the Asian states that just a few years earlier had scorned the United States as a "has-been" economic power, found themselves knocking on Washington's doors asking for assistance in their economic plight.

The IMF, with strong U.S. backing, immediately pressured them to undertake liberalizing reforms in finance, corporate governance, and labor markets, and to restrict domestic demand through higher interest rates, lower government spending, and stiffer taxes. Initially, most of the affected Asian states complied, but by the second half of 1998, as domestic turmoil in some of them intensified, they began to adopt measures that countered those demanded by the IMF. In September 1998, Malaysia, in response to speculative attacks on the currency and depletion of its foreign-exchange reserves, imposed exchange controls. Also around this time, the government of Taiwan intervened against speculators by curbing the flow of finance in and out of the country. And Asia's two strongest economies, Japan and China, urged the Group of Seven to review policies toward liberalization. Thousands of miles away, many of Europe's leaders, worried about the fragility of their own financial systems, also called for the imposition of additional regulations on the global economy.[45] For Europe, capital controls meant protecting a financial system dominated by banks, over half of which were government-owned and government-subsidized, and which derived a large portion of their profits from interest income. Opening the financial system would compress the banks' interest rates spread and, as a result, reduce their profits. Moreover, Europe assumed that by imposing controls on capital flows, it would enhance the euro as an international reserve currency and make it more attractive than the dollar.[46]

The United States and the other core market democracies were also at odds with regard to trade. As the 1990s unfolded, the Clinton administration moved aggressively on several fronts to help increase U.S. exports. With renewed vigor, Washington pressured other core states to open their markets more. In addition to demanding that these states lower tariffs and quotas, Washington denounced government regulations that constrained competition, loose antitrust enforcement, deficient implementation of intellectual property rights, and the limited access to product distribution systems. The Clinton administration also intensified its efforts to assist U.S.-based companies to attain contracts abroad. To show that they should take its demands seriously, the Clinton administration resorted more often to enforcing Section 301 of U.S. trade law, which permits the United States to retaliate against entities that refuse to open their markets.[47] These actions were not welcomed by the other core entities, and by the start of 1999, the tension between the United States and the European Union had grown markedly. Finally, in early March, the Clinton administration ordered the imposition of 100 percent duties on a range of European products in retaliation for Europe's failure to stop discriminating against Latin American bananas distributed by American corporations. The scope of Washington's "banana-decision" reached well beyond the product itself. For the Clinton administration, Europe's action was part of a wider trend that included the banning of American hormone-treated beef, subsidies for Airbus, directives on data-privacy that placed American firms at a disadvantage, and a reluctance to share with the United States the responsibility for stimulating the world economy.[48]

By the end of the first quarter of 1999, it seemed clear that the financial crisis had not abated the authority of the United States, and that its economic strength had helped avert a world depression. In late February, with support from Europe's central bankers, the Clinton administration blocked attempts by German and French political leaders to design rules that would coordinate exchange rates between the dominant economies and exert tighter controls over hedge funds. Two months later, the IMF, with strong encouragement from the Clinton administration, approved the creation of new contingent credit lines to make loans available to countries before they are stricken by economic crisis. These developments, however, were unlikely to bring their debate to an end. The United States continued to state that its powerful European and Asian economic counterparts had to open their markets more and be fairer in the way they assisted domestic firms in international competition for major projects. Many of the Asian and European states, in turn, continued to ask for the creation of regimes designed to monitor and regulate derivative transactions, hedge funds, and other short-term financial flows, and to do whatever they could to protect their domestic markets. They also insisted that the World Trade Organization rule against the United States sanction-imposing "Section 301" legislation, and demanded that the U.S. government be less aggressive in its support of American-based corporations seeking foreign contracts.

These clefts, though troubling, will not provoke international instability. To begin with, even if the international economic system were to be divided into several nations or regions, each with its own distinct set of market norms and rules, the United States and the European and Asian states have become too interdependent to fully yield to their parochial economic interests.[49] The United States knows that it needs the explicit support of Europe's and Asia's principal market democracies to keep the global economy open. In turn, the European and Asian states recognize that ultimately their own overall well-being remains tightly linked to the needs and wishes of the system's hegemon. They have not forgotten that though the United States's economic wealth no longer towers over theirs, as it did immediately after the end of the Second World War, it remains the engine of the global economy.

Security concerns will also affect their calculations. The United States has made it clear that its security and economic well being are tightly linked to the welfare of its Asian and European democratic counterparts. Washington realizes that if its relationship with its partners in Asia and Europe were to snap, the United States would have to increase extensively its military power to protect its worldwide economic interests. Fearful that North Korea may decide to deal with its economic plight by launching a military attack on South Korea, or that China may become more assertive toward Taiwan, the United States has pressured Japan to heighten its military presence in the region. Japan, which renounced war as its sovereign right and has maintained a self-defense force designed solely to protect its own territory since the end of the Second World War, will have to resolve this matter before it is able to play the role envisioned by the United States. The chances are that such a day lies in the very near future. The United States's other Asian partners will view Japan's military ascension with some trepidation, but they will also recognize that unless they decide to break fully with the relationships they have developed since 1945 and pin their destinies to China's, their own welfare will continue to depend heavily on the military protection of two of the world's largest economies.

Differences in the security arena had a noticeable effect on the United States's relationship with its European allies. During the early years after the Cold War, some political leaders in the United States wondered whether it should retain its NATO membership. With Russia no longer posing a significant threat, some suggested that it was time for Europe to assume sole responsibility for its own safety. The Clinton administration did not share this view. While it agreed that the United States should waive some of its NATO responsibilities, it also emphasized that because American economic interests were so intertwined with Europe's, the United States could not afford to have its affluent European allies engulfed by chaos. The Clinton administration renewed the United States's commitment with a demand—that NATO expand the alliance to include former members of the Warsaw Pact. Washington reasoned that the incorporation of additional European states would further lessen the likelihood of a European war and strengthen the capacity of the newly born democracies to consolidate and legitimize the power of their regimes. After Russia and some NATO members voiced certain concerns, Hungary, Poland, and the Czech Republic were accepted as the organization's newest partners. Nine other states also expressed their strong desire to see their national emblems raised at NATO's headquarters in Brussels.

During this period, several of NATO's European members began to erect a separate European defense structure under the auspices of the Western European Union (WEU). Since its creation in 1995 until late 1999, the United States and the Europeans debated whether the WEU should become a security organization fully independent of NATO, or whether it should be part of NATO and separated only when necessary. Notwithstanding the belief that Europe had to create its own independent security system, Europe's leaders did not support breaking their ties with the United States.

First, they did not welcome the prospects of dealing solely on their own with the external effects provoked by the domestic political and economic turmoil tormenting Russia, and by the nationalist and ethnic upheavals afflicting eastern and central Europe. Their involvements in Bosnia and Kosovo vividly reminded them that without the backing of the United States they were unable to generate appreciable results. Second, they knew that a military union that fully excluded the United States would impose a severe burden on the major European economies.[50] In the 1990s the joint GNPs of Britain, France, and Germany amounted to close to 70 percent of the United States's GNP, and their joint military expenditures amounted to 44 percent of the United States's military expenditures. Any attempt on their part to increase significantly their defense budgets in order to bring their collective military power to the level of the United States's, would weaken their respective domestic economies and the overall economy of the European Union. Third, they recognized that such an action would impel the United States to augment its own military force, which would make it harder for Europe to meet its original objective. Fourth, they knew that to be an effective military power, a European military organization would have to function as a fully integrated body. It is doubtful that any one of the major European entities would allow one of its counterparts to assume the role the United States has traditionally played as leader of NATO, or that they would be able to put aside their respective domestic political and economic needs and interests and function as a single, united organization. [51] And finally, none of the European entities has forgotten the costs it accrued in the two world wars, and the kind of military might the United States can amass when its interests are threatened. If there was anything they had learned from those two wars and the Cold War, it was that being part of a security organization dominated by the United States was preferable to being part of a security organization competing with the United States. In short, the Europeans understood that the creation of a separate security organization that eliminated all types of military relationships with the United States would have enfeebled, rather than strengthened, their security. [52] Or as Germany's foreign minister, Joschka Fischer, noted at the height of NATO's attack on Serbia, "the United States is an indispensable power for me—even if Europe unites, it will need an Atlantic insurance policy."[53]

The Kosovo conflict, however, proved once again that Europe had become too dependent on the military might of the United States. In an attempt to address this issue, the European Union decided in December 1999 to design a European Strategic Defense Plan. By mid 2000, the main members had agreed to create by 2003 a solely European armed force of some 60,000 troops for the purpose of being deployed quickly in a peacekeeping mission to a troubled area in Europe, and staying at the site for a full year. Remembering too well the opposition it faced at home as it struggled to procure support for American involvement in Kosovo, the Clinton administration formally supported the European Strategic Defense Plan.

Another condition that could help the United States and its core Asian and European partners protect the stability of the international system is the nature of their respective domestic political regimes. It would be premature to propose that because they are all ruled by democratic regimes their relationships will not destabilize the international system. In the years to come, they or the international system may generate contradictions too onerous for their democratic systems to handle peacefully. However, because democracies are readier than non-democratic governments "to reciprocate each other's behavior, to accept third-party mediation or good offices in settling disputes, and to accept binding third-party arbitration and adjudication,"[54] there is a strong likelihood that when at odds with one another, they will strive to reach some type of accord before their differences destabilize the international system.

In sum, by the end of the twentieth century the United States and its principal partners in Asia and Europe had built their relationships on three pillars: military interconnections, economic interdependence, and democracy. Their military interconnections will not be reduced so long as they believe that they share common external threats. If these threats lessen considerably, then they will be less inclined to preserve their military alliance. This decision, however, is unlikely to augment the likelihood of conflict between them, for each party (and here I am assuming the European states would act as a united defense front) would still have enough military power to deter the other. Furthermore, so long as they preserve their economic interdependence, they will be encouraged to try to curb the tension generated by their opposing interests. To be sure, many of the main European states are resentful of the United States's power and role in the international economic arena. As the U.S. ambassador to France, Felix Rohatyn, put it, in Europe there is "the sense that America is such an extraordinary power that it can crush everything in its way." There is a "feeling that globalization has an American face on it and is a danger to the European view of society."[55] This sentiment, however, will have limited effect on their relationships so long as they remain interdependent. Still, interdependence between Europe and the United States could diminish if each increases its economic links with developing countries and regions. Under this new set of conditions, the United States and the other developed states could be less predisposed to accommodate each other's interests. It is too early to say that if they are battered by several major crises concurrently, the democratic nature of their respective political regimes will enable them to always steer away from conflict and to protect the stability of the international system. In a sense, this type of scenario, more than any other, would test the United States's claim that the implementation of its doctrine of enlargement of market democracies will reduce international conflict.

The Doctrine of Enlargement and Its Effects on Russia and Central Europe

Following the disintegration of the Soviet Union, the United States concluded that it would be in its and Europe's interests to help Russia and the newly freed states design stable domestic political and economic systems. Washington was cognizant that it had to be careful not to disregard the fears and concerns of a severely weakened Russia. It understood that conflict often had been the result of an enfeebled power's fear that its adversaries were prepared to capitalize on its frailty. Political leaders on both sides of the fence had good reasons to be concerned.

In December 1989 and June 1990, the United States and the Soviet Union reached two very important agreements. The first accord set the way for the reduction and limitation of conventional weapons in Europe. The second one entailed a non-aggression pact between NATO and the Warsaw Treaty Organization. Following the signing of the second compact, the leader of the Soviet Union and the Communist Party, Mikhail Gorbachev, called for the transformation of the Soviet economic system from a command to a market economy within a 500–day period. The plan provoked intense domestic opposition. Gorbachev offered a compromise, but his action did not allay his opponents' fears. In August 1991, anti-reform members of the Communist Party and discontented government officials mounted a coup. After three days, reformers, aided by massive popular protests in Moscow and other major Russian cities, forced the coup leaders to capitulate.

With the prestige of the Communist Party in tatters, one Soviet republic after another declared its independence. Troubled by the rapid disintegration of the Soviet Union, the United States supported Gorbachev's attempt to create a voluntary union. In the meantime, Russia's president, Boris Yeltsin, decided to go ahead and introduce free-market reforms in his own country. His decision proved to be cataclysmic; within a year's time Russia experienced a 24 percent drop in production and 2,000 percent hyperinflation. Convinced that a chaotic Russia would threaten the stability of the international system, the leaders of the United States and other world economies agreed to help, but conditioned their support on Yeltsin's readiness to initiate additional economic structural reforms. At the 1992 Munich economic meeting, they urged Moscow to rapidly abolish central planning, privatize most state enterprises, and eliminate controls on imports and capital movements. They also demanded that Russia make sharp cuts in public spending and limit money and credit.[56] The implementation of the reforms and austerity programs brought about additional drops in production and increases in unemployment and prices. Nationalists and communists, nostalgic for the era when the Soviet Union was perceived as a superpower, once again tried to seize power. Their attempt failed, and Yeltsin and his administration carried on with their economic reforms. By the end of 1995, many assumed that Russia was beginning to see the light at the end of the tunnel. Economic growth had resumed, inflation had dropped, the budget deficit seemed under control, and the value of the ruble had stabilized.

The signals were only surface deep. In 1998, foreign investors, already handicapped by the Asian financial crisis and conscious that the sharp drop in prices had cut Russia's foreign currency earnings to almost half those of the previous year, started to remove their funds from the country. By August, after defaulting on much of its debt and allowing the ruble to collapse, mayhem descended on Russia's economy and its leaders went knocking on the IMF's doors one more time. Russia's dreadful economic performance afflicted most of its domestic institutions, but few suffered as badly as its military. In 1997, Russia's military received only 56 percent of its budgeted appropriation. This shortfall made it so difficult for its military to purchase new weapons that by 1998 only 30 percent of the weapons on its inventory were classified as modern. Should this trend remain unaltered, by the year 2005 Russia's military will have plunged to the rank of that of a third-world country, with only 5 to 7 percent of its weapons being classified as new.[57]

Russia's economic and military weakness forced its leaders to accept several unsavory developments in the international arena. East Germany, a country that during the Cold War had been one of the Soviet Union's principal allies, stopped being a separate actor in 1990, when it united with West Germany to form one single German state. Poland, the Czech Republic, and Hungary, all former members of the Warsaw Treaty Organization, joined NATO in 1999.[58] As if to add insult to injury, ten other states across Central and Eastern Europe agreed to remake their armies under the guidance of U.S. military advisers. In the words of NATO's military commander, U.S. General Wesley K. Clark, the United States's post–Cold War goal was to design a "security sphere across Eastern Europe."[59]

Meanwhile, national groups that had been under Russia's direct control, or under the sovereign jurisdiction of Eastern European states, began to clamor for independence. In some instances the demands were voiced by ethnic groups within an existing state, as in the case of Chechnyans in Russia, and Croats, Serbs, Slovenes, and Albanians in Yugoslavia; in other cases the calls were initiated by nationalist groups in different states, as occurred between Hungary and Romania over Transylvania. These demands proved to be costly. During the early part of the 1990s, the rivalry between nationalist groups resulted in the deaths of some 50,000 people in Croatia, 50,000 to 200,000 in Bosnia, and 30,000 to 50,000 in Chechnya.[60] Apprehensive about the aftereffects of these wars on the region, Russia's Foreign Minister Andrei V. Kozyrev warned in 1993 that the threat of ethnic violence at that time was "no less serious than the threat of nuclear war yesterday."[61] These conflicts, though serious, did not pose the threat bred by the war over Kosovo between Serbia and NATO.

With the end of the Cold War, the pressure on Yugoslavia to move from a state-controlled economy to a market-based economy intensified. Serbia, which was already experiencing severe economic problems, did not handle the added strain well. Its new leader, a former member of the Communist Party, Slobodan Milosevic, tried to assert Serbian hegemony over the other Yugoslavian republics. Slovenia, a republic composed almost entirely of ethnic Slovenes and which had the most prosperous economy in the federation, rejected Milosevic's attempt and formally declared its independence in June 1991. Croatia, with an 80 percent Croatian population and a sizable Serb minority, also announced its independence that same month. Milosevic, determined to save the Yugoslavian federation, dispatched Serbian troops to the two republics, and a few days later a full-fledged civil war had erupted. Shortly afterward, Macedonia copied Slovenia's and Croatia's actions. As the conflict in Yugoslavia moved into Bosnia, following the latter's declaration of sovereignty in April 1992, the United Nations, backed by NATO, dispatched troops to provide neutral "safe havens" for its civilian populations. Bosnia, a republic made up of Muslims (the single largest demographic group within the republic), Serbs (most of whom are Orthodox Christians), and Croats (who are predominately Catholic), proved to be a perplexing challenge. Starting in 1992, the UN and NATO launched a series of diplomatic initiatives designed to bring the fighting to a halt. It was not until 1994, however, when an attack against a major market in Sarajevo killed and wounded over 200 civilians, that the Clinton administration concluded that without the United States's active involvement the peace process would go nowhere. The United States's participation did not pay off immediately, largely because it relied mostly on threats and limited force. It was not until Bosnian Serbs marched into one of the "safe areas" controlled by the United Nations in July 1995 and methodically slaughtered thousands of Muslims, that NATO, under U.S. leadership, decided to intensify its attacks by launching a series of air strikes.[62] The Bosnian Serbs, weakened by their military losses and the imposed economic sanctions, finally accepted the Dayton Accord brokered by Washington in November 1995.[63] This action, however, did not bring peace to Yugoslavia and its former republics.

Following the signing of the agreement, the United States and its European allies deployed their forces in order to keep the quarreling parties at peace while the different Bosnian factions worked to design a political accord. Four years later, though the truce still remained in place, the different factions had not yet reached a permanent agreement. In the process, conflict in Kosovo, a province of Serbia, gained disastrous proportions. In the second half of the 1990s, Albanians, who make up 90 percent of Kosovo's population, launched a drive to break away from Serbia. Milosevic responded in form. As the new civil war gained momentum, the United States and its NATO partners put together a peace deal that granted Kosovo broad autonomy, but not independence, and authorized the deployment of some 28,000 NATO-led peacekeeping forces. In late March 1999, the United States and its NATO partners, after many failed attempts to persuade Milosevic to join the Albanians in the signing of the peace accord, launched air strikes against Serbian forces.

As the war between NATO and Serbia intensified, the relationships between the United States and Russia deteriorated. Unable to restructure its political and economic systems and to break its dependence on the financial charity of the West, alienated by the actions of its former Warsaw partners, and encumbered by widespread domestic neurosis, Moscow began to regard the war on Serbia both as an attempt to further humiliate Russia and as a means to eliminate the disrepute its failings had spawned both at home and abroad. Early in the war, Yeltsin warned the United States and NATO that the bombing on Serbia could provoke a wider conflict in Europe or even a "third world war" unless it was ended immediately. This threat was followed by claims that only a political defeat would stop NATO from becoming "the world's gendarme."[64] And yet, aware that Russia's economy could not regain its strength without the good will of the West and that the Russian military lacked the preparedness and capability to stand against the United States and a united NATO, Moscow attempted to regain some of its lost prestige by serving as moderator. In June, the Russian leaders accepted NATO's peace terms and helped convince Milosevic that the bombing would not stop unless he did the same.

Developments in Russia and Central and Eastern Europe will continue to cause alarm in many quarters, but they will not generate the type of international conflict common to previous eras. Even the most fervent Russian nationalists understand that their military is no longer the military of yesteryears and that if Russia ever hopes to revive its economy it cannot totally alienate its most powerful potential financial backers: the West. Equally as significant, the United States and its Western European allies will continue to hammer the message that they are no longer interested in gaining control over additional territories. Prior to 1914, the major European powers were divided into two hostile alliances, with members of each alliance striving either to protect the territory under its control or to enlarge it. By the 1990s, however, neither the United States nor any one of the major European powers had the craving, or the need, to enlarge its power by augmenting its territory. This message could be lost if Russia's failures to stabilize its domestic political and economic systems persist, and if the United States's effort to create a security sphere across Eastern Europe by expanding NATO is not balanced by scrupulously crafted reassurances that the policy is not designed to further undermine Russia's power and security.[65] However, in view of President Clinton's appeal to the Western Europeans to admit Russia, eventually, to both NATO and the European Union, and President Vladimir V. Putin's claim that Russia's future is tightly linked to Europe's, one has good reason to infer that all the major parties will endeavor to abate their differences.

The Doctrine of Enlargement and Its Effects on China

With the unraveling of the Soviet empire, analysts wondered which country would emerge as the United States's principal international rival. The immediate consensus was that no other entity matched China's potential. Analysts acknowledged that the GNP of the United States was more than twice the size of China's, its military expenditures more than four times greater, and its nuclear arsenal perhaps 20 to 30 times larger. However, they also projected that in 25 years, China's population will be nearly five times the size of the United States's, and its economy one and a half times greater.[66] Based on these estimates, they inferred that China's armed personnel would remain larger than the United States's and that it would continue to augment its military expenditures and the size of its nuclear arsenal.

The above forecast generated a major debate about how the United States should respond to China's emergence as an international rival. Containment advocates were convinced that as China's military power and economic wealth increased, its leaders would attempt to satisfy a long list of unrealized territorial and political ambitions. Relying on a traditional realpolitik perspective, they noted that the only alternative left to the United States was to strengthen its alliances on the Chinese periphery and to increase its military deployment in Asia. Engagement advocates agreed that China's power potential was substantial, but contended that its intentions remained unclear and that it would be premature for the United States to implement belligerent policies. They recommended that Washington continue to conduct dialogues on matters of security and human rights, and expand economic relations.[67]

History is awash with examples of countries that failed to realize their potential.[68] An entity's power is determined not only by its size and productive capability but also by its location, the characteristics of its population, and the nature of its political and economic systems. During the twentieth century, the United States was surrounded north and south by considerably weaker neighbors, and east and west by two vast oceans that kept it safe from the power aspirations of Europe's and Asia's major entities. These conditions made it easier to project its power worldwide. China will not experience this freedom. In the north, it still faces Russia, a rival with the strength to play, if no longer a major role worldwide, at least a critical part regionally. In the southwest, China shares its border with India—a former adversary housing the second largest population in the world. And to the east, it confronts Taiwan, an entity still unwilling to defer to Beijing, and Japan, the proprietor of a formidable economy and an ally of the United States.

The presence of a major military gap in a power rivalry will ordinarily impel the trailing state to narrow it. China was the only major power that decided to increase its defense budget substantially at the end of the Cold War. This decision seems to have been spurred by the Gulf War. As the war ensued, the leaders of the People's Liberation Army realized that if China ever hoped to compete with the United States in the international arena as an equal, it had to improve its armed forces rapidly.[69] Notwithstanding the many steps China will most likely continue to take to modernize its military, the measures must be kept in perspective. China's defense budget in the 1990s was still one-third that of the United States. Considering that its navy and air force were primitive compared to those of the United States, the only way Beijing could close the gap would be to spend more on defense than the United States for a great number of years, and to develop highly sophisticated technology. In addition, the United States would have to fail to respond with a military drive of its own.[70] If history is any guide, the prospects of these three conditions coming to pass simultaneously are small.

China's domestic structure will also act as an obstacle to its global aspirations. Committed to the notion that without economic wealth a country cannot become a world power, the Chinese government sanctioned the design of a "socialist-market economy." The doctrine has been guided by the principle that the state must contribute to the creation of conglomerates that can compete worldwide. These conglomerates, which have adopted many of the values and ideas championed by advocates of a free-market economy, such as modern management, foreign investment, applied technology, and shareholder structures, exist not for the sake of their stockholders but for the well being of the state's national interest. By relying on this approach, China was able to quadruple its GDP in less than 20 years, and to increase its foreign trade by more than 16 percent per year from 1974 to 1994. The implementation of the doctrine, however, also prompted harmful results.[71]

In the long run, all state-run economies induce corruption. China has not been the exception. Most members of China's Communist Party, which totals some 55 million, work for the government or manage state enterprises. Their privileged position, along with the high level of corruption they have helped spawn, has provoked intense resentment among the Chinese populace. This anger has been intensified by China's decision to tone down its commitment to meeting basic human needs. Until the first half of the 1990s, China's comparative record at providing adequate food intake, safe drinking water, sufficient clothing and shelter, literacy, sanitation, health care, and employment was laudable. In 1994, its rank in the Human Development Index (HDI) was far ahead of its GNP per capita rank. According to the United Nations Human Development Report, the variance between both ranks indicated that China had made more judicious use of its income to improve the capabilities of its people than any other country in the world.[72] By 1997, however, China had decided to retreat from its earlier commitment. While in 1994 it was ranked 143 in GNP per capita and 94 in HDI, by 1997 its GNP per capita rank had improved to 105 but its HDI rank had descended to 108. The costs of this change were not distributed evenly among China's regions and ethnic groups. Most of the burden was shouldered by regions inhabited by China's non-Han minorities, such as the Mongolians, Tibetans, and Muslims. Fearful that its economic policies might instigate social instability, the Chinese government attempted to rectify regional imbalances, albeit unsuccessfully. It also enlarged its People's Armed Police, a national force trained in riot control. "By increasing the size of the People's Armed Police, the leadership in Beijing implicitly acknowledge[d] that internal unrest [was] a greater threat to the regime's survival than [was] foreign invasion."[73]

China's economic and social problems will continue to be compounded by its political system. After communism lost its credibility as a viable ideological alternative to liberalism, the Chinese Communist Party increased its dependence on nationalism. It appealed to Chinese nationalist sentiments both to protect its own standing within the political system and to generate support for its domestic and international policies.[74] But as China's economy continues to grow and becomes more complex and intertwined with foreign markets, the state will be pressured to cede its economic authority to the market. This action, in turn, will intensify the push on the Communist Party to open the political system. Economic liberalization does not always end in democracy. Over the long run, however, it is nearly impossible both to promote economic growth and to maintain a closed political system, particularly in an increasingly interdependent global economic system. It is unlikely that the party will voluntarily open China's political system if the leaders of the People's Liberation Army retain their domestic political power and decide that such an action would weaken China's relative power in the region. This reaction, however, could also help provoke additional internal instability.

Considering the obstacles it must surmount, it is highly improbable that China will reach the crest of the international system within the next two decades. Assuming that other factors remain constant (always a dubious assumption in a rapidly changing environment), to succeed, China would have to: i) maintain the existing rate of economic growth, ii) augment its offensive military power expeditiously, iii) restrain the tension its growth in military and economic strength will generate with its immediate neighbors and the United States; iv) ensure that its economic growth is not so unevenly distributed between the regions and minority groups that those who are left behind are compelled to challenge the authority of the central government, and v) cope effectively with the pressure to open the political system as the state curtails its economic functions and more Chinese enjoy the fruits of a rapidly developing economy.

Whether or not China's drive to become a major world player will induce instability in the region depends on how threatened it feels. The Clinton administration concluded this much when it decided, after a series of mishaps, to place its trust primarily on the market component of its broader doctrine of enlargement. It accepted that it could not coerce China to open its political system and nurture human rights, and at the same time persuade it to open its market and establish closer economic ties with the United States. As Deputy Secretary of State Talbott noted, the U.S. policy toward China had to be "predicated on the conviction that continued economic and cultural engagement" was the best way to induce political openness and regional stability.[75] It was not evident, however, that subsequent U.S. administrations will be able to, or will want to, adhere to this doctrine. If China refuses to open its market and political system further, tries to encroach on Taiwan's independence, or acts against Japan, future U.S. administrations will be hard pressed not to yield to congressional demands that the United States develop a more militant China policy. Under such conditions, the stability of the international system will depend on the intensity of the tension generated by Washington's and Beijing's incompatible foreign policies, and on the costs the United States and China are ready to pay—the former to preserve the region's power balance, the latter to alter it.

The problem would be compounded were the United States to decide to implement a limited missile defense system. In his final year as president, Bill Clinton sought to persuade China, Russia, and Europe that the creation of a limited missile defense system to protect the United States against attacks by rogue states such as North Korea and Iraq, would be in their interest and would not engender a new arms race.[76] As one might expect, the idea spawned a great deal of controversy. In the United States, the sentiment ran fairly strong in favor of deploying such a system. Abroad, however, opposition proved to be intense. The Europeans feared that the implementation of such a plan would generate an increase in tension and a new arms race. Their concerns seemed justified. Moscow warned that it would destabilize 30 years of arms control agreements between the United States and Russia. More unsettling, Beijing made it clear that deployment by the United States of a limited missile defense system would force China to increase the size of its long-range missile forces.[77] Though the Clinton administration decided against the emplacement of a missile defense system, it would not be surprising if its successor reverses it. It has always been then tendency of the state dominating the status quo to try to maintain a preponderance of power.[78] The deployment of such a system is destined to increase tension considerably. As has been noted: "In seeking to protect the United States against an unknown and undefined challenge, NMD (national missile defense) will stimulate the growth of a potential Chinese threat. . . ."[79]

The Doctrine of Enlargement and Its Effects on the Persian Gulf

A number of positive signs sprang from the Persian Gulf in the 1990s. Arab governments that had depended on Soviet support softened their rhetoric and lowered their profile. Iraq's defeat in the battlefield degraded military threats to oil access in the Gulf. Iran's moderates commandeered some of the powers held by the ayatollahs. Israel and the Palestinians reached a few important compromises. And many Arab governments began to accept that they had no choice but to learn to live with Israel. It would be wrong, however, to assume that the Persian Gulf lost its capacity to generate contradictions that could destabilize the international system, and that the United States did not need to be troubled about its Gulf policy.

Recent history has shown that it is incorrect to contend that as the globalization of market democracies becomes more pervasive, states with different cultural components will be less resistant to additional globalization. The argument is erected on the unsound assumption that though there are domestic pockets of resistance throughout the globe, all the affected entities will ultimately find a common ground. The market has little interest in a society's political order and cultural background. It does not care about an interest group's religious, ethnic, or nationalist affiliation, or whether it strives to preserve its social order, so long as their actions do not hinder economic performance. Conversely, though most of today's societies are interested in fostering economic development, in some there are groups that place greater value on preserving their social order and cultural heritage and, as a result, resort to violence to prevent the utilization of economic instruments that could undermine it.

For decades, Washington's foreign policy toward the Persian Gulf was built on the belief that the continuing prosperity of United States and the stability of the world's economy depended heavily on open access to the region's oil supplies. Convinced that many of the Gulf's producing states were too weak to defend themselves against stronger entities in the region, and that the Europeans were unlikely to take up the burden, the United States assumed the role of protector. In this role, its primary activities in the 1990s entailed helping Israel protect itself; ensuring, via the implementation of a "dual containment" policy, that neither Iraq nor Iran become the region's hegemon; and aiding states such as Egypt, Saudi Arabia, and Kuwait to preserve domestic stability. To the fulfillment of these ends it invested between $30 billion and $60 billion (depending on how calculations are conducted).[80]

The United States, however, built its Persian Gulf policy on a house of cards, one that could be toppled by its own strategy of enlargement. The oil boom of the 1970s made it possible for the leaders of the Gulf states to "take a holiday from politics." Awash in money generated by impressive current account surpluses, they became convinced that they did not need to share power, strengthen their legitimacy, or address some of the most pertinent economic, social, or political issues affecting their states. The United States, afraid that another Gulf state might attempt to replicate Iran's revolutionary experience, turned a blind eye on the Gulf leaders' intransigence. The drop in oil prices in 1986 altered the political reality, but not the disposition of most of the Gulf leaders. Rather than initiating structural political and economic reforms, most of their governments engaged in deficit spending. This decision provoked external and internal challenges. The international economic system began to demand greater market discipline, transparency, and accountability. The governments and the ruling families responded with budget cuts, but refused to initiate meaningful structural changes that might weaken their power, undermine their interests, and undercut their traditional privileges.[81]

The external demands and the internal responses spurred retorts from different domestic voices. In some cases, the disapprovals came from those who demanded that governments free their states of their dependence on foreign support and help the expansive underclass attain the skills it needed to exit its inferior station. In other instances, the objections were initiated by those versed in Western political principles, who demanded greater participation in government and the reduction of privileges bestowed on the ruling families. The strongest censures were uttered by those who clamored for the replacement of the secular state with one guided by radical Islamic fundamentalist principles.[82]

As demonstrated by the Iranian revolution, Washington's competence to abate domestic forces in the Gulf was, and will remain, limited. Washington will continue to back allied states with rigid authoritarian regimes, such as Egypt and Saudi Arabia, but the fate of these relationships will depend less on the United States's support and more on the Arab leaders' ability both to grasp the nature of the tensions that afflict their countries and to defuse them constructively. Deep nationalist, sectarian, and ethnic cleavages will prevent the mounting of a united anti-

U.S. front across the entire region. But these divisions will not make it easier for the United States to assist individual countries in meaningful ways. Its attempts will be hampered by the prospect that its support, regardless of how well intended, will continue to fuel strident domestic opposition.[83]

The Doctrine of Enlargement and Its Effects on Latin America and Africa

Most of the wars fought in the 1990s were civil wars. The vast majority of these conflicts ensued in the developing world. During the Cold War, between 1946 and 1988, the international arena witnessed the start of 60 civil wars, which resulted in the death of some 144,000 people per year. Between 1989, when the Berlin Wall fell, and 1997, there were 103 civil wars, which led to the killing of some 217,000 people per year.[84] Stated differently, while between 1946 and 1988 there was an average of only 1.4 civil wars per year, between 1989 and 1997 the average increased to close to 13 civil wars per year.

Civil wars were not the only ill afflicting developing countries. The ratio of average income of the most powerful country in the world, the United States, to that of the poorest, Ethiopia, increased from about 9 to 1, at the start of the twentieth century, to 60 to 1 at the end.[85] The United Nations estimated that in the early 1990s, 30 percent of the jobs in Latin America and 60 percent of those in Africa existed in the informal sector, where wages were much lower than in the formal area, and job security was virtually nonexistent.[86] With the introduction of higher technology into their industries and a growing service sector worldwide, the number of manufacturing jobs in the developing economies has dwindled. These jobs were often replaced by lower-paying jobs that were more temporary and less likely to be protected by trade unions. The effects of these developments on income distribution were considerable. It was estimated that while the ratio of income inequality in Western Europe was about 5 to 1, and in the United States 10 to 1, in Latin America it was about 16 to 1 (in Brazil it was 25 to 1).[87] In Chile, for instance, the regime of August Pinochet implemented major structural economic adjustments from 1973 until 1988. One of the results of this policy was to bring down the income of the lowest 20 percent by 3 percent, and to increase that of the richest 20 percent by 10 percent. The wage gap between skilled and unskilled labor also increased by more than 30 percent in Peru, and 20 percent in Colombia. As remarked by the *Financial Times,* the free global economy remains an "imperfect force. . . . About two-thirds of the world's population have gained little or no substantial advantage from rapid economic growth."[88] High levels of conflict accompanied by extensive economic inequality, however, do not always induce international instability. Their effects depend on where they ensue and the value placed on them by the international system's core entities.

Latin America

Latin American states have endured wars, civil wars, revolutions, and military coups since their independence in the early decades of the nineteenth century. The rate of these events, however, has changed through time. Since the end of the nineteenth century, few of them have attempted to enlarge their power by gaining control over neighboring territories. Military coups and civil wars, on the other hand, though they continued throughout much of the twentieth century, became less common after the end of the Cold War. These last two changes have not been fortuitous.

Almost since its inception, the United States regarded Latin America as vital to its security interests. This belief played a central role during the Cold War. During that period, Washington supported Latin American leaders willing and able to help the United States contain communism, regardless of whether or not they were committed to democracy. This action on the part of the United States often spawned counteractions that, in turn, engendered military coups, authoritarian regimes, civil wars, or all three. The end of communism as a viable political alternative freed the United States to be more severe toward Latin America.[89] No longer able to use the threat of a communist takeover as a bargaining tool and recognizing that the only game left in town was that dictated by the United States, most Latin American states agreed to initiate major political and economic reforms, which included creating democratic regimes and bringing civil wars and military coups to an end.

With the approach of the new century, nearly every Latin American state remained encircled by the same boundaries that defined it in 1945, almost none faced the prospect of war, and civil wars and military coups were no longer common features of the Latin American political landscape.[90] Still, the region continued to be afflicted by a series of major political, economic, and social problems. High levels of political corruption, accompanied by high unemployment and increasing economic inequality have fueled skepticism about the ability of the newly established democracies both to protect their fragile regimes and to continue implementing market-oriented policies. Latin American entities will not be equal in their ability to cope with the contradictions emanating from their own domestic systems. Their success will depend on the intensity of the internal tensions, the strength of their political regimes, and the decisions by the United States about which countries it considers vital to its economic and security interests and, thus, worthy of its support.[91]

Possibly no case exemplifies more effectively the value the United States has placed, and will continue to place, on the welfare of vital Latin

American entities than its involvement in Mexico's 1994–1995 financial crisis. On December 19, 1994, Mexico devalued the peso, which had been pegged at 3.5 to the dollar. By then, dollar reserves in Mexico had shrunk to $11 billion, which was not enough to pay dollar-pegged bonds that were about to be due shortly. As money continued to leave Mexico, its government announced that it would not be able to guarantee dollars for pesos at any price. Following the announcement, the Mexican peso fell drastically and stocks tumbled. These developments took many people by surprise.[92] Mexico's economy had improved significantly since 1982, when the government ran a deficit equal to 16 percent of GDP and had defaulted on millions of dollars in loan payments. By 1994, Mexico had balanced its budget three years in a row, sold costly state-owned companies, and appropriated an open-market policy by becoming part of the North American Free Trade Agreement (NAFTA). These attractive economic features, however, were tarnished by other less desirable economic activities. By the end of 1994, it had become clear that Mexico had borrowed and bought too much from the international market, and not sold enough. This imbalance increased its current-account deficit to a sum equivalent to 8 percent of the country's GDP. In the words of Stanley Fischer, an IMF deputy managing director, Mexico did "everything right—with one exception, and you can't do that thing wrong."[93]

The Clinton administration moved swiftly to rescue Mexico's economy. On January 12, after Mexico's government had agreed to cut spending and its labor unions to hold wage gains to 7 percent, Clinton proposed a $40 billion Mexican aid package to the U.S. Congress. On January 23, Secretary of Treasury Robert Rubin and Federal Reserve Chairman Alan Greenspan went to Congress to ask for support for Clinton's plan. The following day, Clinton, in his State of the Union address, stated that it was in the interest of the United States to help Mexico resolve the economic crisis. Shortly afterward, however, the U.S. Congress announced that it would not support Clinton's plan. Four days later, Clinton bypassed Congress and used the Exchange Stabilization Fund to authorize $20 billion in loans and loan guarantees to Mexico. Clinton's action instigated rebukes from several members of Congress, but he did not bend.

His decision to assist Mexico was defined by three national interest considerations. First, he and Secretary of State Warren Christopher believed that leadership exerts a decisive influence upon national power, and that leadership is linked to a policy of prestige designed to "impress other nations with the power one's own nation actually possesses, or with the power it believes, or wants other nations to believe, it possesses."[94] Christopher acknowledged this point when he stated that the decision to help Mexico was, probably more than anything else, "a test of American leadership. By extending this package to Mexico, the United States will demonstrate its unwavering commitment to lead this hemisphere toward stability and prosperity. . . . Only the United States has the capacity to offer this leadership."[95] Also implied in the statement, but clarified in another portion of his testimony, was the notion that if the United States hoped to protect the essential rules governing interstate economic relations, it had to protect its weaker partners. The United States provided this service because it recognized that its own welfare was tightly linked to the welfare of the international regime it dominated. The approval of the loan guarantee package, stated Christopher, would "have far-reaching implications for the prosperity and stability of Latin America and of emerging market economies around the world."[96] The third and final consideration referred to by the Clinton administration centered on the economic and political interconnection between Mexico and the United States. The United States, explained Christopher, "has an immense economic and political stake in Mexico's stability. . . . If we fail to act decisively now, American investment in Mexico will be imperiled. American exports—now $40 billion a year—will diminish. And many of the 700,000 American jobs those exports support could be jeopardized. . . . [E]conomic distress and political instability in Mexico could add to the pressure that already pushes thousands of illegal immigrants across the 2,000–mile border that we share. . . . Moreover, Mexico's capacity to cooperate with us on a range of other issues—from narcotics trafficking and money laundering to the environment—could be severely strained."[97]

In short, new financial crises similar to those experienced by Mexico in late 1994 and early 1995, and Brazil in early 1999, will continue to arise during the next two decades. Moreover, political disturbances in Bolivia, Peru, Venezuela, and Colombia in 2000 indicate that the hopes that Latin America would finally join the family of stable democracies were premature. However, after nearly two centuries of attempting, first, to gain tutelage over the region and, second, to keep it under its dominion, Washington has repeatedly demonstrated that it was not about to sit back and permit events in Latin America to debilitate the United States's authority over the area and undermine the stability of the international system. It is doubtful that if new developments threaten the economic interests and political leadership of the United States in Latin America, Washington will not intervene to quell them.

Africa

Africa, like Latin America, has been burdened by extensive political, economic, and social turmoil. However, Africa's much shorter postcolonial history, along with its location, have induced contradictions with a tenor very different from those shaped by Latin America.

For a brief while after the end of the Second World War, Africa was of little concern to the United States and the Soviet Union. Encumbered by challenges in Europe and Asia, Washington and Moscow paid token attention to Africa's pre-independence plight. This attitude changed in the late 1950s and early 1960s, as the struggle for independence in Africa gained momentum and each of the two world giants decided that its power and prestige would suffer if it permitted the other to gain the upper hand in previously unattended regions. For the remainder of the Cold War, Washington and Moscow sided with almost any African group or state willing to support its cause against its ideological rival. Though their involvement was not followed by a rebirth of peace, it curbed significantly the frequency of wars and civil wars. This concern with African affairs faded shortly after the disintegration of the Soviet Union. In 1993, the United States, with the support of 29 other states, intervened in Somalia in an attempt to bring to an end a civil war that had ravaged its population. After 18 U.S. Army rangers were killed in Mogadishu in October, the Clinton administration concluded that the interests of the United States in the area were not sufficiently important to justify paying such a cost. Throughout the remainder of the 1990s, the United States did very little to help terminate the civil conflicts that raged in Algeria, Sudan, Uganda, Angola, the Democratic Republic of Congo, Lesotho, Burundi, Rwanda, Congo Brazzaville, Guinea-Bissau, Senegal, and Sierra Leone.

Since the end of the Second World War, death brought about by wars, civil wars, poverty, and famine have characterized Africa more than any other continent or region of the world. Still, such characterization did not alter the fact that Africa's international significance since the end of the Second World War has been, and will continue to be, dictated by the structure of the international system. During part of the life of the bipolar system, both superpowers viewed Africa as an important pawn; following the demise of the Soviet Union, the United States rapidly put Africa out of its mind. Convinced that an unstable Africa would have limited effect on its interests and on the stability of the international system, the United States channeled its energy and resources to regions that it considered vital. Left to their own devices and with little chance of affecting the destiny of the world's most important entity, parts of Africa will continue to empower their internal demons to dictate events.

Terrorism, the United States, and International Instability

In the 1990s, U.S. policy makers, political analysts, and journalists became obsessed with terrorism.[98] The 1995 nerve gas attack on a crowded Tokyo subway station by a Japanese cult group, the 1995 bombing of the U.S. federal government building in Oklahoma City, the 1996 bombing of the U.S. military compound in Saudi Arabia, the revelation that the former Soviet Union had designed a massive biowarfare program, the discovery of chemical and biological arsenals in Iraq, the bombing of two U.S. embassies in Africa, and the attack on a U.S. vessel in Yemen helped induce this fixation. Indeed, because of some of these developments, President Clinton apportioned to his 1999 budget hundreds of millions of dollars to curtail the dangers of terrorism.

Defined as the "substate application of violence or threatened violence to sow panic in a society, to weaken or overthrow the incumbents, and to bring about political change," terrorism has long been the instrument of the weak against the powerful.[99] Social and economic minorities, along with a wide range of nationalist, ethnic, and religious groups have relied on terrorism to advance their political causes. Paradoxically, the new interest in terrorism was not driven by its frequency. The number of international terrorist incidents had been dropping since 1987, and reached its lowest point in 24 years in 1996.[100] The new concern with terrorism can be attributed to the belief that nuclear, chemical, and biological weapons are not terribly difficult to design and use, that if used they could devastate the population of any major city, and that the world is populated by extremist groups anxious to launch a major attack against a Western power, preferably the United States.[101] It is probable that the international arena will witness a devastating act of terrorism in the next two and a half decades. To acknowledge that such an event is highly likely, however, is not to contend that acts of superterrorism will become common practice and that they will destabilize the United States and the international system.

Acts of terrorism come in different forms.[102] The most common type in the 1990s was mass-casualty conventional terrorism. This type pertains to an act carried out via conventional means and initiated by one individual or a small group sans state support, or by a small group backed by a state. The bombing of the federal building in Oklahoma City fits in the first category, while the bombing of Pan Am flight 103, assuming it was financed by a "rogue state," belongs in the second one.[103] The second type refers to acts of terrorism in which the perpetrators use weapons of mass-destruction for a small-scale attack, and their act is or is not sponsored by a "rogue state." In March 1995, the Aum Shinrikyo group contrived a poison gas attack in the Tokyo subway. The act, which killed 10 people and injured 5,000, was not state-sponsored. In the 1990s there were numerous states that sponsored terrorist groups and that had access to chemical and biological weapons. No single state, however, ever staged or sponsored such an act. Finally, superterrorism refers to the strategic use of chemical or biological agents in order to kill tens or hundreds of thousands of people. This type of act may also be differentiated depending on whether it is or is not state-sponsored. Once again, the world has yet to witness this form of terrorism.

Ideally, an international system's hegemon would want to impede the execution of all types of terrorist acts. Regardless of its power and intelligence-gathering capabilities, however, no hegemon committed to keeping its domestic political system open and competitive will ever be able to fully realize such a goal. Since it cannot, it is in its interest to prevent the execution of the type of act that carries the greatest potential to undermine its power and to destabilize the international system. The fulfillment of this goal is not unrealizable, for as the potential destructive effect of an act increases from the first set to the last one, their likelihood of ensuing decreases.[104] The likelihood will be lessened by three sets of impediments.

According to a 1996 Defense Department report, very few terrorist groups had the financial and technical resources necessary to develop and use weapons of mass destruction effectively. These groups typically encountered problems in the production, manufacture, storage, and delivery of nuclear, chemical, and biological weapons.[105] Other elements will also help abate their zeal to embark on superterrorism. History abounds with groups with extremist political agendas; very few of them, however, have shown any desire to pay the price its execution generally exacts. Those who could achieve their objectives with traditional means have tried to avoid overkill, for they knew that if they destroyed too many lives they would spawn puissant counteractions that, in turn, would reduce greatly their own chances for political and physical survival. The vast majority of them demonstrated that they would much rather enjoy the fruits of their efforts than sacrifice their lives for a cause.

Identifying terrorist groups is not a difficult task; determining what they plan to do, where, when, and how is markedly more complex. Still, the challenge is not insuperable. Because most terrorist groups have political agendas, they try to gain recognition by disseminating information about their concerns and objectives. As of late, most terrorist groups have gone so far as to reveal their violent intents before following through. Furthermore, people and groups do not become killers of thousands of civilians right away. Most terrorist groups precede their acts with protracted processes of radicalization.[106] The increase in intensity and frequency of their actions propels intelligence-gathering organizations to examine and dissect them in order to infer their intentions. The interactive process that takes place between a terrorist group and its potential target does not guarantee that the latter will detect a superterrorist act before it is triggered; it does, however, increase the likelihood that it will.

In sum, there is no reason to assume that the new tensions that will emerge in the international arena in the next few decades will provoke an increase in terrorist acts. It is sensible to assume, nevertheless, that as the accessibility to biological, chemical, and nuclear weapons increases, so will the disposition by terrorist groups to use them.[107] The United States and the other major market democracies will not be able to halt every single terrorist act. Their ability to prevent one will be directly related to the potential target's international prominence, the terrorist group's global reputation, and the damage the terrorist group intends to wreak. The greater the potential target's international notability, the terrorist group's international fame, and the havoc the terrorist group plans to cause, the greater the ability of the target to detect the plan before it is fully implemented.

The Pitfalls of Complacency and Indecisiveness

In the mid-1980s, Oliver Stone wrote and directed the film *Wall Street*. The film's most absorbing protagonist, a merciless Wall Street investor played by Michael Douglas, captures in one short sentence the creed that has epitomized for the past 200 years the source of the United States's lasting power. "Greed," notes Douglas's character, "for lack of a better word, is good." Greed, he adds, is good because it fosters competition and creativity. Adherence to this doctrine has enabled the United States to become the world's dominant entity and to neutralize countless challenges to its authority. Greed alone, however, cannot guarantee indefinite international dominance.

Perils are history's constant. The latest drive by the United States to widen the global community of market democracies does not mark the beginning of a less hazardous era. Its doctrine will continue to create or revive several antipodal undertakings. As in the past, the United States's ability to uncover a growing tension in a timely fashion, and to take the measures necessary to control or reduce it, will be determined by its leaders' ability to view each problem through many different lenses, design each policy free of intense domestic political discord, and persuade the American public that its interests remain tightly linked to the welfare of the international system. But today, more than ever, its success will depend greatly on how skillful it is at warding off two internal problems.

Complacency is one of the worst ailments that can afflict a world hegemon. It typically surfaces when an entity stands alone at the top of system, unburdened by competition from its closest rivals.[108] Rationality is one of the first functions undermined by excessive satisfaction. Rationality requires effort; it cannot be attained unless decision-makers are prepared to endure the demands of energy and time. Intensive competition is the best enticer of rationality. Surrounded by states with similar capabilities, each state understands that to retain its competitive edge it must be willing to pay the procedural costs necessary to assess international problems rationally. The leaders of a state that is markedly more powerful than others, on the other hand, will be less driven by the need to gather substantial amounts of information and carefully examine a wide range of options before making its final decision. Monopoly, as economists have long known, is a major impediment to rationality.[109]

Another domestic condition that could undermine the United States's ability to cope effectively with international tensions is indecisiveness. Before initiating a risky foreign policy, nearly every president has tried to gauge how the Congress and the American public would respond to the decision, the human and material costs they would be willing to tolerate before he started losing their confidence and support, and the effects the action might have on his own political future. This type of pressure can have both constructive and negative effects. On the constructive side, the domestic political pressure stops leaders from taking unnecessary risks. It prevents them from assuming that they can place American interests in harm's way without first exploring alternative avenues and confirming that the threats to the United States's national interest are real. On the negative side, the consequences can be threefold.

The United States's ability and willingness to respond effectively to an international challenge have been heavily influenced by the nature and intensity of the external threat, and the skills of its leaders. Ironically, in a democracy these two factors tend to be inversely related. Certainly, when a state faces a major threat, its leaders must be able to bring together the means necessary to thwart the challenge and minimize the costs it will sustain in the process. These two tasks require substantial leadership skills. Still, leaders of a stable democracy understand that under such circumstances they can expect solid support from political rivals and the vast majority of the domestic population. Such support is unlikely to emerge promptly if the threat emanating from the international arena is not obvious. If the leaders decide that the threat requires an overt and discernible armed response, one that could result in material and human losses to their entity's armed forces, they will first have to persuade their domestic political adversaries and the public that the international challenge merits the action they are proposing. Conscious of the fervent opposition they are likely to encounter and the political costs they may be forced to pay, very few leaders pursue this option.

One of two developments typically follows the decision to avert a public outcry. When conditions permit, leaders may decide that a covert operation is the most attractive alternative. Though U.S. covert operations generally require congressional support, the domestic political costs to the two branches of government are not considerable. However, because of their limited utility, and because it has become increasingly difficult to keep information under wraps, contemporary leaders are now less willing than their predecessors to rely on covert operations. This drawback often leaves democratic leaders with one option—to allow the international event to mature into a major crisis.[110] The shortcomings do not stop there. Prior to a war, the leaders of each rival state must try to persuade the others that they are prepared to use their country's military to achieve their objectives if peaceful alternatives fail, that they will employ as much force as they need to and for as long as they need to in order to achieve their objectives, and that they have the full backing of their people and the military. If war ensues, leaders must repeatedly warn their adversaries that their personal commitment to win the war has not wavered, nor has domestic support for their policy. In a rivalry between a state controlled by an authoritarian regime and one led by a democratic government, the leaders of the latter will generally be at a disadvantage. In the past, knowledge that the freedom of U.S. leaders to rely on force had been hampered by strong domestic opposition has encouraged the United States's rivals either to dismiss its military threats or to resort to violence. Likewise, knowledge that U.S. presidents have come under heavy criticism for failing to achieve their war objectives rapidly and without accruing heavy human casualties, and that this pressure has forced them to limit their goals, has licensed the United States's adversaries to intensify their resolve and fight longer.

The significance of the last two conditions has risen considerably since the advent of instant global communication. With CNN and other international news organizations reaching almost every corner of the world, authoritarian leaders assume that by following closely what is being reported they can estimate better than ever the kind of domestic political support U.S. presidents can count on. But this assumption has not always been justified. Vendors of information do not prosper because they furnish great quantities of news objectively. Their success is dictated by their ability to sell controversy. As an international political issue takes shape and the U.S. president and his advisors begin to mold a policy, the first reaction by most news organizations is not to elicit a balanced analysis but to focus on those leaders and pundits who find fault with its design. Driven by the adage that good news is no news, the global media unintentionally leads authoritarian leaders to miscalculate the resolve and support of U.S. leaders. To be sure, news organizations commonly rely on instant polls to depict the extent of the support and opposition. But this representation can be highly misleading. Unless the United States becomes the target of a direct military attack, the majority of the American public initially will tend to voice its objection to any type of U.S. military involvement abroad. These polls, however, have seldom captured the intensity of the support of or opposition to a policy during the early days of its implementation. In fact, as U.S. international operations gain momentum, it has not been uncommon for the American public to increase its support. This support has often intensified when the deeds of the authoritarian leader have created widespread human despair, and the news media have reported them at great length.

Complacency and indecisiveness are two domestic conditions the

United States cannot afford to experience for extended periods if it hopes both to be effective in the promotion of its doctrine of enlargement and to protect its international status. Of the two conditions, the former will be the least difficult to uproot. Since complacency is primarily a function of the absence of intense competition, and since the United States will experience greater challenges from a wider range of states regarding a variety of issues, future administrations are not likely to display the conceit disclosed by the Clinton administration during its last years in power. If they do not replace it with a more purposeful attitude, then it is probable that they will be faulted for not being able to detect a major international crisis at an early stage.

Early crisis detection enhances the ability of decision-makers to limit its costly effects. This ability, however, can be enfeebled by decision-makers handicapped by indecisiveness. The openness of the United States's political system has always generated a measure of indecisiveness on the part of its leaders. The presence of indecisiveness in the U.S. foreign policymaking process is fated to become more common as the amount of, and access to, information increases. The long-term effect of this condition on the United States and on the stability of the international system will be determined by the number of intense crises Washington is forced to resolve simultaneously.

APPENDIX

The Cold War Was Not a Matter of Culpability

"Did Stalin . . . seek a Cold War?" The question is like asking: '[D]oes a fish seek water?'" With these words, John Lewis Gaddis, the foremost U.S. analyst of the Cold War, seeks to underscore his conviction that the Soviet leader was responsible for the Cold War.[1] Gaddis acknowledges that, because of the circumstances, even without Stalin a Cold War might have ensued. But he stresses that Stalin's "dispositional behavior," specifically, his lifelong "disposition to wage cold wars" annulled any chance that the United States and the Soviet Union could have overcome their differences at the end of the Second World War.[2]

Two factors led me to question Gaddis's line of argument. According to Gaddis, social psychologists attribute causes to the actions of individuals by categorizing them into either "dispositional" or "situational" behavior. Dispositional behavior, notes Gaddis, reflects deeply rooted personal characteristics that do not change, regardless of the circumstances under which people find themselves. Situational behavior, on the other hand, changes with circumstances; the way individuals respond to events is determined more by the event than by the individuals' personal traits. Gaddis uses this distinction to propose that Stalin's dispositional tendencies prevented him from abandoning in world politics the paranoia that defined his domestic politics.

Gaddis's exceptional qualities as a historian notwithstanding, he wholly misconstrues the distinction between the two forms of behavior, and the intent for creating the categories. To begin with, the difference is spelled out by attribution theorists, who created the two categories not for the purpose of differentiating people according to whether they respond to an event based on their personality or the situation, but in order to contrast the way responses to events are perceived by the actors and those observing the actions of the actors. Both parties, note social psychologists, attribute behavior to different causes: the actors typically attribute their behavior to the requirements of the situation, while the observers attribute the same behavior to the dispositional characteristics of the actors. "The divergent perceptions of actors and observers exemplify the tendency for people to attribute causality to whatever captures their attention or is salient."[3] Equally as significant, Gaddis misinterprets the implications behind the definitions applied to each category. Dispositional causes refer to the enduring characteristics of the individual that, as Gaddis correctly notes, remain much the same regardless of the circumstances. These characteristics, however, do not automatically denote, as he contends, inflexibility. To be sure, based on the past analysis of an actor's behavior it may be possible for the observer to predict the manner in which the observed party will respond in the future, but such a prediction does not always lead to the conclusion that the actor is "inflexible." Gaddis may be right when he proposes that Stalin was determined to wage a cold war on the West, but this action and whatever other actions he may have initiated against other domestic and international political parties do not prove that he always responded inflexibly to whatever happened. If such had been the case, then the Soviet Union would have never agreed to diplomatic relations with the United States in 1933, or signed an agreement with Germany in 1939, or joined forces with the United States and Britain to fight the Germans after 1941. As George Kennan noted: "The [Soviet] leadership is at liberty to put forward for tactical purposes any particular thesis it finds useful. . . ."[4] "[T]he Soviet leaders are prepared to recognize situations, if not arguments."[5]

For my second reason for placing little emphasis on Stalin's personality traits in the inquiry into the start of the Cold War, I refer to a comment by Karl Marx that was acknowledged by Gaddis in his own analysis. "Men," wrote Marx, "make their own history, but they do not make it just as they please; they do not make it under circumstances chosen by themselves, but under circumstances directly found, given and transmitted from the past."[6] Stalin, more than any other Soviet leader, helped shape the structure of the Soviet political, economic, and social system. With the passage of time, Stalin, more than any other Soviet leader, determined the manner in which this system would respond to the external world. And yet, this same system, as became clearly evident following Stalin's death, developed its own separate identity—not one that was at odds with that of its leader, but one that transcended the leader's personality. Stated differently, it is most unlikely that the Soviet political system would have tolerated a leader who was unwilling to exploit the opportunities offered by the international system that emerged at the end of the Second World War.

Notes

Introduction

1. See Daniel Yergin and Joseph Stanislaw, *The Commanding Heights* (New York: Simon and Schuster, 1998), 336. See also Earl H. Fry, Stan A. Taylor, and Robert S. Wood, *America the Vincible* (Englewood Cliffs, N.J.: Prentice Hall, 1994), 257.
2. See Charles W. Kegley Jr. and Eugene R. Wittkopf, *World Politics: Trends and Transformations* 7th ed. (New York: St. Martin's/Worth, 1999), 99–103.
3. See G. W. Hegel, *Reason in History* (New York: The Bobbs-Merrill Publishing Company, 1953); and Robert Heilbroner, *Marxism: For and Against* (New York: W. W. Norton, 1980).
4. See Thomas J. Biersteker, "Dialectical Thinking About World Order: Sixteen Theses on Dialectics," paper presented at the *Annual Meeting of the International Studies Association* (Anaheim, Calif.: March 1986).
5. The reader should not infer from this contention that I assume that all decision-makers are hindered by the same psychological and information-processing defects. As I have proposed elsewhere, decision-making skills can vary significantly from one decision-maker to another. See Alex Roberto Hybel, "A Fortuitous Victory: An Information Processing Approach to the Gulf War," in *The Domestic Sources of American Foreign Policy: Insights and Evidence,* ed. Eugene R. Wittkopf and James M. McCormick (Lanham, Md.: Rowman and Littlefield Publishers, 1999).
6. See Robert Dahl, *Regimes and Opposition* (New Haven: Yale University Press, 1974), 3–9.
7. To avoid confusion, it is important to keep in mind that democratic systems can also vary significantly in their levels of competitiveness. The American political system, with its two-party system, is significantly less competitive than, say, Norway's party system, which for years had a five-party format.

8. See Robert Gilpin, *The Political Economy of International Relations* (Cambridge: Cambridge University Press, 1987), 18.

9. To contend that the market affects every aspect of society, including the issues that dominate the state's political agenda, is not to propose that the market is more important than politics, or that there is a causal relationship between the market and politics, with the market functioning as the cause. It is always the state, that is, the political embodiment of a territory, that decides, as it gauges the market's effects on a peoples' well-being, whether to institute or to abolish regulations that will alter a market's levels of openness or competitiveness.

10. Paradoxically, the legitimacy of authoritarian states is heavily dependent on economic success. It is no wonder, thus, that so many dictators who have been in power for lengthy periods are overthrown as their states' economies falter.

Chapter 1

1. Robert Gilpin, *War and Change in International Politics* (Cambridge: Cambridge University Press, 1983), 106.

2. Ibid., 96–102.

3. Gordon A. Craig and Alexander L. George, *Force and Statecraft: Diplomatic Problems of Our Times* (New York: Oxford University Press, 1983), 18 and 24.

4. Ibid., 31.

5. The figures appear in Paul Kennedy, *The Rise and Fall of Great Powers: Economic Change and Military Conflict From 1500 to 2000* (New York: Random House, 1987), 171.

6. It was not until 1860, when Russia founded the city of Vladivostok in the Far East, after acquiring the surrounding region, that Saint Petersburg gained access to a second warm-water port. This new port enabled Russia to have direct access to the Sea of Japan.

7. This action was instigated by the Ottoman government's decision in 1852 to grant Roman Catholics rights equal to those held by Greek Orthodox Christians.

8. This meant that the Black Sea would be closed to all warships, and that no one would be authorized to set up naval arsenals and dockyards on its shores.

9. Quoted in Kennedy, *The Rise and Fall,* 177.

10. Gordon A. Craig, *Europe Since 1815* (New York: Holt, Reinhart and Winston, 1966), 131–34.

11. Ibid., 187 and 197.

12. Asa Briggs and Patricia Clavin, *Modern Europe, 1789–1989* (London: Routledge, 1997), 111.

13. The members of the German Confederation were not particularly enthusiastic about having Prussia as the leader, and thus, prior to the war, they sided with Austria.

14. Quoted in John Lowe, *The Great Powers, Imperialism and the German Problem, 1865–1925* (London: Routledge, 1994), 30.

15. As if to add insult to injury, the ceremony in which King Wilhelm I of Prussia was proclaimed kaiser (emperor) of Germany took place on January 18, 1871, in the Hall of Mirrors at the Palace of Versailles.
16. Lowe, *The Great Powers,* 35–8. See also Briggs and Clavin, *Modern Europe,* 122–23.
17. Benedict Anderson, *Imagined Communities* (London: Verso, 1993), 4.
18. Torbjön Knutsen, *A History of International Relations Theory* (New York: Manchester University Press, 1992), 163–64.
19. Briggs and Clavin, *Modern Europe,* 86–7.
20. Quoted in Briggs and Clavin, *Modern Europe,* 104.
21. Lawrence Lafore, *The Long Fuse* (Philadelphia, Penn.: Lippincott, 1965), 60.
22. See Gilpin, *War and Change,* 134–36. See also Kennedy, *The Rise and Fall,* 99 and 154–56; and Benjamin Cohen, *The Question of Imperialism* (New York: Basic Books, 1973), 76–7.
23. Few comments capture better Britain's drive to dominate the world's economic system than that expressed by its foreign minister George Canning, after he had convinced the British Parliament to grant diplomatic recognition to the newly liberated Spanish American states: "Spanish America is free and if we do not mismanage our affairs sadly she is English." Quoted in John Gallagher and Ronald Robinson, "The Imperialism of Free Trade," in *International Political Economy: Perspectives on Global Power and Wealth,* ed. Jeffrey A. Frieden and David A. Lake (New York: St. Martin's Press, 1987), 120.
24. Gilpin, *War and Change,* 136.
25. Walter McDougall, *Promised Land, Crusader State* (Boston: Houghton Mifflin, 1997), 7.
26. Some analysts are likely to disagree with my contention that the costs imposed on the United States by its territorial expansion were small. Their challenge would not be unjustified. There is no question that the expansion inflicted enormous costs on Native Americans, and that it contributed, in no small measure, to the start of the Civil War. My rationale for proposing that the costs were low is twofold. First, my assessment is based solely on the costs imposed on white Americans. And second, notwithstanding the fact that the enlargement of the United States's territory badly divided the country and helped provoke the Civil War, the costs were not experienced until more than ten years after the territorial expansion had been completed. I will address the latter issue later in this chapter.
27. Charles E. Lindblom, *Politics and Markets* (New York: Basic Books, 1977), 162.
28. Hannah Arendt, *Between Past and Future* (New York: Meridian, 1963), 157.
29. Giovanni Sartori, *The Theory of Democracy Revisited,* vol. II (Chatham, N.J.: Chatham House, 1987), 285.
30. Ibid., 289. Until the seventeenth century, dissent and diversity were considered to be the causes of discord and disorder that brought down states.
31. Ibid., 337–45. See also Robert Dahl, *Democracy and Its Critics* (New Haven: Yale University Press, 1989), 83–106.

32. Joseph A. Schumpeter, *Capitalism, Socialism and Democracy*, 3rd ed. (New York: Harper and Row, 1950), 269.

33. Giovanni Sartori, *The Theory of Democracy Revisited*, vol. I (Chatham, N.J.: Chatham House, 1987), 156.

34. See Joseph LaPalombara, *Politics Among Nations* (Englewood Cliffs, N.J.: Prentice-Hall, 1974), 314. See also Geriant Perry, *Political Elites* (New York: Praeger Publisher, 1969), 65–6.

35. Competitiveness presupposes a structure of competition.

36. By no means am I suggesting that the parties will compete for the center of the spectrum of opinions in election after election. I do contend, however, that failure by one of the parties to compete for the support of the voters who are located between the two parties will generally lead to its defeat. See Anthony Downs, *An Economic Theory of Democracy* (New York: Harper and Brothers, 1958).

37. Though it is technically inappropriate for me to refer to the United States's party system during the nineteenth century as a two-party system, considering that during one period the system was occupied by only one party and at another time by four parties, the political competition that ensued was, for the most part, centripetally oriented. One of the major exceptions was prior to the Civil War period.

38. Alexis de Tocqueville, *Democracy in America,* vol. II (New York: Vintage Books, 1945), 150–51.

39. See Robert Gilpin, *The Political Economy of International Relations* (Princeton: Princeton University Press, 1987),16–17. See also Paul R. Gregory and Roy J. Ruffin, *Basic Microeconomics* (Glenview, Ill.: Scott, Foresman and Company, 1989), 7, 51, and 387–88.

40. It is important that I introduce a few qualifiers. First, it is imperative to keep in mind that I am not suggesting that all market oriented systems are democracies. Second, it is not uncommon for economists to use the terms "capitalism" and "market economy" interchangeably. I consider this interchange erroneous, for it is possible for a society to have market socialism, that is, an economic system characterized by state ownership of the factors of production, the use of primarily economic incentives, market allocation of resources, and decentralized decision making. And third, I am not assuming that capitalism always fosters the development of a self-regulating market, that is, of a market that is open to all buyers and sellers and in which no buyer or seller can determine the terms of exchange. In fact, if we accept that two of capitalism's defining characteristics are profit motive and the drive to amass capital (the others are private ownership of the means of production and the existence of free or wage labor), then it is not difficult to envision a capitalist system in which one seller succeeds in determining the terms of exchange.

41. See Lindblom, *Politics and Markets,* 162–64.

42. The speech is reprinted in Thomas G. Paterson (ed.), *Major Problems in American Foreign Policy: To 1914,* vol. I (Lexington, Mass.: D.C. Heath and Company, 1989), 74–7.

43. Quoted in Walter LaFeber, *The American Age: United States Foreign Policy at Home and Abroad Since 1750* (New York: W. W. Norton, 1989), 84.

44. Quoted in LaFeber, *The American Age,* 51. For a more detailed discussion of the issue see Theodore Draper, *A Struggle for Power: The American Revolution* (New York: Random House, 1996), 102–31.
45. Quoted in LaFeber, *The American Age,* 83. In 1823 Adams assumed that Cuba, like the other Latin American colonies, would seek to gain independence from Spain. Adams misread Cuba's intention, for in 1823 Cuba's leaders decided to remain linked to Spain. Ultimately, however, Adams's pronouncement proved to be prophetic, for as Cuba got closer to gaining independence from Spain in the 1890s, the United States took the necessary steps to ensure that the island would "gravitate only" toward the United States.
46. LaFeber, *The American Age,* 91–2.
47. Land speculating was a major enterprise in the United States during that period, and some of the most prominent speculators were individuals such as George Washington and Benjamin Franklin.
48. The first census, which was conducted in 1790, classified 95 percent of Americans as rural, that is, living on farms and in small towns. New York, in 1815, had fewer than 150,000 inhabitants.
49. Wayne Cole, *An Interpretative History of American Foreign Relations* (Homewood, Ill.: The Dorsey Press, 1968), 22–6.
50. Though formal political party competition was not present for some ten years, divisions within the Democratic-Republican Party ran deep. This should not be surprising considering that the party attempted to represent and serve competing interests.
51. Cole, *An Interpretative History,* 118–20.
52. The Whig Party controlled the presidency during two four-year periods. In the first instance, William Henry Harrison was elected president in 1840 but died a month after he was inaugurated, in 1841. He was replaced by John Tyler. General Zachary Taylor was elected in 1848 and died in 1850. He was replaced by Millard Fillmore.
53. Quoted in Lawrence S. Kaplan, "America's Advantage From Europe's Distress," in *Major Problems in American Foreign Policy: To 1914,* vol. I, ed. Thomas G. Paterson (Lexington, Mass.: D. C. Heath and Company, 1989), 116.
54. Cole, *An Interpretative History,* 86–8.
55. Quoted in LaFeber, *The American Age,* 77.
56. Portions of George Canning's letter appear in Paterson, ed., *Major Problems in American Foreign Policy,* vol. I, 181–82.
57. Portions of the message appear in Paterson, ed., *Major Problems in American Foreign Policy,* vol. I, 184–85.
58. Portions of the account of the meeting appear in Paterson, ed., *Major Problems in American Foreign Policy,* vol. I, 183–84.
59. Cuba had the largest slave society in the Caribbean. It was estimated that during the middle of the nineteenth century some 324,000 slaves and 425,000 whites inhabited the island.
60. A fourth man, representing the Constitutional Union Party, also ran for president.
61. Craig, *Europe Since 1815,* 276–78.

62. Austria would annex both Bosnia and Herzegovina at the start of the twentieth century.
63. Lowe, *The Great Powers,* 54. See also Craig, *Europe Since 1815,* 276–81.
64. The treaty was not made public.
65. Lowe, *The Great Powers,* 65–6.
66. Ibid., 70. See also Lafore, *The Long Fuse,* 102.
67. The alliances established between Germany and Austria, on the one hand, and France and Russia, on the other hand, were, in principle, binding agreements. The subsequent ententes were less strict, for they limited the provisions to consultation and promises of diplomatic support.
68. Kennedy, *The Rise and Fall,* 228.
69. Quoted in Lowe, *The Great Powers,* 142.
70. Kennedy, *The Rise and Fall,* 252.
71. Robert Gildea, *Barricades and Borders: Europe 1800–1914.* (Oxford: Oxford University Press, 1987), 396–99.
72. Ibid., 399–402.
73. Ibid., 407–8; and Lafore, *The Long Fuse,* 142–46.
74. By 1903, about 90 percent of Serbia's foreign commerce was with the Habsburg Monarchy.
75. Message from Germany's Chancellor Prince Bernard von Bülow to the German Ambassador in Vienna. Quoted in Lafore, *The Long Fuse,* 161.
76. Quoted in Lafore, *The Long Fuse,* 178.
77. William R. Keylor, *The Twentieth Century World* (New York: Oxford University Press, 1996), 50.
78. Of the European powers, only Russia had a larger population.
79. Kennedy, *The Rise and Fall,* 179.
80. For more precise figures, the reader can refer to Kennedy, *The Rise and Fall,* 200–201.
81. Ibid., 179.
82. Quoted in William Appleman Williams, *The Tragedy of American Diplomacy* (New York: Dell Publishing Company, 1972), 29.
83. Quoted in Williams, *The Tragedy of American Diplomacy,* 28.
84. Quoted in Williams, *The Tragedy of American Diplomacy,* 31.
85. Quoted in Williams, *The Tragedy of American Diplomacy,* 35.
86. Quoted in Williams, *The Tragedy of American Diplomacy,* 35.
87. Quoted in LaFeber, *The American Age,* 164. Blaine served as secretary of state first in 1881 and again in 1889–1892.
88. Quoted in LaFeber, *The American Age,* 167.
89. The provisions, which were drawn by President McKinnley and his advisers, were submitted to Congress by Senator Oliver Platt, and came to be known as the Platt Amendment. The Platt Amendment articles are reprinted in Paterson, ed., *Major Problems in American Foreign Policy,* vol. I, 455–56. See also LaFeber, *The American Age,* 197.
90. I discuss in greater detail the foreign policy of the United States toward this region in a later chapter.
91. The warning, which came to be known as the Roosevelt Corollary to the Monroe Doctrine, is reprinted in Paterson, ed., *Major Problems in American Foreign Policy,* vol. I, 461.

92. Quoted in Robert Freeman Smith, "Wilson's Pursuit of Order," in *Major Problems in American Foreign Policy,* vol. I, ed. Thomas G. Paterson (Lexington, Mass.: D. C. Heath and Company, 1989), 516.

93. Secretary of State William Jennings Bryan was the first to challenge this imbalance when he asked Wilson, who had written a note to Germany demanding that it pledge never again to attack a passenger liner, to send London a strong note protesting the British blockade of Germany. Wilson refused his secretary of state's request, and Bryan resigned.

94. LaFeber, *The American Age,* 272–73.

Chapter 2

1. Alexis de Tocqueville, *Democracy in America,* vol. I (New York: Vintage Books 1945), 243.

2. For an extensive discussion of the effects of past experiences on foreign policy making, see Alex Roberto Hybel, *How Leaders Reason: U.S. Intervention in the Caribbean Basin and Latin America* (Oxford: Basil Blackwell, 1990).

3. See Robert Gilpin, *War and Change in International Politics* (Cambridge: Cambridge University Press, 1983), 31–3.

4. Gordon Craig, *Europe Since 1815* (New York: Holt, Rinehart and Winston, 1966), 535.

5. Ibid., 536.

6. William Keylor, *The Twentieth Century World* (New York: Oxford University Press, 1996), 76–7.

7. Gordon A. Craig and Alexander L. George, *Force and Statecraft: Diplomatic Problems of Our Times* (New York: Oxford University Press, 1983), 50.

8. Hybel, *How Leaders Reason,* 1.

9. Quoted in Craig and George, *Force and Statecraft,* 52 and 53.

10. The United States was one of the "Associate" states. Guided by the belief that the new international system should be rebuilt on "American ideals," Wilson had decided that the United States would take part in the war not as an "Allied" power but as an "Associated" power. He considered this distinction crucial. Though he was convinced that it was in the United States's interest to help France and England defeat Germany, he was also of the opinion that the United States had to distance itself from the Europeans who wanted total victory over Germany and the division of spoils among the winners. The strategy advocated by the Europeans, Wilson had argued, would only help perpetuate colonialism, autocracy, and wars. This meant that the American Expeditionary Forces fighting in Europe under the command of General John Pershing were never integrated into the Allied armies and fought primarily on the single front of western Europe. See Walter LaFeber, *The American Age: United States Foreign Policy at Home and Abroad Since 1750* (New York: W. W. Norton, 1989), 279–86.

11. The Italian premier was one of the original members, but he walked out following a major disagreement with President Wilson.

12. My emphasis.

13. Craig, *Europe Since 1815,* 546; and Asa Briggs and Patricia Clavin, *Modern Europe, 1789–1989* (London: Routledge, 1997), 259.

14. The three also forced the United States to accept a mandate over Armenia and Constantinople in the disintegrated Ottoman Empire. Wilson accepted reluctantly, and the U.S. Senate rejected assuming responsibility in 1920.
15. Craig, *Europe Since 1815,* 544; and Briggs and Clavin, *Modern Europe, 1789–1989,* 260.
16. Keylor, *The Twentieth Century World,* 78.
17. Craig, *Europe Since 1815,* 546.
18. In the initial economic bloc the United States had not been included.
19. By the end of the First World War, France owed Britain $3 billion and the United States $4 billion, while Britain owed the United States $4.7 billion. See Charles Kindleberger, *The World in Depression, 1929–1939* (Berkeley: University of California Press, 1973), 40.
20. Keylor, *The Twentieth Century World,* 79–81. Keylor's account, which is based on recent research, questions the common contention that the French were united in their belief that the costs of France's economic recovery should be borne by Germany.
21. Kindleberger, *The World in Depression, 1929–1939,* 34.
22. Keylor, *The Twentieth Century World,* 81–4; Briggs and Clavin, *Modern Europe, 1789–1989,* 261; and Craig, *Europe Since 1815,* 545.
23. LaFeber, *The American Age,* 302.
24. Under Articles 10 and 15, the United States would have had great difficulty justifying to other members of the League of Nations its actions toward Caribbean Basin states during the first 20 years of the twentieth century and enforcing the Monroe Doctrine. U.S. Senators warned Wilson of this problem, and upon his return to Paris he made it clear that the Covenant could not infringe on the United States's right to continue enforcing the Monroe Doctrine.
25. LaFeber, *The American Age,* 303.
26. Lloyd Gardner C., *Safe for Democracy: The Anglo-American Response to Revolution, 1913–1923* (New York: Oxford University Press, 1984), 258–60.
27. Quoted in Edward Hallet Carr, *The Twenty Years' Crisis, 1919–1939* (New York: Harper and Row, 1964), 33.
28. Quoted in Robert Schulzinger, *American Diplomacy in the Twentieth Century* (New York: Oxford University Press, 1984), 106. Wilson, however, never claimed that every state in the international arena was ready to be guided by a democratic regime. People in less developed countries, he added, were not yet prepared to live according to democratic tenets. Business leaders from the United States and other democracies could help these people appreciate the principles of democracy by promoting economic interactions that "would make the world more comfortable and more happy." Quoted in LaFeber, *The American Age,* 256.
29. In all fairness to Clemenceau, he recognized that since he had not been able to convince the Allies to destroy Germany's military and economic base, he would need their commitment to help France defend itself were it to be attacked by Germany. Both the United States and Britain extended such an agreement. In the case of the United States, however, the agreement was dependent on approval by the U.S. Congress. As I will explain shortly, any

alert French politician would have recognized that the U.S. Congress was not going to automatically accept Wilson's recommendation.

30. Quoted in Edwin Rozwenc and Thomas Bender, *The Making of American Society* (New York: Alfred Knopf, 1978), 275.
31. Quoted in Rozwenc and Bender, *The Making of American Society*, 273.
32. On March 19, 1920, the U.S. Senate supported the treaty by a vote of 49 to 35, short of the necessary two-thirds.
33. Quoted in Rozwenc and Bender, *The Making of American Society*, 310.
34. Quoted in Rozwenc and Bender, *The Making of American Society*, 311.
35. This was not the only type of assistance France sought from other parties. It also relied on alliances established with many of the newly created Eastern European states. But these states were not powerful enough to assist France were it to find itself once again facing Germany's military might.
36. The first three factors are described in Kindleberger, *The World in Depression, 1929–1939,* 292; the last two appear in Charles P. Kindleberger, "Dominance and Leadership in the International Economy: Exploitation, Public Goods, and Free Riders," in *International Studies Quarterly* 25, June 1981: 247.
37. David A. Lake, "International Economic Structures and American Foreign Policy, 1887–1934," in *International Political Economy: Perspectives on Global Power and Wealth,* ed. Jeffrey A. Frieden and David A. Lake (New York: St. Martin's Press, 1987), 147–53.
38. Ibid., 159–63.
39. Ibid., 157.
40. Ibid., 159.
41. Schulzinger, *American Diplomacy in the Twentieth Century,* 126.
42. See LaFeber, *The American Age,* 295 and 318–19.
43. Ibid., 323–24.
44. See Lake, "International Economic Structures," 160; and Kindleberger, *The World in Depression, 1929–1939,* 77.
45. See Keylor, *The Twentieth Century World,* 94; and LaFeber, *The American Age,* 325.
46. For a detailed description of the level of duty on imports imposed by different acts going back to 1890, see Lake, "International Economic Structures," 158.
47. Charles Lipson, *Standing Guard: Protecting Foreign Capital in the Nineteenth and Twentieth Centuries* (Berkeley: University of California Press, 1985), 67.
48. Ibid., 67–8. See also Keylor, *The Twentieth Century World,* 113; and Briggs and Clavin, *Modern Europe, 1789–1989,* 290.
49. See Kindleberger, *The World in Depression, 1929–1939,* 36–7; Briggs and Clavin, *Modern Europe, 1789–1989,* 285–86; and Craig, *Europe Since 1815,* 362.
50. The United States did not send its representatives to the commission, as it had not signed the Treaty of Versailles.
51. See Kindleberger, *The World in Depression, 1929–1939,* 38; LaFeber, *The American Age,* 327; and Schulzinger, *American Diplomacy in the Twentieth Century,* 130–31.

52. Craig, *Europe Since 1815*, 562–64.
53. Quoted in LaFeber, *The American Age*, 327.
54. Portions of this analysis are drawn from the works by Gilbert, Briggs and Clavin, Kindleberger, and from Lake's own analysis of Kindleberger's study. See Felix Gilbert, *The End of the European Era, 1890 to the Present* (New York: W. W. Norton, 1979), 255–58; Briggs and Clavin, *Modern Europe, 1789–1989*, 197–304; Kindleberger, *The World in Depression, 1929–1939*, 108–26; and Lake, "International Economic Structures," 147–53.
55. During an eight-year period in the 1930s, U.S. banks received a net inflow of gold amounting to close to $6.6 billion.
56. Gilbert, *The End of the European Era, 1890 to the Present*, 257.
57. Kindleberger, *The World in Depression, 1929–1939*, 85–6.
58. Ibid., 86 and 97.
59. See Briggs and Clavin, *Modern Europe, 1789–1989*, 303; Keylor, *The Twentieth Century World*, 129; Eric Hobsbawm, *The Age of Extremes: A History of the World, 1914–1991* (New York: Pantheon, 1994), 100; LaFeber, *The American Age*, 331–32; Paul Kennedy, *The Rise and Fall of Great Powers: Economic Change and Military Conflict From 1500 to 2000* (New York: Random House, 1987), 283; Kindleberger, *The World in Depression, 1929–1939*, 124; and Craig, *Europe Since 1815*, 638.
60. Though high, these figures do not even compare with the distress endured by Chile's economy, which during that same period experienced an 80 percent reduction in exports.
61. Lake, "International Economic Structures," 151.
62. Those who wonder why the distinction is critical should keep in mind that Lake is attempting to contend that a state's foreign economic policy is determined by its position in the international economic structure. If an analyst were to determine a state's position in the international economic system based on its behavior, then her or his argument would be tautological.
63. The United States invested in Europe $577 million in 1927 and $598 million in 1928, but only $142 million in 1929. See Kindleberger, *The World in Depression, 1929–1939*, 56, 292–93, and 306–7.

Chapter 3

1. Edwin Reischauer, *The Japanese Today* (Cambridge, Mass.: Harvard University Press, 1988), 87–91.
2. Text of document appears in Thomas G. Paterson, ed., *Major Problems in American Foreign Policy Since 1914*, vol. II (Lexington, Mass.: D. C. Heath and Company, 1989), 110–11. Capital ships are warships over 10,000 tons that carry guns larger than eight inches.
3. Article III. See Paterson, ed., *Major Problems in American Foreign Policy: Since 1914*, vol. II, 115.
4. Walter LaFeber, *The American Age: United States Foreign Policy at Home and Abroad Since 1750* (New York: W. W. Norton, 1989), 322.
5. Reischauer, *The Japanese Today*, 95.

6. Charles P. Kindleberger, *The World in Depression, 1929–1939* (Berkeley: University of California Press, 1973); and William Keylor, *The Twentieth Century World* (New York: Oxford University Press, 1996), 227.
7. Reischauer, *The Japanese Today,* 98–9.
8. The terms of the treaty expired in 1936. Most of my discussion in this section comes directly from one of my earlier works. See Alex Roberto Hybel, *The Logic of Surprise in International Conflict* (Lexington, Mass.: D. C. Heath and Company, 1986), 28–9.
9. Nobutaka Ike, *Japan's Decision For War: Records of the 1941 Policy Conference* (Stanford, Calif.: Stanford University Press, 1967), 138–39.
10. Eric Hobsbawm, *The Age of Extremes: A History of the World, 1914–1991* (New York: Pantheon, 1994), 109–12.
11. Ibid., 113–14.
12. Ibid., 116.
13. Until the start of the First World War, Mussolini viewed himself as a Marxist-Leninist. He parted company with communism when, as the managing editor of the socialist paper *Avanti!,* he called for the abandonment of neutralism and the entry of Italy in the war on the side of the Allies.
14. Benito Mussolini, "The Doctrines of Fascism," in *Social and Political Philosophy,* ed. John Somerville and Ronald E. Santoni (Garden City, N.Y.: Doubleday, 1963), 44.
15. David E. Ingersoll and Richard K. Matthews, *The Philosophical Roots of Modern Ideology* (Englewood Cliffs, N.J.: Prentice-Hall, 1986), 252.
16. Quoted in George Mosse, *Toward the Final Solution* (New York: Howard Fertig, 1978), 52.
17. Nazism formally justified expansionism under the concept of *Lebensraum:* "living space."
18. Felix Gilbert, *The End of the European Era, 1890 to the Present* (New York: W. W. Norton, 1979), 257–58.
19. Gilbert, *The End of the European Era,* 270; and Asa Briggs and Patricia Clavin, *Modern Europe, 1789–1989* (London: Routledge, 1997), 306–7.
20. Much of my discussion on the nature of democratic regimes is based on Robert Dahl's work. See Robert A. Dahl, *Democracy and Its Critics* (New Haven: Yale University Press, 1989).
21. For a detailed comparative analysis of the relationships between constitutional designs and political performances, see Bringham G. Powell, *Contemporary Democracies* (Cambridge, Mass.: Harvard University Press, 1982).
22. There is no question that there are significant differences within multi-party systems. At this juncture, however, it is sufficient to point out the difference between a party system in which only two parties compete, and one in which three or more compete.
23. Gordon A. Craig, *Europe Since 1815* (New York: Holt, Reinhart and Winston, 1966), 620 and 635.
24. Adolf Hitler, *Mein Kampf* (Boston: Houghton Mifflin Company, 1943), 649, 653, and 654.
25. The Locarno agreement stated that Germany accepted the German-Franco frontier, as well as the Rhineland, as a demilitarized zone.

26. The suggestion has been forwarded by certain analysts that the United States recognized that Japan was justified in trying to gain access to Asia's raw materials and markets but was opposed to Japan's autarchic approach. This hypothesis disregards the fact that the United States started to act in a similar fashion at the beginning of the twentieth century when it forced the newly independent Cuban government to incorporate into its constitution the Platt Amendment. As I explained earlier, this amendment granted the United States the right to intervene in Cuba's domestic affairs whenever events in that country threatened U.S. economic or political interests. The United States imposed a similar restriction on Haiti in 1915, and subsequently on other Caribbean Basin or Central American states.

27. The so-called Stimson Doctrine appears in Thomas G. Patterson, ed., *Major Problems in American Foreign Policy: Since 1914*, vol. II, 125–26.

28. Portions of Gerald Nye's May 28, 1935, speech, in which he explains the results of the investigation conducted by his committee, are reprinted in Thomas G. Paterson, ed., *Major Problems in American Foreign Policy: Since 1914*, vol. II, 167–69.

29. In a Gallup poll conducted in early 1937, 70 percent of those interviewed believed that it had been a mistake for the United States to enter the First World War. *The Gallup Poll*, vol. I (New York: Random House, 1972), 54.

30. Quoted in Robert D. Schulzinger, *American Diplomacy in the Twentieth Century* (New York: Oxford University Press, 1984), 172.

31. Edwin Rozwenc and Thomas Bender, *The Making of American Society* (New York: Alfred Knopf, 1978), 427. Moreover, 54 percent believed that the United States should withdraw its troops from China to ensure that they would not get involved in the fighting. *The Gallup Poll*, vol. I, 68.

32. Quoted in Robert A. Devine, "Roosevelt the Isolationist," in *Major Problems in American Foreign Policy: Since 1914*, vol. II, ed. Thomas G. Paterson (Lexington, Mass.: D. C. Heath and Company, 1989), 194.

33. Quoted in Devine, "Roosevelt the Isolationist," 194.

34. It is important to note, however, that 63 percent opposed military training for men of 20 and over. *The Gallup Poll*, vol. I, 132 and 129.

35. Quoted in Rozwenc and Bender, *The Making of American Society*, 433.

36. Quoted in Rozwenc and Bender, *The Making of American Society*, 435.

37. *The Gallup Poll*, vol. I, 183.

38. The public sentiment on this matter was very strong. By the end of September 1939, 95 percent remarked that the United States should not send troops to fight Germany. *The Gallup Poll*, vol. I, 184.

39. Robert Dallek, "Roosevelt's Leadership, Public Opinion, and Playing Time for Asia," in *Major Problems in American Foreign Policy: Since 1914*, vol. II, ed. Thomas G. Paterson (Lexington, Mass.: D. C. Heath and Company, 1989), 208.

40. Devine, "Roosevelt the Isolationist," 199.

41. Quoted in Schulzinger, *American Diplomacy in the Twentieth Century*, 172.

42. Quoted in Schulzinger, *American Diplomacy in the Twentieth Century*, 172.

43. Dallek, "Roosevelt's Leadership, Public Opinion," 214.

44. I discuss Roosevelt's rationale for the Atlantic Charter in the next chapter, as I address his postwar plans for the United States.

45. One of Roosevelt's first foreign policy acts was to grant the Soviet Union full diplomatic recognition. I address this decision also in the next chapter, as I discuss the type of world order he envisioned.
46. Dallek, "Roosevelt's Leadership, Public Opinion," 219.
47. Exchange between Roosevelt and his adviser, Harry Hopkins. Ibid., 220.
48. Statement by Secretary of War Henry Stimson to a congressional investigating committee. Ibid., 220–21.
49. See Paul Kennedy, *The Rise and Fall of Great Powers: Economic Change and Military Conflict From 1500 to 2000* (New York: Random House, 1987), 332.

Chapter 4

1. Prior to the Industrial Revolution, it was not uncommon for states with advanced economies and great wealth to be plundered by states that were weaker on both counts. States with less advanced economies sometimes had greater military power because they possessed numerical superiority, had a more effective military organization, had developed a new form of warfare technology, or were more prone to martial affairs. See Robert Gilpin, *War and Change in International Politics* (Cambridge: Cambridge University Press, 1983), chapter 3.
2. Ibid., 135–38.
3. John Lewis Gaddis has argued that the Cold War was provoked by the "dispositional behavior of Joseph Stalin, the leader of the Soviet Union". See John Lewis Gaddis, *We Now Know* (Oxford: Clarendon Press, 1997). For my critique of Gaddis's analysis, please refer to Appendix I.
4. Daniel Yergin, *Shattered Peace* (Boston: Houghton Mifflin Company, 1978), 46.
5. The sixth and seventh principles broadened the political and economic scopes of the first five principles. The last principle expressed the determination by the charter's creators to disarm those states that "threaten, or may threaten, aggression outside their frontiers [Japan, Italy, and Germany]"; and encouraged other states to lighten "the crushing burden of armaments."
6. William Keylor, *The Twentieth Century World* (New York: Oxford University Press, 1996), 182.
7. Quoted in William Taubman, *Stalin's American Foreign Policy: From Entente to Détente to Cold War* (New York: W. W. Norton, 1982), 34.
8. Quoted in Taubman, *Stalin's American Foreign Policy,* 34.
9. Quoted in Walter LaFeber, *The American Age: United States Foreign Policy at Home and Abroad Since 1750* (New York: W. W. Norton, 1989), 300.
10. See Point Six of Wilson's Fourteen Points peace plan.
11. Quoted in Taubman, *Stalin's American Foreign Policy,* 13.
12. Japan was the only power that kept its forces in Russia for a while longer. It stayed in Siberia until 1922 and in the northern part of Sakhalin Island until 1925.
13. Joseph Stalin, *Works,* vol. 4 (Moscow: Foreign Languages Publishing House, 1952–1955), 240 and 293.

14. Britain extended full diplomatic recognition to the Soviet Union in 1923.
15. Taubman, *Stalin's American Foreign Policy,* 15–6.
16. Quoted in Taubman, *Stalin's American Foreign Policy,* 17.
17. Its population decreased from 171 million in 1914 to 132 million in 1921. By losing Poland, Finland, and the Baltic states, the Soviet state lost many industrial plants, railways, and farms. Moreover, by 1920, manufacturing had declined 13 percent from its 1914 output, while only 1.6 percent of the prewar iron ore was being produced, 2.4 percent of the pig iron, 4.0 percent of the steel, and 5.0 percent of the cotton. During this same period, per capita national income declined by 60 percent. Agricultural output did not return to its prewar level until 1926, and industrial output until 1928. See Paul Kennedy, *The Rise and Fall of Great Powers: Economic Change and Military Conflict From 1500 to 2000* (New York: Random House, 1987), 321.
18. Quoted in Taubman, *Stalin's American Foreign Policy,* 21.
19. One of the agreements reached by the Molotov-Ribbentrop Pact was that the Soviet state and Germany would divide between them parts of Eastern Europe.
20. Gaddis, *We Now Know,* 15; and LaFeber, *The American Age,* 396. Gaddis's depiction of Stalin's behavior during this event is surprising. He writes: "Stalin showed no sense of shame or even embarrassment about this, no awareness that the methods by which he obtained these concessions could conceivably render them illegitimate in the eyes of anyone else. When it came to territorial aspirations, he made no distinction between adversaries and allies: what one provided the other was expected to endorse." I have great difficulty understanding why anyone would expect Stalin, or for that matter any other leader, to show any sense of shame or embarrassment. In international politics, territory had always been a greatly desired commodity. Washington, for instance, had not shown much shame or embarrassment in 1848, after the United States had defeated the Mexicans and enlarged its territory considerably, nor during the first two decades of the twentieth century when its troops moved from one Caribbean Basin country to another demanding that their governments bow to U.S. hegemony. Moreover, Gaddis overlooks the obvious fact that for Stalin the alliance with Britain and the United States was no different from the agreement he had reached with Hitler in 1939: both were designed to further the interests of the Soviet Union.
21. A document of the meeting between Roosevelt and Molotov is reproduced in Thomas G. Paterson, ed., *Major Problems in American Foreign Policy: Since 1914,* vol. II (Lexington, Mass.: D. C. Heath and Company, 1989), 232–34.
22. Quoted in Gary R. Hess, "Roosevelt as a Practical Idealist," in *Major Problems in American Foreign Policy: Since 1914,* vol. II, ed. Thomas G. Paterson, 249.
23. Quoted in Yergin, *Shattered Peace,* 65.
24. "The Churchill-Stalin Percentage Deal, 1944," appears in Paterson, ed., *Major Problems in American Foreign Policy: Since 1914,* vol. II, 238–39.
25. Yergin, *Shattered Peace,* 61.

26. Ibid., 62.

27. "The Yalta Protocol of Proceedings, 1945," appears in Paterson, ed., *Major Problems in American Foreign Policy: Since 1914*, vol. II, 239–43.

28. Quoted in Yergin, *Shattered Peace*, 63.

29. Quoted in Hess, "Roosevelt as a Practical Idealist," 253.

30. Quoted in Hess, "Roosevelt as a Practical Idealist," 253.

31. Much has been written about the effect of Roosevelt's death, and the subsequent ascension to the presidency of Vice President Harry Truman, on the relationship between the Soviet Union and the United States. Were one to focus on the counsel Truman received upon assuming the presidency, and on the policies he initiated, the interest seems justified. By the summer of 1945, Truman was being advised principally by individuals who recommended that the United States take a much "tougher" posture toward the Soviet Union than it had during Roosevelt's days, and the foreign policies of the new president began to reflect this new stand. However, though it might be interesting to speculate about what would and would not have happened had Roosevelt been able to complete his new term in office, there are three reasons why the matter cannot be addressed intelligently.

First, it goes without saying that any answer propounded would be nothing more than a conjecture. Second, regardless of the care applied to the design of the conjecture, invariably it would be erected on a faulty analytical framework. Roosevelt and Truman led the United States under very different circumstances. Roosevelt was empowered to develop the political, economic, and military means necessary to defeat both the Germans and the Japanese. Though during his tenure as president he spent long hours thinking about, and trying to design, a new world structure, death robbed him of the responsibility of actually creating it. Truman, on the other hand, had to ensure that the war the United States was expected to win would come to its end rapidly and at the lowest possible cost; and he had to help create a new world structure that would both protect and promote the interests of the United States. Thus, inferences about what Roosevelt might have done as president had he not died in April 1945 would have to be matched with inferences made about what Truman might have done as president had he been in power during Roosevelt's last two presidential terms. And third, it is very difficult to predict the extent to which the actions of a leader may or may not change with a change in circumstances. Though there is no doubt that Roosevelt was hoping to create a world system dominated by a partnership between the Soviet Union and the United States, albeit with competing interests, it is impossible to predict whether he would have continued to hold such hope had he faced the challenges Truman confronted during his tenure as president.

32. Quoted in Gaddis, *We Now Know*, 31.

33. Quoted in Gaddis, *We Now Know*, 31.

34. It is worth noting, however, that until February 1945, about 55 percent of the U.S. public still believed that the Soviet Union could be trusted to cooperate with the United States after the end of the Second World War. See *The Gallup Poll*, vol. II (New York: Random House, 1972), 492.

35. Quoted in Yergin, *Shattered Peace,* 99.
36. Quoted in Yergin, *Shattered Peace,* 119.
37. Churchill, who faced elections back in Britain, attended only the earlier meetings. Upon losing the elections, he was replaced by the newly elected prime minister, Anthony Eden. Eden, who had attended the earlier meetings as Britain's foreign secretary, returned to Potsdam on July 28.
38. Robert D. Schulzinger, *American Diplomacy in the Twentieth Century* (New York: Oxford University Press, 1984), 198.
39. A poll showed that 85 percent of the U.S. public approved the using of the atomic bombs on the two Japanese cities. See *The Gallup Poll,* vol. II, 521–22.
40. Azerbaijan borders the Soviet Union. In November of 1945, its provincial government had declared its autonomy from Iran.
41. Quoted in Norman A. Graebner, *America as a World Power* (Wilmington, Del.: Scholarly Resources, 1984), 128.
42. *The Gallup Poll,* vol. II, 498, 557, 581–82, and 604.
43. Quoted in LaFeber, *The American Age,* 453.
44. Full document reprinted in Paterson, ed., *Major Problems in American Foreign Policy: Since 1914,* vol. II, 297–300.
45. Document reprinted in Paterson, ed., *Major Problems in American Foreign Policy: Since 1914,* vol. II, 284–88.
46. The recommendations appear in the same document reprinted in Paterson, ed., *Major Problems in American Foreign Policy : Since 1914,* vol. II, 284–88.
47. John Lewis Gaddis, *Strategies of Containment* (New York: Oxford University Press, 1982), 21–2.
48. Ibid., 22.
49. *The Gallup Poll,* vol. II, 636, 639, and 672.
50. The letter is reprinted in William Lanouette and Bela Szilard, *Genius in the Shadows: A Biography of Leo Szilard, the Man Behind the Bomb* (New York: C. Scribner's Son, 1992), 205–6.
51. Quoted in McGeorge Bundy, *Danger and Survival* (New York: Random House, 1988), 44. A significant portion of my analysis of the decisions made by the United States and the Soviet Union regarding their nuclear arsenals and strategies is derived from McGeorge Bundy's exceptional study. I am also greatly indebted to Robert Peurifoy. Mr. Peurifoy helped clarify a wide range of technical issues and made sure that my arguments never strayed into unsubstantiated contentions.
52. Quoted in Bundy, *Danger and Survival,* 51.
53. Quoted in Bundy, *Danger and Survival,*134.
54. *The Gallup Poll,* vol. II, 525.
55. Quoted in Bundy, *Danger and Survival,* 141.
56. Quoted in Yergin, *Shattered Peace,* 239.
57. Quoted in Bundy, *Danger and Survival,* 144.
58. Quoted in Bundy, *Danger and Survival,* 177.
59. Bundy, *Danger and Survival,* 213.
60. See Michael Mandelbaum, *The Nuclear Revolution* (Cambridge: Cambridge University Press, 1983), 87–116.

61. The quote appears in Robert Gilpin, *The Political Economy of International Relations* (Princeton: Princeton University Press, 1987), 132. The argument was originally presented by John Ruggie, "International Regimes, Transactions, and Change: Embedded Liberalism in the Postwar Economic Order," in *International Organization* 36, 1982: 393.
62. See Joan Edelman Spero, *The Politics of International Economic Relations* (New York: St. Martin's Press, 1985), 36; and Melissa H. Birch, "The International Monetary Fund," in *Dealing With Debt,* ed. Thomas J. Biersteker (Boulder: Westview Press, 1993), 20–1.
63. Melissa H. Birch and Thomas J. Biersteker, "The World Bank," in *Dealing With Debt,* ed. Thomas J. Biersteker (Boulder: Westview Press, 1993), 37–8.
64. Keylor, *The Twentieth Century World,* 262–63.
65. Spero, *The Politics of International Economic Relations,* 41–2.
66. Quoted in Spero, *The Politics of International Economic Relations,* 93.
67. Ibid., 91.
68. Ibid., 94.
69. Jock A. Finlayson and Mark W. Zacher, "The GATT and the regulation of trade barriers: regime dynamics and functions," in *International Regimes,* ed. Stephen Krasner (Ithaca: Cornell University Press, 1983), 273–74.
70. Gilpin, *The Political Economy of International Relations,* 191.
71. For a more detailed explanation, see Ruggie, "International Regimes, Transactions, and Change."
72. About 56 percent of the 64 percent who had heard or read about the Marshall Plan supported it. The poll was taken in November 1947. Moreover, in a poll taken in April 1948, 80 percent of those interviewed favored the United States's developing closer trade relations with other states. It ought to be noted, however, that though the U.S. public supported Truman's strategic and international economic policies, it did not extend the same support to him. His approval rating in April 1948 was 36 percent. See *The Gallup Poll,* vol. II, 691, 727, and 732.
73. George Kennan, *Memoirs* (New York: Pantheon Books, 1967), 368.
74. Keylor, *The Twentieth Century World,* 270.
75. Adam B. Ulam, *The Rivals* (New York: Penguin Books, 1983), 136–37.
76. Quoted in Taubman, *Stalin's American Foreign Policy,* 168. It is obvious that Dulles's opinion was colored by the mysterious death of Jan Masaryk, the foreign minister of Czechoslovakia and a friend of the West.
77. Quoted in Taubman, *Stalin's American Foreign Policy,* 168.
78. See Ibid., 169.
79. Quoted in Kennan, *Memoirs,* 401.
80. Representatives from Italy, Norway, Denmark, Iceland, Portugal, and Canada also joined the talks.
81. *The Gallup Poll,* vol. II, 748.
82. These polls were conducted in late January 1948, March 1948, and late July/early August 1948. See *The Gallup Poll,* vol. II, 709, 721, and 767.
83. Support by the U.S. public for NATO was also considerable. When asked whether the United States and countries participating in the Marshall Plan should join together in a permanent military alliance, 68 percent of

those queried in November 1948 said yes. By March 1949, the support had increased to 76 percent. I should add, however, that about 54 percent opposed the United States's spending $2 billion to help Western Europe rearm. See *The Gallup Poll*, vol. II, 1972: 771 and 800.

84. Quoted in Kennan, *Memoirs*, 374.
85. Ibid., 374.
86. Ibid., 381.
87. Quoted in Gaddis, *Strategies of Containment*, 41.
88. Ibid., 92.
89. Quoted in Gaddis, *Strategies of Containment*, 93.
90. In a poll conducted in September 1950, 64 percent of those queried stated that the United States should continue fighting North Koreans on their own territory until they surrendered. *The Gallup Poll*, vol. III, 943.
91. Ibid., 955 and 960.
92. Ibid., 989.
93. By early March 1953, 53 percent of the U.S. public believed that the United States made a mistake by going to war in Korea. See *The Gallup Poll*, vol. III, 1052.
94. It has been well established that the communist influence on the Arbenz government was not substantial. See Alex Roberto Hybel, *How Leaders Reason: U.S. Intervention in the Caribbean Basin and Latin America* (Oxford: Basil Blackwell, 1990), chapter 3.
95. It is possible to link the deeper roots of the action to the Monroe Doctrine enacted in 1823. For an analysis of the Monroe Doctrine and its intent, please refer to chapter 1.
96. Quoted in Paul W. Drake, "From Good Men to Good Neighbors," in *Exporting Democracy: The United States and Latin America*, ed. Abraham Lowenthal (Baltimore: The Johns Hopkins University Press, 1991), 13.
97. Ibid., 20.
98. Quoted in Drake, "From Good Men to Good Neighbors," 21.
99. Quoted in Drake, "From Good Men to Good Neighbors," 23.
100. Keylor, *The Twentieth Century World*, 212.
101. Ibid., 217.
102. Lars Schoultz, *National Security and United States Policy Toward Latin America* (Princeton: Princeton University Press, 1987), 179.
103. Guatemala's unwillingness to sign the treaty had nothing to do with its political implications. Guatemala would have signed the treaty had the other signatories accepted its demand that it include the proviso: "Guatemala refuses to recognize British sovereignty over Belize." After the majority of the signatories had rejected the proviso, Guatemala withdrew ratification of the treaty. See Richard Immerman, *The CIA in Guatemala* (Austin: University of Texas Press, 1982), 92–3.
104. Quoted in Larry Berman, *Planning a Tragedy: The Americanization of the War in Vietnam* (New York: W. W. Norton, 1982), 9.
105. The poll was conducted in August, 1953, shortly after the United States, the Chinese, and the Koreans had agreed to end the war in Korea. By June 1954, the percentage, though it remained high, had gone down from 85 to 72 percent. *The Gallup Poll*, vol. III, 1170 and 1236.

106. Quoted in Berman, *Planning a Tragedy,* 9 and 10.
107. It is critical that the reader be aware that each of the regions I am presently analyzing was affected by a great number of issues that were unrelated to the Cold War. My decision not to discuss them should not be interpreted as an attempt on my part to assume that they were not significant. My objective throughout the analysis is always to ascertain the extent to which an issue helped generate or reduce tension in the international system. At the present, thus, my goal is to focus on those issues that affected the relationship between the United States and the Soviet Union.
108. Fawaz A. Gerges, *The Superpowers and the Middle East* (Boulder: Westview Press, 1994), 25.
109. Britain also signed the pact.
110. Gerges, *The Superpowers and the Middle East,* 28.
111. Ibid., 23 and 34.
112. Ibid., 55.
113. Quoted in Gerges, *The Superpowers and the Middle East,* 56.
114. Ibid., 69.
115. Obviously, in this section of my argument I am excluding Africa's Mediterranean region.
116. Benjamin Cohen, *The Question of Imperialism* (New York: Basic Books, 1973), 23–30.
117. John Darwin, "Africa and World Politics Since 1945: Theories of Decolonization," in *Explaining International Relations Since 1945,* ed. Ngaire Woods (Oxford: Oxford University Press, 1996), 202–3.
118. Keylor, *The Twentieth Century World,* 412–13.

Chapter 5

1. Rober Gilpin, *War and Change in International Politics* (Cambridge: Cambridge University Press, 1983), 10.
2. Ibid., 11.
3. Paul Kennedy, *The Rise and Fall of Great Powers: Economic Change and Military Conflict From 1500 to 2000* (New York: Random House, 1987), 515.
4. Walter Russell Mead, *Mortal Splendor: The American Empire in Transition* (Boston: Houghton Mifflin, 1987), 54.
5. Obviously, there have been instances in which international entities have attempted to protect the status quo but did not have the capabilities to do so. Those entities clearly fit in the earlier category. In this case, I am merely referring to those states that do not base their policies on unfounded assumptions and calculations.
6. Quoted in McGeorge Bundy, *Danger and Survival* (New York: Random House, 1988), 246.
7. Ibid., 246–47.
8. Quoted in Bundy, *Danger and Survival,* 252.
9. Quoted in Bundy, *Danger and Survival,* 256
10. In a major Gallup poll conducted in six major cities outside the United States in October 1957, 59 percent answered yes when asked whether

they thought that the Russian satellite was a serious blow to the U.S. prestige. The interviews were conducted in New Delhi, Toronto, Paris, Oslo, Helsinki, and Copenhagen. In the United States, when asked whether they thought that Russia was moving ahead of the United States in the development of missiles and long distance rockets, 49 percent answered yes, while 32 percent said no. See *The Gallup Poll*, vol. III (New York: Random House, 1972), 1519–21.

11. Jonathan Dean, "Berlin in a Divided Germany: An Evolving International Regime," in *U.S.-Soviet Security Cooperation*, ed. Alexander L. George, Philip A. Farley, and Alexander Dallin (New York: Oxford University Press, 1988), 87–90.

12. Quoted in Alex Roberto Hybel, *How Leaders Reason: U.S. Intervention in the Caribbean Basin and Latin America* (Oxford: Basil Blackwell, 1990), 87.

13. The comment was made by Secretary of State Dean Rusk while discussing how to respond to the discovery of Soviet nuclear missiles in Cuba. Obviously, the comment was designed to apply only to core areas, that is, regions such as Japan, Western Europe, and Latin America. Quoted in Ernest R. May and Philip D. Zelikow, eds., *The Kennedy Tapes* (Cambridge, Mass.: The Belknap Press of Harvard University Press, 1997), 127.

14. Quoted in John Lewis Gaddis, *Strategies of Containment* (New York: Oxford University Press, 1982), 202.

15. Quoted in Gaddis, *Strategies of Containment,* 203.

16. Ibid., 202–3.

17. Ibid., 202 and 217.

18. Quoted in Gaddis, *Strategies of Containment,* 205

19. See Thomas D. Lairson and David Skidmore, *International Political Economy: The Struggle for Power and Wealth* (New York: Harcourt Brace College Publishers, 1993), 76–7. See also Robert Keohane, "U.S. Foreign Economic Policy Toward Advanced Capitalist States," in *Eagle Entangled: U.S. Foreign Policy in a Complex World,* ed. Kenneth A. Oye, Donald Rothchild, and Robert Lieber (New York: Longman, 1979), 93.

20. John O. Odell, *U.S. International Monetary Policy* (Princeton: Princeton University Press, 1982), 84.

21. Lairson and Skidmore, *International Political Economy,* 78.

22. For my analysis of Triffin's study I have relied on Gilpin's and Odell's separate discussions of his work. See Robert Gilpin, *The Political Economy of International Relations* (Princeton: Princeton University Press, 1987), 134–35; and Odell, *U.S. International Monetary Policy,* 93–5.

23. Odell, *U.S. International Monetary Policy,* 94.

24. Quoted in Odell, *U.S. International Monetary Policy,* 89.

25. Ibid., 90–1.

26. Ibid., 99 and 101.

27. The three others were: i) the anti-colonial insurrection in Portuguese Angola; ii) the white minority regime in South Africa and its program of apartheid; and iii) Ghana's and Guinea's decision to stray from "true" neutralism. See Thomas J. Noer, "New Frontiers and Old Priorities in

Africa," in *Kennedy's Quest for Victory,* ed. Thomas G. Paterson (New York: Oxford University Press, 1989), 260.

28. Ibid., 262–63.
29. See Hybel, *How Leaders Reason,* 118.
30. Ibid., 92–8. Analysts have typically placed blame for the Bay of Pigs fiasco on the shoulders of the CIA. Though there is little doubt that the CIA's plan was highly flawed, no one was more responsible for the failure than President Kennedy.
31. The U.S. public's support of Kennedy after the Bay of Pigs fiasco was in the 80 percent range. The public's attitude varied significantly, however, when it was asked what steps the United States should take against Cuba. When asked whether the United States should refuse to buy from or sell products to Cuba so long as Castro remained in power, 63 percent agreed that the United States should refuse. When asked whether the United States should aid the anti-Castro forces with money and war material, 44 percent favored the action while 41 percent opposed it. When asked whether the United States should send its own armed forces into Cuba to help overthrow Castro, only 24 percent favored the policy while 65 percent opposed it. *The Gallup Poll,* vol. III, 1717 and 1721.
32. William R. Keylor, *The Twentieth Century World* (New York: Oxford University Press, 1996), 307.
33. Quoted in Dean, "Berlin in a Divided Germany," 91.
34. Quoted in May and Zelikow eds., *The Kennedy Tapes,* 31.
35. When asked whether the United States should keep its forces in Berlin along with the British and French forces even at the risk of war, 82 percent answered yes. *The Gallup Poll,* vol. III, 1729.
36. In fact, just a few days before the presidential election was held in the United States, Eisenhower had written a letter to the president of South Vietnam, Ngo Dinh Diem, promising that the United States would "continue to assist Vietnam in the difficult yet hopeful struggle ahead." Quoted in Larry Berman, *Planning a Tragedy: The Americanization of the War in Vietnam* (New York: Norton and Company, 1982), 15.
37. Gaddis, *Strategies of Containment,* 241.
38. Berman, *Planning a Tragedy,* 17.
39. Ibid., 19.
40. Quoted in Berman, *Planning a Tragedy,* 23.
41. Lawrence J. Bassett, and Stephen E. Pelz, "The Failed Search for Victory: Vietnam and the Politics of War," in *Kennedy's Quest for Victory,* ed. Thomas G. Paterson (New York: Oxford University Press, 1989), 240.
42. Transcript of the conversation appears in May and Zelikow, eds., *The Kennedy Tapes,* 174–76.
43. Ibid., 175.
44. Ibid., 176.
45. Ibid., 276–79.
46. Ibid., 391. My emphasis.
47. Ibid., 630–35 and 636–37.

48. Quoted in Walter LaFeber, *The American Age: United States Foreign Policy at Home and Abroad Since 1750* (New York: W. W. Norton, 1989), 570.
49. Quoted in May and Zelikow, eds., *The Kennedy Tapes,* 690.
50. Two things need to be taken into account while reviewing the figures. First, a very large amount of the funds allocated by the United States for 1969 were to pay for the Vietnam War. Second, it is very likely that the Soviet figures are lower than the actual amount spent by the Soviet Union. See Kennedy, *The Rise and Fall,* 384 and 395.
51. Edward P. Haley, David M. Keithly, and Jack Merritt, eds., *Nuclear Strategy, Arms, Control and the Future* (Boulder: Westview Press, 1985), 10.
52. See Bundy's February 16, 1965, letter to Johnson in Berman, *Planning a Tragedy,* 43–4.
53. Ibid., 70–1.
54. Statement by Assistant Secretary of Defense for International Security William Bundy. Quoted in Gaddis, *Strategies of Containment,* 272.
55. Edwin Rozwenc and Thomas Bender, *The Making of American Society* (New York: Alfred Knopf, 1978), 554–55.
56. Quoted in Rozwenc and Bender, *The Making of American Society,* 560.
57. Ibid., 556–60.
58. By December 1965, unemployment had fallen to 4 percent.
59. David P. Calleo, *The Imperious Economy* (Cambridge, Mass.: Harvard University Press, 1982), 26–8.
60. *The Gallup Poll,* vol. III, 1922, 2014, and 2101.
61. Henry Kissinger, *White House Years* (Boston: Little, Brown and Company, 1979), 56–7.
62. Probably few comments can capture Kissinger's concern with the credibility of the United Sates as clearly as his response to a question posed by President Charles de Gaulle. At their first meeting, which took place in Paris in late February 1969, de Gaulle asked Kissinger why the United States did not simply pull out of Vietnam. Kissinger's response was: "Because a sudden withdrawal might give us a credibility problem." Ibid., 110.
63. Ibid., 62.
64. As noted by Gaddis, past efforts by the United States to surpass the Soviets had only provoked comparable efforts on their part. As a result, the Nixon administration reasoned that it would be in the interests of both sides to exhibit mutual restraint. Gaddis, *Strategies of Containment,* 279–80.
65. Quoted in Gaddis, *Strategies of Containment,* 281.
66. Kissinger, *White House Years,* 83 and 85–6.
67. Ibid., 119, 126–27, and 128–29.
68. Ibid., 163–67.
69. Ibid., 234.
70. Gaddis, *Strategies of Containment,* 339.
71. Kissinger, *White House Years,* 228.
72. Ibid., 69.
73. Ibid., 950.
74. Quoted in Odell, *U.S. International Monetary Policy,* 183.

75. Gilpin, *The Political Economy of International Relations*, 135–40; and Calleo, *The Imperious Economy*, 32–3.
76. Odell, *U.S. International Monetary Policy*, 200–201.
77. Real GNP shrank by $3.5 billion and unemployment reached 6 percent. See Calleo, *The Imperious Economy*, 29.
78. Kissinger, *White House Years*, 952.
79. Ibid., 953.
80. It increased from a $9.8 billion deficit in 1970 to nearly $30 billion in 1971. See Odell, *U.S. International Monetary Policy*, Table 4, Column 4—Official Reserve Transactions Balance, 205.
81. Kissinger, *White House Years*, 955.
82. See Odell, *U.S. International Monetary Policy*, 235–39; and Calleo, *The Imperious Economy*, 30–1.
83. Odell, *U.S. International Monetary Policy*, 287–88.
84. Kissinger, *White House Years*, 1072. Clearly Nixon was referring also to his July 1971 speech in Kansas City, when he proposed that those five countries/regions "will determine the economic future," of the world. See Gaddis, *Strategies of Containment*, 280.
85. See Kissinger, *White House Years*, 1060 and 1062.
86. Of great concern to many American leaders was whether Nixon in his negotiations with the Chinese had yielded on the question of Taiwan.
87. Condoleezza Rice, "SALT and the Search for a Security Regime," in *U.S.-Soviet Security Cooperation*, eds. Alexander L. George, Philip J. Farley, and Alexander Dallin (New York: Oxford University Press, 1988), 294.
88. Quoted in Rice, "SALT and the Search for a Security Regime," 294.
89. One missile could carry more than one reentry vehicle, each carrying a warhead, which could be guided to different targets.
90. Kissinger, *White House Years*, 1250.
91. By then Nixon had already been reelected.
92. For a description of the content of the agreement, see Kissinger, *White House Years*, 1466–68.
93. By no means am I suggesting that hegemonic states will invariably behave in the manner I am proposing. Clearly, as demonstrated by Eisenhower, certain leaders will be more inclined than others to recognize critical contradictions.
94. Most analysts have viewed the Vietnam War as the United States's greatest foreign policy failure. This assessment cannot be contested if one considers that Washington's basic intent since the early 1950s had been to prevent the Communists from gaining control over all of Vietnam. However, with the help of hindsight one can also propose that the Vietnam War proved to be a blessing in disguise for the United States, for it forced its leaders to acknowledge that its international outlook had to change.

Chapter 6

1. See James McCormick, *American Foreign Policy and Process* (Itasca, Ill.: F. E. Peacock, 1998), 125.

2. See Joan Edelman Spero, *The Politics of International Economic Relations* (New York: St. Martin's Press, 1985), 48–54.

3. Ibid., 55–6.

4. Alex Roberto Hybel, *The Logic of Surprise in International Conflict* (Lexington, Mass.: D. C. Heath and Company, 1986), 39.

5. For a detailed account of Kissinger's negotiations see Henry Kissinger, *Years of Upheaval* (Boston: Little, Brown and Company, 1982). For an overview of the war and the negotiations that ensued, see Steven L. Spiegel, "The United States and the Arab-Israeli Dispute," in *Eagle Entangled: U.S. Foreign Policy in a Complex World*, ed. Kenneth A. Oye, Donald Rothchild, and Robert Lieber (New York: Longman, 1979), 336–65; and William B. Quandt, *Decade of Decisions* (Berkeley: University of California Press, 1977), chapters 3–9.

6. Kissinger, *Years of Upheaval*, 872–73; and Robert Keohane, *After Hegemony: Cooperation and Discord in the World Political Economy* (Princeton: Princeton University Press, 1984), 222.

7. Kissinger, *Years of Upheaval*, 854.

8. See Michael Mandelbaum and William Schneider, "The New Internationalisms: Public Opinion and American Foreign Policy," in *Eagle Entangled: U.S. Foreign Policy in a Complex World*, ed. Kenneth A. Oye, Donald Rothchild, and Robert Lieber (New York: Longman, 1979), 35–6.

9. Ibid., 36.

10. Stanley Hoffman, 'The Hell of Good Intentions," *Foreign Policy* (Winter 1977–1978): 3.

11. See Ernest B. Haas, "Human Rights: To Act or Not to Act?" in *Eagle Entangled. U.S. Foreign Policy in a Complex World*, ed. Kenneth A. Oye, Donald Rothchild, and Robert Lieber (New York: Longman, 1979, 179.

12. James M. McCormick, *American Foreign Policy and American Values* (Itasca, Ill.: F. E. Peacock Publishers, 1985), 93.

13. Quoted in McCormick, *American Foreign Policy and Process*, 126.

14. Richard Thorton, *The Carter Years: Toward a New Global Order* (New York: Paragon House, 1991), 7.

15. "Jimmy Carter, Commencement Address at the University of Notre Dame," in *A Reader in American Foreign Policy*, ed. James M. McCormick (Itasca, Ill.: F. E. Peacock Publishers, 1986), 152–54.

16. Cyrus Vance, *Hard Choices* (New York: Simon and Schuster, 1983), 45.

17. Quoted in Thorton, *The Carter Years*, 8.

18. Quoted in Thorton, *The Carter Years*, 9.

19. Vance, *Hard Choices*, 50.

20. Ibid., 52. See also Gaddis Smith, *Morality, Reason, and Power* (New York: Hill and Wang, 1986), 76.

21. Thorton, *The Carter Years*, 23.

22. This was the same missile Carter would have been willing to forego had Moscow accepted the original comprehensive deep-cut proposal. See Smith, *Morality, Reason, and Power*, 81.

23. National Security Study Memorandum 39 (NSSM 39). Quoted in Stephen Ambrose, *Rise to Globalism* (New York: Penguin Books, 1988), 283.

24. Donald Rothchild, "U.S. Policy Styles in Africa: From Minimal Engagement to Liberal Internationalism," in *Eagle Entangled: U.S. Foreign Policy in a Complex World*, ed. Kenneth A. Oye, Donald Rothchild, and Robert Lieber (New York: Longman, 1979), 305.

25. Ibid., 311; and Ambrose, *Rise to Globalism*, 289.

26. Quoted in Rothchild, "U.S. Policy Styles in Africa," 311.

27. Thorton, *The Carter Years*, 168.

28. Ibid., 168–69.

29. Vance, *Hard Choices*, 73.

30. Ibid., 72–5. See also Smith, *Morality, Reason, and Power*, 153.

31. Vance, *Hard Choices*, 85; and Smith, *Morality , Reason, and Power*, 155.

32. The analysis and citation in this section is based on an earlier work. See Alex Roberto Hybel, *How Leaders Reason: U.S. Intervention in the Caribbean Basin and Latin America* (Oxford: Basil Blackwell, 1990), 234–62.

33. Presidents Kennedy and Johnson limited the United States's arms sales and economic assistance to Iran, claiming that the shah was a dictator who could not be trusted. Nixon, however, reversed this policy immediately upon assuming power.

34. Vance, *Hard Choices*, 314.

35. Carter requested approval for the sale of seven AWACS aircraft.

36. Vance, *Hard Choices*, 323.

37. It was also during this time that the CIA produced an analysis that contended that Iran was in neither a revolutionary nor a prerevolutionary stage.

38. Vance, *Hard Choices*, 332–33. Vance advocated the creation of a moderate civilian government, while Brzezinski proposed that the only way to prevent the revolutionaries from succeeding was by allowing the military to use its "iron fist."

39. Spero, *The Politics of International Economics*, 60–1.

40. Calleo, *The Imperious Economy*, 140–41.

41. Still, in 1977 the United States imported more crude oil than it had during the past four years. U.S. net imports of crude oil were distributed as follows (in millions of barrels per day): 1973, 6.0; 1974, 5.8; 1975, 5.8; 1976, 7.0; 1977, 8.5. See Thorton, *The Carter Years*, 78 (note 2).

42. Calleo, *The Imperious Economy*, 142–43.

43. Quoted in Thorton, *The Carter Years*, 48.

44. See Spero, *The Politics of International Economics*, 68; and Thorton, *The Carter Years*, 53–60.

45. Thorton, *The Carter Years*, 57.

46. Spero, *The Politics of International Economics*, 68.

47. See Thorton, *The Carter Years*, 59–60; Spero, *The Politics of International Economics*, 71; and Calleo, *The Imperious Economy*, 143.

48. Keohane, *After Hegemony*, 226.

49. This increase was the first one in 18 months.

50. See Thorton, *The Carter Years*, 421–34. For a detailed account of the negotiation between the United States, Israel, and Egypt, see Vance, *Hard Choices*, 1983.

51. Thorton, *The Carter Years*, 426–39.

52. Quoted in Robert D. Schulzinger, *American Diplomacy in the Twentieth Century* (New York: Oxford University Press, 1984), 329.
53. Nitze's comments are printed in P. Edward Haley, David M. Keithly, and Jack Merritt, eds., *Nuclear Strategy, Arms Control, and the Future* (Boulder: Westview Press, 1985), 248.
54. The United States and NATO did not begin the deployment of the intermediate missiles and cruise missiles in Europe until late 1983. I analyze the effects of this action on the relationship between the Western powers and the Soviet Union during my discussion of the defense policy initiated by the Reagan administration.
55. See Vance, *Hard Choices,* 360–61.
56. Ibid., 358–64.
57. Quoted in Thorton, *The Carter Years,* 483.
58. John Lewis Gaddis, *The United States and the End of the Cold War* (New York: Oxford University Press, 1992), 131.
59. See Glenn H. Snyder and Paul Diesing, *Conflict Among Nations* (Princeton: Princeton University Press, 1977), 40–2.
60. The Intermediate-Range Nuclear Forces Treaty (INF) was signed at a summit meeting in Washington on December 8, 1987. For a discussion of opposition to INF from conservatives, and political leaders such Robert Dole, Jesse Helms, and Dan Quayle, see George P. Schultz, *Turmoil and Triumph* (New York: Charles Scribner's Sons, 1993), 1006–8.
61. Quoted in James Scott, *Deciding to Intervene: The Reagan Doctrine and American Foreign Policy* (Durham, N.C.: Duke University Press, 1996), 17.
62. National Security Decision Directive 75. Quoted in Scott, *Deciding to Intervene,* 21. See also Condoleezza Rice, "U.S.-Soviet Relations," in *Looking Back on the Reagan Presidency,* ed. Larry Berman (Baltimore: The Johns Hopkins University Press, 1990), 73–5.
63. "Jimmy Carter's Commencement Address at the University of Notre Dame," in *A Reader in American Foreign Policy,* ed. James M. McCormick (Itasca, Ill.: F. E. Publishers, 1986), 180–87.
64. Anthony Campagna, *The Economy in the Reagan Years* (Westport, Conn.: Greenwood Press, 1994), 42.
65. Scott, *Deciding to Intervene,* 20–1.
66. The authorization was denied.
67. See Hybel, *How Leaders Reason,* 265–76.
68. Quoted in Scott, *Deciding to Intervene,* 51.
69. Quoted in Schultz, *Turmoil and Triumph,* 262.
70. Quoted in Schultz, *Turmoil and Triumph,* 262.
71. Quoted in Schultz, *Turmoil and Triumph,* 262.
72. Quoted in Jonathan Stein, *From H-Bomb to Star Wars* (Lexington, Mass.: Lexington Books, 1984), 55.
73. The U.S.-NATO strategy has been commonly referred to as the "dual-track decision" because it committed them to negotiations with Moscow at the same time they were deploying missiles. See Lawrence T. Caldwell, "Soviet Policy and Nuclear Weapons and Arms Control," in *Soviet International Behavior and U.S. Policy Options,* ed. Lawrence T. Caldwell (Lexington, Mass.: Lexington Books, 1985), 215–16.

74. See William Schneider, "Rambo and Reality: Having it Both Ways," in *Eagle Resurgent? The Reagan Era in American Foreign Policy*, ed. Kenneth A. Oye, Donald Rothchild, and Robert J. Lieber (Boston: Little, Brown, and Company, 1987), 42.

75. Ibid., 68.

76. John Reshetar, *The Soviet Polity: Government and Politics in the USSR* (New York: Harper and Row, 1989), 224.

77. Ibid., 225.

78. Gordon Smith, *Soviet Politics: Struggling With Change* (New York: St. Martin's Press, 1992), 234.

79. Ibid., 50–1.

80. Ibid., 55–6. See also Edward Hewett, *Reforming the Soviet Economy* (Washington, DC: Brookings Institution, 1988), 52.

81. Smith, *Soviet Politics,* 62–4.

82. Ibid., 310–33. See also Jeffrey Checkel, *Ideas and International Political Change: Soviet/Russian Behavior and the End of the Cold War* (New Haven: Yale University Press, 1997), 24–7. According to Checkel, by the middle of the 1980s a great number of Soviet leaders and analysts accepted that the deductive framework based on Marxist-Leninist principles they had been using was being challenged by a series of domestic and international failings. This realization led them to adopt an inductive framework of analysis, one that accepted that the world was changing according to laws that were at odds with those postulated by the original Marxist-Leninist approach.

83. In two separate articles, Richard Ned Lebow and Kenneth A. Oye investigate how effective the "Realist" model is at explaining the decision by the Soviet Union to terminate its bipolar rivalry with the United States. Since Oye's article is a direct response to Lebow's piece, I will highlight his argument. At the outset Oye challenges Lebow's contention that learning rather than environmental conditions brought about changes in the Soviet Union's domestic structure and foreign policy. According to Oye, external environmental conditions were a significant cause of political and economic liberalization within the Soviet Union. These changes, in turn, fostered learning. Oye then contends that the decision by the Soviet Union to retreat from Eastern Europe and the Third World and to reduce its military spending were not at variance, as claimed by Lebow, with realism. Each of these changes, adds Oye, was in accord with prudential realism.

I agree with Oye's assessment. In his analysis, Lebow fails to take into account two things. First, he does not take into consideration that learning that leads to a radical change in behavior is unlikely to take place until an entity is forced by costly experiences or events, all emanating from the external environment, to reassess and then modify its behavior. Second, though Lebow is correct when he notes that the Soviet Union's decision to retreat from Eastern Europe and the Third World and to reduce its military spending compromised traditionally defined vital security interests, he fails to keep in mind that a rational entity faced with two difficult choices will always select the least costly. Cognizant that it lacked the economic resources to continue competing with the United States, Moscow faced two choices: launching a preemptive attack or retreating. Knowing fully well that an attack would have inflicted heavy costs not only on the United States but also the Soviet Union, Moscow chose to retreat. As Realists have long acknowledged, for the state there is no security interest more important than ensuring its own survival. See Richard Ned Lebow, "The Long Peace, the End of the Cold War, and the Failure of Realism," in *International Relations Theory and the End of the Cold War,* ed. Richard Ned Lebow and Thomas Risse-Kappen (New York Columbia University Press, 1995), 23–56; and Kenneth A. Oye, "Explaining the End of the Cold War: Morphological and Behavioral Adaptations to the Nuclear Peace?" in *International Relations Theory and the End of the Cold War,* ed. Richard Ned Lebow and Thomas Risse-Kappen (New York: Columbia University Press, 1995), 57–83.

84. Gorbachev was in fact responding to a direct demand from President George Bush, who had warned Gorbachev that the continuation of Soviet aid to Nicaragua would affect the nature of the relationship between the United States and the Soviet Union. See William M. LeoGrande, *Our Own Backyard: The United States in Central America, 1977–1992* (Chapel Hill: The University of North Carolina, 1998), 558.

85. Walter Russell Mead, *Mortal Splendor: The American Empire in Transition* (Boston: Houghton Mifflin, 1987), 204.

86. Ibid., 213–14.

87. Paul Kennedy, *The Rise and Fall of Great Powers: Economic Change and Military Conflict From 1500 to 2000* (New York: Random House, 1987), 444.

88. Paul Kennedy, "Does America Need Perestroika?" *New Perspectives Quarterly* 6 (Spring 1988).

89. Kennedy, *The Rise and Fall,* 533–534.

90. David P. Calleo, *Beyond American Hegemony* (New York: Basic Books, 1987), 123.

91. See Stephen Weatherford and Lorraine M. McDonnell, "Ideology and Economic Policy," in *Looking Back in the Reagan Presidency,* ed. Larry Berman (Baltimore: The Johns Hopkins University Press, 1990), 124–27. Reagan was particularly opposed to governmentally sponsored welfare and social programs.

92. Quoted in Benjamin Cohen, "An Explosion in the Kitchen? Economic Relations With Other Advanced Industrial States," in *Eagle Resurgent? The Reagan Era in American Foreign Policy,* ed. Kenneth A. Oye, Donald Rothchild, Robert J. Lieber (Boston: Little, Brown and Company, 1987), 124.

93. Lou Cannon, *The Role of a Lifetime* (New York: Harper and Row, 1990), 109.

94. Reagan had no difficulty linking his personal experience to the "supply siders" argument. He was fond of telling about his own personal experience while a movie actor: "You could only make four pictures and then you were in the top bracket. So we all quit working after four pictures and went off to the country." Quoted in Cannon, *The Role of a Lifetime,* 91.

95. Campagna, *The Economy in the Reagan Years,* 33–5, 53, and 55–6.

96. Every 10 percent appreciation of the trade-weighted value of the dollar dampens the U.S. price level by 1.5 percentage points. From mid-1980 to

early 1985, the trade-weighted value of the dollar rose from 40 percent to 60 percent, depending on the precise time period and weights chosen. This increase sharply cut foreign demand for U.S. products and directed a good portion of U.S. demands toward foreign goods. It has been estimated that this appreciation of the value of the dollar exported part of the inflationary pressure generated by the recovery, thus limiting inflation by 1 to 2 percent annually during that period. Starting in 1985, the dollar began to depreciate, and by 1988 the U.S. trade finally experienced a lowering of its trade deficit, the first one since 1980. See Fred Bergsten, *America in the World Economy* (Washington, DC: Institute for International Economics, 1988), 35 (see also footnote 4); and Campagna, *The Economy in the Reagan Years,* 155–57.

97. Cannon, *The Role of a Lifetime,* 829–30.

98. Quoted in Cannon, *The Role of a Lifetime,* 829. Reagan's economic policies had unequal effects on domestic income distribution. Using the household unit to measure income distribution from 1981 to 1989, all fifths, except the top fifth, lost ground. In 1981, the lowest fifth received 4.1 percent of the aggregate income, while the highest fifth received 44.2 percent. In 1989, the lowest fifth received 3.8 percent, while the highest fifth received 46.8 percent. This means that during the 1981–1989 period, the aggregate income of the lowest fifth went down 7.3 percent while the aggregate income of the highest fifth went up 5.6 percent. See Bergsten, *America in the World Economy,* 40–1; and Campagna, *The Economy in the Reagan Years,* 69 and 184–85.

99. Earl H. Fry, Stan A. Taylor, and Robert S. Wood, *America the Vincible* (Englewood Cliffs, N.J., 1994), 253–54.

100. The reader should keep in mind that a significant portion of the foreign aid provided by the United States to developing countries during the Cold War was for the purpose of containing Soviet expansion.

101. Josef Joffe, "America the Inescapable," *The New York Times Magazine* (8 June 1997): 41.

Chapter 7

1. Alexis de Tocqueville, *Democracy in America* (New York: Vintage Books, 1945), vol. 2, book 4.

2. Quoted in Ronald Steel, *Walter Lippmann and the American Century* (Boston: Little, Brown, 1980), 112.

3. Woodrow Wilson's Fourteen Point Speech to the Joint Session of Congress, 8 January 1918. Reprinted in David F. Long, ed., *A Documentary History of U.S. Foreign Relations—The Mid-1890's to 1979* (Lanham, Md.: University Press of America, 1980), 58.

4. Quoted in Tony Smith, "In Defense of Intervention," *Foreign Affairs* 73, no. 6 (November/December1994): 40.

5. Anthony Lake, speech entitled "From Containment to Enlargement." (Washington, DC: Johns Hopkins University Press, School of Advanced International Studies, 21 September 1993): 4–5.

6. See John Lewis Gaddis, *Strategies of Containment* (Oxford: Oxford University Press, 1982), 92.

7. The United States did intervene in Somalia for a short while in the early 1990s.

8. See Robert S. Chase, Emily B. Hill, and Paul Kennedy, "Pivotal States and U.S. Strategy," *Foreign Affairs* 75, no. 1 (January/February 1996).

9. Critics who challenged Clinton's decision to go to war against Serbia in 1999, often argued that the United States should not be in the business of ending ethnic cleansing throughout the world. Notwithstanding the Clinton administration's repeated claims that the United States intervened in Kosovo to stop the ethnic cleansing ordered by Yugoslavia's president, Slobodan Milosevic, that was never its sole, nor primary, reason. As Clinton noted the day he authorized the launching of the air attacks on Serbia, his decision was driven not just by morality, but also by the belief that failure to stop the ethnic cleansing in Kosovo would destabilize the region and Western Europe. Many analysts have questioned this contention and argued that ethnic cleansing in Kosovo would have little effect on the strategic and economic interests of both Western Europe and the United States. Such argument, however, remains open to debate, depending on the analyst's definition of the United States's national interest. Still, had Clinton's decision to intervene in Kosovo been driven solely by the belief that it was the moral responsibility of the United States to end such form of behavior, then he would have also engaged the United States militarily to stop the ethnic cleansing that ensued throughout Africa during much of the 1990s.

10. Agnostics about whether globalization was becoming a fact of life in the 1990s were few, but their objections resonated. Robert Wade, for instance, contended that though the world economy was markedly more interconnected in the 1990s than in the 1960s, it was still significantly more international than global. In turn, Robert Boyer warned that past predictions about the globalization of the market economy had not fared well, and then added that few of the new mechanisms that promoted economic convergence were powerful enough to break down differences in economic performances.

Skeptics formulated the debate in terms of several questions. For present purposes, it will suffice to posit just one. Was the world economy in the 1990s "operating in a new more internationalized, or less nationally or regionally segmented way[?]" According to Wade, by focusing on a few pieces of information one would have recognized that it was premature to contend that the world economy was functioning in a more internationalized manner in the 1990s. First, 90 percent or more of the economies of the United States, Japan, the single-unit Europe, and the Asian and Latin American states consisted of production for the domestic market, and in those same entities 90 percent of consumption took place in the home market. Second, not only was most of the world trade concentrated among the northern countries, but this concentration was rising. Third, trade between the developed and the developing countries was regional, not global. Latin America traded primarily with North America; Eastern Europe, Africa, and the Middle East traded predominantly with Western Europe; and East and Southeast Asian countries sent most of their exported goods to North America and Japan. Fourth, while developing countries liberalized their trade regimes by lowering direct controls of imports and reducing the degree of overvaluation of the exchange rate, developed countries, led by the United States, raised new barriers in the form of quotas, voluntary trade restraints, and managed trade.

The picture, continued Wade, was not altered significantly when the focus was turned to the analysis of trends in Foreign Direct Investment (FDI). To begin with, as was the case with trade, domestic investment by domestic capital was measurably greater than direct investment overseas and foreign investment at home. Few cases were likely to authenticate this contention better than the United States. The stock of the United States's capital invested abroad in the 1980s represented less than 7 percent of its GNP, which was slightly less than what it was in 1900. Moreover, though in the 1990s the flow of FDI to less developed economies rose dramatically, most of it continued to be directed toward the United States and the European Union. And finally, FDI showed the same regional characteristics found in trade. In short, to the extent that investment capital left a developed country, most of it was reinvested in another developed state and secondarily in a less developed economy within the same region. See Robert Wade, "Globalization and Its Limits: Reports of the Death of the National Economy are Greatly Exaggerated," in *National Diversity and Global Capitalism,* ed. Suzanne Berger and Ronald Dore (Ithaca: Cornell University Press, 1996), 60–88; Robert Boyer, "The Convergence Hypothesis Revisited: Globalization but Still the Century of Nations?" in *National Diversity and Global Capitalism,* ed. Suzanne Berger and Ronald Dore (Ithaca: Cornell University Press, 1996), 29–58.

11. International Monetary Foundation, *World Economic Outlook* (Washington, DC: International Monetary Foundation, May 1994), 65. One study predicted that the implementation of the Uruguay Round's Final Act, which was designed in part to lower trade barriers worldwide across a broad spectrum of goods and services, could increase the incomes of developing countries by over $70 billion by the year 2002. See Ian Goldin, Odin Knudsen, and Dominique van der Mensbrugghe, *Trade Liberalization: Global Economic Implications* (Paris: OECD Development Center, 1993). This figure was estimated in 1992 dollars.

12. Proponents of structural adjustment pointed out that countries that had privatized faster, such as Argentina and Malaysia, or had privatized earlier, such as Chile and Mexico, generally experienced faster and more extensive growth.

13. As explained by one analyst, the second industrial revolution in the twentieth century changed conditions for industrialization of peripheries drastically. No longer could capital goods be produced using traditional goods, even under high tariff protection. Production required modern goods, and these had to be imported from the developed countries. Under these conditions, the import capacity of the economy, severely constrained by unequal exchange, has become the bottleneck of industrialization. By providing foreign exchange, and amid considerable evidence that success

in promoting manufactured exports was critical to the stimulation of industrial development, trade reform and liberalization were supposed to allow countries to industrialize at a faster pace. See Alain de Janvry, "The Political Economy of Rural Development in Latin America: An Interpretation," in *Agricultural Development in the Third World*, ed. Carl K. Eicher and John Staatz (Baltimore: Johns Hopkins University Press, 1984), 84–5. See also Hollis B. Chenery, "Interaction Between Industrialization and Exports," *American Economic Review* (1980); 281–87. Chenery uses Hong Kong, Singapore, South Korea, and Brazil as examples of export-led growth leading to industrialization.

14. Anna O. Krueger, "Trade Policy as an Input to Development," *American Economic Review* (1980): 92. This process occurs via "the spread of new wants and activities and new methods of production and economic organization through a greater degree of international mobility of resources and human contacts." See Hla Myint, "Exports and Economic Development in Less Developed Countries," in *Agricultural Development in the Third World*, ed. Carl K. Eicher and John Staatz (Baltimore: Johns Hopkins University Press, 1984), 230.

15. Jeffrey Frieden, "Invested Interests: The Politics of National Economic Policies in a World of Global Finance," *International Organization* 45 (1991): 425. For more on the trend away from capital controls see John B. Goodman and Louis W. Pauly, "The Obsolescence of Capital Controls? Economic Management in an Age of Global Markets," *World Politics* 46 (1993): 79. The authors compare the extent of capital controls in the post–Second World War monetary order to their use today. Using Germany, France, Japan, and Italy as case studies, they conclude that between the late 1970s and the present, "a broad movement away from capital controls was evident across the industrialized world."

16. International Monetary Foundation, *World Economic Outlook* (Washington, DC: International Monetary Foundation, October 1994), 48.

17. See Anne de Julius, *Global Companies and Public Policy: The Growing Challenge to Foreign Direct Investment* (New York: Council on Foreign Relations, 1990).

18. In the United States, for instance, FDI soared during the 1980s, from a total market value of $83 billion in 1980 to more than $407 billion in 1991. See Robin Gaster, "Protectionism With Purpose: Guiding Foreign Investment," *Foreign Policy* no. 88 (Fall 1992): 91.

19. David B. Yoffie, ed., *Beyond Free Trade: Firms, Governments and Global Competition* (Boston: Harvard Business School Press, 1993), x.

20. David J. Collis, "Bearings: The Visible Hand of Global Firms," in *Beyond Free Trade: Firms, Government, and Global Competition*, ed. David B. Yoffie (Boston: Harvard Business School Press, 1993), 302. For more on this global mentality, see C. Bartlett and S. Ghoshal, *Managing Across Borders* (Boston: Harvard Business School Press, 1989). The authors propose that a firm must not only plan globally but also act globally in order to successfully coordinate a geographically dispersed strategy.

21. IBM's workforce in the 1990s, for instance, was 40 percent foreign, including 18,000 Japanese employees. With annual sales of $6 billion,

IBM Japan became one of that country's major exporters of computers. General Electric, Singapore's largest private employer, was also an "American" firm; and one-third of Taiwan's notorious trade surplus with the United States was for a time generated by American corporations manufacturing and purchasing products there, and then selling or using them back in the United States.

22. Gaster, "Protectionism With Purpose, " 93.
23. Gerald Meier, *Leading Issues in Economic Development* (New York: Oxford University Press, 1989), 264.
24. Frieden, "Invested Interests," 428.
25. Joan Edelman Spero, "Guiding Global Finances," *Foreign Policy* no. 73 (Winter 1988–89): 113.
26. See John B. Goodman, *Monetary Sovereignty: The Politics of Central Banking in Western Europe* (Ithaca: Cornell University Press, 1992), 18. The Bank for International Settlements (BIS) estimated that international bond and bank lending was at $440 billion in 1989, up from $180 billion just five years earlier. In the same report, the BIS estimated that capital outflows from the 13 leading industrialized countries averaged $444 billion in 1989, with almost two-thirds of that amount consisting of portfolio investment. See Bank of International Settlements, *Sixtieth Annual Report* (Washington, DC: 1990), 63 and 82.
27. Spero, "Guiding Global Finances," 114.
28. Ibid., 115.
29. J. Pelkmans, *The Economics of the European Community* (The Hague: Martinus Nijhoff, 1984), 3.
30. International Monetary Foundation, *World Economic Outlook* (Washington, DC: International Monetary Foundation, May 1993), 111.
31. See John Ruggie, "Territoriality and Beyond: Problematizing Modernity in International Relations," *International Organization* 36 (1993): 139–74. Ruggie offers the concept of "unbundled territoriality" as a lexical starting point for exploring contemporary international transformation. He writes that, "the terrain of unbundled territoriality . . . is the place wherein a rearticulation of international political space would be occurring."
32. Miroslav N. Jovanovic, *International Economic Integration* (New York: Routledge, 1992), 3.
33. Spero, "Guiding Global Finance," 117.
34. Richard O'Brien, *Global Financial Integration: The End of Geography* (New York: Council on Foreign Relations, 1992), 97. For more on the role of technology, especially with regard to global finance, see his chapter 2.
35. In fact, even when restrictions are in place to direct economic flows, states are often unable to effectively control the movement of investment and trade, which, as a result of the technological innovations described above, has become too mobile and intangible to be harnessed by traditional policy tools.
36. Bruce Russett, "A Community of Peace: Democracy, Interdependence, and International Organization," in *The Global Agenda,* 5th ed., ed. Charles W. Kegley, Jr., and Eugene Wittkopf (New York: St. Martin's/Worth, 1998), 244–45.

37. For a criticism of the Clinton administration's foreign policy, see Michael Mandelbaum, "Foreign Policy as Social Work," *Foreign Affairs* 75, no. 1 (January/February 1996).

38. Strobe Talbott, "Democracy and the National Interest," *Foreign Affairs* 75, no. 6 (November/December 1996): 52.

39. Dani Rodrik, "Nonsense in the Globalization Debate," *Foreign Policy* no. 107 (Summer 1997): 27.

40. Very few analysts seemed as convinced as Kenichi Ohmae and Wolfang Reinicke that the state was destined to lose its economic rationale. In terms of the global economy, noted Ohmae, "nation-states have become little more than bit actors . . . they have become—first and foremost— remarkably inefficient engines of wealth distribution." These states, he added, were replaced by "region-states." Region-states were the natural economic zones of the new international system. They were defined not by politics but by consumer preferences, access to critical information, ability to attract corporations, and the flow of capital. Whether they fell within the borders of a particular region was purely an accident of history and was irrelevant. Reinicke, in turn, proposed that "globalization has ended the nation-state's monopoly over internal sovereignty, which was formerly guaranteed by territory. This change deprives external sovereignty of its functional value. The nation-state as an externally sovereign actor in the international system will become a thing of the past." Richard Barnet and John Cavanagh concurred with Ohmae and Reinicke. As they noted, the leaders of states "are losing much of the control over their own territory they once had. More and more, they must conform to the demands of the outside world because the outsiders are already inside the gates."
   Richard Rosecrance was not convinced that the state was destined to experience the fate of dinosaurs. He believed, however, that in a world structured by a market economy, the state of the future will be the virtual- state—an entity less concerned about its territorially based production capability and more interested in developing an economy that depends on mobile factors of production. Finally, Susan Strange proposed that in the past 25 years the center of gravity in world politics has shifted "from the public agencies of the state to private bodies of various kinds, and from states to markets and market operators." In this new world, she added, politics occurred at almost every level and among a diverse group of actors, from the state to organized crime to transnational corporations to international regimes. See Kenichi Ohmae, *The End of the Nation State: The Rise of Regional Economies* (New York: Free Press, 1995), 80; Wolfang Reinicke, "Global Public Policy," *Foreign Affairs* 76, no. 6 (November/ December 1997): 127–28; Richard Barnet and John Cavanagh, *Global Dreams: Imperial Corporations and the New World* (New York: Simon and Schuster, 1994), 19; Richard Rosecrance, "The Rise of the Virtual State," *Foreign Affairs* 75, no. 4 (July/August 1996): 56; and Susan Strange, *The Retreat of the State: The Diffusion of Power in the World Economy* (New York: Cambridge University Press, 1996), 95.

41. Ruggie, "Territoriality and Beyond," 151.

42. A major example in 1999 was Brazil. In March 1999, the IMF, with strong backing from the United States, made it clear that it would not release a second $9 billion aid package until Brazil's government agreed to additional spending cuts.

43. As noted by Benedict Kingsbury: "In terms of their capacity to manage issues of national economic and social policy, their political ability to represent and regulate, their provision of a rule-of-law system and guarantees of property rights and basic civil rights, many putative states have only the trappings but not most of the effective functions of states. The activities of some state institutions appear to make human flourishing and economic activity more rather than less difficult. In some cases they have neither monopolized the use of force nor achieved the maintenance of basic order; in other cases, there is order, but it is not provided by the institutions of the state." See Benedict Kingsbury, "Sovereignty and Inequality," in *Inequality, Globalization, and World Politics,* ed. Andrew Hurrell and Ngaire Woods (New York: Oxford University Press, 1999), 84.

44. Daniel Yergin and Joseph Stanislaw, *The Commanding Heights* (New York: Simon and Schuster, 1998), 158.

45. Robert Wade, "The Fight Over Capital Flows," *Foreign Policy* no. 113 (Winter 1998–1999): 48–53.

46. Ibid., 45–51.

47. Jeffrey Garten, "Is America Abandoning Multilateral Trade," *Foreign Affairs* 74, no. 6 (November/December 1995): 53–7.

48. See *The Economist,* 6–12 March 1999: 20 and 65.

49. A similar conclusion is arrived at by Tammen et al, when they suggest that "[e]conomic interactions among satisfied nations, including such issues as trade and capital flows, generally are resolved cooperatively." See Ronald L. Tammen, Jacek Kugler, Douglas Lemke, Allan C. Stam III, Carole Alsharabati, Mark Andrew Abdollahian, Brian Efird, and A.F.K. Organski, *Power Transitions: Strategies for the 21ˢᵗ Century* (New York: Chatham House Publishers, 2000), 109.

In 1997, the world traded a total of $6.4 trillion. Profits earned from this exchange were not equally divided. The developed economies pocketed about 65 percent of the profits received from exports, while the developing economies, which are much larger in number, secured only 35 percent of the proceeds. The difference regarding per capita figures was more striking. The exports from developed economies brought a return of $4,026 per capita, while those from less developed economies generated only $372 per capita. For the United States, the need to keep the international economic system open was especially important. In 1985, U.S. exports supported 7 million American jobs; by the year 2000 they were expected to support some 16 million jobs. Moreover, in 1995 the United States's combined exports and imports totaled 23 percent of its GDP. Foreign direct investment reflected the same pattern. The total world foreign direct investment in 1996 was over $2 trillion. Most of it originated in highly developed economies, and only one-third was sent to countries outside their domain.

50. The NATO war against Serbia forced many European leaders to acknowledge that Europe needed to do a lot to catch up with the United States in defense terms. It revealed the tremendous asymmetry of military power between the United States and Europe, and the need for the latter the do something to remove the imbalance. However, it also disclosed that in order to catch up, Europe would have to spend much more in defense than it had until recently. See *The New York Times* (15 June 1999): A1 and A14.

51. Interestingly, during the Kosovo crisis, the military entity that responded to Yugoslavia's actions was not the Western European Union but NATO. A powerful and united Western European Union would have been able to claim that because the problem was a European problem, one which did not affect the United States and Canada, their involvement would not be necessary.

52. States in both Asia and Europe also recognize that though their policies toward the Middle East often conflict with Washington's, the United States remains the only entity with a chance to prevent the Middle East from fracturing the world economy. It is questionable whether the United States could prevent the domestic breakdown of Saudi Arabia or Egypt were either state to be challenged by a radical domestic group. It is not questionable, however, that of the major powers, the United States would have the greatest chance.

53. *The New York Times Magazine* (30 May 1999): 31.

54. Russett, "A Community of Peace," 244–45.

55. *The New York Times* (9 April 2000): A8.

56. David Kotz, "Capitalist Collapse: How Russia Can Recover," in *World Politics 99/00: Annual Report* (Guilford, Conn.: Dushkin/McGraw-Hill, 1999), 149.

57. NATO's countries stood between 60 to 80 percent. See Dale R. Herspring, "Russia's Crumbling Military," in *World Politics 99/00. Annual Report* (Guilford, Conn.: Dushkin/McGraw-Hill, 1999), 151.

58. Formally, the Czech Republic was never a member of the Warsaw Pact. Formal membership belonged to Czechoslovakia, which split into Slovakia and the Czech Republic after the end of the Cold War.

59. Dana Priest, "U.S. Military Builds Alliances Across Europe: Effort to Expand Influence and Security Called Risky," *World Politics 99/00: Annual Report* (Guilford, Conn.: Dushkin/McGraw-Hill, 1999), 80. Very few analysts who have criticized the Clinton administration's Kosovo policy have taken into account that from the very beginning it has been driven by the belief that Yugoslavia was a central component of the United States's security sphere across Eastern Europe. As Clinton noted in an Op-Ed in The *New York Times,* had the United States and its NATO allies not intervened, "[t]he Balkan conflict would have continued indefinitely, posing a risk of a wider war and of continuing tensions with Russia. NATO itself would have been discredited for failing to defend the values that it gives meaning." He then added: "[T]he region's democracies are responding to the pull of integration by sticking with their

reforms, taking in refugees and supporting NATO's campaigns. A democratic Serbia that respects the rights of its neighbors can and should join them." William Jefferson Clinton, "A Just and Necessary War," The New York Times (22 May 1999): 17.

60. Samuel Huntington, The Clash of Civilizations and the Remaking of World Order (New York: Simon and Schuster, 1996), 253.

61. Quoted in Charles W. Kegley, Jr., and Eugene R. Wittkopf, World Politics: Trends and Transformations, 7th ed. (New York: St. Martin's/Worth, 1999), 184.

62. The U.S. Congress, reflecting public unwillingness to get involved in the conflict, refused to support military intervention by the United States.

63. For a discussion of the Dayton Accord, see Radha Kumar, "The Troubled History of Partition," Foreign Affairs 76, no. 1 (January/February 1997): 22–34; and Richard Holbrooke, "Richard Holbrooke on Bosnia," Foreign Affairs 76, no. 2 (March/April 1997): 170–72.

64. The Economist (1 May 1999): 48.

65. For a related argument see Tammen et al., Power Transitions, 136.

66. It has also been projected that Germany's, France's, and Japan's economies will remain significantly smaller than the United States's economy.

67. Robert Ross, "China II: Beijing as a Conservative Power," Foreign Affairs 76, no. 2 (March/April 1997): 33.

68. Russia is the twentieth century's most renowned example.

69. Richard Bernstein and Ross Munro, "China I: The Coming Conflict With America," Foreign Affairs 76, no. 2 (March/April 1997): 23.

70. For a similar argument, see Ross, "China II: Beijing As a Conservative Power," 38.

71. Kenneth Lieberthal, "A New China Strategy," Foreign Affairs 74, no. 6 (November/December 1995): 35 and 45.

72. United Nations Development Programme, Human Development Report, 1994 (New York: Oxford University Press, 1994), 94–5.

73. Quoted in The New York Times (28 March 1999): 8.

74. As Thomas J. Christensen notes: "[N]ationalism is the sole ideological glue that holds the People's Republic together and keeps the CCP (Chinese Communist Party) in power. Since the Chinese Communist Party is no longer communist, it must be even more Chinese." Thomas Christensen, "Chinese Realpolitik," Foreign Affairs 75, no. 5 (September/October 1996): 46.

75. Talbott, "Democracy and the National Interest," 57.

76. To create such a system, the United States would have to persuade Russia to amend their 27–year-old Anti-Ballistic Missile Treaty.

77. See The New York Times (4 June 2000): 6; and Jack Mendelsohn, "And it still won't work," in American Foreign Policy, 6th ed., ed. Glenn Hastedt (Guilford, Conn.: Dushkin/MacGraw-Hill 2000), 224.

78. See Tammen et al., Power Transitions, 103.

79. Mendelsohn, "And it still won't work," 224.

80. See Graham E. Fuller and Ian O. Lesser, "Persian Gulf Myths," Foreign Affairs 76, no. 3 (May/June 1997): 42–3. See also Zbigniew Brzezinski,

Brent Scowcroft, and Richard Murphy, "Differentiated Containment," *Foreign Affairs* 76, no. 3 (May/June 1997); and Vahan Zanoyan, "After the Oil Boom," *Foreign Affairs* 74, no. 6 (November/December 1995).

81. See Zanoyan, "After the Oil Boom," 2.

82. As Fawaz A. Gerges notes: "Growing unemployment and the maldistribution of resources create armies of angry, disillusioned, and resentful youths who become natural recruiting grounds for Islamists." See Fawaz A. Gerges, *America and Political Islam* (Cambridge: Cambridge University Press, 1999), 239.

83. Tension in the region increased notably following the attack on the U.S.S. *Cole* in Yemen in October 2000, along with the eruption of a new wave of violence between Palestinians and Israelis.

84. I estimated the figures based on a table prepared by Kegley and Wittkopf, *World Politics,* 368.

85. Nancy Birdsall, "Life is Unfair: Inequality in the World," *Foreign Policy* no. 111 (Summer 1998): 76.

86. United Nations Development Programme, *Human Development Report,* 25.

87. Birdsall, "Life is Unfair," 78.

88. Quoted in Eric Hobsbawm, *The Age of Extremes: A History of the World, 1914–1991* (New York: Pantheon, 1994), 574.

89. Though Fidel Castro managed to remain in power in Cuba through the 1990s, and is likely to be president until his death, the demise of the Soviet Union transformed him into an inconsequential leader outside his country. The Sandinistas in Nicaragua, on the other hand, aware that they could no longer depend on Soviet and Cuban support, and with the national economy ravaged by the civil war against the contras, had no choice but to agree to hold new elections. In February 1990, Violeta Barrios de Chamorro, who headed the National Opposition Union, a unified anti-Sandinsta coalition, was elected president. The Sandinistas accepted the popular verdict and since then have adhered to the role expected of the loyal opposition in a democratic regime.

90. Peru and Ecuador have yet to fully resolve their boundary disputes; the prospects of civil war in Colombia are still measurable; and Venezuela risks being overtaken by a leader with dictatorial aspirations.

91. A most telling signal of the United States's desire to dictate which countries should and should not become the benefactors of external support is the debate that ensued at an IMF gathering in Washington in late April 1999. While Washington favored "a case by case" approach to economic crises, the Europeans, fearful that this type of format would allow the United States to dictate which countries should be helped and under what conditions, called for guidelines that would delineate the rules of the game. See *The Economist* (1 May 1999): 72.

92. I am not suggesting that everybody was caught by surprise. The IMF presumably warned Mexican officials privately that the country's current-account problem could cause problems, but chose not to go public for fear that it would instigate a run on the peso. See Lee Smith, "Time to Buy Mexico?" *Fortune* (6 February 1995): 124.

93. Ibid., 123.

94. Hans Morgenthau, *Politics Among Nations* (New York: Knopf, 1985), 87.
95. Warren Christopher, "Statement Before the House Committee on Banking, Finance, and Urban Affairs," *U.S. Department of State, Office of the Spokesman* (Washington, DC: U.S. Department of State, 25 January 1995).
96. Ibid.
97. Ibid.
98. By no means am I suggesting that concern about terrorist acts was born in the 1990s. The killing of the Israeli athletes at the Munich Olympic Games in the early 1970s triggered a new awareness on the part of some U.S. agencies regarding the threat of terrorism.
99. See Walter Laqueur, "Postmodern Terrorism," *Foreign Affairs* 75, no. 5 (September/October 1996): 24.
100. The 1980s were the worst period.
101. Ehud Sprinzak, "The Great Superterrorism Scare," *Foreign Policy* no. 112 (Fall 1998): 112.
102. Though I rely on Sprinzak's categorization, I modified it in some significant ways. See Ibid., 116–17.
103. It is generally assumed that the bombing of Pan Am flight 103 was in response to the shooting down of the A-30 Iranian commercial jet by the United States during the prelude to the Iraqi war.
104. It goes without saying that my argument is based on the assumption that the hegemon is the aggressor's principal target.
105. Quoted in Laqueur, "Postmodern Terrorism," 29.
106. Sprinzak, "The Great Superterrorism Scare," 113.
107. It is worthwhile noting that the argument made by gun control advocates in the United States differs little from the contention that terrorism's prospects increase with the availability of weapons and their destructive potential.
108. Complacency, needless to say, comes in different forms. A case in point is China in the late 1400s and early 1500s. It seems that China's culture of complacency, that is, the belief by its intellectual leaders that they had nothing to learn from abroad, their tendency to look inward, their devotion to past ideals and methods, and their respect for authority and suspicion of new ideas, may help explain why, though it had the material capacity to become the world's dominant power, it did not do so.
109. When various firms compete, resources are usually allocated more efficiently than when a single firm rules the market. Moreover, the assumption of profit maximization may lead to accurate predictions of behavior where competition is vigorous, but the same assumption may not be valid in instances in which the conditions of competitions are weak. See Oliver E. Williamson, "A Model of Rational Managerial Behavior," in Richard Cliffs and James G. March, *A Behavioral Theory of the Firm* (Englewood Cliffs, N.J.: Prentice-Hall, Inc., 1963), 238. From this, it could be inferred that the "greater an international actor's sense of invulnerability, the greater its reluctance to pay the procedural costs necessary to assess international problems rationally." See Alex Roberto Hybel, *Power Over Rationality* (Albany, New York: SUNY Press, 1993), 94.

110. A similar argument can be made with regard to economic problems. A president who is aware that an international financial crisis is about to ensue is unlikely to try to prevent it if he believes that his action will elicit extensive domestic political opposition.

Appendix

1. John Lewis Gaddis, *We Now Know* (Oxford: Clarendon Press, 1997), 25.
2. Ibid., 22–3.
3. I purposely depend on Deborah Larson's explanation of the two behavioral categories, because Gaddis himself relies on her analysis to posit his own explanation. See Deborah Larson, *Origins of Containment: A Psychological Explanation* (Princeton: Princeton University Press, 1985), 37. Also see Gaddis, *We Now Know,* 20, in particular refer to note 98.
4. Quoted in John Lewis Gaddis, *Strategies of Containment* (New York: Oxford University Press, 1982), 34.
5. Ibid., 50.
6. Quoted in Gaddis, *We Now Know,* 24.

Bibliography

Ambrose, Stephen. *Rise to Globalism*. New York: Penguin Books, 1988.

Anderson, Benedict. *Imagined Communities*. London: Verso, 1993.

Arendt, Hannah. *Between Past and Future*. New York: Meridian, 1963.

Bank of International Settlements. *Sixtieth Annual Report*. Washington, DC: 1990.

Barber, Benjamin R. *Jihad Vs. McWorld*. New York: Random House, 1995.

Barnet, Richard J., and John Cavanagh. *Global Dreams: Imperial Corporations and the New World*. New York: Simon and Schuster, 1994.

Bartlett, C., and S. Ghoshal. *Managing Across Borders*. Boston: Harvard Business School Press, 1989.

Bassett, Lawrence J., and Stephen E. Pelz. "The Failed Search for Victory: Vietnam and the Politics of War." In *Kennedy's Quest for Victory*. Edited by Thomas G. Paterson. New York: Oxford University Press, 1989.

Bergsten, Fred. *America in the World Economy*. Washington, D.C.: Institute for International Economics, 1988.

Berman, Larry. *Planning a Tragedy: The Americanization of the War in Vietnam*. New York: Norton and Company, 1982.

Bernstein, Richard, and Ross H. Munro. "China I: The Coming Conflict with America." *Foreign Affairs* 76, no. 2 (March/April 1997).

Biersteker, Thomas J. "Dialectical Thinking About World Order: Sixteen Theses on Dialectics." Paper presented at the *Annual Meeting of the International Studies Association*. Anaheim, Calif. (March 1986).

Birch, Melissa H. "The International Monetary Fund." In *Dealing With Debt*. Edited by Thomas J. Biersteker. Boulder: Westview Press, 1993.

Birch, Melissa H., and Thomas J. Biersteker. "The World Bank." In *Dealing With Debt*. Edited by Thomas J. Biersteker. Boulder: Westview Press, 1993.

Birdsall, Nancy. "Life is Unfair: Inequality in the World." *Foreign Policy* no. 111 (Summer 1998).

Boyer, Robert. "The Convergence Hypothesis Revisited: Globalization but Still the Century of Nations?" In *National Diversity and Global Capitalism*. Edited by Suzanne Berger and Ronald Dore. Ithaca: Cornell University Press, 1996.

Briggs, Asa, and Patricia Clavin. *Modern Europe, 1789–1989*. London: Routledge, 1997.

Brzezinski, Zbigniew, Brent Scowcroft, and Richard Murphy. "Differentiated Containment." *Foreign Affairs* 76, no. 3 (May/June 1997).

Bundy, McGeorge. *Danger and Survival*. New York: Random House, 1988.

Caldwell, Lawrence T. "Soviet Policy and Nuclear Weapons and Arms Control." In *Soviet International Behavior and U.S. Policy Options*. Edited by Lawrence T. Caldwell. Lexington, Mass.: Lexington Books, 1985.

Calleo, David P. *Beyond American Hegemony*. New York: Basic Books, 1987.

———. *The Imperious Economy*. Cambridge, Mass.: Harvard University Press, 1982.

Campagna, Antony S. *The Economy in the Reagan Years*. Westport, Conn.: Greenwood Press, 1994.

Cannon, Lou. *President Reagan: The Role of a Lifetime*. New York: Simon and Schuster, 1990.

Carr, Edward Hallet. *The Twenty Years' Crisis, 1919–1939*. New York: Harper and Row, 1964.

Chase, Robert S., Emily B. Hill, and Paul Kennedy. "Pivotal States and U.S. Strategy." *Foreign Affairs* 75, no. 1 (January/February 1996).

Checkel, Jeffrey. *Ideas and International Political Change: Soviet/Russian Behavior and the End of the Cold War*. New Haven: Yale University Press, 1997.

Chenery, Hollis B. "Interaction Between Industrialization and Exports." *American Economic Review* (May 1980).

Chicago Council on Foreign Relations, The. *American Public Opinion and U.S. Foreign Policy 1999*. Waukegan, Ill.: Lake County Press, 1999.

Christensen, Thomas J. "Chinese Realpolitik." *Foreign Affairs* 75, no. 5 (September/October 1996).

Christopher, Warren. "Statement Before the House Committee on Banking, Finance, and Urban Affairs." *U.S. Department of State, Office of the Spokesman*. Washington, D.C.: U.S. Department of State (25 January 1995).

Clinton, William Jefferson. "A Just and Necessary War." *The New York Times*, 23 May 1999.

Cohen, Benjamin. "An Explosion in the Kitchen? Economic Relations With Other Advanced Industrial States." In *Eagle Resurgent? The Reagan Era in American Foreign Policy*. Edited by Kenneth A. Oye, Donald Rotchild, and Robert J. Lieber. Boston: Little, Brown and Company, 1987.

———. *The Question of Imperialism*. New York: Basic Books, 1973.

Cole, Wayne S. *An Interpretative History of American Foreign Relations*. Homewood, Ill.: The Dorsey Press, 1968.

Collis, David J. "Bearings: The Visible Hand of Global Firms." In *Beyond Free Trade: Firms, Government and Global Competition*. Edited by David Yoffie. Boston: Harvard Business School Press, 1993.

Craig, Gordon A. *Europe Since 1815*. New York: Holt, Rinehart and Winston, 1966.

Craig, Gordon A., and Alexander L. George. *Force and Statecraft: Diplomatic Problems of Our Time*. New York: Oxford University Press, 1983.

Dahl, Robert A. *Democracy and Its Critics*. New Haven: Yale University Press, 1989.

———. *Regimes and Opposition.* New Haven: Yale University Press, 1974.

Dallek, Robert. "Roosevelt's Leadership, Public Opinion, and Playing Time for Asia." In *Major Problems in American Foreign Policy: Since 1914,* vol. II. Edited by Thomas G. Paterson. Lexington, Mass.: D. C. Heath and Company, 1989.

Darwin, John. "Africa and World Politics Since 1945: Theories of Decolonization." In *Explaining International Relations Since 1945.* Edited by Ngaire Woods. Oxford: Oxford University Press, 1996.

Dean, Jonathan. "Berlin in a Divided Germany: An Evolving International Regime." In *U.S.–Soviet Security Cooperation.* Edited by Alexander L. George, Philip A. Farley, and Alexander Dallin. New York: Oxford University Press, 1988.

Devine, Robert A. "Roosevelt the Isolationist." In *Major Problems in American Foreign Policy: Since 1914,* vol. II. Edited by Thomas G. Paterson. Lexington, Mass: D.C. Heath and Company, 1989.

Downs, Anthony. *An Economic Theory of Democracy.* New York: Harper and Brothers, 1958.

Drake, Paul W. "From Good Men to Good Neighbors." In *Exporting Democracy: The United States and Latin America.* Edited by Abraham Lowenthal. Baltimore: The Johns Hopkins University Press, 1991.

Draper, Theodore. *A Struggle for Power: The American Revolution.* New York: Random House, 1996.

Economist, The. 1 May 1999.

Economist, The. 6–12 March 1999.

Finlayson, Jock A., and Mark W. Zacher. "The GATT and the regulation of trade barriers: regime dynamics and functions." In *International Regimes.* Edited by Stephen Krasner. Ithaca: Cornell University Press, 1993.

Frieden, Jeffrey A. "Invested Interests: The Politics of National Economic Policies in a World of Global Finance." *International Organization* 45 (1991).

Fry, Earl H., Stan A. Taylor, and Robert S. Wood. *America the Vincible.* Englewood Cliffs, N.J.: Prentice Hall, 1994.

Fuller, Graham E., and Ian O. Lesser. "Persian Gulf Myths." *Foreign Affairs* 76, no. 3 (May/June 1997).

Gaddis, John Lewis. *We Now Know.* Oxford: Clarendon Press, 1997.

———. *The United States and the End of the Cold War.* New York: Oxford University Press, 1992.

———. *Strategies of Containment.* New York: Oxford University Press, 1982.

Gallagher, John, and Ronald Robinson. "The Imperialism of Free Trade." In *International Political Economy: Perspectives on Global Power and Wealth.* Edited by Jeffrey A. Frieden and David A. Lake. New York: St. Martin's Press, 1987.

Gallup Poll, The, vols. I, II, and III. New York: Random House, 1972.

Gardner, Lloyd C. *Safe for Democracy: The Anglo-American Response to Revolution, 1913–1923.* New York: Oxford University Press, 1984.

Garten, Jeffrey E. "Is America Abandoning Multilateral Trade?" *Foreign Affairs* 74, no. 6 (November/December 1995).

Gaster, Robin. "Protectionism With Purpose: Guiding Foreign Investment." *Foreign Policy* no. 88 (Fall 1992).

Gerges, Fawaz A. *America and Political Islam.* Cambridge: Cambridge University Press, 1999.

———. *The Superpowers and the Middle East.* Boulder: Westview Press, 1994.

Gilbert, Felix. *The End of the European Era, 1890 to the Present.* New York: W. W. Norton, 1979.

Gildea, Robert. *Barricades and Borders: Europe 1800–1914.* Oxford: Oxford University Press, 1987.

Gilpin, Robert. *The Political Economy of International Relations.* Princeton: Princeton University Press, 1987.

———. *War and Change in International Politics.* Cambridge: Cambridge University Press, 1983.

Goldin, Ian, Odin Knudsen, and Dominique van der Mensbrugghe. *Trade Liberalization: Global Economic Implications.* Paris: OECD Development Center, 1993

Goodman, John B. *Monetary Sovereignty: The Politics of Central Banking in Western Europe.* Ithaca: Cornell University Press, 1992.

Goodman, John B., and Louis W. Pauly. "The Obsolescence of Capital Controls? Economic Management in an Age of Global Markets." *World Politics* 46 (1993).

Graebner, Norman A. *America as a World Power.* Wilmington, Del.: Scholarly Resources, 1984.

Gregory, Paul R, and Roy J. Ruffin. *Basic Microeconomics.* Glenview, Ill.: Scott, Foresman and Company, 1989.

Haas, Ernest B. "Human Rights: To Act or Not to Act?" In *Eagle Entangled: U.S. Foreign Policy in a Complex World.* Edited by Kenneth A. Oye, Donald Rothchild, and Robert J. Lieber. New York: Longman, 1979.

Haley, P. Edward, David M. Keithly, and Jack Merritt, eds. *Nuclear Strategy, Arms Control, and the Future.* Boulder: Westview Press, 1985.

Hegel, G. W. F. *Reason in History.* Translated and with an introduction by Robert S. Hartman. New York: The Bobbs-Merrill Publishing Company, 1953.

Heilbroner, Robert. *Marxism: For and Against.* New York: W. W. Norton, 1980.

Herspring, Dale R. "Russia's Crumbling Military." *World Politics 99/00: Annual Report.* Guilford, Conn.: Dushkin/McGraw-Hill, 1999.

Hess, Gary R. "Roosevelt as Practical Idealist." In *Major Problems in American Foreign Policy: Since 1914,* vol. II. Edited by Thomas G. Paterson. Lexington, Mass.: D. C. Heath and Company, 1989.

Hewett, Edward A. *Reforming the Soviet Economy.* Washington, DC: Brookings Institution, 1988.

Hitler, Adolf. *Mein Kampf,* Boston: Houghton Mifflin Company, 1943.

Hobsbawm, Eric. *The Age of Extremes: A History of the World, 1914–1991.* New York: Pantheon, 1994.

Hoffman, Stanley. "The Hell of Good Intentions." *Foreign Policy* (Winter 1978).

Holbrooke, Richard. "Richard Holbrooke on Bosnia." *Foreign Affairs* 76, no. 2 (March/April 1997).

Holzman, Franklin D. *International Trade Under Communism.* New York: Basic Books, 1976.

Huntington, Samuel P. *The Clash of Civilizations and the Remaking of World Order.* New York: Simon and Schuster, 1996.

Hybel, Alex Roberto. "A Fortuitous Victory: An Information Processing Approach to the Gulf War." In *The Domestic Sources of American Foreign Policy:*

Insights and Evidence. Edited by Eugene R. Wittkopf and James M. McCormick. Lanham, Maryland: Rowman and Littlefield Publishers, 1999.

————. *Power Over Rationality.* Albany, New York: SUNY Press, 1993.

————. *How Leaders Reason: U.S. Intervention in the Caribbean Basin and Latin America.* Oxford: Basil Blackwell, 1990.

————. *The Logic of Surprise in International Conflict.* Lexington, Mass.: D. C. Heath and Company, 1986.

Ike, Nobutaka. *Japan's Decision for War: Records of the 1941 Policy Conference.* Stanford, Calif.: Stanford University Press, 1967.

Immerman, Richard. *The CIA in Guatemala.* Austin: University of Texas Press, 1982.

Ingersoll, David E., and Richard K. Matthews. *The Philosophic Roots of Modern Ideology.* Englewood Cliffs, N.J.: Prentice-Hall, 1986.

International Monetary Foundation. *World Economic Outlook.* Washington, D.C.: International Monetary Foundation, October 1994.

————. *World Economic Outlook.* Washington, D.C.: International Monetary Foundation, May 1994.

————. *World Economic Outlook.* Washington, D.C.: International Monetary Foundation, May 1992.

Janvry, Alain de. "The Political Economy of Rural Development in Latin America: An Interpretation." In *Agricultural Development in the Third World.* Edited by Carl K. Eicher and John Staatz. Baltimore: Johns Hopkins University Press, 1984.

Joffe, Josef. "America the Inescapable." *The New York Times Magazine.* (8 June 1997).

Jovanovíc, Miroslav N. *International Economic Integration.* New York: Routledge, 1992.

Julius, Anne de. *Global Companies and Public Policy: The Growing Challenge to Foreign Direct Investment.* New York: Council on Foreign Relations, 1990.

Kaplan, Lawrence S. 1989. "America's Advantage From Europe's Distress." In *Major Problems in American Foreign Policy: To 1914,* vol. I. Edited by Thomas G. Paterson. Lexington, Mass.: D. C. Heath and Company.

Kegley, Charles W., Jr., ed. *Controversies in International Relations Theory: Realism and the Neoliberal Challenge.* New York: St. Martin's Press, 1995.

Kegley, Charles W., Jr., and Eugene R. Wittkopf. *World Politics: Trends and Transformations,* 7th ed. New York: St. Martin's/Worth, 1999.

Kennan, George. *Memoirs.* New York: Pantheon Books, 1967.

Kennedy, Paul. "Does America Need Perestroika?" *New Perspectives Quarterly* (Spring 1988).

————. *The Rise and Fall of Great Powers: Economic Change and Military Conflict From 1500 to 2000.* New York: Random House, 1987.

Keohane, Robert O. *After Hegemony: Cooperation and Discord in the World Political Economy.* Princeton: Princeton University Press, 1984.

————. "U.S. Foreign Economic Policy Toward Advanced Capitalist States." In *Eagle Entangled: U.S. Foreign Policy in a Complex World.* Edited by Kenneth A. Oye, Donald Rothchild, and Robert Lieber. New York: Longman, 1979.

Keylor, William, R. *The Twentieth Century World.* New York: Oxford University Press, 1996.

Kindleberger, Charles P. "Dominance and Leadership in the International Economy: Exploitation, Public Goods, and Free Riders." *International Studies Quarterly* 25 (June 1981).

————. *The World in Depression, 1929–1939.* Berkeley: University of California Press, 1973.

Kingsbury, Benedict. "Sovereignty and Inequality." In *Inequality, Globalization, and World Politics.* Edited by Andrew Hurrell and Ngaire Woods. New York: Oxford University Press, 1999.

Kissinger, Henry. *Years of Upheaval.* Boston: Little, Brown and Company, 1982.

————. *White House Years.* Boston: Little, Brown and Company, 1979.

Knutsen, Torbjörn. *A History of International Relations Theory.* New York: Manchester University Press, 1992.

Kotz, David M. "Capitalist Collapse: How Russia Can Recover." *World Politics 99/00: Annual Report.* Guilford, Conn.: Dushkin/McGraw-Hill, 1999.

Krueger, Anna O. "Trade Policy as an Input to Development." *American Economic Review* (May 1980).

Kruzel, Joseph. "American Security Policy in a New World Order." In *American Defense Annual,* 8th ed. Edited by Joseph Kruzel. New York: Lexington Books, 1993.

Kumar, Radha. "The Troubled History of Partition." *Foreign Affairs* 76, no. 1 (January/February 1997).

LaFeber, Walter. *The American Age: United States Foreign Policy at Home and Abroad Since 1750.* New York: W. W. Norton, 1989.

Lafore, Laurence. *The Long Fuse.* Philadelphia, Penn.: Lippincott, 1965.

Lairson, Thomas D., and David Skidmore. *International Political Economy: The Struggle for Power and Wealth.* New York: Harcourt Brace College Publishers, 1993.

Lake, Anthony. "From Containment to Enlargement." Washington, D.C.: Johns Hopkins University Press, School of Advanced International Studies, 21 September 1993.

Lake, David A. "International Economic Structures and American Foreign Policy, 1887–1934." In *International Political Economy: Perspectives on Global Power and Wealth.* Edited by Jeffrey A. Frieden and David A. Lake. New York: St. Martin's Press, 1987.

Lanouette, William, with Bela Szilard. *Genius in the Shadows: A Biography of Leo Szilard, the Man Behind the Bomb.* New York: C. Scribner's Son, 1992.

LaPalombara, Joseph. *Politics Among Nations.* Englewood Cliffs, N.J.: Prentice-Hall, 1974.

Laqueur, Walter. "Postmodern Terrorism." *Foreign Affairs* 75, no. 5, (September/October 1996).

Larson, Deborah Welch. *Origins of Containment: A Psychological Explanation.* Princeton: Princeton University Press, 1985.

Lebow, Richard Ned. "The Long Peace, the End of the Cold War, and the Failure of Realism." In *International Relations Theory and the End of the Cold War.* Edited by Richard Ned Lebow and Thomas Risse-Kappen. New York: Columbia University Press, 1995.

LeoGrande, William M. *Our Own Backyard: The United States in Central America, 1977–1992.* Chapel Hill: The University of North Carolina Press, 1998.

Lieberthal, Kenneth. "A New China Strategy." *Foreign Affairs* 74, no. 6, (November/December 1995).

Lindblom, Charles E. *Politics and Markets.* New York: Basic Books, 1997.

Lipson, Charles. *Standing Guard: Protecting Foreign Capital in the Nineteenth and Twentieth Centuries.* Berkeley: University of California Press, 1985.

Long, David F., ed. *A Documentary History of U.S. Foreign Relations: The Mid-1890s To 1979.* Boston: University Press of America, 1980.

Lowe, John. *The Great Powers, Imperialism and the German Problem, 1865–1925.* London: Routledge, 1994.

Maksimova, Margarita Matveena. "Comments on Types of Economic Integration by B. Balassa." In *Economic Integration Worldwide, Regional, Sectoral.* Edited by F. Machlup. London: Macmillan, 1976.

Mandelbaum, Michael. "Foreign Policy as Social Work." *Foreign Affairs* 75, no. 1 (January/February 1996).

———. *The Nuclear Revolution.* Cambridge: Cambridge University Press, 1983.

Mandelbaum, Michael, and William Schneider. "The New Internationalism: Public Opinion and American Foreign Policy." In *Eagle Entangled: U.S. Foreign Policy in a Complex World.* Edited by Kenneth A. Oye, Donald Rothchild, and Robert J. Lieber. New York: Longman, 1979.

May, Ernest R., and Philip D. Zelikow, eds. *The Kennedy Tapes.* Cambridge, Mass.: The Belknap Press of Harvard University Press, 1997.

McCormick, James M. *American Foreign Policy and Process.* Itasca, Ill.: F. E. Peacock, 1998.

———, ed. "Jimmy Carter's Commencement Address at the University of Notre Dame." Reprinted in *A Reader in American Foreign Policy.* Itasca, Ill.: F. E. Peacock Publishers, 1986.

———. *American Foreign Policy and American Values.* Itasca, Ill.: F. E. Peacock Publishers, 1985.

McDougall, Walter A. *Promised Land, Crusader State.* Boston: Houghton Mifflin, 1997.

Mead, Walter Russell. *Mortal Splendor: The American Empire in Transition.* Boston: Houghton Mifflin, 1987.

Meier, Gerald M. *Leading Issues in Economic Development.* New York: Oxford University Press, 1989.

Mendelsohn, Jack. "And it still won't work." In *American Foreign Policy,* 6th ed. Edited by Glenn P. Hastedt. Guilford, Conn.: Dushkin/McGraw-Hill, 2000.

Morgenthau, Hans. *Politics Among Nations.* New York: Knopf, 1985.

Mosse, George. *Toward the Final Solution.* New York: Howard Fertig, 1978.

Mussolini, Benito. "The Doctrine of Fascism." In *Social and Political Philosophy.* Edited by John Somerville and Ronald E. Santoni. Garden City, N.Y.: Doubleday, 1963.

Myint, Hla. "Exports and Economic Development of Less Developed Countries." In *Agricultural Development in the Third World.* Edited by Carl K. Eicher and John Staatz. Baltimore: Johns Hopkins University Press, 1984.

New York Times, 9 April 2000.

New York Times, 15 June 1999.

New York Times, 28 March 1998.

New York Times Magazine, The, 30 May 1999.

Noer, Thomas J. "New Frontiers and Old Priorities in Africa." In *Kennedy's Quest for Victory.* Edited by Thomas G. Paterson. New York: Oxford University Press, 1989.

Nye, Joseph S., Jr., and William A. Owens. 1996. "America's Information Edge." *Foreign Affairs* 75, no. 2 (March/April 1996).

Nye, Joseph S. *Bound To Lead: The Changing Nature of American Power.* New York: Basic Books, 1990.

O'Brien, Richard. *Global Financial Integration: The End of Geography.* New York: Council on Foreign Relations, 1992.

Odell, John O. *U.S. International Monetary Policy.* Princeton: Princeton University Press, 1982.

Ohmae, Kenichi. *The End of the Nation State: The Rise of Regional Economies.* New York: Free Press, 1996.

Oye, Kenneth A. "Explaining the End of the Cold War: Morphological and Behavioral Adaptations to the Nuclear Peace?" In *International Relations Theory and the End of the Cold War.* Edited by Richard Ned Lebow and Thomas Risse-Kappen. New York, Columbia University Press, 1995.

Paterson, Thomas G., ed. *Major Problems in American Foreign Policy: To 1914,* vol. I. Lexington, Mass.: D. C. Heath and Company, 1989.

Paterson, Thomas G., ed. *Major Problems in American Foreign Policy: Since 1914,* vol. II. Lexington, Mass.: D. C. Heath and Company, 1989.

Pelkmans, J. *The Economics of the European Community.* The Hague: Martinus Nijhoff, 1984.

Perry, Geriant. *Political Elites.* New York: Praeger Publisher, 1969.

Powell, G. Bingham. *Contemporary Democracies.* Cambridge, Mass.: Harvard University Press, 1982.

Priest, Dana. "U.S. Military Builds Alliances Across Europe: Effort to Expand Influence and Security Called Risky." *World Politics 99/00: Annual Report.* Guilford, Conn.: Dushkin/McGraw-Hill, 1999.

Quandt, William B. *Decade of Decisions.* Berkeley: University of California Press, 1977.

Reinicke, Wolfang. "Global Public Policy." *Foreign Affairs* 76, no. 6, (November/December 1997).

Reischauer, Edwin O. *The Japanese Today.* Cambridge, Mass.: Harvard University Press, 1988.

Rejai, Mostafa. *Comparative Political Ideologies.* New York: St. Martin's Press, 1984.

Reshetar, John S. *The Soviet Polity: Government and Politics in the USSR.* New York: Harper and Row, 1989.

Rice, Condoleezza. "U.S.–Soviet Relations." In *Looking Back on the Reagan Presidency.* Edited Larry Berman. Baltimore: The Johns Hopkins University Press, 1990.

———. "SALT and the Search for a Security Regime." In *U.S–Soviet Security Cooperation.* Edited by Alexander L. George, Philip J. Farley, and Alexander Dallin. New York: Oxford University Press, 1988.

Rodrik, Dani. "Nonsense in the Globalization Debate." *Foreign Policy,* no. 107 (Summer 1997).

Rosecrance, Richard. "The Rise of the Virtual State." *Foreign Affairs* 75, no. 4 (July/August 1996).

Ross, Robert S. "China II: Beijing as a Conservative Power." *Foreign Affairs* 76, no. 2 (March/April 1997).

Rothchild, Donald. "U.S. Policy Styles in Africa: From Minimal Engagement to Liberal Internationalism." In *Eagle Entangled: U.S. Foreign Policy in a Complex World.* Edited by Kenneth A. Oye, Donald Rothchild, and Robert Lieber. New York: Longman, 1979.

Rozwenc, Edwin, and Thomas Bender. *The Making of American Society.* New York: Alfred Knopf, 1978.

Ruggie, John. "Territoriality and Beyond: Problematizing Modernity in International Relations." *International Organization* 47 (1993).

————. "International Regimes, Transactions, and Change: Embedded Liberalism in the Postwar Economic Order." *International Organization* 36 (1982).

Russett, Bruce. "A Community of Peace: Democracy, Interdependence, and International Organization." In *The Global Agenda,* 5th ed. Edited by Charles W. Kegley Jr. and Eugene R. Wittkopf. New York: St. Martin's/Worth, 1998.

Sartori, Giovanni. *The Theory of Democracy Revisited,* vols. I and II. Chatham, N.J.: Chatham House, 1987.

Schneider, William. "Rambo and Reality: Having It Both Ways." In *Eagle Resurgent? The Reagan Era in American Foreign Policy.* Edited by Kenneth A. Oye, Donald Rothchild, and Robert J. Lieber. Boston: Little, Brown and Company, 1987.

Schoultz, Lars. *National Security and United States Policy Toward Latin America.* Princeton: Princeton University Press, 1987.

Schultz, George P. *Turmoil and Triumph.* New York: Charles Scribner's Sons, 1993.

Schulzinger, Robert D. *American Diplomacy in the Twentieth Century.* New York: Oxford University Press, 1984.

Schumpeter, Joseph A. *Capitalism, Socialism and Democracy,* 3rd. ed. New York: Harper and Row, 1950.

Scott, James. *Deciding to Intervene: The Reagan Doctrine and American Policy.* Durham, N.C.: Duke University Press, 1996.

Smith, Gaddis. *Morality, Reason, and Power.* New York: Hill and Wang, 1986.

Smith, Gordon. *Soviet Politics: Struggling With Change.* New York: St. Martin's Press, 1992.

Smith, Lee. "Time to Buy Mexico?" *Fortune* (6 February 1995).

Smith, Robert Freeman. "Wilson's Pursuit of Order." In *Major Problems in American Foreign Policy: Since 1914.* Edited by Thomas G. Paterson Lexington, Mass.: D.C. Heath and Company, 1989.

Smith, Tony. "In Defense of Intervention." *Foreign Affairs* 73, no. 6 (November/December 1994).

Snyder, Glenn H., and Paul Diesing. *Conflict Among Nations.* Princeton: Princeton University Press, 1997.

Spero, Joan Edelman. "Guiding Global Finance." *Foreign Policy* no. 73 (Winter 1988–1989).

———. *The Politics of International Economic Relations.* New York: St. Martin's Press, 1985.

Spiegel, Steven L. "The United States and the Arab–Israeli Dispute." In *Eagle Entangled: U.S. Foreign Policy in a Complex World.* Edited by Kenneth A. Oye, Donald Rothchild, and Robert Lieber. New York: Longman, 1979.

Sprinzak, Ehud. "The Great Superterrorism Scare." *Foreign Policy* no. 112 (Fall 1998).

Stalin, Joseph V. *Works,* vol. 4. Moscow: Foreign Languages Publishing House, 1952–1955.

Steel, Ronald. *Walter Lippmann and the American Century.* Boston: Little, Brown and Company 1980.

Stein, Jonathan B. *From H-Bomb to Star Wars.* Lexington, Mass.: Lexington Books, 1984.

Strange, Susan. *The Retreat of the State: The Diffusion of Power in the World Economy.* New York: Cambridge University Press, 1996.

Talbott, Strobe. "Democracy and the National Interest." *Foreign Affairs* 75, no. 6 (November/December 1996).

Tammen, Ronald L., Jacek Kugler, Douglas Lemke, Allan C. Stam III, Carole Alsharabati, Mark Andrew Abdollahian, Brian Efird, and A.F.K. Organski. *Power Transitions: Strategies for the 21ˢᵗ Century.* New York: Chatham House Publishers, 2000.

Taubman, William. *Stalin's American Foreign Policy: From Entente to Détente to Cold War.* New York: W. W. Norton and Company, 1982.

Thorow, Lester C. *The Future of Capitalism: How Today's Forces Shape Tomorrow's World.* New York: William Morrow and Company, 1996.

Thorton, Richard C. *The Carter Years: Toward a New Global Order.* New York: Paragon House, 1991.

Tocqueville, Alexis de. *Democracy in America,* vols. I and II. New York: Vintage Books, 1945.

Ulam, Adam B. *The Rivals.* New York: Penguin Books, 1983.

United Nations Development Programme. *Human Development Report, 1997.* New York: Oxford University Press, 1997.

United Nations Development Programme. *Human Development Report, 1994.* New York: Oxford University Press, 1994.

Vance, Cyrus. *Hard Choices.* New York: Simon and Schuster, 1983.

Vogel, Steven K. *Freer Markets, More Rules: Regulatory Reform in Advanced Industrial Countries.* Ithaca: Cornell University Press, 1996.

Wade, Robert. "The Fight Over Capital Flows." *Foreign Policy* no. 113 (Winter 1998–1999).

Wade, Robert. "Globalization and Its Limits: Reports of the Death of the National Economy Are Greatly Exaggerated." In *National Diversity and Global Capitalism.* Edited by Suzanne Berger and Ronald Dore. Ithaca: Cornell University Press, 1996.

Weatherford, Stephen, and Lorraine M. McDonnell. "Ideology and Economic Policy." In *Looking Back on the Reagan Presidency.* Edited by Larry Berman. Baltimore: The Johns Hopkins University Press, 1990.

Williams, William Appleman. *The Tragedy of American Diplomacy.* New York: Dell Publishing Company, 1972.

Williamson, Oliver E. "A Model of Rational Managerial Behavior." In Richard
    Cliffs and James G. March. *A Behavioral Theory of the Firm.* Englewood Cliffs,
    N.J.: Prentice-Hall, Inc, 1963.
Yergin, Daniel. *Shattered Peace.* Boston: Houghton Mifflin Company, 1978.
Yergin, Daniel, and Joseph Stanislaw. *The Commanding Heights.* New York: Simon
    and Schuster, 1988.
Yoffie, David B., ed. *Beyond Free Trade: Firms, Government and Global Competition.*
    Boston: Harvard Business School Press, 1993.
Zanoyan, Vahan. "After the Oil Boom." *Foreign Affairs* 74, no. 6 (November/
    December 1995).

Index

About the Index: All the headings are arranged alphabetically. The subheadings are not always grouped alphabetically. First, when continent/region/country-subheadings are under a particular heading; they are always placed at the top of the list. If there are other subheadings under that heading, those that mark the beginning of a set of subheadings are also organized alphabetically. Within a subset of subheadings, however, those that follow the first item are sometimes presented chronologically.